Sustainable
Poetry

Sustainable Poetry

Four American Ecopoets

LEONARD M. SCIGAJ

THE UNIVERSITY PRESS OF KENTUCKY

Publication of this volume was made possible in part by a grant
from the National Endowment for the Humanities.

Scholarly publisher for the Commonwealth,
serving Bellarmine College, Berea College, Centre
College of Kentucky, Eastern Kentucky University,
The Filson Club Historical Society, Georgetown College,
Kentucky Historical Society, Kentucky State University,
Morehead State University, Murray State University,
Northern Kentucky University, Transylvania University,
University of Kentucky, University of Louisville,
and Western Kentucky University.

Editorial and Sales Offices: The University Press of Kentucky
663 South Limestone Street, Lexington, Kentucky 40508-4008

99 00 01 02 03   5 4 3 2 1

Library of Congress Cataloging-in-Publication Data

Scigaj, Leonard M.
Sustainable poetry : four American ecopoets / Leonard M. Scigaj.
p.   cm.
Incudes bibliographical references (p.   ) and index.
ISBN 0-8131-2120-5 (cl. : alk. paper)
1. American poetry—20th century—History and criticism. 2. Nature in literature.
3. Merwin, W.S. (William Stanley), 1927-   —Knowledge—Natural history.
4. Berry, Wendell, 1934-   —Knowledge—Natural history. 5. Ammons, A.R., 1926-
—Knowledge—Natural history. 6. Snyder, Gary, 1930-   —Knowledge—Natural
history. 7. Environmental protection in literature. 8. Nature conservation in literature.
9. Ecology in literature. I. Title.
PS310.N3S38   1999
811'.5409355—dc21   99-18166

Manufactured in the United States of America

For William T. Hendricks, M.D.
who saved my life three times
and for my Literature and Ecology students
who save my spirit every year

The love of wilderness is more than a hunger for what is always beyond reach; it is also an expression of loyalty to the earth which bore us and sustains us, the only home we shall ever know, the only paradise we ever need—if only we had the eyes to see.

Edward Abbey, *Desert Solitaire*, 190

Wisdom does not inspect, but behold. We must look a long time before we can see.

Henry David Thoreau, "The Natural History of Massachusetts," 29

True philosophy consists in re-learning to look at the world . . . .

Maurice Merleau-Ponty, *The Phenomenology of Perception*, xx

When philosophy ceases to be doubt in order to make itself disclosure, explicitation, the field it opens to itself is indeed made up of significations or of essences—since it has detached itself from the facts and the beings—but these significations or essences do not suffice to themselves, they overtly refer to our acts of ideation which have lifted them from a brute being, wherein we must find again in their wild state what answers to our essences and our significations.

Maurice Merleau-Ponty, *The Visible and the Invisible*, 110

The pictographic glyph or character still referred, implicitly, to the animate phenomenon of which it was the static image. . . . With the phonetic *aleph-beth*, however, the written character no longer refers us to any sensible phenomenon out in the world, or even to the name of such a phenomenon (as with the rebus), but solely to a gesture to be made by the human mouth. There is a concerted shift of attention away from any outward or worldly reference of the pictorial image. . . .

David Abram, *The Spell of the Sensuous*, 100

Contents

Preface

Niagara-on-the-Lake, Ontario, is a picturesque resort town, complete with white picket fences, manicured lawns, elegant flower gardens, antique bed and breakfasts, yupscale curio shops, posh pubs where one can sip one's pint o' bitter, and sunset dinner cruises up the Niagara. The town is situated where the Niagara River empties into Lake Ontario, which is picturesque enough, but it is a resort town primarily because the world-renowned Shaw Festival resides there, offering some of the best live theater in North America. Having dabbled in the theater as an undergraduate in my hometown of Buffalo, New York, a short drive from Ontario, I would take in a play every summer I returned home to visit my parents. In the summer of 1989 I decided to stay overnight in Niagara-on-the-Lake and see two days of shows, including *Man and Superman.* The odyssey that produced the following study began the morning after the overnight when, while strolling along the waterfront, I noticed a beautiful beach near the center of town that displayed a large "No Swimming" sign. Yachts at anchor, sailing boats tacking in the gentle breezes, dinner cruises up the river, but no swimming at a gorgeous beach in clear view of where the Niagara empties into Lake Ontario?

I was shocked. I knew Love Canal was being cleaned up, but that spot of polluted soil was in a small, well-defined area of the city of Niagara Falls, at least ten miles away. What could possibly create so much pollution that swimming in Lake Ontario was *verboten*? As I returned to Virginia Tech to prepare fall classes, I began to meditate on why the poststructural language theory I was reading to keep abreast of critical theory for my modern and contemporary poetry classes seldom engages environmental problems in the real world that we traverse daily. Though I had recently signed contracts to complete two books for G.K. Hall, I resolved to begin reading whatever environmental criticism I could find that discussed contemporary literature, especially poetry. I had audited a sophomore-level ecology course in Virginia Tech's Biology department in 1981, for my own enrichment, but never found the time to continue the interest. I soon learned that toxins from the chemical plants on the American side of the Niagara River travel hundreds of miles through the limestone layers of the Niagara escarpment and that heavy industry in Buffalo, Niagara Falls, Hamilton, and Toronto still dumps tons of waste each day into the water. Then I remembered the Canadian swimmer Vicki Keith: when she was preparing to complete the last of her swims across all five Great Lakes with a swim across Lake Ontario in August 1988, her support crew teased her often about the polluted water she would swallow.

The more I read, the more convinced I became that I should develop a new environmental literature course for my department. Literature and Ecology began in Virginia Tech's English department in the spring of 1995 with one section per year. Four years later, we have three or four sections every semester. Each semester I show short video clips from the National Audubon Society Special *Great Lakes: A Bitter Legacy* (Lucas 1991). The clips summarize a famous study by the Wayne State researchers Joseph and Sandra Jacobson about how PCBs in the umbilical cord blood of women who ate Lake Michigan sport fish several times a month for at least six years prior to pregnancy have permanently harmed their children, who test at subnormal levels for memory retention at age four. The impairment was more measurably pronounced and visible also in verbal functioning, attention, and reading in the same 212 children when retested at age eleven (Jacobson). As my students leave the classroom in ashen-faced silence, I meditate on how Niagara Falls, a favorite haunt of my youth, now vies with Cancer Alley, the southern Mississippi, as the most polluted body of water on the North American continent. As I lock up the VCR, I have bleak visions of how every day thousands of globe-hopping tourists take snapshots of what is possibly the greatest open sewer in the world. There ought to be a position in contemporary poetry theory that accounts for poetry that addresses environmental disasters such as this.

In 1994 I read John Elder's excellent *Imagining the Earth* (1985) and Wendell Berry's wonderful *Standing by Words* (1983) in the same month and slowly realized that one could separate nature poetry and environmental poetry from ecopoetry, develop a critical position for ecopoetry that responds to poststructural language theory, and in the process account for levels of sophistication in the ecopoetry I was enjoying. Elder laid the foundation for further studies of environmental poetry, and primarily articulated how the nature poetry of Ammons, Berry, Jeffers, and Snyder shares themes with canonical nineteenth- and twentieth-century writers such as Wordsworth and Eliot on the inhabitation of place, pollution as cultural decay, etc. I wanted to update Elder's work, add W.S. Merwin (who was just beginning to make environmental poetry his primary focus in the 1980s), and explore new ways of developing a *theoretical* position for what I call ecopoetry that would critique poststructural language theory and provide an alternative. My own reading of the phenomenology of Merleau-Ponty at about this time, with the help of M.C. Dillon's lucid *Merleau-Ponty's Ontology* (1988), looked promising. In the late summer of 1997, as I was composing the last chapter of this study, I read David Abram's recent study of Merleau-Ponty, *The Spell of the Sensuous* (1996), and incorporated some of his fine insights into that Snyder chapter.

I originally hoped to include a chapter on Adrienne Rich's ecopoetry in this volume. But as I researched the lengthy careers of Ammons, Berry, Merwin, and Snyder, I accumulated more than enough manuscript pages to fill a critical volume. In the process I also recognized that these four males were publishing ecopoetry by 1965, whereas ecofeminist poetry began to appear about a decade later. Enough women environmental poets with established careers exist to fill an entire volume (Louise Gluck, Joy Harjo, Susan Howe, Denise Levertov, Mary Oliver, Marge Piercy, Adrienne Rich, Pattiann Rogers), and in such a volume I could explore at length the subtle differences in allegiance to feminism and ecofeminism among these poets. I hope to write that volume after I complete a collection of Sylvia Plath's unpublished letters, already substantially underway, that I am entitling "Plath's Letters to Women." The three publications listed under my name in the works cited section attest to my interest in ecofeminism and in poetry written by women.

In February of 1998, I sent a copy of the introductory chapters plus the appropriate chapter of the main text to each of the four poets. None found the material inimical or at variance with their poetic intent; only Merwin remembered having read any Merleau-Ponty—he "admired immensely" the few things he had read here and there, years ago. Berry has a standard policy, in place for decades, of not commenting on interpretative scholarship concerning his own work; otherwise he would never find the time to continue that work. Ammons, though he found the text "life-enhancing" and quipped that "between us we have established the probability that there is a planet here," was unfortunately hospitalized and unable to peruse the manuscript in detail. He did respond "excellent" to a query concerning whether my approach to phenomenology was consistent with his thinking about the nature of perception in the creation of environmental poetry. Merwin found the research and theoretical base impressive and offered helpful biographical background about his years in France as well as suggestions about my interpretations of some of the poems of *The Vixen*, his most recent volume. Snyder offered comments on my use of Zen and Dogen in his most recent volume, *Mountains and Rivers without End*. He found my poem interpretations "generous," was pleased that the "Dharma-labors" of *Sustainable Poetry* will reach print, and felt "inclined to go read" Merleau-Ponty now.

I suppose one reason why environmental poetry has not received much attention by theorists is the unspoken assumption that it depends on an outmoded, naive mimesis, or the misguided notion that language automatically conveys the full presence of the speaker and the essence of the referential object, or that environmental poems are restricted to a passive representationalism, a purely objective recording of incidents in the natural world. On the contrary, my own reading of the poetry often indicated an acutely self-conscious awareness of the limits of language, an emphasis on the process of perception, and a lively comprehension of how the act of perception welds the subjective human psyche to phenomena in the natural world while respecting that natural world as an equal and separate other, an other seriously maimed by the hands of humans. Though poetry becomes one-dimensional doggerel when it sinks to propaganda, environmental poetry seldom stoops to that level. I agree with Ammons that poetry provides exemplary models of human behavior (SM 33), and environmental poetry challenges us to alter our perceptions from the anthropocentric to the biocentric. In my estimation changes in personal behavior and voting patterns are more likely to appear after the reader has altered his or her perceptions about how humans ought to relate to the environment. Living in harmony with our environment will happen once we recognize that the pollution we have created is the result of considering nature as a subordinate entity, a natural resource to be dominated and exploited by humans, whereas our perceptions of beauty as well as our survival as a species depend on achieving a balance between the needs of humans and the needs of nature.

In my opening chapters I develop a theoretical position for ecopoetry in part by critiquing the work of Charles Altieri and Marjorie Perloff. I have learned much from these two first-rate senior scholars, and since they are extremely sharp, articulate, and representative spokespersons for poststructural theory as it intersects with an aesthetic position on contemporary poetry, I thought that responding to the limitations of that theory would help readers to understand how contemporary ecopoetry differs. By embracing Derrida in the 1980s and Wittgenstein in the 1990s, Altieri and Perloff have solidified an aesthetic approach to contemporary poetry based on language theory, but this approach is unhelpful for ecopoetry and ecocriticism. In my estimation, this approach is also unhelpful for readers who want contemporary poetry to confront with honesty the actual world we live in daily. In my introductory chapters I critique the work of Robert Hass and Jorie Graham as exemplary of a poststructural language poetry that nevertheless remains blind to the needs of nature. A phenomenological approach that grants nature an equal and separate status is necessary, and Merleau-Ponty in my estimation offers exactly that. Because my use of Merleau-Ponty has no precedent in contemporary poetry criticism (Abram does not discuss poetry in *The Spell of the Sensuous* [1996]), I decided to take an historical approach to each of the four poets I treat, cover all recent volumes, and prove that a great body of ecopoetry actually does emphasize a phenomenological approach that grants nature the status of a separate and equal other in the search for biocentric harmony. Professor Ronald Bruzina of the University of Kentucky Philosophy department offered important clarifications for Merleau-Ponty's concepts of the visible and the invisible and sound advice about phrasing Merleau-Ponty's categories.

Ecocriticism is conducted, according to Lawrence Buell, "in a spirit of commitment to environmentalist praxis" (1995, 430 n). I believe, with Salman Rushdie, that politics and literature "are inextricably mixed," that "passivity always serves the interests of the status quo," and that "if resistance is useless, those whom one might otherwise resist become omnipotent" (1991, 97, 100). But the best resistance may simply reside in articulating an ecological poetic that already does exist in the poetry. This should aid in changing perceptions. I also remembered what Shaw's Don Juan said to the Statue—that we can make the passive man "brave by simply putting an idea into his head" (622).

The aestheticist position in contemporary poetry criticism often represses or naturalizes the actual state of the nature that grounds the poetry. It also fails to take into account the inevitable consequences for college classroom instruction of the academic power structure. Critics such as Altieri and Perloff, well placed in the Modern Language Association, exert a great influence not only in choosing certain kinds of special sessions and excluding others at the annual conference but in their letters of recommendation for tenure and promotion cases they affect in no small measure the critical allegiances of the instructors who teach the best and the brightest of the next generation. If students in our literature classes are regularly taught to admire the aesthetic blooms of textuality and language theory and devalue referential reality, how do we prepare them to cope with the toxic blooms our generation has bequeathed them? Horace's *Ars Poetica*, one of the oldest works of literary criticism in the West, tells us to consider both the *dulce* and the *utile*, the aesthetic delight *and* the practical instruction value of literature: "He who combines the useful and the pleasing wins out by both instructing and delighting the reader" (1952, 56).

In the discussion portion of William Howarth's "New Nature Writers" session at the 1996 MLA Conference in Washington, D.C. (9 P.M. Sunday, December 29), an intrepid student at the back of the room raised his hand and stated that no one in his generation believes that he or she can simply don a bathing suit and jump into the nearest creek or lake. His generation is the first generation of Americans to have to make such a statement. In less than four hundred years we have turned this fresh green breast of the new world into a brave new degraded world. Not only must this student confront the fact that without graduate degrees his college diploma, given chronic corporate downsizing, will probably earn him only a temp job with no security and no benefits, but with his fresh young mind he must also resign himself to working all his adult life in an environment that his parents have already placed in dire need of intensive care. And we wonder at the ennui and anomie of Generation X and Generation Next. I composed every page of this study with that student in mind.

Earlier drafts of portions from three chapters of *Sustainable Poetry* have been accepted for publication. The editors of all three publications have graciously granted me permission to reprint these works: "Contemporary Ecological and Environmental Poetry: *Différance* or *Référance?*" *Interdisciplinary Studies in Literature and Environment*, 3 (fall 1996): 1-25; "'The World Was the Beginning of the World': Agency and Homology in A.R. Ammons's *Garbage.*" In *Reading the Earth: New Directions in the Study of Literature and Environment.* Ed. Michael Branch, Rochelle Johnson, Daniel Peterson, and Scott Slovic. Moscow: U of Idaho P, 1998; and "Dōgen's Boat, Fan, and Rice Cake: Realization and Artifice in Snyder's 1996 *Mountains and Rivers without End.*" *Studies in Humanities*, 25, no. 2 (1999). Forthcoming.

For permission to quote extensively from the copyrighted poetry and prose of A.R. Ammons, Wendell Berry, W.S. Merwin, and Gary Snyder, we are especially grateful to the following:

W.W. Norton & Company, for quotation from the Ammons volumes published by them: *Collected Poems 1951-1971,* © A.R. Ammons 1972, *Sumerian Vistas,* © A.R. Ammons 1987, *Garbage,* © A.R. Ammons 1993, *Brink Road,* © A.R. Ammons 1996, *Glare,* © A.R. Ammons 1997. The University of Michigan Press, for quotation from the Ammons essay "A Note on Incongruence," published by them in *Set in Motion,* © A.R. Ammons, 1996. "A Note on Incongruence" first appeared in *Epoch* 15 (winter 1966): 192.

Farrar, Straus & Giroux, Inc., for quotation from the following poems published by them and collected in Berry's *Collected Poems 1957-1982*: "The Design of a House," "Elegy," "The Gift of Gravity," "The Handing Down," "The Law That Marries All Things," "Observance," and "Leaving Home," © 1984 Wendell Berry. Wendell Berry, for quotation from the following poems in his *Collected Poems 1957-1982*: "The Silence," "The Sycamore," "Window Poems," "Meditation in the Spring Rain," "The Farmer, Speaking of Monuments," "Enriching the Earth," and "Manifesto: The Mad Farmer Liberation Front," © Wendell Berry, 1984. Counterpoint Press, Inc., for quotation from the Berry volume published by them: *A Timbered Choir: The Sabbath Poems 1979-1997,* © Wendell Berry, 1998. Random House/Knopf, Inc., and Pantheon Books, for quotation from the Berry volume published by them: *Entries,* © 1994 Wendell Berry.

Random House/Knopf, for quotation from the Merwin volumes published by them: *The Rain in the Trees,* © W.S. Merwin 1988, and *Travels,* © W.S. Merwin 1992.

New Directions Publishing Corporation, for quotation from the Gary Snyder volumes published by them: *Regarding Wave,* © Gary Snyder 1970, and *Turtle Island,* © Gary Snyder 1974. Farrar, Straus, & Giroux, Inc., for quotation from the Gary Snyder volume published by them: *Axe Handles,* © Gary Snyder 1983. Random House/Knopf, Inc., and Pantheon Books, for quotation from the Gary Snyder volume published by them: *No Nature,* © Gary Snyder 1992. Counterpoint Press, Inc., for quotation from the Snyder volume published by them: *Mountains and Rivers Without End,* © Gary Snyder 1996.

For permission to quote from the copyrighted works of other poets, we are also grateful to the following:

University of Illinois Press, for quotation from the Brendan Galvin volume published by them: *Great Blue,* © Brendan Galvin 1990.

Abbreviations Used in the Text

ACP   Ammons, A.R. *Collected Poems: 1951-1971*. New York: Norton, 1972.

BCP   Berry, Wendell. *Collected Poems: 1957-1982*. San Francisco: North Point, 1984.

CH   Berry, Wendell. *A Continuous Harmony: Essays Cultural and Agricultural*. New York: Harcourt, Brace, Jovanovich, 1972.

G   Ammons, A.R. *Garbage*. New York: Norton, 1993.

MRWE   Snyder, Gary. *Mountains and Rivers Without End*. Washington, D.C.: Counterpoint, 1996.

NA   Stevens, Wallace. *The Necessary Angel: Essays on Reality and the Imagination*. New York: Random House/Vintage, 1951.

NN   Snyder, Gary. *No Nature: New and Selected Poems*. New York: Pantheon, 1992.

PI   Wittgenstein, Ludwig. *Philosophical Investigations*. 3d ed. Trans. G.E.M. Anscombe. New York: Macmillan, 1968.

PP   Merleau-Ponty, Maurice. *The Phenomenology of Perception*. Trans. Colin Smith. London: Routledge & Kegan Paul, 1962; New York: Humanities P, 1962.

PriP   Merleau-Ponty, Maurice. *The Primacy of Perception*. Trans. James M. Edie. Evanston: Northwestern UP, 1964.

PW   Snyder, Gary. *The Practice of the Wild*. San Francisco: North Point, 1990.

RE   Berry, Wendell. *Recollected Essays: 1965-1980*. San Francisco: North Point, 1981.

RT   Merwin, W.S. *The Rain in the Trees*. New York: Knopf, 1988.

RW   Snyder, Gary. *The Real Work: Interviews and Talks, 1964-1979*.
        Ed. William Scott McLean. New York: New Directions,
        1980.

SEFC   Berry, Wendell. *Sex, Economy, Freedom, & Community*. New
        York & San Francisco: Pantheon, 1993.

SM   Ammons, A.R. *Set in Motion: Essays, Interviews, & Dialogues*.
        Ed. Zofia Burr. Ann Arbor: U of Michigan P, 1996.

SV   Ammons, A.R. *Sumerian Vistas*. New York: Norton, 1987.

SW   Berry, Wendell. *Standing by Words*. San Francisco: North Point,
        1983.

TC   Berry, Wendell. *A Timbered Choir: The Sabbath Poems 1979-
        1997*. Washington, D.C.: Counterpoint, 1998.

UA   Berry, Wendell. *The Unsettling of America: Culture &
        Agriculture*. San Francisco: Sierra Club, 1986.

UW   Berry, Wendell. *The Unforeseen Wilderness: Kentucky's Red River
        Gorge*. San Francisco: North Point, 1991.

VI   Merleau-Ponty, Maurice. *The Visible and the Invisible*. Trans.
        Alphonso Lingis. Ed. Claude Lefort. Evanston: Northwestern
        UP, 1968.

Ecopoetry and Contemporary American Poetry Criticism

God's in His

heaven, but not all is right with the world:
the nest's foul, befouled: the planet's

riddled, stink flows down the mighty rivers; dirty water
climbs sores up the children's

legs

Ammons, *Glare*, 248

The Hands of Humans

In 1902, at the beginning of the twentieth century, Alfred Stieglitz exhibited his photograph "The Hand of Man" at his Little Galleries of the Photo-Secession at 291 Fifth Avenue, in New York. He passionately wanted his audience to reperceive the ordinary and transform its aesthetic potential into an art that would lift life beyond the decay of time and organic matter, as did William Carlos Williams in poems such as "The Rose" and "Spring Strains." Stieglitz's photo depicted a grimy locomotive belching smoke in a railway yard, but the compositional arrangement—the contrast of light and darkness, the tense, foregrounded lines of rails intersecting at the locomotive's head, and the chuffing engine with its agitated column of smoke at the center balancing the rigid telephone poles to the left and the squat city building to the right—transformed the tawdry iron horse into a vibrant visual image reminiscent of the active space relished in Cubist art.

Dada Invades New York, the Dada retrospective at the Whitney Museum in the fall and winter of 1996-97, reminded us that one of the central impulses in the fabulous explosion of talent in modern art was to transform the aesthetic potential within the everyday, an everyday that included the technological extensions of the hands of humans—the machines, skyscrapers, bridges, and subways of urban life. But as I write in February 1998, at the end of this century, celebrating the hands of humans and their technological extensions has become a much more problematic endeavor. Today it is questionable to create poetry that purifies the ordinary natural world by transforming it into a superior aesthetic museum of art or limiting critical interest to language and textuality when that natural world is so stressed, so endangered by the hands of humans.

In December 1997, delegates from every major world nation convened in Kyoto, Japan, to produce the Kyoto Protocol, the first step in global cooperation to reduce the dangerous levels of carbon dioxide, sulphur dioxide, methane, and other greenhouse gasses that ring the troposphere and produce global warming. The protocol stipulates that by 2012 the United States must lower its greenhouse emissions to seven percent below 1990 levels, whereas in 1996 our emissions were already 8.8 percent above 1990 levels (Brown 1998, 115). Meeting the protocol's target will call for massive changes in the ways American consumers and industry use energy. With less than five percent of world population, the United States produces from its automobiles and factories, the technological extensions of the hands of humans, an incredible twenty-three percent of global carbon dioxide emissions (Brown 1997, 8; Gore 1992, 176). Further, 1998 was the warmest year on record, and the ten warmest years on planet earth occurred in the past twelve years. Deforestation in the Amazon rain forest, which adds carbon dioxide and methane pollution to the troposphere, increased thirty-four percent from 1991 to 1994 (Brown 1997, 15), and more recent statistics are not available because our government refuses to release the four hundred thousand dollars needed to analyze the Landsat photos. Apparently the recent deforestation is so staggering that some believe the statistics would embarrass the Brazilian government, the hosts of the 1992 United Nations Earth Summit in Rio (Astor 1997). Meanwhile Malaysian and Indonesian lumber companies have bought 8.6 million acres of the Brazilian Amazon to clear cut for mahogany and teak, hardwoods whose market price has tripled in recent years (*Roanoke Times* 1997). The hands of humans in developing countries have learned to mimic the hands of their former overlords, as they strip their own assets with capitalistic glee.

Scientists have compiled enough evidence to suggest that global warming causes such volatile weather that major companies in the insurance industry, an industry that invests most of its $1.4 trillion of yearly premium income, are openly advising all insurance companies to stop investing in fossil fuel conglomerates and shift investments to alternative energy and energy conservation enterprises (Hertsgaard 1996). This is in part a reaction to hurricane Andrew, which on one Florida day (August 24, 1992) created an estimated $30 billion of damage and bankrupted eight insurance companies (Brown 1996, 15, 26-28). Unpredictable and volatile weather patterns, a consequence of global warming, have also caused widespread floods and droughts that have damaged world crop harvests, left hundreds of thousands homeless, and created the conditions for epidemics that could outstrip our most advanced antibiotics and scientific deterrents.

In January 1998, sixteen hundred scientists from around the world signed a document stating that the ecological health of our oceans, which we once thought a limitless repository for wastes produced by the hands of humans, is severely endangered. Coral reefs, which provide shelter and food for fish, are dying, fish species and numbers are dwindling at an alarming rate, thirteen of the world's fifteen major ocean fisheries are in decline (Brown 1996, 5), and one—the cod fishery off the shores of Newfoundland—has been so overfished that the Canadian government has closed it to commercial fishing. Red tide blooms and pfiesteria outbreaks, caused by warmed water and high nutrient levels in water, have killed countless fresh and salt water fish off the coast of Africa and in the rivers of the United States. Factories and chemical companies pour toxic waste into our rivers and oceans, and chemical runoff from agricultural lands and animal wastes from huge livestock farms (beef and dairy cattle, chickens, pigs) raise the nutrient content in water to levels that also poison fish. A National Resources Defense Council study found that sewage from antiquated municipal treatment plants deposits fecal coloform bacteria in our shoreline waters, causing more than two thousand beach closings in one year in America, though this is but a tiny fraction of what should be closed, since many states do not monitor shoreline water quality with any regularity (*Roanoke Times,* 24 July 1992). Not a single American company has been convicted at the federal level for illegally dumping toxic waste since the 1986 Superfund Amendments and Reauthorization Act took effect, for companies provide data voluntarily and the law lacks enforcement funding. Yet America produces more than half of the world's toxic waste (Caldicott 1992, 66).

Preliminary research indicates that global warming, influenced by the hands of humans, aggravates the disastrous effects of El Niños. El Niños have occurred for centuries, normally alternating with La Niñas. But today El Niños occur with far greater frequency. Dubbed "the Christ child" by South American Catholics in the sixteenth century because its disastrous effects occur near Christmas, an El Niño occurs when the trade winds that blow across the Pacific Ocean weaken. When especially strong, these trade winds keep the warmest ocean water on the planet on the western end of the Pacific and create heavy but predictable (and needed) monsoons in Southeast Asia. During periods when La Niña ("the girl child") prevails, the United States has a colder than normal winter. When the trade winds weaken, the warmest water in the Pacific slides eastward toward Peru and Central America and ocean currents take this water northward to the west coast of North America. In this El Niño scenario, the warmed water creates tumultuous storms and tidal waves on the west coast of the Americas and droughts in southern Africa, Indonesia, and western Australia. Hence the floods and mudslides in California in January and February of 1998 and the tornadoes in Florida that killed twice as many as Hurricane Andrew and cost fruit farmers hundreds of millions of dollars in crop failures when trees flowered too early and froze before sluggish bees could pollinate them.

Dr. Neville Nicholls of the Australia Bureau of Meteorology, in Melbourne, an acknowledged El Niño expert and the father of El Niño forecasting, has developed sophisticated computer models that reveal enhanced carbon dioxide levels to aggravate the volatility of El Niños. He also notes that, since the 1970s, we have had only two significant La Niñas, in 1975 and 1988. This parallels the carbon dioxide increases monitored on Mauna Loa on the Big Island of Hawaii: carbon dioxide counts have steadily risen during this period—by sixty parts per million in the past forty years. Doubling the carbon dioxide levels in the atmosphere will cause El Niños every third year instead of the present five-year cycle and will ultimately create a positive feedback loop with global warming that could place our planet in a permanent El Niño (Bristow 1997). NOAA, the National Oceanographic and Atmospheric Administration, has strung seventy high-tech buoys throughout an area of the Pacific twice the size of the United States to collect data that warns us of coming El Niños, but the force of this phenomenon is entirely beyond the technological capacities of the hands of humans. Our auto and factory exhausts are definitely altering the global climate in destructive ways.

Though we would like to believe that the above examples are simply problems in the politics of resource management, the hands of humans have so changed the environment of our entire planet that the problem cuts to the bone of what we can depict with honesty in our creative endeavors. We have despoiled nature, the necessary context for any aesthetic act, to the point where we must pause before composing poems that present nature as a benign and reliable backdrop for human quests for an authentic voice. We can no longer conceive of nature as a bucolic idyll, a type of Christian resurrection, a rational exemplar of God's harmonious design, a romantic refuge from urban factories, an indifferent or hostile Darwinian menace, or an echoing hollow filled by poststructural language theory. What we need is a sustainable poetry, a poetry that does not allow the degradation of ecosystems through inattention to the referential base of all language. We need a poetry that treats nature as a separate and equal other and includes respect for nature conceived as a series of ecosystems—dynamic and potentially self-regulating cyclic feedback systems. These ecosystems sustain every moment of our lives, and, because they have been so bruised by humans, we cannot naturalize them into benign backdrops for human preoccupations or reduce them to nonexistence by an obsessive focus on language in our literary creations.

For more than a century, ecologists have labored to comprehend, as much as we can with human logic, the laws and operations of the ecosystems that humans need to survive on planet earth. As we inhabit the twenty-first century, we will need a poetry that does not ignore nature or simply project human fears or aesthetic designs on it. Nature must have its own voice, separate and at least equal to the voice of humans, in the quest to create a balance where both humans and nature can survive into the next century, when the hands of humans will become even more powerful. Today, more than ninety percent of world population increases come from developing countries (Sitarz 1994, 43) and, as the global population swells from 5.8 to 10 billion people by 2050, many of these developing countries will continue their rapid industrialization and strong economic growth, creating millions of middle-class citizens whose desire for consumer goods will place enormous stress on ecosystems. China alone has five times the present population of America; in 1995 it had two million cars on its roads, but it expects to have twenty-two million cars polluting earth's atmosphere by 2010 (Brown 1997, 27).

At the end of the twentieth century the ubiquitous evidence of the worldwide despoliation of nature at the hands of humans boggles the mind. Evidence pours in like effluent and taxes the mind as well as the publishing industry. By the time this book reaches store shelves, all of the above examples of environmental deterioration will be outdated, almost always to be replaced with more alarming examples and statistics. Every week on network television news we watch still more examples of environmental stress or catastrophe somewhere in the world; they arrive with the numbing regularity of the body counts we watched daily during the Vietnam War.

With grim humor I will end this opening position statement with one final example before turning to literary criticism and theory. When humans recently tried to mimic nature and reproduce the ecosystems necessary for survival, the very revealing results placed the limits of our technological hands into perspective. Corporate investors in 1991 spent $150 million to construct Biosphere 2. In Arizona's Sonoran Desert, scientists placed eight humans in a glass and steel greenhouse to determine whether modern technology could reproduce nature's ecosystems and keep the eight alive and well. Though the integrity of the building's seals was broached at least twice (once to expel dangerous levels of carbon dioxide and the other time to augment low food supplies), most called the experiment a success when all eight emerged alive two years later. Needless to say, the Biospherians did not deforest their land or produce the levels of air, soil, and water pollution that we have grown accustomed to on planet earth. Few noticed, however, that it took more than $9 million per person per year and an incredibly complicated network of technological gear to replicate the ecosystem services that nature offers all humans everyday for free (Avise 1994).

Humans cannot afford to take nature's free services for granted. Nor can creative writers and literary critics ignore the environment by ensconcing themselves in claustral searches for the authentic human voice where they focus primarily on the logic of linguistic systems. The situation of poetry at the end of the twentieth century cries out for an appreciation of the authentic nature that grounds language and supports every human instant of aesthetic as well as ordinary consciousness. Because human hands so directly affect ecosystems, we cannot postulate a benign and reliable nature as the scenic backdrop for our aesthetic and linguistic quests. As Bill McKibben (1989, 18, 48, 58, 77-91) and Al Gore (1992, 30-34, 61, 73-74, 79, 90) have warned, the hands of humans are the coarchitects of nature, and we must comprehend, examine, and critique the whys and hows of our actions before regional environmental crises turn to planetary catastrophe. Because all that we know of ourselves happens through interacting with nature's life support systems, we cannot ignore nature or conceive of it as a repository for human fears and projections. Nature must stand as a separate and at least equal other in our literary meditations. We cannot limit the other beyond the self in our literary creations to other humans, human institutions, and human culture. At the end of this century our new situation on planet earth brings with it a new imperative, a new need for an enhanced understanding and a finer appreciation of context, the referential world of nature.

From Nature Poetry to Ecopoetry

Poetry that addresses our connection to the natural world has enjoyed a renaissance over the past thirty years. Authors such as A.R. Ammons, Wendell Berry, Philip Booth, Brendan Galvin, Louise Gluck, Donald Hall, Joy Harjo, William Heyen, Susan Howe, Denise Levertov, W.S. Merwin, Mary Oliver, Robert Pack, Marge Piercy, Adrienne Rich, Pattiann Rogers, Gary Snyder, and others have written dozens of fine volumes exploring the many ways that humans relate to nature. Most of these treat nature not as a convenient background for human concerns but acknowledge that it sustains human, as well as nonhuman, life in ecosystems that have been deeply bruised by human exploitation and pollution. Many nature poets writing today are also environmental poets who have captured the attention of thousands of readers and have gained significant recognition: Ammons won the 1993 National Book Award for his book-length poem *Garbage;* Rich has since won a McArthur Award; and Merwin two six-figure poetry prizes, the Lila Wallace–Readers' Digest Prize, and the Tanning Prize from the Academy of American Poets.

Humanistic research on environmental topics has also burgeoned over the past thirty years. Roderick Nash, in *The Rights of Nature* (1989), catalogued how, since the late 1960s, hundreds of British and American ecologists, theologians, philosophers, ethicians, sociologists, intellectual historians, philosophers of religion, anthropologists, creative writers, animal rights activists, ecofeminists, and environmentalists have engaged in interdisciplinary research and debate to extend environmental ethics to include all living beings on earth. Though areas of disagreement have appeared, most agree with Theodore Roszak's statement in *Person/Planet* that for the survival of the earth and human civilization "nature must also have its natural rights" (1978, 32). Nash's exhaustive research led him to conclude that the development of environmental ethics over the past few decades is "arguably the most dramatic expansion of morality in the course of human thought" (1989, 7).

Though the work of many contemporary American poets has been intimately involved with both nature poetry and environmental ethics, interest among senior American poetry critics has lagged far behind, possibly because poetry primarily concerned with the environment has not yet acquired the status of being a theoretically interesting subject. Though in journals significant studies of nature writers have appeared, incorporating theoretical approaches that range from awareness or consciousness-raising to the ecological, ethical, ecofeminist, ecopastoral, dialogical, phenomenological, history of ideas, and social constructionist, primers or handbooks summarizing the gist of these approaches have not been published. The very first *Ecocriticism Reader* (1996), edited by Cheryll Glotfelty and Harold Fromm, has just recently appeared. One will not find a single essay devoted to environmental poetry in the *Contemporary Literature* issues entitled "The Poetry of the Seventies" (fall 1982) or "The Poetry of the Eighties" (summer 1992).

The literary establishment still valorizes approaches dominated by poststructural language theorists. Dorothy Nielsen, for instance, placed an environmental essay on Snyder and Levertov in the winter 1993 issue of *Contemporary Literature,* but to gain acceptance she buttressed her argument with Paul de Man's poststructural theory. She organized her essay around his term "prosopopoeia"—using personifications of nature to construct historicized and politicized voices for nonhuman life. De Man's lofty theory, however, never knelt on the greenswards of life. Nielsen, in adopting a social constructionist stance, emphasized that Snyder and Levertov created "the illusion of intersubjective relationships between the poetic speaker and the world" (691). She followed Charles Altieri's position that one branch of postmodern poetry is a "poetry of immanence," where "ecological thinking" is limited to a subjectivist stance (Altieri 1973 ["From Symbolist Thought to Immanence"], 612).

Can nature ever be anything more than an impossibly alien "other," trapped in a dualistic paradigm, that humans must subjectivize and personify, imbue with human qualities, in order to understand? The actual poetry written over the past thirty years often argues otherwise. Nature and environmental poets often record moments of nondualistic inhabitation in specific places where the experience occurs only when the noise of human ratiocination, including the fabrications of language, has been silenced or revel in moments of phenomenological participation in Being where the activity of seeing intertwines the human and nonhuman worlds. When Wendell Berry, for instance, desires to experience the prereflective world of his moment-to-moment experience, he knows he cannot articulate its colors in language, but he cannot otherwise communicate his silent experience. What he can do is bear witness to how the leaves fall with a "golden" silence, with "a sound / that is not a name" ("The Silence," BCP 156). Or in meditation he frees himself of egocentricity so that he can "see" the interconnectedness of experience among all sentient beings in a given locale. He is "Seen by more than I see" (TC 26). Light becomes not only the reassurance of nature's sustaining energy but contains a phenomenological dimension as the shared medium that enables ecologically interdependent vision. In the next chapter we will inquire more deeply into the phenomenological dimensions of nondualistic silence and sight as distinctive features of environmental poetry and ecopoetry.

Many anthologies of nature poetry have appeared in recent years, and creative writing journals in America have devoted entire issues to nature poetry: the winter 1989 issue of *Witness*, the spring 1993 issue of the *Georgia Review*, and a 1993 issue of the *Ohio Review* (no. 49) come to mind. Terry Gifford (1995, 2-3, 21-22) saw a similar green revolution in the United Kingdom in the British government, in poetry anthologies, and in journals such as *Poetry Review* (summer 1990) and *Poetry Wales* (vol. 26, no. 1). Anthology editors in their introductions have broached the knotty problem of defining just what is contemporary nature poetry, with mixed results. In *Poems for a Small Planet*, for instance, a 1993 anthology of contemporary American nature poetry edited by Robert Pack and Jay Parini, Parini ended his introduction with a definition of nature poetry as "poems that in some way reflect a highly developed consciousness of the natural world" (xv). This is too broad and simple a definition; in previous paragraphs he focused more on the necessity of a biocentric, politicized poetry that responds to global environmental degradation. Pack's excellent afterword explored the necessity to "reinvent ourselves" (272), to develop a "morality of restraint," "reverence," appreciation of natural beauty and a "capacity for empathy" toward nonhuman nature (273). Through discussions of classic examples from Homer through Shakespeare, Blake, Wordsworth, Dickinson, Hopkins, Frost, Stevens, William Carlos Williams, Rachel Carson, and Bill McKibben, Pack argued (289-90) that we need to return to the humility and the sense of human limits that these poets articulated and that Roderick Nash developed in *Wilderness and the American Mind* (1982).

Robert Finch and John Elder, in their introduction to the *Norton Book of Nature Writing* (1990), take a historical view, affirming that nature writing is "a recognizable and distinct tradition in English prose." They delineate distinct features such as wilderness exploration, pastoral nostalgia, a critique of industrialism and "cold science," playful associations and interactions of the human with the nonhuman, and a sense of responsibility for preserving the health of the land. Finch and Elder conclude that the purpose of nature writing is to *connect* humans to planetary biological processes (19-25). They note that "in a time when the natural context of fiction has been attenuated and when much literary theory discovers nothing to read but constructs of self-reflexive language, nature writing asserts both the humane value of literature and the importance to a mature individual's relationship with the world of understanding fundamental physical and biological processes" (25). Don Scheese, in an essay on Thoreau's *Journals*, similarly stresses the inhabitation of place, whether through a journey or meditation, as central to the genre (1992, 140). Fostering that sense of inhabitation and connectedness with planetary processes occurs in both the aesthetic and phenomenological dimensions of ecopoetry. Most poststructural theory, as we shall soon see, does more than attenuate our sense of connectedness to and responsibility for those fundamental physical and biological processes.

All nature poetry is obviously not automatically environmental poetry, even in the contemporary present. Lawrence Buell, in *The Environmental Imagination*, lists four characteristics that define environmental literature (1995, 7-8). First, the nonhuman environment cannot simply function as a background or framing device but must maintain "a presence that begins to suggest that human history is implicated in natural history." This criterion evinces a biocentric view where humans are but one of many species interacting with other organisms to create natural history. Buell's second criterion, that "the human interest is not understood to be the only legitimate interest," suggests a shift from anthropocentric thinking toward environmental ethics, for here the environmental writer allows nonhuman living things to have habitats and histories of their own. Next Buell implies that environmental ethics is a necessary component of an environmental text, for his third criterion states that "human accountability to the environment is part of the text's ethical orientation." An implicit sense of the environment as a "process rather than a constant" forms the fourth characteristic. In the ensuing chapters of his comprehensive study of American environmental literature, Buell is most compelling when he elucidates how environmental writers manage to make landscape an active agent in the text, with its own voice and ethical position, that often critiques the anthropocentric concerns of major characters, social groups, and the assumptions of Western civilization itself.

Environmental writers, then, emphasize the relationship between the ethical dimensions that humans find in nature and environmental praxis. If environmental writers constitute a smaller group within the class of nature writers, ecopoets comprise an even smaller subgroup within the environmentalist group. In this study, I focus on the recent work of four contemporary American poets—A.R. Ammons, Wendell Berry, W.S. Merwin, and Gary Snyder—whose poetry has consciously been influenced by a sensitivity to ecological thinking, especially in the areas of energy flow/retention, cyclic renewal, bioregionalism, and the interdependency of all organisms within an ecosystem. These broad areas become not just themes or subjects of discussion in poems and essays but suffuse in strikingly different ways the very poetic and phenomenological dimensions of each major text. Aesthetic theory, phenomenological perception, poetic practice, and creative uses of basic ecological principles fuse in complex and arresting ways in each poet. Each poet also affirms that human language is much more limited than the ecological processes of nature and uses postmodern self-reflexivity to disrupt the fashionably hermetic treatment of poetry as a self-contained linguistic construct whose ontological ground is language theory.

Ecopoets present nature in their poems as a separate and equal other in dialogues meant to include the referential world and offer exemplary models of biocentric perception and behavior. Born within eight years of each other (1926-34), the four poets I discuss established publishing careers before the impact of Derrida and European poststructuralism in the late 1960s, and they reject the Derridean postponement of meaning along an endless chain of signifiers, nor do they agree with Wittgenstein's statement in the *Tractatus* that "*the limits of my language* mean the limits of my world" (5.6). This statement expresses the conviction of a logician concerned with the utterability of a statement or proposition in language conceived as a logical system. Ecopoets and environmental poets are much more concerned with affirming the integrity of the lived body of quotidian, prereflective experience as the base of all thinking, and treat statements such as Wittgenstein's as the hubris of humans habituated to dominating nature. Since humans are a subset of nature and in all respects dependent on nature for survival, it follows that the restrictions of human logic are far less important than living in harmony with nature's speech—the fluctuations of ecosystems and biological processes. Ecopoets are more in agreement with Pack, who presented an interesting view of Wordsworth as he asserted that both our human origin and the origin of language derive from the natural world:

In Wordsworth . . . the quest for self-identity and self-knowledge necessarily involve the search for human origins. "How shall I seek the origin?" Wordsworth asks, and, typical of the way he seeks to answer his own question is his representation of moments of looking and listening, attending to the world of natural images: "and I would stand, / If the night blackened with a coming storm, / Beneath some rock, listening to the notes that are / The ghostly language of the ancient earth, / Or make their dim abode in distant winds." Again, listening to the winds, now in their less gentle and grimmer aspect, Wordsworth senses a connection between mere physical sounds—perceived, however, as "notes"—and human language, which has emerged from matter itself. To understand our humanity we must, according to Wordsworth, understand the medium of nature out of which language, our distinguishing human characteristic, has been born. (284)

Ecopoets distill ecological processes into aesthetic techniques to restore our lost sense of connectedness to the planet that bore and sustains us. But they are not Ph.D. ecologists. Karl Kroeber observes, in his *Ecological Literary Criticism* (1994), that environmental poets are obviously not scientists and do not have a command of the intricacies of ecological research. They follow Wordsworth, who rejoiced in the superiority of the poet's more democratic social stance over the scientist's search for recondite law. Kroeber reminds us that "later Shelley, who often followed scientific research carefully, would assert that 'we have more knowledge than we can digest,' and urged poets to 'imagine what we know,' an education clearly to be carried out less through scientific research than humanistic learning" (16). Ecology today is a very complex scientific discipline involving complicated computer research and field work by Ph.D. researchers in one of the areas of the biological sciences who study the energy flow and interdependencies of organisms in closed ecosystems. Contemporary ecopoets usually become interested in responding creatively to the broad outlines of ecological thinking; they seldom write poems that demand particular knowledge of the technical intricacies of scientific theory.

Nevertheless, creative ideas in ecopoets do not occur in total ignorance of basic ecological thinking. Ammons, early in his career, adapted a Plotinian/Emersonian interest in centers and peripheries to his formal method of composition and developed intricate homologies and discussions of spindles of energy flow in his most recent work. He admits deriving many creative ideas from reading *Scientific American* (SM 48). Wendell Berry developed a complex sociobiological mystique of the soil and hydrological cycles in his poems; he derived some of his ideas from the field work of the soil ecologist Sir Albert Howard. Berry, like Merwin, often evokes through rhythm and language a Heideggerian search for the moment when Being haunts him in the prereflective instant of experiencing silent nature. Gary Snyder read J.E. Lovelock's *Gaia* and Ramon Margalef's use of the climax theory of ecosystem development and fashioned in his poems since the 1970s a complex series of analogies to the poet as a cultural fungus who digests the symbol-detritus. In the "Tiny Energies" section heading of *No Nature* (1992), Snyder quoted the ecologist H.T. Odum on how language stores bits of information energy just as ecosystems retain a small portion of their energy flow (NN 354). Merwin, the most postmodern of ecopoets, has for the past decade embarked on an ontological program of using language very self-reflexively to dislocate it from sedimented meaning and restore to it the child's moment of experiencing first sight, first smell, first hearing, first taste, first touch. Or he deliberately lards a poem with cliches, sedimented language, to make his reader realize how little of our actual sensuous experience we typically expect to convey on paper and how thinking in abstractions leads to planetary exploitation. Chapters 3-6 will detail the ecological poetics of these four ecopoets.

Ecopoetry and Contemporary American Poetry Criticism

Joseph Meeker introduced the term "ecology" into literary criticism in his 1972 *The Comedy of Survival*. When Kroeber introduced "ecology" into journal criticism two years later in his *PMLA* article on Wordsworth's "Home at Grasmere," he spoke of how Wordsworth foreshadowed contemporary thinking about nature as an "ecological unity" by celebrating Grasmere as a "complexly interdependent, self-sufficient 'place'" (1974, 132) where a "*continuity* of natural existence" in "earthly actuality truly perceived" offered an "authentic alternative" (134) to the industrialization and the political and economic upheaval of the Napoleonic era. Kroeber affirmed that Grasmere, Wordsworth's chosen dwelling place, offered the opportunity to create fine poetry from "the commonest and most everyday *beingness*," to celebrate nature's "unified interdependence," and to suggest to his readers that we must perceive "civilization as healthiest when most adroitly adapted to the necessities of the total framework of the natural balances within which it must function" (136-37). Because in Wordsworth's poem the human mind and nature are exquisitely fitted one to the other, and because the poem asserts that language enriches our lives by allowing us to fuse our bodily sensations and our thoughts, we can liberate ourselves from passivity and from enchainment to rote impulse by recognizing that, in Kroeber's words, "liberation depends upon conscious participation in the living yet nonperceptible unity of the vale, in fine, in its ecological equilibrium" (140).

In this essay, Kroeber identifies many of the defining aspects that ecocriticism regularly addressed over the next decades: (1) the need to assert a holistic sense of interdependence, requiring that humans see themselves as a subset of nature, not its dominator; (2) a celebration of everyday "beingness"; (3) the joys of dwelling within a distinct locale, a bioregion that is known and appreciated; and (4) an inquiry into the knotty question of what attitude toward language, what poetic best serves the purposes of ecocriticism. The concept of interdependence, where humans are one of many species interacting to maintain a complex natural system, is central to ecology and to ecocriticism. Twenty years later, in his *Ecological Literary Criticism*, Kroeber solidified this aspect of ecocriticism by quoting a definition of an ecosystem from Robert P. McIntosh: an ecosystem is "a group of organisms of different kinds . . . with reciprocal relations to the nonliving environment and, especially, having mutual relations of varying kinds and degrees among themselves" (Kroeber 1994, 26). This emphasis on a holistic approach to interactions of organisms with their context, their environment, is consonant with the approach taken by the German zoologist Ernst Haeckel when he coined the term "ecology" (he spelled it "oecologie") in his 1866 *Generelle Morphologie*. To this understanding of ecology one might add Anna Bramwell's normative use of the term, derived in part from the 1970s focus on the increasing scarcity of nonrenewable energy resources, as the economy of energy flow within a closed system (4). Like interdependency, energy-flow economy places a premium on sharing and cooperation.

In *Ecological Literary Criticism* Kroeber affirms that literary criticism ought to seek its theoretical models not in language theory or the aesthetics of consciousness but in the physical sciences, especially biology. By studying the physical sciences one can gain an adequate grasp of nature as an equal other, the necessary referential context where all poetic meditations occur. He argues that Wordsworth and Shelley were "less concerned with transcending natural existence than transfiguring" our "internalized cultural presuppositions" about how humans relate to their environment (3,

9). In passing comments and throughout his final chapter, Kroeber likens the program of the Romantics to the recent work of the Nobel Prize-winning biologist Gerald M. Edelman on the biological basis of human consciousness. Edelman emphasizes an interdependence of the human brain with its referential context and with the act of perception. For Edelman the brain develops and changes groupings of nerve cells in response to received perceptions, and "the context for any one brain function thus encompasses both the continuously changing operation of other brain functions as well as the continuous changes in the 'outside' environment with which the brain engages" (Kroeber 1994, 145). Neurological groupings change their adhesive properties and hence their functional groupings as the brain adapts and readapts "to the demands of its shifting relationships with its unstable environment" (146).

Carolyn Merchant, in the preface to her 1990 *The Death of Nature*, also suggests that the proper models for environmental inquiry and literature should come from referential reality—the physical sciences. She notes that recent scientific advances in physics indicate a shift away from the mechanistic scientific objectivity that is still Western culture's normative way of experiencing the world (193, 229) and toward more process-oriented organic field models. Merchant directs our attention to the work of the physicist David Bohm, who argues that twentieth-century advances in relativity and quantum theory suggest that matter behaves not according to the regularities of mechanistic thinking but according to processes of stable versus fluid energy fields, with unpredictable leaps in the flowing stream of energy-charged matter. Hence, "context dependence . . . is a fundamental characteristic of matter" (xvii). In *Radical Ecology* (1992) Merchant reaffirms her advocacy of Bohm's work (93-94). In ecopoetry's restoration of context to text we will often see the twin themes of inhabitation and connectedness to planetary ecosystems.

Thirty years ago, the ecologist Paul Sears identified a social purpose within the study of ecology. This is perhaps a final defining aspect of ecoliterature and ecocriticism. He called ecology a "subversive subject" because, when it studies an entire ecosystem, it cannot help but "critique man's operations within the ecosystem." Hence "man is not just an observer and irresponsible exploiter but an integral part, now the world's most dominant organism. He has come into the system and survived thus far by the bounty of that system plus his own marvelous power of adjustment. Even so, the historical record is replete with his failures" (1964, 12). The recent history of environmental degradation—deforestation; ozone depletion; chemical pollution of air, water, and soil; the loss of species diversity; and human overpopulation—is largely attributable to human exploitation of nature's economy. When we read the work of ecologists such as Paul and Anne Ehrlich (*The Population Explosion* [1990]; *The Stork and the Plow* [1995]), of the philosopher of science Carolyn Merchant (*The Death of Nature*; *Radical Ecology*), of science writers such as Bill McKibben (*The End of Nature* [1989]), and the environmental research incorporated into Lester Brown's yearly *State of the World* (1996, 1997, and 1998) from the Worldwatch Institute, we realize that for the first time in planetary history the bounty of nature is itself in question. This is sufficient reason for treating nature as an equal other in environmental poetry.

Kroeber, in *Ecological Literary Criticism*, posits an ancillary social function for literary ecocriticism, following Jonathan Bate's lead. Bate, in his introduction to *Romantic Ecology* (1991), critiques the exaltation of the human imagination and human society, and the total lack of attention to the natural world context of humans, in treatments of the Romantics by such critics as Geoffrey Hartman, Harold Bloom, and Jerome McGann. Bate's work attests to the fact that Wordsworth, far from being a sleepy recluse who preferred to escape the madding crowd of industrialists and day laborers, was seriously engaged in legal debates over deforestation, ecosystem degradation, and social issues such as the enclosure of land and the conservation of scenic areas. Wordsworth offered his poems as models of a way of life sanctioned by nature and sanctified by simple, unalienated labor in direct opposition to reductive capitalist emphasis on ownership and productivity. Bate argues that Wordsworth's nonaristocratic pastorals may not create radical activists but "do have the capacity to alter mentalities" (33).

Kroeber concurs with Bate on the severely anthropocentric exaltation of human concerns among contemporary literary critics and states that, just as ecologically oriented poets ask us to revise our perceptions of our relation to the natural world (9), so ecological literary criticism "requires us to reassess the fundamental presuppositions undergirding recent literary theorizing" (25). Kroeber worries over the New Historicist position that all is discourse, that "there is no nature" (Kroeber, 17; Liu 38) and, like Bate (7), chafes over Paul de Man's exaltation of the poetic consciousness in Wordsworth's *Prelude* as independent "of all relationship with the outside world" (Kroeber 37; de Man 16). Kroeber levels some harsh words at "high-tech critics" who "enter into debates with themselves far too abstract to be connected with specific and immediate realities of injustice, poverty, and devastation of the natural environment." The "distaste for ordinary language" in such critics "and their preference for esoteric jargon may be read as symptomatic of a subconscious desire to escape from the responsibilities of involvement with real and 'hot' socioeconomic problems" (40). Kroeber affirms that the Romantics' emphasis on environmental practicality kept them from sterile debates confined to an aesthetic "art for art's sake" mode (14-15).

The exaltation of anthropocentric consciousness and high culture certainly appears in postmodern American literary criticism. Helen Vendler, a fine Stevens scholar and one of the most important book reviewers of contemporary American poetry, has throughout her career remained faithful to this domination of aesthetic mind over nature. Vendler offers a very different view of Wordsworth and poetic language in the following paragraph from "What We Have Loved, Others Will Love," her 1980 MLA Presidential address: "What we can be certain of is the persistence of art, and of literary art, in some form, since in every culture, as Wordsworth said, the mind of man becomes, by its aesthetic inventions, 'A thousand times more beautiful than the earth / On which he dwells.' For Wordsworth, as he closed *The Prelude*, this was the highest possible compliment to the mind, that it should be, by its aesthetic capacity, more beautiful than this frame of things, the earth" (1980, 33). Vendler treats Stevens as another master of the sublimity of consciousness in her research on his poetry. In 1980 one could still have sublime confidence in the elegant words of Stevens, who could place the entire planet on his literary table, but the worldwide degradation of planetary ecosystems that surrounds us in the late 1990s suggests that we may be better served by strengthening the relationship of poetic language to its referential source. As Gyorgyi Voros argues in her recent *Notations of The Wild: Ecology in the Poetry of Wallace Stevens* (1997), the referential, environmental side of Stevens needs more emphasis. Ariel at the end of "The Planet on the Table" is glad that his poems retained "some affluence . . ./ Of the planet of which they were part." After all, Stevens did affirm in "Looking Across the Fields and Watching the Birds Fly" that "the spirit comes from the body of the world." Even in his early poetry Stevens asserted that man's "soil is his intelligence," not the reverse ("The Comedian as the Letter C"). In *The Necessary Angel*, his collection of essays on poetry, he affirmed the necessity of contact with the natural world for poetic activity: to write literature one must regard "the pressure of reality" (1951, 20, 22, 28, 36) and recognize "the interdependence of the imagination and reality as equals" (27, 24, 33). Interestingly enough, Stevens conceived of the imagination as "a part of what is real" (60, 63, 67) and the final poem as "an agreement with reality" (54, 57-59).

The problems Bate and Kroeber perceive with nineteenth-century literary criticism are somewhat similar for criticism of contemporary American poetry. In 1990 Glen Love wondered why, given the publication of such seminally important studies of environmental ethics and literature as Joseph Meeker's *The Comedy of Survival,* Donald Worster's *Nature's Economy: The Roots of Ecology* (1979), John Elder's *Imagining the Earth* ([1985] 1996), and Roderick Nash's *The Rights of Nature* (1989), critics of American literature have so resisted ecologically oriented research? "Given the fact that most of us in the profession of English would be offended at not being considered environmentally conscious and ecologically aware," stated Love, "how are we to account for our general failure to apply any sense of this awareness to our daily work?" (203). Love pressed the issue with a hard question: "In the context of this widespread disciplinary revaluation, why, one wonders, have literary criticism and theory remained so peculiarly unaffected, so curiously unwilling or unable to address questions which are at the forefront of public concern?" (205). (Indeed, *Time* in its November 16, 1992, issue reported that exit polls for the 1992 U.S. presidential election revealed that 74 percent of respondents who voted for Clinton/Gore listed concern for the environment as their top issue.) Love answered his own question by pointing toward the discomfort literary critics experience with interdisciplinary research and by noting "our discipline's limited humanistic vision, our narrowly anthropocentric view of what is consequential in life." Ecocriticism for Love presents us with the challenge "to outgrow our notion that human beings are so special that the earth exists for our comfort and disposal alone" (205).

One can readily apply Kroeber and Bate's acute awareness of the limiting assumptions that undergird current nineteenth-century poetry criticism to postmodern American poetry criticism. Contemporary American poetry critics have been beguiled for the past two decades by what they perceive as the hegemony of poststructural language theory. Altieri has put the matter very succinctly:

> The entire [poststructural] enterprise is haunted by the models of subjection developed by Lacan and Althusser—the one in terms of family romance, the other in terms of the interpellation that gives agents a place in the social order. Both perspectives prove disturbingly essentialist, asserting necessary structures for the psyche which divide subjective agency from itself and force it to live its imaginative life in thrall to some other that it

internalizes as the means of attributing to itself powers of subjectivity. . . . Derrida and Foucault are more abstract, but perhaps also even more trapped, since for them the depersonalizing force is a property of all categories: categories and hence concepts force third-person frameworks necessary for intelligibility on first-person states and thus necessarily banish subjective agency to the margins of a public world. (1992 ["Contemporary Poetry as Philosophy"], 221-22)

Yet Altieri's response to this poststructural dilemma is worth investigating, for it provides a perfect illustration of criticism that produced Love's quandary over why environmental literature is not attracting interest among contemporary literary critics. The answer is that the interest of most senior American poetry critics runs in the completely opposite direction, toward language theory. Altieri tried to establish a measure of temporal referentiality and subjective agency for postmodern establishment poetry by applying Wittgensteinian categories—deictic shifters such as "now" and "this"—which, in postmodern poets such as John Ashbery and C.K. Williams, appear to create a self-reflexive consciousness of how one wills the self and disposes the self toward what is being told rather than by idealizing what actually gets told. This, however, requires that the reader appreciate the poem on a rarefied, secondary semiotic level, discounting the primary action, event, or experience that actually is told. As the reader attends the persona's experience of overturning the past in a present moment of new awareness, he places the emphasis on lexical process rather than on the referential context with its knotty socioeconomic, ethical, and environmental dimensions. Appreciating this subtle activity on a rarefied, secondary semiotic level seems to seal off the poem from any connectedness to the referential world. Deictic shifters also offer slender criteria for distinguishing between good and mediocre poetry.

Altieri's Wittgensteinian methodology limits discussions of literature to language theory. His resistance to social issues, an aspect of the referential side of literature, appears in a critique of what he calls "oppositional postmodernism" and in his largely negative review of Paul Smith's *Discerning the Subject*. In "The Limits of Oppositional Postmodernism," Altieri critiques the visual art of Sherrie Levine, Barbara Krueger, Hans Haake, David Salle, and other postmodern artists who proclaim political positions but exhibit no "actual specific political filiations" (1990, 456) or refer to no specific political events. Altieri believes that such art traps itself in simplistic oppositions, is narcissistic or at least self-congratulatory (456), and is prone to the charge of "manipulat[ing] symbolic capital without incurring any real ideological debts" (459). Altieri openly advocates a bourgeois art, as in the work of Elizabeth Murray and Jennifer Bartlett, which is politically accommodationist but explores rich, intense, complex, distinctive states of feeling with a fine intelligence and thus resists commodification. Altieri conveys just how politically accommodationist his admittedly bourgeois position becomes in his use of high-level abstractions like "investments." Here the language echoes that of the mutual-fund broker:

> Most art that engages our attention does so by its ability to make us reflect on our models of human agency, the economies governing our imaginative investments, and the particular quality of social relations for which our relation to the artwork becomes an emblem. (464)

> [Art] has a politics, in the most general sense of that term, to the degree that it carries certain qualities or makes comprehensible and attractive certain attitudes which propose modifying the investments that its audience makes in its own social relationships. Thus it becomes possible to argue that there is now a bourgeois art worth honoring for its social effects, because of the intelligence and intensity of the qualitative resistance it exerts on problems of commodification (such as Krueger and Haake address). If images and positions become simulacra when they lose any claim to individual distinction, then art can wield social power simply by virtue of its efforts to take responsibility for its own purposiveness, its own capacity to shape a significant particularity. (462-63)

The abstract language—"certain qualities," "certain attitudes," "investments," "social relationships," "social effects," "problems"—strips the discussion of any referential particularity, any specificity that would relate the art to any *actual* social relationships or problems. What if the "significant particularity" concerns only ruminations on the failure of language within a naturalized landscape that never foregrounds the serious environmental degradation within that landscape, as in the poetry of Robert Hass, or brackets social issues by treating the entire social environment as corrosive while being possessed by anguished fears about self-realization, as in the poetry of Jorie Graham? The "significant particularity" may be so naturalized or so introspective that it masks significant social and environmental issues or conveys a smug cynicism that all one can do is reflect, sigh, and return one's nose to the careerist grindstone. When Hass muses on social injustice in *Human Wishes*, he habitually voices a hollow defeatism that he reinvests in brash careerism: "I knew that I had my own work to do. / The ones who wear the boots decide all that" (1989, 61).

With its emphasis on referential context, environmental poetry must contain an activist dimension to foreground particular acts of environmental degradation and degraded planetary ecosystems. Ecopoets and their audiences do have specific political filiations: a green position on particular issues informs their politics and frequently influences their votes at the ballot box. And environmental poetry is capable of much subtlety, rich and complex states of feeling and participation in nature, if one finds the right theoretical approach to elucidate that complexity. In the next chapter and throughout ensuing chapters, I will present the work of Merleau-Ponty as the proper aesthetic and phenomenological guide for appreciating ecopoetry and elucidating its complexity.

Ecocriticism versus Poststructural Language Theory

Altieri's strong negative response to Paul Smith's (1988) excellent critique of poststructural language theorists in *Discerning the Subject* certainly confirms an agenda, representative of poststructural language critics, that desires to valorize textuality and devalue referential context. Smith, in evaluating the systems of Derrida, Lacan, Barthes, Althusser, and others, finds a disturbing lack of concern for the subject as an individual capable of resistance to hegemonic social systems—as a force capable of initiating or helping to produce significant social change. Smith sees in these poststructural theoretical systems a subject that is subjected to the superior powers of social systems as it adopts the ideology inscribed in their language practices. In his review of this book, Altieri accuses Smith of an irresponsible desire to "stage a responsibility that has no clear grounds and imposes no clear obligations" (262). Because Smith does not himself develop at length an adequate model for agency that accounts for how the unconscious distorts and limits each person's attempts to understand a "self," and because he never articulates how his belief in a Hegelian negativity of the mind working through the pressure of contradictions actually produces political resistance, Smith's "inadequate foundations" lead him to idealize resistance in a way that for Altieri is typical of the "lies that our disciplinary practices allow us to maintain to ourselves" (262-63). Why Altieri seems to find all attempts at introducing social concerns into poetry to be self-congratulatory is itself open to question, and one detects an elitism behind his flat statement that "to this reader political commitments are a sorry and dangerous criterion for assessing intellectual positions" (258). Smith does not advocate a political agenda; he simply tries to locate a position in poststructural theory where it is possible to alter perceptions and social values in ways that promote action and change in the historical process.

Though Auden opined in his Yeats elegy that "poetry makes nothing happen," his own poetry was aften able to "show an affirming flame" ("September 1, 1939") by witnessing atrocities, mirroring the unvarnished actuality of historical situations, warning us of political ineptitude and the blindness of capitalism, and revealing possible choices. Ecopoets and environmental poets often accomplish the same consciousness-raising ends as they warn us of how deeply we have bruised the ecosystems on which the survival of all life on this planet depends and convince us that responsible social action depends on altered perceptions of our relationship with planet earth. Environmental poets and ecopoets subscribe to the twin truths that "the Eye altering alters all" (Blake, "The Mental Traveller") and "where there is no vision, the people perish" (Proverbs 29:18). Their poems provide models of altered perception that promote environmental awareness and active agency.

In *Canons and Consequences* (1990), Altieri repeats his criticism of Smith but at least offers a more accurate and detailed account of what Smith actually does say and credits him with a realistic and conscious effort to avoid projecting political goals for an entire society. An agent acts in particular situations to reduce the pressures of internal contradictions between being (1) interpellated into master discourses and (2) understanding himself as a free agent through remembering his past subject positions as incapable of being incorporated into a master text. So it seems that Altieri did finally see how Smith's use of Hegelian negativity can produce resistance. But Altieri's negative statements about Smith remain unnecessarily harsh in *Canons and Consequences*, especially given the intricacy and clarity of Smith's critiques of poststructuralist theoretical systems. Altieri's own ethical model of a Wittgensteinian/Rawlsian grammar of pronouns for agency appears after hundreds of pages of highly abstract diction that average only one or two concrete literary examples per chapter. Though highly critical of Smith, Altieri integrates some of Smith's approach into his final model: he speaks of "mobile first-person states," for instance, where "egos can share a variety of positions" (300, 304). But the mobile surplus of negativity that Smith develops from Hegel and associates with freedom and conscious choice becomes worthwhile to Altieri only when he finds similar material in Derrida's *The Ear of the Other* (1990, 213-15). Altieri also agrees, in much more sophisticated language, with some of Smith's own critique of Derrida's endless chains of textual significations with no positive terms: "[Derrida's] demand for rigor must reduce all relations to textual fragments with no privilegeable principle of integration, so it proves impossible not to be suspicious of every construction attributing significant agency to the persons asserting responsibility or being offered it" (1990, 311).

While I applaud Altieri's ability to assess complex postmodern theoretical systems in detail, to negotiate a model from combinations of elements worth preserving from very different, difficult theorists, and to incorporate the faculty of judgment without foundationalism, I find his unwillingness to descend from an Altierian empyrean of theoretical models to offer more concrete analyses of particular literary texts that engage environmental or social issues difficult to accept. His homoginized, generalized language gradually exhausts the patience of all but the most fervent poststructural reader while his focus on how a text's action allows us to assess the agent's ability to gain identity and acceptance within a desired community (249), but never a concrete specific community, seems helplessly relativistic and disconnects us from any sense of inhabitation, of living in a specific place on this planet. What ideological debts does such prose incur? Smith, as much as Altieri, is engaged in articulating what our culture can offer in the way of an imaginative "trying out identities," but Altieri restricts agency to our dreams while foreclosing on engaging actual political situations: "In our world, however, where Reagans are elected and where the many pursue dreams and tribunals that sicken those fostered on alternative communities, one's dreams of reforming the world always border on nightmares of being swallowed up by that same world" (1990, 253).

The limitations of Altieri's aestheticism surface most directly when he constructs his own position on agency in *Subjective Agency* (1994). Here he accepts the poststructural dogma that universals of moral conduct are not possible and there is no such thing as a unified, reliable, coherent self, yet he rightly critiques poststructuralists such as Althusser, Lacan, and Foucault for their unwillingness to consider language beyond its regulatory and punitive aspects, for language has an "enabling dimension" that "facilitates contracts and sustains entitlements" (167). So far this is excellent. And when Altieri develops his own expressivist ethical position on agency, where first-person avowals to take responsibility for positions about what makes a life worth living incorporate modifications from second-person audiences and third-person principles, one may at first be inclined to agree with the dense, sinewy, clear argument.

The problem occurs when one gradually realizes that Altieri restricts the second-person "you" and the third-person principles to the human positions, institutions, and culture housed in linguistic systems. While the ecopoets to be discussed in the ensuing chapters do not consider nature as a moral universal, they are well aware that the "you" or other in the ethical dialogue is not limited to anthropocentric perspectives. Human avowals must also respond to nature's needs; one must reason beyond self-interest and balance one's desires for the good life with the health of planetary ecosystems.

Underneath the cool logic of Altieri's prose resides an arrogant, nineteenth-century desire to dominate nature through language. This is most apparent on pages 133 and 134, where he speaks of the Hegelian labor that creates human identity as a process of working "against an indifferent and indeterminate nature." Here Altieri not only summarizes Hegel but, since he presents no other position for nature in the volume, appears to reveal his own predilections: "Self-consciousness cannot be content with any one image of itself, or any one struggle for lordship. More important are the range of struggles it takes on, often not by combatting other wills but by joining other wills in battles against the inchoate in nature and in the social relations imposed on the agents." Barry Lopez critiqued the sad environmental results of this nineteenth-century heroic notion of battling nature to achieve identity in his accounts of British and American efforts to find a Northern Passage through the Arctic in chapter 9 of *Arctic Dreams* (1986).

Never in *Subjective Agency* does Altieri present nature as part of the "you," the internalized other, or as an other with its own laws, survival rights, and needs. Though the unsubjected self actuates what it can know of its own momentary identity through its avowals and self-reflection on these avowals, one needs clean air and water, warmth, food, clothing, and shelter to sustain the self so that it can make avowals, and these heretofore free services provided by nature are presently severely stressed and endangered by the hands of humans. The "you" or second person audiences will always remain hopelessly vague and relativized in Altieri's aesthetic grammar, for in practice his emphasis rests on first person avowals, on the lexical process that records how the poet takes responsibility for his thoughts and actions. If nature had a place in Altieri's system (it doesn't), it would no doubt reside in the third person neuter, in the colorless, nondescript "it."

An environmental dimension should exist in the ethics of any human free choice or concept of agency, but Altieri's focus on language and grammars walls out the environmental at every turn. In the discussion portion of the "Philosophical Issues in Literature" section of the 1996 MLA Convention in Washington, D.C. (December 28), Altieri exclaimed that "you can't get outside of logic." Whenever he uses the words "grammar" and "logic," he restricts himself to the grammar and logic housed in linguistic systems created by humans. Altieri likes Stanley Cavell's notion of shame as a check to the ego in the construction of identity (1994, 202), but environmentalists would extend the notion of shame to include the environment and bow meekly and often before nature, as Lopez does.

In "Some Problems about Agency and the Theories of Radical Poetics" (1996), Altieri develops comments from Charles Olson to argue that poetic texts function as exemplary models of perspectives that readers can try on to nudge them toward modifying their relationships with "worlds beyond the texts" (228) and in the process become active agents. This is promising, but Altieri in his recent critical orientation ignores environmental poetry and never recognizes nonhuman living nature as a legitimate "world beyond the text." He is a dualist who restricts himself to exploring the aesthetic subtleties of poetic texts. Nature is the inchoate adversary to be overcome by language in the creation of culture. In *Glare* (1997), Ammons argues otherwise. Language is toss-away newsprint for Ammons unless it carries not only the energy of human perception but also the energy of the natural world and "marries" itself to "some body" in the referential world (51).

To better differentiate the concerns of ecopoets from those of poststructural language critics, let me also discuss two more examples of how preoccupation with the aesthetics of language both eliminates ecopoetry by ignoring it and creates more literary criticism hermetically sealed from any discernible reference to the actual events of the quotidian world in which we live. In *Radical Artifice* (1991) Marjorie Perloff reviews the poetics of major post-World War II American poetry movements. Until midcentury, the dominant poetic was the modernist heightened or purified everyday speech of the common man's experience—an aesthetic of presence where poetic language attempted to represent a more refined version of immediate experience that originally took place "out there," in the putative "real world" of speech and action, where the word is not separated from its object. In this mode, Perloff concludes, "the implication is that ideally, if the poet were equal to his task, words could and should represent the realities behind them, realities, so Eliot would have it, that belong to both poet and reader. . . . Writing, by this argument, *makes present* what the poet wishes to say" (32). The fifties shift by the Beats and Black Mountain poets to open form and a breath- or speech-based poetics, exemplified by Gary Snyder and others, changed the locus of reality from the common man to the poet's subjective energy but did not change the fundamental notion that poetic language conveys the presence of the poet's original experience.

Perloff then argues that since the 1960s, Derrida's *Of Grammatology* and other texts critiqued doctrines of logocentric presence. Derrida denounces doctrines that "confine writing to a secondary and instrumental function: translator of a full speech that was fully *present* (present to itself, to its signified, to the other, the very condition of the theme of presence in general), technics in the service of language, *spokesman*, interpreter of an originary speech itself shielded from interpretation" (Derrida 1976, 8; Perloff 1991, 36). Perloff concludes that

> as the speech-based poetics of midcentury has given way, more and more, to the foregrounding of the materiality of the written sign itself, a prosody based on intonational contours has become increasingly problematic. The emphasis upon the moment of enunciation (at best variable and transitory) now seems a questionable procedure, whether for the poet or the reader. For such "momentary" or "instantaneous" rhythm suggests that there is first an experience, something lived and felt *out there,* and only then and secondarily its verbal rendering. But this doctrine goes counter to everything poststructuralist theory has taught us: if writing is regarded, not as the linear representation of a prior "full" or "originary" speech, but as what Derrida calls a "sequence of differences," a sequence in which the phonemic, graphemic, and ideographic elements of language are brought into play, then we may expect to find a poetic composition that is neither conventionally metrical on the one hand, nor breath-determined or "intonational" on the other. (137-38)

Perloff delineates a new poetry of radical artifice that derives its poetics not from an emphasis on the authenticity of prior speech or experience but from a heightened sense of the poem as "made," as construct—an "antireferential" text governed by arbitrarily imposed compositional rules and forms (45-47). Perloff adopts Derridean notions of the play of difference in written language and Lacanian and Wittgensteinian tenets that assume that all experience is mediated by language. To this combination she adds the premise that an intrusive media of talk shows and advertising mediates experience today and in the process offers Americans a daily diet of Baudrillardian simulacra; this creates a hyperreal, bytes of language that are "models of a real without origin or reality" (39). Such radical artifice does describe the compositions of John Cage and the poetry of John Ashbery, Louis Zukofsky, Leslie Scalapino, Lyn Hejinian, Charles Bernstein, Ron Silliman, Susan Howe, and others, whose work Perloff interprets approvingly.

Yet Perloff's short history of twentieth-century American poetics ignores the environmental poetry and ecopoetry in dozens of poetry collections published by Ammons, Berry, Merwin, Snyder, and others and buttressed by several collections of critical essays published by Berry and Snyder, from the mid-1960s to the present. She mentions only in passing Snyder's earliest, breath-based poetic (34-35) and dismisses all ecopoets and ecocriticism by ignoring them.

The Derridean play of differences and the postmodern premise that all experience is mediated by language, principally developed by Lacan, often result in creating poetry and literary criticism characterized by a hermetically sealed textuality that avoids recognizing the fact that all writing is situated in the socioeconomic and environmental present of its moment of composition, influencing it and being influenced by it. Perloff emphasizes her antireferential bent when she says that radical artifice poetry mirrors not "actual speech" or the "exchange of a 'man speaking to men'" but a hyperreal speech "emptied of all particularity of reference" (40). Furthermore, a poetics divorced from referentiality aids little in offering the reader an awareness of oneself as a potential agent of historical change. The divorce of text from socioeconomic and environmental context legitimates the status quo by never calling it into question, by adopting a tacitly laissez-faire posture.

Perloff's position concerning referentiality is typical of establishment poststructural criticism. One further example, from Jerome Klinkowitz's *Rosenberg/Barthes/Hassan: The Postmodern Habit of Thought* (1988), should suffice to underscore this point. While emphasizing the influence of action painting and Derridean textual play in creating the postmodern aesthetic,

Klinkowitz manages to equate politics with "extraneous elements" and seal off the text from any referential context:

> Arising out of movement, the work is received as movement, and for once the essence of art can be located in an identity of production and reception. As long as contact with this process is maintained, the artwork continues to exist; on the other hand, a sense of contact prevents extraneous elements from interfering and diverting the imaginative act—in this way postmodernism prevents political misreadings motivated by materials outside the textual or painterly activity . . . . Here is the field of action for the maker, who invests the truth of a work not in its messages or psychological expressivity, but in the evidence of his or her hand pressing down to create a trace in paint or language. Inside no longer commands outside; there is no kernel of meaning to be cracked, only a texture of activity to be experienced in its making. (5)

From Altieri, Perloff, Klinkowitz, and others one can readily see how contemporary American poetry criticism is moving far away from a poet's originary experience in nature and in real communities struggling to survive their socioeconomic and environmental problems. Are all materials outside the "textual or painterly activity" in the moment of creation "extraneous" and "political," as Klinkowitz argues, or is this a deliberate attempt to seal off the text from anything other than aesthetic activity? Edward Said argues forcefully in *The World, the Text, and the Critic* that texts are always situated, as is literary criticism. One cannot disconnect the text from what Said calls its "worldliness" (1983, 4, 26, 27, 32, 34, 39). What the text valorizes and what it suppresses, as Raymond Williams proved brilliantly in his analyses of eighteenth-century English country-house poems in *The Country and the City* (1973), may legitimate the will to power of a dominant class, a class whose political power allowed them to enclose land and then glorify the aesthetic dimensions of their holdings (pleasant vistas, manicured gardens), while hiding from the reader the displaced peasants and the toil of undernourished day laborers who made the views and gardens possible (96-119). Pollution in America today is so rife and yet so systematically repressed in establishment American poetry that one cannot help but extend Williams's analysis of the perception of nature within the dominant class. Rather than discomfort their readers and critics, establishment American poets today cleanse their texts of all references to the pollution created by middle class consumption. This could be the political agenda of a class that must repress the actual environmental consequences of its actions in order to sustain privileges and pleasures without guilt.

For Said a text solicits the world's attention and engages the reader in a dialectic of production where the writer responds to his historical situation and the reader must make some sense of this response (40-41). The notion of a hermetically sealed textual universe of free Derridean play runs counter to what Said sees as the text's "worldliness, circumstantiality, the text's status as an event having sensuous particularity as well as historical contingency . . . [as] an infrangible part of its capacity for conveying and producing meaning. This means that the text has a specific situation . . . [and that this] situation exists at the same level of surface particularity as the textual object itself" (39). Hence, Said argues, contra Derrida, that "any simple diametric opposition asserted on the one hand between speech, bound by situation and reference, and on the other hand the text as an interception or suspension of speech's worldliness is, I think, misleading and largely simplified" (33).

Similarly, as critics valorize certain texts as superior cultural artifacts and create notions of canonicity, they participate in a worldly struggle for authority and power. Said's discussions of Swift and Conrad in *The World, the Text, and the Critic*, and of numerous third-world prose writers in *Culture and Imperialism* (1993), amply prove how an oppositional criticism can reveal and critique our historical choices and how it can restore a sense of worldliness while questioning the prerogatives of a dominant culture.

Ecopoets and Language

Ecopoets are not indifferent to language or to poststructural critiques of the function of language. They argue the reverse of the poststructural position that all experience is mediated by language. For ecopoets language is an instrument that the poet continually refurbishes to articulate his originary experience in nature—the origin, as Pack asserted, of language. For Ammons language is a secondary "reflection" of what is initially a "non-verbal experience of reality." A poem occurs when a writer stretches or dislocates, to borrow Eliot's term, sedimented language into language that will provide as accurate as possible a reflection of an originary perception initiated by stimuli from events in the natural world. These events Ammons calls "facts." The preverbal experience is primary; what we can retain of its richness and its energy is kept alive in language (SM 8-9). For the ecopoet, language preserves the historical record of the percept.

Merwin's recent poetry explores the fine line between the cliches of sedimented language and language that evokes the preverbal experience that the poet struggles to convey in language. Merwin has faith in language as the "ultimate achievement" of our species. Language offers humans "the most flexible articulation of our experience," but it can never convey "the full unique intimacy of that experience" (Hirsch 1987, 76). Naming gives humans a conceptual "control" over things that can all too readily create "barriers" between the self and things. The feeling of control soon leads to the anthropocentric exploitation of nature. In his best poems Merwin tries to evoke the Zen moment of preverbal suchness, the experience of joyous participation in a world of things with no names (Elliott 1988, 16-17).

Snyder in his essays often takes an anthropological view to remind us that language originated in tribal societies from an intense desire to connect the inner world of hopes and fears with the outer world of sensuous experience. So the origin of language resides in the songs, rituals, and myths of a community rooted in the natural world, as reflected in their oral traditions and in the healing art of the shaman (1979 ["Poetry, Community, & Climax"], 33). Instead of theoretical flights, Snyder would like to see people "grounded" in a sense of place. Get people "in touch" with their lives, their bodies, and the environment, said Snyder, "and the poetry'll take care of itself." The work of poetry for Snyder is "the work of social change," and it occurs not by propaganda or taking stands on particular social issues but by "bringing us back to our original, true natures" through a language that helps us to see "the universe freshly, in eternity" (RW 72).

In *The Practice of the Wild* (1990), Snyder states that "when logos-oriented philosophers uncritically advance language as a unique human gift which serves as the organizer of the chaotic universe—it is a delusion" (77). "Language belongs to our biological nature and writing is just moose-tracks in the snow" (69). Snyder does not believe that all experience is mediated by language; he believes that "the unconditioned mind-in-the-moment . . . eats, transforms, goes beyond, language. Art, or creative play, sometimes does this by going directly to the freshness and uniqueness of the moment, and to direct, unmediated experience" (70-71). Two paragraphs from *Practice* state unequivocally that Snyder believes that language derives from our biological being, from our connectedness to natural ecosystems, and it arises spontaneously. It does not structure all that we can

know of our world, as Wittgenstein believes, but is our most creative way
to articulate our unique experiences:

> Language and culture emerge from our biological-social natural
> existence, animals that we were/are. Language is a mind-body
> system that coevolved with our needs and nerves. Like imagi-
> nation and the body, language rises unbidden. It is of a com-
> plexity that eludes our rational intellectual capacities. All attempts
> at scientific description of natural languages have fallen short of
> completeness, as the descriptive linguists readily confess, yet the
> child learns the mother tongue early and has virtually mastered
> it by six.
>
> Language is learned in the house and in the fields, not at
> school. Without having ever been taught formal grammar we
> utter syntactically correct sentences, one after another, for all
> the waking hours of the years of our life. Without conscious
> device we constantly reach into the vast word-hoards in the
> depths of the wild unconscious. We cannot as individuals or
> even as a species take credit for this power. It came from some-
> place else: from the way clouds divide and mingle (and the arms
> of energy that coil first back and then forward), from the way
> the many flowerlets of a composite blossom divide and redi-
> vide, from the gleaming calligraphy of the ancient riverbeds
> under present riverbeds of the Yukon River streaming out the
> Yukon flats, from the wind in the pine needles, from the chuck-
> les of grouse in the ceanothus bushes. (17)

Wendell Berry is perhaps the most outspoken and provocative among
ecopoets on the question of language. In *Standing by Words* (1983), Berry
argues that "the subject of poetry is not words, it is the world." Poetry has
always had a traditional social allegiance to the values of the spirit, and "this
ancient allegiance gives poets the freedom, and perhaps the moral impera-
tive, to turn outward" (SW 8). He is wary of poetry written as a self-ab-
sorbed, hermetic exercise in wordcraft:

> One of the oldest doctrines of specialist poets is that of the
> primacy of language and the primacy of poetry. They have vir-
> tually made a religion of their art, a religion based not on what
> they have in common with other people, but on what they *do*

that sets them apart. For poets who believe this way, a poem is not a point of clarification or connection between themselves and the world on the one hand and between themselves and their readers on the other, nor is it an adventure into any reality or mystery outside themselves. It is a seeking of self in words, the making of a word-world in which the word-self may be at home. The poets go to their poems as other people have gone to the world or to God—for a sense of their own reality. (SW 7)

Berry agrees with Snyder that the poet is responsible for "possibilities opening both inward and outward" (Snyder 1979 ["Poetry, Community, & Climax"], 21), and when "the connection between inward and outward is broken . . . then language fails" (SW 31). Conversely, Berry uses the metaphor of a healthy, balanced ecosystem where the inner world intersects with the outer, referential world: "To be bound within the confines of either the internal or the external way of accounting is to be diseased. To hold the two in balance is to validate both kinds, and to have health" (SW 42).

Berry uses cognates of the word "reference" many times in *Standing by Words*; in a passage that alludes to the title of his book, Berry reserves his sharpest criticism for those who use words that are deliberately meant "to refer to nothing in particular," where "attention rests upon percentages, categories, abstract functions. The reference drifts inevitably toward the merely provisional. It is not language that the user will very likely be required to stand by or to act on, for it does not define any personal ground for standing or acting" (52). In *Sex, Economy, Freedom & Community* (1993), Berry sees the Gulf War as "the failure of those who most profit from the world to be able to imagine a world except in terms of abstract quantities" (82). He even dislikes the words "environment," "ecology," and "ecosystem," for these words lack particularity and convey no responsibility. These terms "come from the juiceless, abstract intellectuality of the universities which was invented to disconnect, displace, and disembody the mind (35). Language that is healthy connects us to nature's songs, whose rhythms in the poet have the "profoundest *reference*" (SW 17).

All four ecopoets emphasize the *relationality* of language, the instrumental ability of language—how it articulates and codifies ways that humans relate to nature and to themselves. In chapter five we will explore how Merwin uses Heidegger's emphasis on the relationality of language to realize new perceptions of our participation in Being. In the postscript, we will see how the poststructural historian Michel de Certeau emphasizes the relationality of language. For de Certeau language is a positive instrument that can promote authentic social and environmental relations between humans and their environment—relations that can lead to emancipatory social change.

2

Sustainable Poetry

A Poetry of *Référance*

Must literature always lead us away from the physical
world, never back to it?
> Buell, *The Environmental Imagination*, 11

A Poetry of *Référance*

The literature that Altieri, Perloff, Klinkowitz, and other poststructural
language critics valorize derives from an aesthetics heavily influenced by
Derrida's deconstruction of the metaphysics of presence in language. For
Derrida the written word, not the spoken word, is primary in contempo-
rary culture, and the concepts (the signified) that signifiers (signs such as
orthographic squiggles, pictographs, and so on) are supposed to grasp are
characterized by absence, for any signified is itself only positional and de-
pendent on more language and borrowings from other concepts in a
synchronic view of a language system. Referential pointing is purely con-
ventional and impossibly unstable, for the signifiers are always in motion,
signifying away from each other and forever supplementing an originary
absence with ephemerally disseminating meaning. For establishment
postmodern poets such as Robert Hass, the word "blackberry," for instance,
"is elegy to what it signifies" (1979 [*Praise*], 4). Meaning is constantly de-
ferred and needing supplement because language, according to Saussure in
his *Course in General Linguistics*, is a system of differences with no positive
terms (1966, 120). Derrida's *différance*, the interplay of delay (to defer) and

dissimilarity (to differ) in language, is at the heart of much postmodern poetry ("*Différance*" 18). Enjoying the *jouissance* of Roland Barthes, the pleasure of playing with a highly self-conscious, self-reflexive poetic language, where meaning is carefully restricted to engagements with lexical systems, is the goal of much postmodern establishment poetry. How does one cross such a chasm to the referentiality needed for environmental poetry?

In denying any extralinguistic grounding for language, Derrida takes a reductionist position, for Saussure clearly posits a social, communal ground for language (113). Language has at least a mediate connectedness to the referential world from the standpoint of social praxis. As a culture completes its synchronic system, concepts are locked into signifiers, and communication is possible only with relatively stable signifiers that normally do relate words to referents (Ellis 1989, 45-60; Dillon 1988, 182-84). At least two people must agree over relatively stable signifiers to create a language; otherwise, one only has an indecipherable secret code, or an endless chain of deferred signification. By promoting infinite play and dissemination cut off from referentiality, Derrida has, as John Ellis notes, "abolished language" as a communication tool among humans (54). Saussure clearly states that "the signifier, though to all appearances freely chosen with respect to the idea that it represents, is fixed, not free, with respect to the linguistic community that uses it" (71). Arnold Krupat calls writers who have completely jettisoned referentiality "antihumanists" and laments that for the first time in history poetry has divorced itself from *utile* in its obsession with *dulce* (1989, 26, 40-42). Because its postmodern aesthetic depends on a complete divorce from referentiality, the poetry of *différance* is unable to confront even the most basic facts of our global environmental degradation: that world population will double by 2050 while various forms of soil, water, and air pollution or erosion may poison, suffocate or starve most humans on our planet by that date.

To describe the hermetic treatment of language as a freedom-filled lexical playfield, establishment poststructural poetry critics often cite Derrida's statement in *Of Grammatology* (1978, 158) that "*il n'y a pas de hors-texte*"—"there is nothing outside of the text" or "there is no outside-text." John Mowitt, however, argues that Derrida's own texts or readings bring persistently interdisciplinary combinations of phenomenological, semiotic, psychoanalytic, and cultural preoccupations into "play," thus nudging the language read into new "signifying structures" (1992, 83-103). This, plus the antidisciplinary thrust of the entire *Tel Quel* movement, leads Mowitt to conclude his book with a strong plea, authorized by Derrida's reading practices, that we must deconstruct the limited disciplinary readings of the literary establishment, for here is where the discipline perpetuates itself—through disciplining its members' critical practices (pace Foucault). Marjorie Perloff, for instance, moves from the speech-based and "deep image" poetics of American verse from midcentury through the seventies to the radical artifice of Derridean language play in the poetry of the eighties while enforcing disciplinary limits that ignore the very strong ecological and environmental poetry that flourished in the eighties. By refusing to widen her disciplinary boundaries beyond a poetics derived from poststructural language theory, she reinforces disciplinary limits that privilege the play of language while excluding referentiality and marginalizing most interdisciplinary readings. Derrida apparently does not authorize such practices, but our disciplinary-bounded poetry establishment regularly enforces them.

Mowitt (97) notes that Derrida ended his analysis of "Freud and the Scene of Writing" in *Writing and Difference* with the statement that "the *sociality* of writing as *drama* requires an entirely different discipline" (1978, 227). Derrida seems to authorize texts that are the products of different combinations of interdisciplinary preoccupations in the psyches of the purveyors of books. Now, if we extend the disciplinary boundaries of literary criticism to include the *inter*disciplinary preoccupations of ecopoetry, especially its referential concern with environmental context, what we often observe from reading the past thirty years of ecopoetry and environmental poetry is the reverse of the free play of *différance*. The real "play" or nudge that one often finds in reading ecopoetry and environmental poetry is a self-reflexive heightening of language that reveals language's limitations. Ecopoets and environmental poets often foreground language only to reveal language as "*sous rature*" ("under erasure"—inadequate but necessary: *Grammatology* xiv-xv, 19, 31) in the quest to transform human behavior into patterns that augment planetary survival.

One might define ecopoetry as poetry that persistently stresses human cooperation with nature conceived as a dynamic, interrelated series of cyclic feedback systems. Wendell Berry's celebration of the hydrological cycle in "The River Bridged and Forgot" and "The Gift of Gravity" (BCP 255-59) and the malathion-laced opening poem of Adrienne Rich's *An Atlas of the Difficult World* (1991, 3–5) are archetypal ecopoems. Environmental poetry reveres nature and often focuses on particular environmental issues, but without the ecopoet's particular concentration on nature as an interrelated series of cyclic feedback systems. Within ecopoetry and environmental poetry, language is often foregrounded only to reveal its limitations, and this is accomplished in such a way that the reader's gaze is thrust beyond language back into the less limited natural world that language refers to, the inhabited place where humans must live in harmony with ecological cycles. I believe that the adequate term for this process that has often occurred in the last thirty years of ecopoetry is *référance*, from the French verb *se référer*, which means "to relate or refer oneself to." In practice, *référance* turns the reader's gaze toward an apprehension of the cyclic processes of wild nature after a self-reflexive recognition of the limits (the *sous rature*) of language. After this two-stage process, a third moment often occurs, the moment of atonement with nature, where we confide our trust in (*s'en référer*) nature's rhythms and cycles, where reading nature becomes our text. In other words, a text informed by *référance*, by the interdisciplinary practices of ecological and environmental poetry, involves (1) reaching a self-reflexive acknowledgment of the limits of language, (2) referring one's perceptions beyond the printed page to nature, to the referential origin of all language, and (3) in most cases achieving an atonement or at-one-ment with nature. The "at-one-ment" of this third stage, occasionally absent in satiric ecopoetry, is, of course, borrowed from a famous Wendell Berry statement (CH 13) derived from John Stewart Collis's *The Triumph of the Tree* (1954). Language and nature under *référance* constitute two opposite but interdependent systems, with the former (language) only temporarily deferring the latter, nature, where language had its origin.

One can define *référance* another way, through a useful contrast. Ezra Pound, in his famous "Vorticism" essay, wrote that Imagists were "trying to record the precise instant when a thing outward and objective transforms itself, or darts into a thing inward and subjective" (1914, 467). Ecopoets often record *référance* as the precise moment when one recognizes that phonetic language is a reified, limited conceptual system of abstract rules and concepts, a product of human logic and reason, whose major function is to point us *outward*, toward that infinitely less limited referential reality of nature. Wittgenstein himself was just as interested in the work or ordinary use value of language, language that points toward objects and referential events, as he was with language as imaginative display, which to him was "an engine idling" (PI, no. 132), or language that self-reflexively foregrounds its grammatical form, its syntax, or shows its logical propositions, its "mode of saying" (Guetti 1993, 4–9). For a quick moment ecopoets reveal language idling or displaying its dependence on human logic, only to turn that moment against itself. James Guetti believes that for Wittgenstein "it is the *action* of language that is important; in meaningful verbal activity, words themselves are relatively self-effacing in favor of the changes their uses achieve" (Guetti 1993, 4). For ecopoets the meaningful changes are changes in perception and consequent changes in social conduct—social praxis.

Recent research on Andy Warhol's 1960s silkscreens offers yet another instructive approach to *référance*. Critics have discussed Warhol's deconstruction of Abstract Expressionism mainly by taking as his subjects the simulacra of mass consumption products. But Hal Foster, in *The Return of the Real* (1996), draws on Lacan's definition of trauma as a missed encounter with the real to uncover an obsessively melancholic fixation on the missed representational object in the traumatized screening process of Warhol's 1963 disaster silkscreens. Because the encounter has been missed, it can only be repeated, as is the case in Warhol's 1963 silkscreened camera film photos of disasters such as *White Burning Car III, Green Burning Car I, Nine Times, Orange Car Crash, Ten Times,* and *Ambulance Disaster.* In these silkscreens of multiple camera shots of the same disaster, complete with blemishes from handling that appear on the film and empty corners of the canvas that readily reveal the materiality and the surface quality of the representation, what happens aesthetically for Foster is something much more complex than a return to representation: "Somehow in these repetitions, then, several contradictory things occur at the same time: a warding away of traumatic significance *and* an opening out to it, a defending against traumatic effect *and* a producing of it" (132). Thus, for Foster an antirepresentational element in these Warhol silkscreens points the viewer's gaze back toward that traumatic missed encounter with referential reality:

> Repetition in Warhol is not reproduction in the sense of representation (of a referent) or simulation (of a pure image, a detached signifier). Rather, repetition serves to *screen* the real understood as traumatic. But this very need also *points* to the real, and at this point the real *ruptures* the screen of repetition. It is a rupture less in the world than in the subject—between the perception and the consciousness of a subject *touched* by an image. In an allusion to Aristotle on accidental causality, Lacan calls this traumatic point the *tuché;* in *Camera Lucida* (1980) Barthes calls it the *punctum.* (132)

Foster asserts that, for Warhol, the *punctum* "works less through content than through technique" (134); though the repetition of the camera image on the silkscreen may screen us from the first order of shock in absorbing the graphic reality of dead, torn bodies, what Warhol manages to produce almost simultaneously is "a second order of trauma, here at the level of technique, where the *punctum* breaks through the screen and allows the real to poke through" (136).

One of the techniques of *référance* that Merwin uses, for instance, concerns generating a string of sedimented, dead language, of tired cliches or flattened prose (which would correspond to the repeated disaster images of Warhol), highlighting these cliches self-reflexively and then turning away from this exhausted language into a minimalist, pure language of firsthand experience perceived freshly, for the first time, as in "The First Year" from *The Rain in the Trees* (1988):

> When the words had all been used
> for other things
> we saw the first day begin
>
> out of the calling water
> and the black branches
> leaves no bigger than your fingertips
> were unfolding on the tree of heaven
> against the old stained wall
> their green sunlight
> that had never shone before
>
> waking together we were the first
> to see them
> and we knew them then
>
> all the languages were foreign and the first
> year rose
> (5)

By first introducing the "used" language of sedimented ordinary ex-perience, and heightening this language self-reflexively *as language*, what follows in the poem appears more fresh, unique, true to an immersion in firsthand experience in the referential world. The technique creates a *punc-tum* reinforced by the repetitions of first sight and phrases such as "green" or new sunlight and by the implied presentation of Merwin and his wife

Paula as Adam and Eve reborn in an environmental garden of Eden where all is fresh, vivid. The spare, minimalist language manages to convey a phenomenologically intense state of perception, especially because Merwin contrasts this originary experience with the dead language of sedimented speech at the beginning and end of the poem.

Merwin's technique in "The First Year" is merely representative of how one ecopoet uses *référance* at one point in his career. Each ecopoet uses *référance* in distinct and unique ways; Merwin developed other techniques in *Travels* (1993) and *The Vixen* (1996), his most recent volumes. Not every ecopoem contains moments of *référance*, but in each poet enough poems do to suggest that the ecopoet is aware that, though language cannot capture essences in the referential world, the poet is actively searching for an originary language that tries to close the gap between words and intense, firsthand experience in that referential world. By juxtaposing and highlighting sedimented language as just that, worn-out, followed by language teased out slowly with fresh and arresting metaphors and images, ecopoets demonstrate what Heidegger calls for in his late essays in *On the Way to Language* (1971) and in *What Is Called Thinking* (1968)—the fresh, originary language that reveals the poet as the true philosopher actively engaged in the moment-to-moment quest toward self-realization on the way toward Being, where he "risk[s] *asking* the question" of how one arrives at authentic Being and "get[s] underway toward the call," the active "blossoming" of Being (Heidegger 1968, 165, 169, 220). If words cannot capture referential reality in any essentialistic way, what an ecopoet can do is to direct our gaze beyond the printed page toward firsthand experiences that approximate the poet's intense involvement in the authentic experience that lies behind his originary language.

Ecopoets do not valorize the completed poem as modernist product, ready for a green museum of art; instead they want the poem to challenge and reconfigure the reader's perceptions so to put the book down and live life more fully in all possible dimensions of the moment of firsthand experience within nature's supportive second skin and to become more responsible about that necessary second skin. The ecopoem is a momentary pause for a reconfiguration of perception, for the altering of the Eye, because without that alteration we trudge on mechanically as consumers in commodified simulacra with blinkered eyes and habits that will one day wreck this planet's supportive second skin.

For the past three decades Wendell Berry, A.R. Ammons, Gary Snyder, and W.S. Merwin have incorporated a healthy self-reflexivity into their poetry without denying the more ordinary mediatory or instrumental value of poetry to effect changes in our perceptions that encourage a sharpened appreciation of the referential world and our ecological interrelatedness to it. Each made a separate peace with postmodernism without building a poetics on its pyrotechnics, and collectively this group has influenced contemporaries such as Marge Piercy and Adrienne Rich, as well as dozens of younger environmental poets—Brendan Galvin, Joy Harjo, Pattiann Rogers, and William Heyen, to name a few—whose careers developed during the late seventies and eighties. More responsive to our current global environmental crisis, *référance*, a technique that has its own measure of linguistic sophistication, characterizes the poetics of many poems from this older generation of ecopoets. These poets recognize the limits of language while referring us in an epiphanic moment to our interdependency and relatedness to the richer planet whose operations created and sustain us.

Of course, the mentor and spiritual father of all four ecopoets discussed in this volume is Robinson Jeffers (1887-1962). Aloof in his Tor House stone tower at Carmel, California, Jeffers taught these poets the stoic endurance and antianthropocentrism of the Inhumanist, especially in his late volume *The Double Axe* ([1948] 1977). Yet, though Jeffers studied medicine and forestry and did have a sense of the oneness and dynamic flux of nature (53), he usually used the beauty of nature as an austere, impersonal backdrop (120, 122) that exposed how overwhelmingly dysfunctional is human behavior. Confident that humanity is a "botched / experiment that has run wild and ought to be stopped" (144), Jeffers felt that this "most repulsive of all hot-blooded animals" (145) will disappear from the earth, that one day "the earth / Will scratch herself and smile and rub off humanity" (105). The Indian gods of "The Inquisitors" who inspect these "fragile" and "noxious" creatures called humans, convey an optimism that contemporary ecopoets would find repellant. The gods agree that "It is not likely they can destroy all life: the planet is / capacious. Life would surely grow up again . . ." (147-49). Enmeshed in their Freudian love and power struggles with others, the most humans can achieve in Jeffers's poems is a conscious acceptance of pain and the final ability to shift their gazes beyond their limited struggles to appreciate the vast, inhuman beauty of nonhuman life and order in the cosmos (Hunt 1990, 248; Zaller 1990, 258-62).

Contemporary ecopoets have a somewhat more optimistic view of the educability of humans and a less optimistic view of our negligible effects on ecosystems. We know from McKibben's *The End of Nature* (1989) that through global warming and genetic manipulation humans are becoming godlike in their capacity to alter and harm the major components of life on planet earth. Whereas in Jeffers humans and nature are usually foils for each other or operate in dialectical relationships, contemporary ecopoets see humans and nature as equal and necessarily interdependent partners in the maintenance of ecological health. The severity of Jeffers's stoic detachment is understandable because it derives at least in part from his having lived as an adult through both of the major wars of this century. When in the longer narratives humans experience nature's power, the result is often a Dionysian sexual frenzy or a Nietzschian will to power, both of which typically end tragically. In contrast to this destructive clash of opposites in Jeffers (Elder 1996, 1–25, 161, 168), most contemporary ecopoets focus on interactive processes shared by humans and ecosystems as they strive to delineate gentler survival strategies for humans to be, in Berry's words, "at home in the world" (BCP 111), living in harmony with nature.

Jeffers died before the widespread development of ecological consciousness in the general public and before the onrush of poststructural language theory, so his poetry and prose do not emphasize nature conceived as a series of interdependent feedback systems, nor does he incorporate into his poems self-reflexivity and responses to the problematics of representation and referentiality in language. Contemporary ecopoetry, however, conveys a profound distrust of language severed from the "real" world where it originated and to which its meanings refer. Wendell Berry, whose poetry emphasizes the interdependence of humans and nature, has created verse from a lifetime of active labor on his Port Royal, Kentucky, farm. His essays on language mark him as one of ecopoetry's most eloquent spokespersons. In *Standing by Words* (1983), Berry admits he is deeply suspicious of those who sever language from its intimacy with action and referentiality, for, as with Swift's projectors or Milton's Satan, a language impoverished of referential specificity also lacks responsibility. The language that is its own place resists the claims of family, community, and nature and the elaborate system of dependencies that constitute planetary ecology (SW 46, 57).

Yet this does not mean Berry opts for some impossible version of linguistic essentialism—speech-based, "deep image"-based, or whatever. Language for Berry is a tool with the "power to designate" (SW 59), to forge an interdependent "balance" (42) between inner and outer needs (31, 46, 59). Although language can never do more than imitate the rhythms of nature, its rhythms resonate with "the profoundest reference" (17) when human needs and labor intersect in just proportions with the needs of family, community, and nature (46). When poetry achieves these "right relations," we have planetary "health" (42). Language separated from responsibility for the referential supports "ecological degradation, pollution, poverty, hatred, and violence" (57).

One fine example of Berry's acknowledgment of the limits of language and the necessity of connectedness with nature occurs in his "Window Poems," from his 1968 volume *Openings* (BCP 72-95). As he meditates on our tragic involvement in Vietnam inside his "long-legged house," his writing studio—a cabin on the Kentucky River—Berry labors at writing poetry in a mood of severe despondency. The window is the location where the anguished, to-fro movement of consciousness meets external nature. As Berry slowly clears his mind of bile and wrath at his country, his smudged window becomes progressively clearer, achieving a fragile "balance / in transparence, delicately / seamed." At the poem's conclusion, he exits the house of art for the world of nature in peace. Yet he achieves his at-one-ment with the world only after recognizing the limits of language. He has learned that his words, however imaginatively strong and capable, will never fly like the birds outside his window feeder, and he deliberately chooses the world of nature after a moment of *référance*: "the world is greater than its words. / To speak of it the mind must bend" (BCP 86).

Moments of *référance* in Berry's poetry appear too frequently to list all of them here. One particularly evocative moment occurs in "The Silence" (BCP 111). As in "Window Poems," Berry again learns that his true home is nature. *Référance* immediately points outward, toward a heightened sense of being enveloped by a system stronger and more supportive than that of language:

> What must a man do to be at home in the world?
> There must be times when he is here
> as though absent, gone beyond words into the woven shadows
> of the grass . . . .
> into the shadows that grow out of the ground
> so that the furrow he opens in the earth opens
> in his bones . . . .

Berry's poetry testifies to his faith in our ability to develop an alertness and imaginative strength sufficient to our environmental needs. He believes "we will understand the world, and preserve ourselves and our values in it, only insofar as we have a language that is alert and responsive to it, and careful of it" (CH 171).

Ammons has spent his entire career convincing us that nature, not the anthropocentric thinking of humans, provides the standards, the norms, the locus of values. No naive pastoralist, Ammons in one of his earliest statements on poetics ("A Note on Incongruence" [1966]) wrote that "poetry is not made out of 'reality,' but out of an invented system of signs," and "language, an invented instrument, is not identical with what it points to" (SM 8). Yet poets do manage to create works that do ample though momentary justice to the human condition by mediating among our feelings, the facts behind these feelings, and changeable referential reality. In 1965, Ammons proclaimed that "ecology," with its "centers & peripheries / in motion, / organic, / interrelations," was his formal model (*Tape* 1965, 112). Many of his early poems are sophisticated human colloquies with nature, where nature is often introduced with deliberate, highly self-reflexive pathetic fallacy. In "The Ridge Farm," a fine example of his more recent work, moments of *référance* occur in sudden, very direct discussions of his aesthetic principles. Again he avers that, since language cannot help but be stained with the redolence and flux of the "real" world, the sanguine optimist in him cannot help but "implicate" language with "barklike beeps" and "floppy turf" to "lift up . . . the whatnot" (SV 16). Language is like shit because it is the "unmistakable assimilation" of all we have gathered from the environment (SV 12). Because poetry is the place where light, nature, and the human spirit dwell to produce the visible (SV 40), for Ammons there can be no outside-text because the visible intertwines with his highly interdisciplinary consciousness in each poetic act.

Throughout Ammons's work nature, not language, provides the bedrock of values. Harold Bloom, a committee member when Ammons won the National Book Award in 1973, praised Ammons in *Ringers in the Tower* (1971) as the "central poet" of his generation. In his 1986 Chelsea House collection of critical essays on Ammons, Bloom repeated this judgment and added a reason for it—"because he alone has made a heterocosm, a second nature in his poetry" (5). In "The Arc Inside and Out," a poem dedicated to Bloom (ACP 390-91), Ammons critiqued Bloom's attempt to place the linguistic product in a superior position to nature. Here Ammons deconstructed Bloom's textual heterocosm:

> neither way to go's to stay, stay
> here, the apple an apple with its own hue
> or streak, the drink of water, the drink,

> the falling into sleep, restfully ever the
> falling into sleep, dream, dream, and
> every morning the sun comes, the sun.

Here the doubling of the apple, the drink of water, and the sun, a perfect moment of *référance*, brings the reader simultaneously into an awareness of the limits of language as well as a finer appreciation of the primacy of the "real" entities in the referential world. The doubling, a technique of *référance*, thrusts the reader's perceptual gaze beyond signifiers on the page toward the referential apple, drink, and sun. Any attempt to totalize in language simply delays or suppresses its opposite—the referential entities to which these words refer.

In his ecopoem *Garbage* (1993), Ammons meditates on the Interstate 95 landfill outside Miami. In the process, he reflects on how "we are not alone in language," for the bluejay has an "extensive vocabulary" and "elephants network even distant / air with sound waves too low for us to hear." Though "we may be alone in words," Ammons takes the biocentric position that "words do for us what other / languages do for others—they warn, inform, // reassure, compare, present" (49-50). Then Ammons gestures outward toward the world in a perfect moment of *référance*:

> the world was the beginning
> of the world; words are a way of fending in the
>
> world: whole languages, like species, can
> disappear without dropping a gram of earth's
>
> weight, and symbolic systems to a fare you well
> can be added without filling a ditch or thimble:
> (50-51)

Perloff, in *Radical Artifice* (1991, 34-35), critiqued Gary Snyder's speech-based Buddhist poetics from a 1967 essay ("Poetry and the Primitive") as naively heroic, an aggressive attempt to block out the consequences of the "information revolution." Yet her very abbreviated discussion of Snyder and speech-based poetics contains special pleading, for Snyder has developed a more thoroughly ecological basis for poetry in subsequent essays. This is a perfect instance of disciplinary discipline marginalizing the interdisciplinary by ignoring it. In a 1979 essay, "Poetry, Community, &

Climax," Snyder defined poetry as a "tool, a net or trap to catch and present; a sharp edge; a medicine, or the little awl that unties knots." Poetry brings "the outer world of nature and the inner world of the unconscious" into "a single focus." For Snyder the wordsmith is a "weaver of rich fabric to delight the mind with possibilities opening both inward and outward." Snyder presents nature and humans as equals. Following the ecologist Ramon Margalef's use of climax theory, Snyder presents the poet, always rooted in place and community, as a recycler of dead cultural biomass and inner potential (29, 21, 34-35; RW 71, 173-74). This is not a speech or breath-based poetics but a poetics of environmental *référance*.

Snyder's *Axe Handles* (1983) contains many such climax/recycling poems about the writing of poetry, all of which present language as a limited tool to assist in the much more important ecological health of the referential world: "On Top," "Soy Sauce," "Fence Posts," and "Working on the '58 Willys Pickup," among others. In "White Sticky" the connotations of the homespun nickname prove more adequate in referring to the actual mushroom than the Latin species name that no one can locate in books. The poet in "Old Pond" uses language only to direct the reader to his actual splash into the referential pond. "Painting the North San Juan School," one of the finest uses of *référance* in *Axe Handles* (21-22), concerns the interjection of self-referential language to convey how skewed and environmentally destructive are the American cultural assumptions preached in elementary school texts. Here the children learn "games of numbers," names for their landscape that have been "Assigned it by the ruling people of the last / three hundred years," and history "told by those who / think they know it." Snyder's actual labor of painting the physical edifice proves more central to the maintenance of education in this very "shaky" culture. Internal, textual, and referential reality fuse in "On Top" (11), Snyder's poem about the writing of ecological poetry; here he presents his poet as a recycler of cultural detritus just as a gardener works compost:

> All this new stuff goes on top
> turn it over   turn it over
> wait   and water down.
> From the dark bottom
> turn it inside out
> let it spread through, sift down,
> even.

Watch it sprout.

A mind like compost.
(11)

The surprise embedded in final line raises one's awareness of ecological interdependence. The reader until then assumes he is reading a description of an activity in the referential world, but the word "mind" in the last line indicates that Snyder has been describing a mental process. The aporia or indecision is intentional; in a poet's daily life the inner and outer processes happen simultaneously, one feeding off the other.

Merwin, the most postmodern of environmental poets, has throughout his career followed his own project to realize "the imagination / Before the names of things" (1975 [*First Four*], 114). Like Heidegger and Merleau-Ponty, who distinguished between sedimented and originary language (Dillon 1988, 175-76, 208-22), Merwin has attempted to awaken his readers from the cliches and abstractions of an exhausted language that seems useful only for capitalist technological domination and environmental destruction—especially in the exploitation of Hawaii, his adopted home since 1979. Language for Merwin can either become a vehicle for domination and control, because it erects concepts between the self and reality, or it can, in the hands of a skillful poet, impede the signifying process until the reader's gaze is thrust beyond language to perceive objects in their rich, colorful, precognitive suchness. Through an erosion of the conventional signifying process, things can suddenly appear "without their names" (Elliott 1988, 16-17)—the Zen "no-time" of stillness and silence, where the ontological being of objects can be revealed (1978 ["Foreword"], 15). Merwin regularly conveys this impedance or erosion in moments of *référance* where self-reflexive language self-destructs, revealing in awe and splendor the beauty of nature cherished by the poet in a moment of Edenic, originary vision, as in the previously discussed "The First Year" (RT [1988*a*] 5) or in noticing for the first time the luscious apricots of "West Wall" (RT 4).

Too often, however, humans see things only as words on pieces of paper, where sedimented, trite language presents objects and experiences without their color. Hence the wistful lament of Merwin's poem "Paper" (RT 45 [1988*a*]), where he suggests how limited is phonetic language printed on a two-dimensional repository:

What an idea
that you can put it on a piece of paper

> what is a piece of paper and how can you tell
> put it on a piece of paper
> . . . .
> everything is white so it can disappear
> everything that is not white
> is alone
> the colors are all white
> the night is white in a place not remembered
> everything is the same color as the other planets
> here in this place hard to see
> on a piece of paper

Merwin also recognizes that language originated by conventionalizing our responses to referentiality, and therefore many words and their richness will die as capitalist technology destroys the environment, the referential source of words. In "Tracing the Letters" (RT 77) Merwin meditates about how the word "green" will gradually fall out of use and disappear from our language once there is no green left in the world. With rain forests falling at one and one-half acres per second (Gore 1992, 118, 223, 252) and topsoil losses at twenty-five billion tons per year (Ehrlich and Daily 1995, 174), that day may come soon. Then our eyes will truly be left to compose readings by tracing letters on pages, with no outside-text worth contemplating:

> already for all
> the green of the years
> there is only one word
> even when the green is not there
> and now the word is written down
> and not only spoken
>
> so it can be closed in the dark
> against an unknown page
> until another time

The purpose of such self-reflexive highlightings of the limits of the printed word in Merwin and in other ecopoets is to force a *punctum*, a moment of *référance*, where the absent referent, the colors of nature, pierces through the technology of newsprint.

Contrary to the flight from referentiality and social praxis of poststructural language criticism exemplified in Altieri, Perloff, and Klinkowitz, William Spanos affirms that the self-reflexivity of some postmodern art does generate a worldly, paradoxically referential "commitment to emancipatory sociopolitical change"; one can find a strong emphasis on referentiality in the oppositional poststructural criticism of Jameson, Said, Lentricchia, Eagleton, Deleuze and Guattari, and others. By emphasizing "disruptive differences" in reading practices between itself and the privileged, hegemonic (mimetic, modernist, or mass consumer) practices intended to repress the reader's freedom to deconstruct or revise, some postmodern theory does "refer to and engage" the "repressive cultural practices that reproduce the sociopolitical world of late (consumer) capitalism" (Spanos 1990, 108-15). Most of the work of these alternative poststructural critics, however, has been directed toward evaluating prose texts. From my foregoing account of *référance*, one can see that contemporary ecopoetry does not depend on a naive realism and does engage in social emancipation. I cannot imagine anything more disruptive of the contemporary consumer practices that abet our global ecological crises than ecopoetry's substitution of biocentrism for the anthropocentrism that has elevated the utilitarian ego to a position of dominance in consumer capitalism. Ecopoetry regularly deconstructs this position through a self-effacement of the speaking subject as he or she becomes absorbed in a biocentric position of nonhierarchical interconnectedness. In this respect, ecopoetry participates in the positive side of poststructuralism—its emphasis on emancipation and social change.

Ammons's early poem "So I Said I Am Ezra" (ACP 1 [1972]), where the subject tries to dominate nature with his voice and, reproved by the wind, is left to splash in biocentric equality with sea oats and sand dunes, defines an entire biocentric area of disruptive *référance* in contemporary ecopoetry. When Berry sows clover and grass into a fallow field in "Enriching the Earth" (BCP 110 [1984]), he learns to "serve the earth" with both body and mind, so that what was "most mute," the disjunction of subject and referential world, is "at last raised up into song." When Merwin in "Conqueror" (RT 62) expatiates on capitalist exploitation, he deconstructs its dominance at the end of the poem, where the entire third world is "praying // for you not to be there." That "you" is of course the conquering American tourist/consumer. Without the recycling that insect life and decomposers accomplish (they account for more than half of the organisms on this planet), human life would not be possible. Hence, in a moment of disruptive *référance*, Merwin in "After the Alphabets" (RT 50) affirms that the speakers of insect language "are their own meaning in a grammar without horizons."

Snyder, in one of the most beautiful Gaia songs in *Axe Handles* (1983, 51), offers a moment of disruptive *référance* through the use of an extended simile to suggest the nonhierarchical and biocentric interconnectedness of life. In longevity, humans occupy only a middling position between the short-lived crickets and the longer-lived trees, rocks, and hills:

> As the crickets' soft autumn hum
> is to us,
> so are we to the trees
>
> as are they
>
> to the rocks and the hills.
> (51)

In all ecopoetry of *référance* the artist, in creating his or her poems, is engaged in an act of reading nature; the armchair Derridean critic or postmodern reader is actually overhearing and rereading a reading and should pay some attention to the original reading. *Référance* marks the difference between the linguistic and referential world and immediately directs the reader toward that richer, less limited, world of nature; thus, difference does not lead to continual delay or infinitely disseminating textual meaning.

Other environmental poets recognize the limitations of language at the same time that they direct the reader toward the richer referential world. Marge Piercy, in the title poem of *Mars and Her Children* (1992), renews her support each year for environmentally friendly whale research near her Cape Cod home. In return she receives a photo of her adopted humpback, named Mars. Here linguistic signification is a "naming" that "makes valuable to us / what is unique in itself." Her secure village vantage point is, comparatively speaking, a "question mark" in a questionable culture. Piercy reminds us that "To name is not to possess what cannot / be owned or even known in the small words / and endless excuses of human speech." In the final sections of the poem she points the reader's gaze toward the humpback's "plume of praise" as it moves "arching out of the grey green moil of water" (138–43). In "The Gift," from William Heyen's *Pterodactyl Rose: Poems of*

Ecology (1991), the "rainforest governor Amazonino Mendes distributed / two thousand free chain saws" to relieve his peasants of their poverty. But Mendes's capitalistic assumptions then impoverish the earth. As Mendes profits he finds it is "easy / for me to speak with a chainsaw tongue // as the trees fall" (44). Heyen's poems glory in postmodern disruption.

Adrienne Rich has enriched her feminism with ecofeminism over the past decade. Her recent volumes specify planetary degradation as the result of the twin oppression of women and nature in patriarchal society. Her essays decry the separation of literature from politics as "the political declarations of privilege" (1986a [*Blood*], 178); this is but one facet of capitalist practices that alienate citizens from their own roots, their memories, dreams, their language, and their power to work as creative agents in changing the historical process through actions and art (Rich 1986a, 185). Staunchly political, Rich is less concerned with the phenomenological roots of language than its instrumental or power use and the hermeneutics of communication. Her moments of *référance* occur when her meditations on nature suddenly inscribe the reader as interlocutor, when the "you" engages the reader's conscience to create a community of historical agents. In "North American Time" (1986b [*Your Native*], 34), language is secondary and accountability should lead to environmental action:

> Try sitting at a typewriter
> one calm summer evening
> at a table by a window
> in the country, try pretending
> your time does not exist
> that you are simply you
> that the imagination simply strays
> like a great moth, unintentional
> try telling yourself
> you are not accountable
> for the life of your tribe
> the breath of your planet

Altieri recognizes the inability of a semiotically based poetics to incorporate agency, for a poetics narrowly based on language theory inevitably collapses into binary systems that privilege one term and suppress the opposite. He calls for work that encourages its readers to create "proleptic communities" of potentially active historical agents (1992 ["Temporality"],

155). He need look no further than Rich for a master in the art of putting "critical pressure on an environment and . . . realiz[ing] potential features of the cultural constitutions framing his or her imaginative activity" (137). A contemporary Parsifal on an environmental quest, Rich passionately believes in the instrumental and exchange values of language. Community begins by sharing our pain and concern with wounded readers in our environmental waste land. Rich interweaves interdisciplinary perspective with textual edge and yet continues to engage the reader through naked sincerity and unabashed sociability: "What are you going through, there on the other edge?" (1991 [*Atlas*], 51).

"Running" for Brendan Galvin is a process of divesting himself of human language, of finding the point where "the last shred of // human song just flew out of my head." "There's no name" for this biocentric awakening, but impressions of nature's ongoing celebration of life survive. Here "that kingfisher / dips and rises over the marsh // like a lesson in scansion." When he slows to a trot his consciousness becomes one with nature's celebration of life; he is for a moment "the least piper's / whistling, and my pulse begins its // shorebird glossolalia" (1990, 114-15). In the title poem of *Great Blue* (1990) Galvin, like Dylan Thomas before him, hopes for the occasional heron, the "Egyptian sign for the generation of life," to parallel his movements. When he does see one while driving, the silent experience of nature's plenitude is so riveting that both automobile and the abstractions of language disappear in a moment of *référance*:

> I look up at the mere
> abstract silhouette *bird* but am taken
> by the dragged beat of wings
>
> translucent at their tips,
> and the cocked spurs trawled behind,
> and have to swerve to hold the lane.
> (161-62)

Since Native American poetry generates a mythic dimension where the isolated individual is restored to family, tribe, landscape, and the Great Spirit, as Paula Gunn Allen has argued (1983, 3–22), one can say that all Native American poetry incorporates an ecological dimension. This is definitely the case in Joy Harjo's *In Mad Love and War* (1990). Through the rhythms and language of Native American ritual, Harjo informs her reader that "We Must Call a Meeting" to "give me back my language," a "language of lizards and storms" with its complex web of ancestors, sky, sun, moon, and "stars to guide us called promise" (9–10). When Harjo wants to reconcile with her lover after a quarrel, the "stark words" of conversational language are insufficient. More persuasive than rational argument is love spoken through ancestral codes of communal love—a referential language of "sunlight / on a scarlet canyon wall in / early winter" (22). A memory of adolescent fishing with her grandfather in "Crystal Lake" (33) brings Harjo to the recognition that the landscape has its own voices calling her home. As she loses language she becomes absorbed in a referential bonding with all dimensions of life:

> Bats fly at perfect random from the limestone cliffs, follow the invisible moon. I don't remember any words, but the shushing of the sun through dried grass, nibble of carp at the bottom of the boat, the slow melting of my body. My grandfather towed us through the lake. We skimmed over mythical fish he once caught, over fish who were as long as rainbows after the coming storm. (33)

In the summer 1992 issue of *Contemporary Literature*, Altieri and Perloff published essays opting for a poetics of textuality rather than referentiality by promoting Wittgenstein's focus on language games. But Wittgenstein was a logician, not a phenomenologist. Guetti emphasizes Wittgenstein's statement that "the meaning of a word is its use in the language" (PI no. 43; Guetti 1993, 31). As I noted previously, Wittgenstein carefully differentiated linguistic "use" (Guetti 1993, 5, 31-32, 43, 55, 58, 166-71) from linguistic "displays" (85, 93), the former of which occur only when language has demonstrable consequences in the referential world or at least asserts a proposition about that reality that is purposive, that leads to work or to applications of experience. Linguistic displays, or what Wittgenstein calls language "idling" (PI no. 132; Guetti 1993, 9), can open up the richness of our "experience of meaning" (Guetti 1993, 55, 73, 93) through the magical effects of aesthetic language, where a heightening of syntactical arrangements and reflexivity can extend the imagination into the illusory or the merely possible. But for Wittgenstein this is never the same as describing the properties of the perceptible world.

Linguistic "use" in Wittgenstein is circumscribed by his concept of "language games" in *Philosophical Investigations* (PI no. 116) and by his strict adherence to human logic. In her recent *Wittgenstein's Ladder* (1996), Perloff emphasizes language as a cultural construct and the influence of human cultural assumptions embedded in any given language as used by a community of human speakers (59-67). Yet Wittgenstein has precious little to say about how creative writers extend a given language by inscribing new perceptions *about the referential world* into it, perceptions not known to the community of speakers at any historical moment. While Perloff (27-41) is correct in noting that Wittgenstein's preface to the *Tractatus*, which mentions aesthetic pleasure, and the last three pages of comments, which discuss ethics, life, and death, were written after Wittgenstein experienced human suffering as a captured German soldier in an Italian internment camp, the experience of human suffering did not affect the iron logic of the rest of the *Tractatus*. Wittgenstein did want to expose the emptiness of war rhetoric like "the nobility of tradition" and the "saving of civilization," but he always limited linguistic use to human actions on the referential world. Wittgenstein's "language games" concept does not explain how new perceptions become part of human use and encoded into the games, and a narrow focus on the games also represses how power structures marginalize some language games and privilege others—how the aesthetic "language games" of poetry critics shoulder out the environmental, for instance (Bloor 1983, 46-49, 152-59).

At the heart of an environmentalist critique of Wittgenstein is his *Tractatus* statement 6.41: "The sense of the world must lie outside the world. In the world everything is as it is and happens as it does happen. *In* it there is no value—and if there were, it would be of no value." Perloff, in *Wittgenstein's Ladder* (1996, 44–45), sees this as a mysterious leap or *clinamen* (42) from the proposition immediately preceding it: "All propositions are of equal value" (PI no. 6.4). Though Perloff finds such jumps from the world of fact to the world of value interesting conundrums, an environmentalist must realize that Wittgenstein is arguing that only humans create value. Assuming that "the world" in itself has no value is anthropocentric hubris. It suggests that all of earth's life-support systems are valueless in themselves, that human logic alone creates value, and that humans do not influence nature. Nature is just a mindless force where "everything is as it is and happens as it does happen."

Environmentalists reverse the terms and point out that nature bats last, that we are a subset of nature and completely dependent on its life-support systems for our survival. Without photosynthesis, carbon burial, and ocean phytoplankton that produce oxygen, the higher vertebrates, in-

cluding humans, could not have evolved. This has no value in itself? It
behooves us to be referentially oriented, to learn nature's biocentric, eco-
logical logic, and conform to it. The exaltation of human logic as the source
of all value follows the mechanistic domination and exploitation paradigm
that threatens major ecosystems. The physicist David Bohm believes that
"it is a mistake to think that the world has a totally defined existence sepa-
rate from our own," for Einsteinian relativity and quantum physics argue
otherwise. "Because we are enfolded inseparably in the world," argues Bohm,
"with no ultimate division between matter and consciousness, *meaning and
value are as much integral aspects of the world as they are of us*" (1988, 67).

    Though establishment postmodern writers such as Jorie Graham and
Robert Hass have proven first-rate poets in the art of imaginative displays,
their poetics of textuality, based on Derridean linguistic gaps or
Wittgensteinian logic, removes us from the practical world we must en-
gage, moment to moment. Too often this poetry deteriorates into a formal-
ism preoccupied with the process of poetic composition. In this scenario,
the aesthetics of textuality reign supreme. The roots of our racial, gender,
socioeconomic, and environmental problems are seldom engaged; when
social issues are raised, the poet typically shrinks back from what is only
seen as a corrosive materialism or politics into the comforts of private self-
exploration. Wallace Stevens could take that route in the first half of this
century, but world ecology and human survival were not issues then. Today
poets who make sweeping, totalistic critiques of contemporary history as
corrosive in order to privilege private self-exploration, merely allow the
wasteful imperialism of dominant cultures to continue—an imperialism
that Edward Said, among others, believes is wrecking our planet (1993,
225, 330).

    Hass, in *Human Wishes* (1989), composes poems from the fragments
of failed human relationships. In his mind these failures follow a Derridean
logic; they confirm the failure of language to offer any reliable connected-
ness to the referential world. Poetry becomes the process of creating a safe
harbor—ballast against the emptiness left in the wake of dead relation-
ships, as in "The Harbor at Seattle" (25-26). Human wishes that anticipate
any satisfaction in the perceptible world beyond intrapersonal reverie are
vanity. The three poems in the volume that venture into social conscious-
ness ("*Rusia en 1931*," "Pascal Lamb," and "Between the Wars") suggest
that attempting social action is futile, even grotesque. Only in the reveries
of the careerist poet, a safe haven where language perpetually idles, can
human wishes be satisfied. Throughout *Human Wishes*, the California land-

scapes offer reliably benign, picturesque parks for bourgeois meanderings. One never sees the brushfires, soil salinization, smog, fresh water shortages, El Niño floods and mudslides, or the polluted shorelines from antiquated city sewage systems that plague the referential California we experience today.

Hass deserves praise for assisting in the organization of the April 1996 *Watershed* environmental literature conference in Washington, D.C., and for his weekly *Washington Post* column, in which he often introduces readers to socially oriented and minority poets. But Hass's own poetry has not been influenced by environmentalism or social activism. *Sun under Wood* (1996) contains many excellent poems that valorize the capacity of human consciousness to make choices and endure pain. The longer poems, especially "Regalia for a Black Hat Dancer," convince us that turning the experience into the aesthetic object—writing the poem—is the way to accept the pain by finding images of the right "size" (57). Early poems in the volume introduce the theme of human pain by exploring Hass's adolescent experiences of enduring his mother's alcoholism. But only the human has value for Hass. Nature throughout the volume is subordinated to human aesthetic and practical use. To sustain Hass's attention it must serve humans ("the sweet medicinal / scent of mountain grasses") or provide aesthetically pleasant names, as with the sunflower called "pearly everlasting" (76). Hass resigns himself to callous images of how Alaskan snow is laced with the "precipitate" of car exhausts, "the burnt carbons / of pre-Cambrian forests." This becomes an example of "life feeding life / feeding life in the usual, mindless way" (25). Like Vendler, Hass magnifies the human mind and minimizes nature as "mindless." Nature's iron law holds the trees as well as "the whole thing up," but leaves and birds are just examples of the orders of life where beauty is "unconscious of itself" (30). So deer blend with the forest (31), for they, unlike the superior humans, are "almost mechanical" in their inability to exercise conscious choice (33). The raccoon's world exists "entirely apart" from Hass's own. Hass cannot enter its silence; he can only enter his own. Otherwise "there was nothing there" (35–37). One suspects that Hass would cast off his ennui and existential angst only if the raccoon could translate four languages or trade aesthetic quips.

In other poems in *Sun Under Wood* Hass depicts nature stereotypically as a ruthless raven's eye (28) or a convenient poststructural place for the mind to locate itself (27). Nature is not an equal other for Hass; it is only a stage or convenient backdrop where human consciousness struts and displays its pain. *Sun under Wood* even contains "Shame: An Aria," a four-page poem praising the power of language to extricate humans from the infinite agony of being caught picking one's nose when an elevator door suddenly opens. All human "congealed lubricants," including the "shit streaks" and "odorous pee-blossoms" in underwear (44), are evidence of our participation in being, and language is a wonderful device that we can use to praise this participation in being. But the focus remains anthropocentric. The most trivial human discomfort can prompt an investigation into how one can use language to "save yourself" (43) from shame and blunt the analytic gaze of other humans ("Hell is—other people," said Sartre in *No Exit* [1955, 47]), for in Hass the human mind is always magnified and nature neutralized. A steady reading diet of such poetry will massage our youth into a perilous self-indulgence that will also render them oblivious to the needs of nature.

Jorie Graham, in her most recent volumes, has developed truly audacious leaps of imaginative thought and reach that have enriched contemporary poetry immeasurably, but she, too, finds comfort only in intrapersonal reverie, especially when uncovering traumatic incidents in her past ("Patience," *Erosion* [1983], 42) during the existential process moment of self-confrontation in the act of writing. Typically she recoils in horror whenever she attempts successful action in the perceptible world. She often emphasizes the most sensationalistic aspects of urban life, and regularly her response is flight into the personal reveries that textuality, not referentiality, affords. The male technocrat hero must be swallowed up by the Great Mother of the feminine (poetic) unconscious, as with the B-52 NORAD base in North Dakota in "What the End Is For" (*End* [1987], 26-29). To know the world is to know its corrosive imperialism, a dirty river Ganges from which the nine-year-old shrinks in fright ("Imperialism," *End*, 94-99). A tourist visit to Rome brings only demonic epiphanies of materialism ("Manifest Destiny," *Region* [1991], 22–28). Memories of participating in the Paris student revolt in the late 1960s uncover the trauma of flight from counterterrorist police ("The Region of Unlikeness," *Region*, 37-40). When she must consent to placing her parents in retirement homes, Graham likens herself to a Nazi war criminal ("From the New World," *Region*, 12-16). History regularly immobilizes us in a false historical consciousness ("Fission," *Region*, 3–8); it can become an open-ended, Heideggerian blossoming of Being in the moment of consciousness only in private self-colloquy ("History," *Region*, 89-93), preferably in the process of creating the poem ("Pollock on Canvas," *End*, 81-89).

When Graham writes of her solitary aesthetic experiences, she does try to counter dualism and prove that our moments of consciousness are imbricated in the natural world. This is especially true of the number of poems entitled "Notes on the Reality of the Self" in *Materialism* (1993). Yet the astringent, demonstrative lines only stanch the wounds inflicted by the corrosive materialism. Consciousness raising does not enable; it reveals a cultural dead end that rationalizes taking refuge in an aesthetic diary. Graham has an inadequate sense of agency, a defect common to contemporary establishment poets. Nor does Graham ever consider nature as a separate and equal series of interdependent ecosystems. In the *Erosion* poem "Two Paintings by Gustav Klimt," for instance, the torn bark and bullet holes of the Buchenwald trees merely reflect the human destructiveness that the poet gilds in the pursuit of pleasure. Graham convicts herself of complicity here; like Klimt, with his decadent gauze and gold filigree, a decadence that preceded the horrors of Nazi death camps, the poet seems condemned to cover her anger with aestheticizing gauze. The complex resignation at the end of the poem, however, argues that this process is inevitable and that nothing can be done either about the trees or the poet's credulous desire to satisfy the aesthetic impulse. The Buchenwald trees, as is the case in all Graham landscapes, never possess an ecological dimension.

Graham's gorgeous, ambitious poems contain the questionable message that the social world can only be corrosive, an impediment to self-realization. The filmic crosscuts and intrusive media (the television in "Breakdancing"; the movie projector in "Fission"; the Walkman in "What Is Called Thinking"; the building security camera in "Relativity: A Quartet") usually lead to anguish about the reality of the self and a pattern of flight into the tortuous recesses of introspection. At best this is a complacent bourgeois elitism that cannot affirm our human potential for positive social action in the referential world. In *Materialism*, pages of bald quotes from Plato through Bacon, Edwards, Whorf, and Wittgenstein alternate with poems displaying an extreme self-analysis that broods over scenes of sensationalistic violence, from random subway shootings to Nazi death camps. While this serves to raise human consciousness of the evils of capitalism, these poems also appear to argue that the violent consequences of Western thinking are inevitable; they reveal our persistent urge to conquer and colonize the world. Graham's conception of history, of possible social action in the referential world, is fatalistic; agency is restricted to keeping the bourgeois domicile and nuclear family safe, and the only relief from the corrosive materialism is lonely anthropocentric introspection.

Poststructural Dualisms

The focus of poststructural language theorists and critics on textuality and grammaticality has the effect of foregrounding textuality and subordinating referentiality. Wittgensteinian grammars like the one being developed by Altieri emphasize theoretical and linguistic models and deemphasize the primary literature, which is usually treated as the less important instantiation of the model being perfected. On occasion, the discussion seems to suggest that the model has somehow generated the poem. Language becomes a self-contained system completely divorced from the "real" world, operating under its own self-contained laws. Allen Thiher found in Wittgenstein's *Tractatus* a dualism where the limits of one's world "coincide" with the limits of one's language, and the only voice that can speak is one that is "certain of a limited number of atomistic propositions." Furthermore, this voice "can say nothing about itself, for the speaking voice is excluded from the world that discourse can represent: 'The subject does not belong to the world: rather, it is a limit of the world' (no. 5. 632). Thus, in a strict sense, the speaking voice can say nothing about what it is saying. It can only record states of affairs . . ." (1983, 81). Thiher found further alienation in the later *Philosophical Investigations*, for here Wittgenstein limited himself to discussions of "language games" that, by reducing all to the linguistic boundaries of the sayable, never predicate an active agent capable of changing whatever is the present cultural case:

> In the *Philosophical Investigations*, voices arise as forms of participation in the various language games that, with their innumerable overlappings, make up that entity we give the name "language." Language games are thus the multiple public spaces and the rules for their arrangement that go to make up the world. And if one asks where is the self that lies behind the speaking voice, the answer seems to be that the self is only a kind of abbreviation for talking about the multiple ways in which voices enter into language games. Or, if taken as a substantial notion, the self can only be viewed as a metaphysical error arising from a misunderstanding about the nature of language. There is no self to be spoken, no inner locus that is the source of meaning, for the locus of speaking is merely speaking itself. (1983, 81-82)

Derrida's system, by reducing the real to the textual, also created a dualistic split between the textual and the impossible other, the natural world. As Paul Smith has shown, at every juncture where Derrida could enlist human agency—the ability to influence social systems in the "real" world—into questions of decidability and empowerment, he systematically avoids making such choices. By focusing on the impossibility of locating origins and emphasizing the materiality of the signifier at the same time that he systematically refuses to grant any reality or even the concept of subjectivity, Derrida creates a dualistic divorce between the textual world and the other of nature (Smith 1988, 45-48).

Lacan, who believes that all experience is mediated by language, also asserts that we can experience the unconscious only through linguistic mediation, for language both creates and structures the unconscious. At the point of its creation, the unconscious is forever alienated from the other, nature, and the signifier forever displaces the desire for the other. Language fills the lack or hole where the other was severed, and until death no possibility exists for healing this dualistic split: "Man's freedom is entirely circumscribed within the constituting triangle of the renunciation that he imposes on the desire of the other by the menace of death for the enjoyment of the fruits of his serfdom" (1977, 104; see also 164-69, 200, 215, 263-65, 285-86). At another juncture in *Écrits* Lacan confidently asserts that "it is the world of words that creates the world of things" (65), a position that contradicts our commonsense experience of nature and is inimical to our survival on this planet. Ammons in particular responds with blunt derision to such irresponsible faith in humanly created abstract systems at the end of section thirteen of *Garbage*:

we'll live no more on
this planet, we'll live in the word: what:

we'll get off: we'll take it with us: our
equations will make any world we wish anywhere

we go: we'll take nothing away from here but
the equations, cool, lofty, eternal, that were

nowhere here to be found when we came
. . . .

we'll kick the *l* out of the wor*l*d and cuddle
up with the avenues and byways of the word:
(76-77)

In creating a hermetically sealed universe of textuality or grammaticality, many poststructural theorists grant textuality a privileged status. Their systems suggest that from written language humans derive an immanent reality beyond which they cannot penetrate. This amounts to claiming that literary language is ontologically distinct—the same major premise that both Krieger (1963, 125-55) and Lentricchia (1980, 218-26) find at the base of the New Criticism. Ransom, in *The New Criticism*, argued that poetic language is ontologically distinct from scientific abstractions, but his intent was to recover the referential world of immediate experience, a project that ecopoets and Merleau-Ponty, as we shall soon see, would consider laudable: "Poetry intends to recover the denser and more refractory original world which we know loosely through our perceptions and memories. By this supposition it is a kind of knowledge which is radically or ontologically distinct" (1941, 281). Lentricchia, echoing Jameson, notes that the postmodern theoretical systems of "Barthes, Derrida, de Man, and their followers . . . . all tell the same story: we are trapped in the prison-house of language; we have access to no substance beyond language but only to words in their differential and intrasystematic relations to one another. We have no right, after such assumptions, to say anything except that all utterances are fictions which never break out of their fictionality." One page later, Lentricchia, anticipating Kroeber and Said, asks a probing, anguished question: "Is it not urgent to grasp what one believes to be the actual interconnections in human experience and refuse to detain oneself by meditating on admittedly fictional entities?" (220-21). Separating language from its relational bond to the referential world can serve an elite that enjoys privileges and leisure; to keep these intact, they shrink from exerting the energy that might produce social change. Environmental and ecological literature certainly does find ways to reassert and invigorate interconnections between the potential agent and the referential world.

Derrida conceded that for him the whole world is a text, including all possible referents, or all is context (1988, 136, 148), but in his deconstructive practices he regularly becomes absorbed in linguisticality, and literary critics influenced by Derrida similarly focus on the aesthetics of textuality. Derrida's attempt to treat the referential world as text soon breaks down under the simplest commonsense scrutiny. If one fails to read a book, no discernible consequences ensue in the referential world, unless, of course, one is enrolled in courses where grades and graduation may depend on understanding certain texts or where our failure to read an instruction manual causes mistakes in operating a machine. On the other hand, America's failure to prosecute the abuse of toxic substances by its chemical companies has resulted in somewhat permanent consequences: damage to our lakes, our soil, our fresh air. Helen Caldicott, for instance, estimates that a third of the water in U.S. aquifers contains measurable chemical contamination (1992, 71). Thousands of oceanfront beaches close each year in America because of chemical pollution, mostly from fecal coloform bacteria emanating from inadequate city sewage treatment plants. The referential world today is not a text we can simply choose to read or not read at our leisure without important referential consequences. The greatest ecodisaster on this planet, the release of six million barrels of oil per day for months into the air of Kuwait and the release of four million gallons of oil into the water of the Persian Gulf in 1991 (*Information Please Environmental Almanac* 1992, 16-18), probably began as a one-paragraph order spoken and written in Arabic by Saddam Hussein. Here referential meaning was not perpetually displaced along a chain of signifiers or confined to a purely textual "language game," and the consequences of this "reading" cannot be erased with each new reading of that paragraph.

Actually the poststructuralist emphasis on language that creates a hermetically sealed textuality, a position that Said finds abhorrent to a recognition that literature is conceived in worldliness and has worldly consequences, is just another form of the Western philosophical dualism, the mechanistic legacy of Bacon, Descartes, and Locke, that ecologists and environmentalists have identified as the single most important paradigm that needs alteration to comprehend the world as an ecological web of interrelated systems sustaining human as well as nonhuman life. Just as Derrida refuses to try to recoup the other beyond the text, so for Lacan the human unconscious is forever alienated from this other. For the environmentalist Paul Shepard, however, dualism has created the faulty perception that "nothing in nature has inherent merit" (1969, 5). For the geneticists David Suzuki and Anita Gordon, the Descartian tradition of dualistic divorce between mind and matter has created the misperception that "the scientist is an objective observer of an external reality" and that the objective study of economics leads us to try to argue environmental causes from pleas for human economic health. However, according to Suzuki and Gordon, "the economy is really a subset of the natural world. So it is the economy that has to fit into the environment, not the other way around" (1991, 165-66). For historian of science Carolyn Merchant, the tradition of dualism "must be reevaluated" because, by "reconceptualizing reality as a machine, [it] sanctioned the domination of both nature and women" and this "mechanical view of nature now taught in most Western schools is accepted without question as our everyday common sense reality" (1980, xxi, 193). For Snyder, Cartesian dualism was a product of city dwellers whose work was characterized by "a profound rejection of the organic world. For a reproductive universe they substituted a model of sterile mechanism and an economy of 'production'" (PW 18-19). For Wendell Berry, dualism is simply "the most destructive disease that afflicts us" (SEFC 105).

For Vice President Al Gore, whose work on current environmental research for more than a decade in Congress qualifies him as an environmentalist, this dualism not only divorces mind from matter and thought from feeling but the "disembodied mind" also separates science from religion and nature from both. This separation insulates individuals from nature. Wittgensteinian grammars, as well as Derridean plays of differences along chains of signifiers, do create machine-like systems that buffer us from the quotidian reality in which we live. Today Scott Adams parodies humdrum office work in his wonderful Dilbert cartoons, but Wendell Berry well knows that Americans are the most dangerous people let loose on this planet, for in their insulated office and careerist activities most know nothing of how to survive or how the global environment beyond one's backyard is being degraded daily to provide consumer goods (SEFC 36-37). They know little about growing their own food or husbanding the livestock they rely on for protein. Gore summarizes in eloquent terms the moral consequences of Western culture's tradition of dualism and the need for an ecological vision:

> If we feel no connection to those in our own communities whose lives are being wasted, who are we? Ultimately, as we lose our place in the larger context in which we used to define our purpose, the sense of community disappears, the feeling of belonging dissipates, the meaning of life slips from our grasp. Believing ourselves to be separate from the earth means having no idea how we fit into the natural cycle of life and no understanding of the natural processes of change that affect us and that we are affecting. It means that we attempt to chart the course of our civilization by reference to ourselves alone. No wonder we are

lost and confused. No wonder so many people feel their lives are wasted. Our species used to flourish within the intricate and interdependent web of life, but we have chosen to leave the garden. Unless we find a way to dramatically change our civilization and our way of thinking about the relationship between humankind and the earth, our children will inherit a wasteland. (1992, 162-63)

Merleau-Ponty's Flesh of the Visible

The most promising philosophical response for environmental literature to both poststructuralism and to philosophical dualism, one that avoids solipsism and skepticism at the same time that it is very congenial to an ecological vision, is that of Maurice Merleau-Ponty. His life immediately precedes the historical development of contemporary ecological poetry, and his response to dualism concerns the same return to the lived body of concrete experience that environmental poets and ecopoets emphasize. Though he died prematurely of a heart attack in 1961, before he could complete *The Visible and the Invisible*, the final synthesis of his thinking, all of his work counters ontological dualism by taking a new phenomenological approach, the objective of which is to restore to the referential world its transcendence without postulating either a theological foundationalism or an initial divorce between human subjectivity and the world that humans inhabit.

Merleau-Ponty argues that the Cartesian legacy has left the West with two positions, empiricism and intellectualism, both of which presuppose dualistic splits between the subjective knower and the objects of perception. For Descartes the mind must remain passive, uninfluenced by the will or the imagination, and of all possible knowledge it can discern only the simple things that have extension and motion. Descartes never asserted either in his *Rules* or his *Meditations* that things exist apart from the clear distinctions formulated by the perceiving consciousness, which reduces objects to immanence. Though Locke and the empiricists attacked Cartesian notions of innate ideas, they, too, limited what can be known of the referential world to combinations of logical atoms within the mind—another reduction to immanence.

Taking the transcendental idealism of Husserl and the radical dualism of Sartre as examples of the intellectualist position, Merleau-Ponty argues that, for Husserl, the only transcendent entity is the ego. Referential reality is that which the conscious cogito constitutes intentionally—a meaning construct of the cogito and hence restricted to immanence. Beginning by setting the nothingness of consciousness (being-for-itself) against the presence of the world (being-in-itself) as complete opposites, Sartre is unable to mediate them to recover the unity of lived, concrete experience for an actual being in the world. Human consciousness identifies a "this" out there by an act of negation (it is what is not consciousness), but this "not," this portion of being in itself, is what is realized by consciousness—an immanence. Any attempt to realize a transcendent object in Sartre founders because temporality is a mode peculiar to consciousness within being-for-itself and can only realize a present "this" out of a negative relation to other "thises," past and future, which transcend the present determinate "this." The attempt to realize a transcendent "this" is limited to what the immanent consciousness can absorb in a present moment, while the transcendent object itself escapes our gaze (Dillon 1988, 9–50).

Merleau-Ponty develops and transforms Husserl's conscious cogito and his notion of intersubjective experience by beginning with a foundational assertion that the world of perception is the source of all value and existence, the final referent of human understanding (PriP 13). The ground and origin of the perceptual world is the invisible, the source of the all-inclusive field of perception as well as the lived body of all sensible existence. He posits this foundation, however, without ascribing any god or theological source for the world of perception. He also asserts that perception is neutral, prepersonal, and primary (PP 215). At the point of first perception no subject-object separation has taken place, for the ego is relativized in the body of perception. Perception remains partial, incomplete; humans can never grasp all of a given object in any one act of perception. Perception, hence, is paradoxical: it reveals a partial, perspectival view of a referential object within a field (PP 4) at the same time that the object withdraws, withholds a portion of itself (PriP 16). Perception is not an action-reaction of physical forces, of one entity in response to another, for all bodies are functions of the predifferentiating field. Subject-object separation begins only when humans reflect on what they have perceived, when the inquiring "I" enters. According to M.C. Dillon, one of the central facets of Merleau-Ponty's phenomenology is that consciousness is always an embodied consciousness which in humans develops into thought. When an infant tries to grasp an object, he views his hand in juxtaposition to the object and at the same time lives through his hand in the act of exploration (Dillon 1988, 110-24). Consciousness would have nothing to be conscious of, and nothing to meditate about, without this constant crisscrossing of the visible and the sentient/sensible during the act of perception.

In *The Phenomenology of Perception*, Merleau-Ponty critiques the atomism of Descartes and the empiricists by recognizing that perception is not a matter of isolated logical atoms or quanta of perception happening within the mind of the perceiver; indeed simple, isolated atoms have never been seen; they are ideal constructs that are in fact inconceivable and unprovable (PP 4). Humans focus on particular sensory phenomena within a certain field (PP 221). Phenomena are ontologically primary and intrinsically meaningful, and the perceptual world is autochthonous, inherently pregnant with form—that is, unity and meaning inhere within the phenomena and are not simply ascribed by the human mind (PriP 15; PP 291). The human mind and human culture are parts of the perceptible world that contains within all of its manifestations an intrinsic Gestalt.

Another way to say this is that every act of perception displays an inherent primordial level of meaning common to living phenomena (Dillon 1988, 66). Transcendent phenomena contain an ambiguous richness, and the unreflective perceptual act, the founding term for Merleau-Ponty (PP 394), occurs at differing levels of complexity in all living beings, and displays in its process its own formal unity, coherence. This is a general property of the world of perception, not an activity of immanence. The world of perception in nature is, somewhat analogous to Gestalt theory, the underlying "horizon of all horizons," whose rich ambiguity and persistent becoming cannot be reduced or thematized. Just as in Gestalt theory humans perceive figures within a field or relational background, so for Merleau-Ponty meanings consolidate from within the all-inclusive horizon that nature presents to humans. Yet these human constructs and meanings are partial realizations whose logic and worth do not affect or exhaust the natural world, that "horizon of all horizons" (PP 327-30). One of the primary goals of ecopoetry, as we shall soon see, is to recover the rich ambiguity and all-inclusiveness of that irreducible natural world that exists prior to language and the subject/object bifurcations of idealism and realism (PP 343).

Merleau-Ponty believes that humans experience portions of the world because we are portions of the world's flesh, the living parts of which (from vegetative life to animal and human life) have the ability to sense. Until we reflect on our sensory experience, it is true to say that the world "perceives in me, not that I perceive" (PP 215). This tacit or prereflective cogito is an anonymous and silent manifestation of being within the world at its most elementary, nonthematized, undifferentiated core. Toward the end of *The*

Phenomenology of Perception, Merleau-Ponty rejects dualism as he discusses how subjective consciousness knows the objective world. There he asserts that we know ourselves through our relations with other things, and the world knows us because our bodies are situated in the flesh of the world (PP 383, 404-8). Even at this early point in his work Merleau-Ponty held the view that "inside and outside are inseparable. The world is wholly inside and I am wholly outside myself" (PP 407). In the later *Visible and Invisible*, he affirms that perceiver and perceived are intertwined in an elementary reversibility so that "we are the world that thinks itself" while simultaneously "the world is at the heart of our flesh" (VI 136 n). Language awakens the reflective "I" and reifies the world, so that humans usually rehearse sedimented perceptions and assumptions accumulated from past experience. Even when ecopoets speak of the silence of the world in wilderness experience or in breakthrough moments when they gain a sense of wild being at the heart of nature, they can only attempt to find fresh language as far removed from cliches as possible to evoke what one cannot completely convey in language, but can experience fully in the lived moment.

For Merleau-Ponty the corporeal body of a sentient being is not separated from consciousness, as in typical dualistic suppositions of immanence and transcendence, but is an instance of the flesh of the visible world. The lived body is situated within the world, and interacts with other living bodies in the search for understanding. Just as the sensation of touching and being touched alternates from one hand to the other when a person touches his or her hands together (PP 93; VI 123, 133), or as one apprehends consciousness in another living being by perceptions of concrete similarities among lived bodies (PriP 118), so corporeal reflexivity operates throughout the body's lived experience. Tacit, prereflective reversibility between consciousness and sensation operates continually in the lived experience of the body, or else simple eye-hand coordination would be impossible. According to Merleau-Ponty, one apprehends one's body "as a subject-object, as capable of 'seeing' and 'suffering'" (PP 95). The lived human body is capable of sympathy and shared suffering with other humans as well as with other orders of sensible/sentient life because it dwells in a shared practical, expressive space with other living bodies that simultaneously "see" or sense (PP 146), not in linguistic gaps between the signified and referentiality. Ammons conveys this sympathy with all of sentient life as well as a sophisticated appreciation of nonhuman language as part of the natural structure of the visible world in *Garbage* (1993):

our cousins the birds talk in the morning: I
can tell the weather by their voices before

I open my eyes: I know some of their "words"
because I know, share with them, their states

of being and feeling . . . .
. . . .
      I know the entire language of chickens,
from rooster crows to biddy cheeps: it is a

language sufficient to the forms and procedures
nature assigned to chicken-birds but a language,

as competition goes, not sufficient to protect
them from us:
(51)

This Ammons meditation is consonant with Merleau-Ponty's belief
that within the human self there is an ongoing alternating, reversible rela-
tion between the body as sensible and the body as consciously sentient, as
well as between the phenomenal body and other phenomena in the world,
though other orders of being are not sentient in the same ways that hu-
mans are (VI 250).

In the crucial fourth chapter of *The Visible and the Invisible*, "The
Intertwining —the Chiasm," Merleau-Ponty discusses reversibility as a fun-
damental property of all flesh within the world. Reversibility is an ambigu-
ously visible identity that incorporates difference. Here he states that "it is
not *I* who sees, not *he* who sees, because an anonymous visibility inhabits
both of us, a vision in general, in virtue of that primordial property that
belongs to the flesh, being here and now, of radiating everywhere and for-
ever, being an individual, of being also a dimension and a universal" (VI
142). Elsewhere in this text Merleau-Ponty asserts that the human body
feeling itself also admits of its visibility for the other (VI 245), for all living
things are portions of the flesh of the world, intertwined and interwoven in
a complex Gestalt, and the human body has that particular sentience that
allows the flesh of the world to be seen. This happens because in the act of
prereflective perception, a decentering or dehiscence (*écart*) occurs that al-
lows the perceiver to distance that which is perceived, else there would be

no differentiation between perceiver and perceived (VI 123). Rather than create a dualistic split, this decenters the flesh of the world into an ambiguous, asymmetrical texture.

In the prereflective moment of perceptual faith, we float in the general sea of being of flesh anonymously sensing itself through the five senses—an experience often prized by nature writers, though Merleau-Ponty never mentioned such. What he does mention is the painter's perception of becoming so intensely absorbed in the act of perception that perspective reverses, and he experiences the trees observing him (PriP 167; VI 139). This experience, conceptually speaking, is not difficult to comprehend when one accepts the premise that all of the world is visible flesh sensing different orders of itself. This state of absorption in a decentered oneness of the flesh of the world may seem to approximate the Zen experience of *satori*, of a fully experienced moment of primordial unity with all of existence, but Merleau-Ponty is more interested in the richness of the process of differentiation and how these differentiations come about—how we see things in such a way that the sense we make of them is what they are, what form they take, phenomenologically speaking.

Dehiscence also preserves the transcendent referentiality of the perceived as being mysteriously more than is ever absorbed in any perceptual act. Reinforcing the anonymous ambiguity of the reversible flesh of the world, Merleau-Ponty states that "the seer and the visible reciprocate one another and we no longer know which sees and which is seen. It is this Visibility, this generality of the Sensible in itself, this anonymity innate to Myself that we have previously called flesh, and one knows there is no name in traditional philosophy to designate it" (VI 139).

Language for Merleau-Ponty is "another flesh" (VI 153) that emanates from dehiscence and speaks not only the voices of humans but the sounds and colors of the referential world from which it grew (VI 155). Language develops from the dehiscence or folding back on itself of the flesh of the world. Indeed, Merleau-Ponty believes that fresh, creative, originary language actually does in the movement from sign to sign provide an example of the reversibility and reciprocity of the visible folding and unfolding into the seeing:

> Why not admit—what Proust knew very well and said in another place—that language as well as music can sustain a sense by virtue of its own arrangement, catch a meaning in its own mesh, that it does so without exception each time it is conquer-

ing, active, creative language, each time something is, in the strong sense, said? . . . . Language as a system of explicit relations between signs and signified, sounds and meaning . . . [becomes] caught up in something like a second life and perception . . . [a] second visibility . . . . [for it realizes] that openness ever to be reopened between the sign and the sign, as the flesh is, we said, the dehiscence of the seeing into the visible and of the visible into the seeing. (VI 153)

What Derrida sees as a continual deferral of meaning in a sequence of signifiers Merleau-Ponty sees as the opening of a furrow in the soil of the visible that at its most creative and originary gives us more than a trace—it gives us a Keatsian envelopment in the flesh of the world, a sense of being enveloped within the sensuous redolence of being for the first time, the special three-dimensional state courted by nature writers and readers. Heidegger approaches this in some of his late essays on language, when he speaks of the poet's ability to bring together in his saying the momentary encounter of self with the four-fold elements of the earth to create "world" (1971 [*On the Way*], 57-108).

But a narrow reading of Heidegger, aided by Derrida's views on language and by Lacan's denatured treatment of Freud, can lead one to the skepticism whereby we never experience the flesh of the world, for all experience is mediated by language, signs can only refer to other signs, and signs cannot encompass extralinguistic reality—can never open furrows in the flesh of the visible. Here the complexities of nature are reduced to the laws of language, and texts and readings of texts become the only reality. M.C. Dillon, in a lengthy chapter on language in his *Merleau-Ponty's Ontology* (1988, 177-243), discusses this reductionism as a variety of "posthermeneutic skepticism" that persistently views language only as a "groundless immanence" (184).

All thinking may be influenced by sedimented assumptions within language, but one can resist being interpellated into monolithic social discourses and Lacan's Name of the Father. Frankly, both Merleau-Ponty and Lacan noted that a child's first experiences of selfhood happen long before the acquisition of language. Merleau-Ponty noted that a baby's cries in a maternity ward regularly induce crying in other babies who are present but not discomfited, but after the age of three months the baby learns to differentiate his own bodily state from those of others (PriP 124). Lacan posited a mirror stage where the infant first differentiates self from not-self somewhere between the ages of six and eighteen months (1977, 1–7). In both cases, a sense of self appears without a knowledge of language.

If we are always subjected to language and are never the resistant subjects that Smith advocates but so seldom finds in poststructural systems, then how can one account for the list of environmental freedom fighters in chapter 14 of Al Gore's *Earth in the Balance*? What about the tenacious efforts of Lois Gibbs and the homeowners association of Love Canal to fight chemical soil and water pollution, Chico Mendes and the Brazilian rubber tappers to fight rain forest depletion, Wangari Matthai and the Greenbelt Movement in Kenya to combat deforestation, Mechai Viravayda and the condom cabbies of Thailand to counter overpopulation, Pat Bryant's fight in the lower Mississippi Cancer Alley area to curb toxic chemical water pollution, and Lynda Draper's struggle to curb General Electric's chlorofluorocarbon emissions that lead to ozone depletion? Under poststructural conceptions of the thrall in which language subjects us to prevailing linguistic discourses, all of these freedom fighters should have capitulated to the discourses of big business and government bureaucracy. Instead, all resisted, persisted, and won important environmental fights.

Toward the conclusion of *The Phenomenology of Perception*, Merleau-Ponty equates the original grasp of the phenomenal world by the prereflective or tacit cogito with the state of silence. Silence is the founding term, the first "meeting of the human and non-human," the moment when human consciousness opens on the perceptual world (PP 403-4). Merleau-Ponty could not accept the position that every experience is mediated by language, for this denies the referential origins of language, cannot account for how language evolved (was each language present in the Garden of Eden onward?), and disallows the intuitive aspect of creative thinking as it searches for an originary expression to speak what had never been perceived before. Between the silent first apprehension of the referential world and the cliches of conventional speech, Merleau-Ponty suggests a gestural connection between the desire to communicate, to express ideas as well as emotion, and to express the sound/body aspect of actual speech developing into language in a group of individuals moving from a pretribal existence toward the position of an evolved culture. This is consonant with the biological/anthropological origins of language that Snyder affirms.

To argue that the concepts of language have always mediated our experience forces one into a doctrine of innate ideas or the equally untenable position that complex languages evolved by happenstance from a situation where signifiers and signifieds were purely arbitrary. Merleau-Ponty believes that at some point in our cultural past every speech act was an originary "singing of the world" (PP 187), a recurrent theme in Berry's poetry, to express the emotional state of the human responding to the silent world and endowing it with new meaning-for-humans: "We need, then, to seek the first attempts at language in the emotional gesticulation whereby man superimposes on the given world the world according to man" (PP 188). And the gesture is the reflective response of the lived body of humans to the phenomena it perceives; hence language expresses "the subject's taking up of a position in the world of his meanings. The term 'world' here is not a manner of speaking: it means that the 'mental' or cultural life borrows its structures from natural life and that the thinking subject must have its basis in the subject incarnate" (PP 193). Thus, Merleau-Ponty takes the position that language is "a revelation of intimate being and of the psychic link which unites us to the world and our fellow men" (PP 196). In the reversibility of the visible flesh of the world, in the ability of all living entities to self-reflexively "turn the world back upon itself" through their sensible/sentient natures, we see the ground in humans for the development of language:

> In a sense, if we were to make completely explicit the architec-
> tonics of the human body, its ontological framework, and how
> it sees itself and hears itself, we would see that the structure of
> its mute world is such that all of the possibilities of language are
> already given in it. Already our existence as seers (that is, we
> said, as beings who turn the world back upon itself and who
> pass over to the other side, and who catch sight of one another,
> who see one another with eyes) and especially our existence as
> sonorous beings for others and for ourselves contain everything
> required for there to be speech from one to the other, speech
> about the world. (VI 155)

Returning the lived corporeal body to the creative space of language is an important part of ecopoetry's attempt to restore the primacy of referentiality. Whether he meditates on the "chunky intermediacy" of trash or of "gooey language densely managed," the size of penises or breasts, the formless Tao as "heaven's daunting asshole," or the act of "blithely oozing / a porch fart" (1993, 22, 98-100, 104), Ammons, in *Garbage*, wants his readers to experience in their reading the sense of corporeal existence as something richer and more satisfying than relating what happens as a pair of eyeballs follows a chain of signifiers in infinitely deferred meaning across a computer screen. When Wendell Berry wants to direct our attention to the physical body's prereflective existence, he presents his sparrow as one who "flies / before he knows he's going to." This sparrow lives the body; "he goes / by the eye-quick / reflex of his flesh / out of sight" (BCP 17). When Gary Snyder desires to step aside of the cultural glacier "eased along by Newton and Descartes" (PW 61), he meditates in "Under the Skin of It" about whether the body and the spirit "know the other's real delight." He decides that flesh, "a type of clay," and spirit, a "gas" floating "in the hollow / Of the Skull," are both "under the skin," and physical pleasure pleases both (NN 316). And when Merwin tries to convey the fullness of sensual experience on this earth, he thinks of his childhood immersion in the life of the sensual body at the end of a day-long romp in a pasture:

> we hid
> in the chill twilight
> face down hearing our breaths
> our own breaths
> full of the horizon
> and the smell of the dew
> on the cold ferns
> (RT 21)

These perceptions by ecopoets support Merleau-Ponty's point that language understood as originary gesture partaking of and articulating the flesh of the world does not reduce speech to either a thought process or a motor activity of the body but synthesizes both as it recovers the referential world of lived experience (PP 194-99).

For Merleau-Ponty language is not autonomous: the laws of form and syntax are culled out of sedimented language after decades and centuries of usage, and originary language over time creates new usages that modify syntax. The periodic desire to sing the world anew happens as "the perceptible world's implosion within us" (1964a [*Signs*], 20), and our response to the silent world that precedes language is to generate "wild" meaning, originary speech acts that grant human meaning to our fresh perceptions (VI 13, 102, 110, 158) of the perceptual world, the world of Heideggerian Being (VI 165-70). The world's silent visibility and our speech acts continually convert one to the other (VI 129) in a reversible intertwining as the interdependent infolding of one flesh forever impelled to burst into

song and significance, to make visible part of the incommensurable total-
ity, the great unthought (VI 118-19). Merleau-Ponty wants us to realize
that in the silent world, as well as in the act of perception, structurings
occur that predate language.

Merleau-Ponty's notions of silence as the world of our immediate,
unreflective, unthematized perception (VI 170-71) and of the visible as the
amorphous, sensible flesh of the world in which all living matter partici-
pates, account for two recurrent themes in environmental poetry and in
the four ecopoets I treat in this volume. Both themes attempt to render in
words the poets' ineffable experiences of bonding with nature, of being as
much "at one" with nature as is possible for humans. To be most "at home
in the world," as well as to find those Heideggerian moments when Being
blossoms, Wendell Berry recognizes the periodic need to go "beyond words"
and "beyond thought" and in silence connect with the land as did the
inhabitants of earlier tribal cultures (BCP 111–12). In silence "the world /
lives in the death of speech / and sings there" (BCP 157). At dusk, when
the noise of manmade engines such as jet planes and automobiles stills,
Berry experiences being grounded in nature as the inverse of human maps,
as the tree of Being, whose reflection stirs on the river's surface as well as
points downward toward "the water's inward life," with "a quietness" so
profound that "no question can be asked in" it (BCP 63). The sole epi-
graph to Berry's *A Timbered Choir* (1998), from Isaiah (14:7), highlights
one of its major themes: "The whole earth is at rest, and is quiet: they break
forth into singing."

In "Utterance," one of the shortest and most subtle poems of *The
Rain in the Trees*, Merwin experiences "the echo of everything that has ever
/ been spoken" while laboring over words and soulfully recognizes that
words impede one's ability to experience the earth during moments of
prereflective silence. Words screen us from the earth and its silence; they
spin their "one syllable / between the earth and silence" (RT 44). Children,
less habituated to ratiocination and abstract concepts, enjoy the ability to
talk to the trees "without anything," in the silence of imaginative play (RT
7). Ammons experiences the ridge line of "The Ridge Farm" as a limit of
the visible, the pressure of reality, and when he finally does drive to the
ridge farm, he experiences the depth of Being, a silence that is "ineluctable"
but that he hears and hears so profoundly that the "silence / deepens down
and picks up ground" (SV 27).

Snyder infrequently writes of experiencing the state of silence, prob-
ably because in zazen and other forms of meditative spiritual discipline he

has lived with it all his adult life. When he composes his poems—most often during physical labor, occasionally in silent meditation—visual images kindred to the original experiences well up from his unconscious. Often in his poems, when humans stop their labors and become silent, they can recognize a "talkless landscape" full of the sounds of nonhuman nature (NN 317, 350; MRWE 145). When Snyder achieves the *śūnyatā* state of nothingness "On Vulture Peak," the residence of the Buddha, he experiences a positive grounding in Being where he apprehends the allness of existence without dualistic separations. At such times Snyder realizes that for forty years the Buddha "said nothing," and "Vulture Peak is silent as a tomb" (NN 332).

Significantly, this *śūnyatā* experience happens for Snyder only after he has traced karmic debt back to its origins, "To the simple garden in my eye" (NN 329). Our human experiences of the visible, sensible flesh of the world, according to Merleau-Ponty, are necessarily self-reflexive, for this is how the human body sees, hears, and comes to know itself. We are "beings who turn the world back upon itself and who pass over to the other side, and who catch sight of one another, who see one another with eyes" (VI 155). Other orders of beings also "see" and sense, and it is no wonder that on occasion environmental poets and ecopoets experience the oneness of life as a paradoxically reciprocal state of seeing and being seen. In *The Practice of the Wild* Snyder affirms that, if we look at the history of the world as something other than a Darwinian "rat race" of survival, we can see hundreds of other ecological interactions: "If the background and foreground are reversed, and we look at it from the side of the 'conditions' and their creative possibilities, we can see these multitudes of interactions through hundreds of other eyes" (1990, 109). The famous lines of Snyder's early poem "Piute Creek," "A clear attentive mind / Has no meaning but that / Which sees is truly seen," occur after words drop away, in a state of vision where the poet recognizes that "Cold proud eyes / Of Cougar or Coyote / Watch me rise and go" (NN 6). In "As for Poets," Snyder begins with one stanza each on earth, air, fire, and water poets. In the fifth stanza, he describes the space poet, and then he comes to the "Mind Poet," whose house is the entire planet and whose vision encompasses all of its life at the same time that his work is seen by all of its life. Snyder ends by stating that the poem "Is seen from all sides, / Everywhere, / At once" (NN 261).

Similar experiences of biocentric oneness with all creation through a reciprocal seeing and being seen occur in the poetry of Merwin, Ammons, and Berry. In the final poem of *The Vixen*, when Merwin experiences "the clear spring of being," when all divisions and barriers between self, loved ones, and friends past and present vanish, the poet experiences a biocentric moment of unity with all creation, including "the eyes of the animals upon me they are all here" (1996, 70). Ammons characteristically is moved to compose when he notices resemblances among all orders of life, as he often explains in his "Essay on Poetics." In the short poem "Poetics" he states that, instead of actively looking for poetic material, he remains "available" for any "shape that may be / summoning itself / through me / from the self not mine but ours" (1972 [ACP], 199).

At the climax of Berry's "Window Poems," when the poet finally leaves the writing shed of art to embrace all of nature,he finds himself "watched / by more than he sees" (BCP 94). In "The Heron," the poet is seen by the heron's "living eye," and thus "I see that I am seen." The experience opens the poet to *référance*, to a biocentric awareness of nature's otherness; the poem ends with the lines "suddenly I know I have passed across / to a shore where I do not live" (BCP 138). In *A Timbered Choir,* Berry echoes the completed vision of St. Paul's I Corinthians 13:11–12 as he records a "face-to-face" encounter with a deer. This occurs only after Berry has deliberately left the workday rut for a sabbath meditation in the woods to appreciate work "Beyond the work of mortal hand, / Seen by more than I see" (26).

Poetic renditions of states of silence, and of the reciprocity of seeing and being seen by the sensible flesh of the world, are attempts by environmental poets and ecopoets to open poetry toward a biocentric interaction with nature without reducing it to an immanence of humanly crafted voices. They take Wittgenstein's ordinary use value of language beyond the human in altering and expanding our perceptions of the nature we see when we shift our referential gaze beyond the printed page. Wittgenstein ended the *Tractatus* with the proposition that "what we cannot speak about we must pass over in silence" (no. 7), but he found no value in nature's silence. Merleau-Ponty's phenomenology can account for these features of environmental poetry and ecopoetry. In the following chapters, we will call on Merleau-Ponty's program frequently as we sketch out the ecological and phenomenological dimensions of the poetry of Ammons, Berry, Merwin, and Snyder.

Sustainable Poetry

Aldo Leopold believes that "a thing is right when it tends to preserve the integrity, stability, and beauty of the biotic community. It is wrong when it is otherwise" (1949, 224-25). His land ethic depends on a sense of interdependency within a community or ecosystem that affirms the right of nonhuman living nature to continued existence, and his sense of community includes "soils, waters, plants, and animals, or collectively: the land" (203-4). The ethics behind sustainability derive from the same principle of biocentric harmony. Simply stated, sustainability means that humans can harvest a sufficient amount of a natural resource for consumption so long as we do not deplete the resource base. It means being aware of the carrying capacity of a given locale, its limit of human habitation or use, and assisting in the replenishment of a resource so that it can maintain its health and integrity. According to Sandra Postel of the Worldwatch Institute, the basic goals of sustainability are "ecological integrity, efficiency, equity, and participatory decision-making" (Brown 1996, 54). Lester Brown of Worldwatch defines a sustainable economy as one where human needs do not tax the limits of ecosystem renewal; in a sustainable economy

> human births and deaths are in balance, soil erosion does not exceed the natural rate of new soil formation, tree cutting does not exceed tree planting, the fish caught do not exceed the sustainable yield of fisheries, the cattle on a range do not exceed its carrying capacity, and water pumping does not exceed aquifer recharge. It is an economy where carbon emissions and carbon fixation are also again in balance. The number of plant and animal species lost does not exceed the rate at which new species evolve.
>
> With population, the challenge is to complete the demographic transition, to reestablish the balance between births and deaths that characterizes a sustainable society. (1996, 11–12)

What does sustainability have to do with poetry? The above definitions of sustainability all suggest maintaining a balance of needs among humans and other living entities to promote ecological health. The foregoing discussion of language in Ammons, Berry, Merwin, and Snyder also suggests that one maintains ethical health by balancing the textual and the referential, the imaginative needs of humans for pleasure and enlightenment and the referential survival needs of life on earth. Sustainable poetry maintains a healthy balance between these textual and referential needs. It presents nature as a separate and at least equal other and offers exemplary models of biocentric perception and behavior. It does not subordinate nature to a superior human consciousness or reduce nature to immanence.

Establishment poetry that systematically naturalizes nature into reliably benign, National Park landscapes and regularly sanitizes the text by systematically editing out specific social and economic concerns, while restricting interest to aesthetics and language theory, is unsustainable poetry, for it attenuates our grasp of important referential realities. Sustainable poetry sustains a connection between the inner and outer world; it is not written in dualistic gaps. The resource base of poetry is the referential world, and language that evades the referential world through divorcing text from context, *dulce* from *utile*, is not sustainable, nor is a poetic oeuvre driven by theory rather than the actual lived experience of the poet within the stubborn complexities of daily existence. When I spoke to W.S. Merwin at his home on Maui in June 1994, I tried to explain some of the consequences of poststructural language theory for poetry criticism. Merwin smiled ruefully and said "I thought poetry had something to do with living." Altieri would probably respond that, without a conceptual model for "living," we could not assess how poetry best fulfills that objective.

Then we would table discussion until dozens of theorists would write dozens of tortuously complex texts to provide an adequate theoretical model for "life." The project would fail, of course, not simply because that has never been accomplished but because the projectors would have to admit that theorizing at that level of abstract complexity simply leaves out too much of what daily living is about. Meanwhile shelf on shelf of theory texts would accumulate, ultimately to be quadruple-bar-coded and take up space in off-campus storage facilities, erected and maintained at the expense of every state's taxpayers, on land that could produce grain or vegetables. Poets grounded in the real world are still the antennae of the race, not academic critics; the role of the critic interested in planetary survival should be to use appropriate theoretical approaches to elucidate and illuminate what actually does appear in the primary creative literature, not to develop models through which poems are processed, boxed, and evaluated according to the tenets of language theory.

Stevens, in *The Necessary Angel*, opined that poetry helps us to live our lives (1951, 29-31, 36). Though phenomenologically inclined, he did not mean only our theoretical lives. The problem is that our lives in the late 1990s are lives with more than double the population and pollution and significantly fewer natural resources than the lives of the people of Stevens's generation. One of the delights of poetry is that it does help us to live our lives, and new poems, as Ammons as well as Stevens reminds us, need to be written when our lived experience and our linguistic reflection of that experience no longer mesh. At the end of the twentieth century, we learn every week of environmental stresses that indicate that nature may someday exhaust the capacities of its ecosystems to sustain humans, and hence we must alter the linguistic reflections of our experience--our poems—to incorporate a more discerning awareness of what nature needs to maintain its health.

When postmodern theorists attempt to locate ontological ground within language, they trap themselves in an embarrassing dilemma, for Derrida's account of language as an absence that disseminates constantly changing meaning precludes ontological stability. On the contrary, by grounding poetry in the phenomenology of the percept, one locates a flexible meeting ground for the human psyche as it interacts with its referential context. Thus ecological context receives sufficient weight at the same time that this paradigm most clearly and succinctly approximates our own commonsense experience. Here environmental and ecological poets can articulate and investigate the complex "tissues of sense, spun out // of sense filaments" (SV 121) that Ammons believes accrue in any intelligent act of perception at the same time that they strive to strike a balance between the needs of humans and the needs of nature.

A sustainable poem is the verbal record of the percept, of the poet's originary perception. It is the verbal record of an interactive encounter in the world of our sensuous experience between the human psyche and nature, where nature retains its autonomy—where nature is not dominated, reduced to immanence, or reduced to a reliably benign aesthetic backdrop for anthropocentric concerns. Ecopoets ensure that nature retains its status as a separate and equal other through the understanding and respect they accord the operations of nature's ecosystems in the poems. Ecopoems are not restricted to the laws of human logic and language, for these are regularly shown to be subordinate to the laws of nature's ecosystems. Language in ecopoems attains neither primacy nor special ontological status; it is simply the most flexible tool humans have created to convey their experiences and perceptions, in the corporeal body as well as in the deepest recesses of the conscious and unconscious mind. Language can never offer a full or exhaustive account of human experience, but a poet is a poet because he or she experiences depths of feelings and perceptions beyond the ordinary and has developed the power to use language to subvert its sedimentary uses and create truly new, originary uses. Once completed, an ecopoem becomes a tool for altering the reader's perceptions from the anthropocentric to the biocentric, and many ecopoems model biocentric behavior. Ecopoems help us to live our lives by encouraging us to understand, respect, and cooperate with the laws of nature that sustain us. Today we very much need sustainable poetry.

3

Homology and Chiastic Energy
in the Lived Body

A. R. Ammons

a light catches somewhere, finds human
spirit to burn on
. . . .
                it dwells:
it dwells and dwells: slowly the light,
its veracity unshaken, dies but moves
to find a place to break out elsewhere:
this light, tendance, neglect
is human concern working with
what is

                             Ammons, SV 40

Born on a Whiteville, North Carolina farm in 1926 and poet in residence at Cornell University since 1964, A.R. Ammons embodies in his poetry the contradictions implied in the two poles of his experience. Sophisticated, witty, and intellectually agile, that poetry nevertheless remains firmly rooted in a sense of place as well as the simple biological realities of everyday living. The forty-year arc of Ammons's career from *Ommateum* (1955) through *Glare* (1997) also represents a movement from the severe isolation, loneliness, and introverted epistemological meditations of the early short poems to the gradually more open-armed acceptance of society and embrace of ordinary living in quotidian reality in the long poems: *Tape for the Turn of the Year* (1965), *Sphere: The Form of a Motion* (1974), "The Ridge Farm" section of *Sumerian Vistas* (1987), *Garbage* (1993), and *Glare*. Once a lofty adventurer in the mysteries of biological minutiae and the laws of physics, Ammons today delights in writing about the backyard squirrels and chipmunks that he sees from his second-floor study window of the Ithaca, New York, home where he has dwelled for the past thirty years. Though the subject matter has become more homey, the intellectual probity of his poetry retains its tensile strength.

Donald Reiman (1985) offers two reasons for the gradually more relaxed embrace of the everyday in Ammons: (1) Harold Bloom's praise of Ammons's poetry and his continued support since the early seventies and (2) the liberation and subsequent bonding with humanity that Ammons achieved after confronting a troublesome father imago in *The Snow Poems* (1977). Reiman also finds that Ammons's development in part depends on his continued willingness to make poetic uses of science in order to see individual fate not only from within but also "from the imagined vantage point of other creatures and of the processes of nature" (1985, 24). This is the ecological pole of what he calls Ammons's "ecological naturalism." At one point in his essay, Reiman reprints a startling quotation from an interview with Philip Fried, where Ammons acknowledges his use of scientific material for poetry at the same time that he both critiques the anthropocentricity of most humanities perspectives and offers a sure gloss for the references to the Sumerian civilization that he occasionally introduces into his poems. Here Ammons emphasizes knowing referential reality, "the nature of the thing out there":

> If you think of the pagan societies as rather carefully paying attention to what the natural forces were around them and then trying to identify with and, as it were, listen to what that force was and appease it, and know something about it, learn its nature, then science does the same thing today.
>
> It puts aside, for the moment, its personal interest in things and tries to know what is the nature of the thing out there. I regard that as a very high value. The humanities often feel opposed to that because that attitude obviously puts human things secondary, whereas the humanities have often claimed that man is the center of everything and has the right to destroy or build or do whatever he wishes. (Quoted in Reiman 1985, 50)

Along with this emphasis on the referential, one can at the same time comprehend Ammons's more recent poetry as a steadily deepening acuity into the nature of language and its relationship to a poetics founded on the perception of ecological interrelatedness. Ammons's outward movement from alienation and loneliness toward a comfortable acceptance and celebration of the natural world parallels a deepening understanding of how the creative act of perception and its recreation in language is homologous to the operations of the energy-driven ecosystems of our planet. Just as ecosystems recoup a portion of their energy, so language is a system wherein the poet's energy dwells. In his more recent poetry, *Sumerian Vistas, Garbage, Brink Road,* and *Glare,* the keen perceptive power of Ammons's biocentric gaze constantly makes his readers aware of the thick textures of interconnectedness among all creatures and elements of planet earth. Nature retains its separate and equal otherness especially in the weight Ammons accords the operations of ecosystems in his poetry.

Consider, for instance, the short poem "Tracing Out" in *Sumerian Vistas.* Ammons begins with a direct question: "What buoys the butterfly"? His answer, "the world's / weight," suddenly makes us aware of a double entendre. Yes, planetary ecosystems sustain the butterfly, give it the air that, displaced, keeps the butterfly afloat. But the repetition of "weight" two more times in the poem also suggests "buoy" as "anchors," for the world's weight in motion produces gravity, which keeps the butterfly from flying off into outer space. Halfway through the poem, though, after a colon (Ammons's trademark that often registers a homological equivalency for the statements on either side), we are just as suddenly made aware that the butterfly's "lightness," its tiny "muscles and plastic / joints," is also the product of the world's "momentarily fined / tissues of sense" and that these tissues, products of the world's sense systems, are homologous to products of the human linguistic system—alternative ways of "making // sense," tissues "spun out // of sense filaments" from the body of the world. The poem ends with the biocentric affirmation that we are all parts of an integrated world. Simultaneously, our human perceptions of that world have been refreshed and enlarged by removing our anthropocentric blinders— "the world's weight [is] the world's." But just how interconnected is nature with human linguistic systems? How are the energy and densely textured arguments of Ammons's recent work connected to the world? By fanciful metaphors in the poet's refined sensibility? If so, then the fabric of "Tracing Out" is more fabulation than fact. The answer to the problem, an answer that also reveals Ammons as an ecopoet, lies in his very consistent poetics of perception and homologous energy.

Very early in his career Ammons published "A Note on Incongruence" (1966), a cryptic, one-page note on the relation of poetic language to experience. Here he set his work apart from naive mimesis as he asserted that "poetry is not made out of 'reality' but out of an invented system of signs." He recognized that "language, an invented instrument, is not identical with what it points to" and that the motivation for a new poem occurs when poets experience "an incongruence between our non-verbal experience of reality and our language reflection of it." Hence, Ammons defines a poem as "a linguistic correction of disorder" (SM 8–9).

Here Ammons appears to agree with the mainstream of poststructural language theory exemplified by Derrida, Lacan, and Wittgenstein. But the last three paragraphs of this "Note" depart markedly from theories that hold that language mediates all experience. Ammons accomplishes this by emphasizing the primacy of perception of the world beyond the self:

> If feeling is an essence that results from the mind's effort to make innumerable sensuous events apprehendable (capable of being acted on), then it may be that as our conscious attention brings more and different events (facts) before the mind, and as these events settle into the unconscious and return as "feelings," we begin to sense a disjointure between our feelings and our linguistic expression of them.
>
> At that point, a new poem becomes necessary. That is, a language system needs to be created which does ampler justice to the facts behind the feelings. A closer congruence needs to be achieved between the reality and the reflection.
>
> Facts change or new facts accumulate, disturbing the habitual response. The mind seeks the new object that can adequately reflect and interpret the new feelings. Disorder becomes incongruence and the poem is a *linguistic* correction to congruence. The facts may stay the same or go on changing, but we are temporarily able to cope. (SM 9)

Referential events are facts that humans perceive with their five senses. Then these sensuous events appear before the mind, gradually settle into the unconscious, and return to the conscious mind as feelings. The poet's job is to make his poetry, his "language reflection," as congruent as possible with his feeling-toned memories of his originary experience. But that originary experience with the referential world is the crucial flash point, the sine qua non for Ammons's compositional practice. Twenty years later, Ammons reaffirmed his epistemological position in an interview comment; with each new poem the poet says, "Here is the poem that most adequately reflects the feelings I have had in my relationship with the world of reality up until now" (SM 50). Because the individual's experience changes, the poet's existing poetic system will never regularize each new originary experience. Hence, as in his poem "The Misfit" (ACP 123), the unique encounter in referential reality is the "unassimilable fact" that forever challenges the mind to inquiry and to linguistic response, that "leads us on" to new poems (SM 53).

If the humanly processed originary experience reproduces or reconfirms what a recent poem expresses, there is no need for a new poem. But, as we all know, our feelings, our moods, and the sensuous events that we bring to consciousness during our experience are inherently changeable. For Ammons, as for Stevens before him, this instability is usually a source of delight. Yet Ammons much more than Stevens gives weight to the referential experience that our senses bring before the mind in the act of perception. Stevens was of his time: influenced by Bergsonian *durée*, he valorized the inner world and its power to find significant relations in a nature that the science of his time often characterized as an elemental chaos informed by entropy. Hence, for Stevens, order is reclaimed within the meditative mind of the poet. For Ammons, the planet earth and its organized ecosystems always retains primacy, and the imaginative act occurs in the continual interplay of perception in dialogue with a referential world that instructs us about its intricate order and survival mechanisms. That referential world can survive quite well without linguistic systems, which become less and less meaningful the more they depart from the ecological systems of our planet: "Whole languages, like species, can / disappear without dropping a gram of earth's // weight" (G 51).

Stevens recognized that his poems were "makings of the sun," but in an age without planetary environmental stress he characteristically accented being entranced with the poetic power of the imagination to put our planet on the table of his poetic memory with "some affluence" ("The Planet on the Table"). But, like Yeats in "Among School Children," Ammons becomes so intoxicated with referential experience that he longs for the organic marriage with the chestnut trees and the "Presences / That passion, piety or affection knows." Yet Ammons also resists aggrandizing the mind in order to fit these presences into anthropocentric Platonic systems or idealized cultural utopias, cerebral Byzantiums. Ammons is incurably biocentric in an age that needs the sanity of his position: "The world was the beginning / of the world" (G 50). That world made us, and we are a subset of it, not vice versa. Curiosity about that world and respect for its nonhuman life has been central to Ammons's epistemology throughout his career. Ammons once characterized a "presence" as a portion of the referential world brought to the attention of the poet in the act of perception: "One can search out another 'presence' for its otherness as for its sameness. I was alone enough as a child to want to know something besides myself. It was easy for me later to adopt the rhetorical device of 'speaking' mountains and winds: I recognized them as presences and wondered, if they spoke, what nature they would speak out of" (Stephenson 1986, 89). The "nature" of presences in the world beyond the self interests Ammons; his poetry explores the ecological balance points between the human self and nature.

Ammons's emphasis on the referential world, where the human body dwells in a corporeal context, is sustained by other important comments he made concerning what psychological state prompts creativity. In a 1986 interview with Jim Stahl, just before he spoke about how his poems reflect the feelings he has had in his relationship with reality, Ammons characterized the poetic state as one where he wants to release rather than intensify verbal pressure. For Ammons, the poet who has to work himself up to a high state of verbal intensity is "the second- or third-rate poet." But "apart from this poet who is constantly trying to intensify, there is the poet who is himself in such an anxious state that he turns to the poem not to create an even more intense verbal environment, but to do just the contrary; to ease that pressure" (SM 45).

Ammons characteristically releases that pressure and creates what Bloom and Ashbery agree is his "oddly negative exuberance" (Ashbery 1986, 58-59) not by a claustral experience with language on a piece of paper but by affirming the integrity of the referential world beyond that anxious self. Instead of imposing a style or artifice on the page, Ammons courts that state of perception where he lets the birch tree in his poem "Poetics" "stand out / wind-glittering / totally its apparent self" (ACP 199). He wants as much as possible to let that tree "unfold" through an "uninterfering" process whereby his biocentric gaze recognizes the equal participation of the referential world in the creative act. Here the table of his poetic intentionality rests secure on a firm planet, while his referentially grounded negative capability remains open,

> available
> to any shape that may be
> summoning itself
> through me
> from the self not mine but ours.
> (ACP 199)

The last word, "ours," suggests that his poetic table rests on the firm ground of our planet, our ecological whole. Always aware of how human intentionality leads to the "merciless" exploitation of nature, Ammons, in *Sumerian Vistas*, states that he goes to nature "because I have filled it with / unintentionality" (SV 15). The referential world of nature for Ammons is a separate and equal other, the place where nature readjusts and corrects human willfulness.

Ammons's "Essay on Poetics" (1972) remains a central statement of his aesthetic principles (ACP 296-317). In this poem, Ammons uses a word, "resemblance," that Stevens also used in his aesthetic theory. But Ammons modifies Stevens's use of it by specifying an ecologically sound series of interpenetrations between human and nonhuman life. Throughout, Ammons reasserts his early emphasis on the primacy of the act of perception as a way of integrating self with other. Here we will find a characteristic crisscrossing of inner and outer energies in the moment of perception and artistic composition that constitutes the heart of Ammons's ecological poetic. After reviewing some of the complications in the acts of perception in "Essay on Poetics," we will explore similarities with Lévi-Strauss's use of homology and the referentially oriented phenomenology of Merleau-Ponty.

Stevens begins his essay "Three Academic Pieces" with the statement that "reality is the central reference for poetry" and proceeds to focus upon "the resemblance between things" as "one of the significant components of the structure of reality" (NA 71). Later Stevens does acknowledge that "the eye does not beget in resemblance. It sees. But the mind begets in resemblance as the painter begets in representation; that is to say, as the painter makes his world within a world; or as the musician begets in music" (NA 76). Nevertheless, Stevens constructs a crucial bridge to the human imagination when he asserts that resemblance "binds together [and] is the base of appearance." Thus, "because this is so in nature, it is so in metaphor," where the transformations of the imagination reign supreme (NA 72-73). Stevens valorizes the world of metaphor in the mind of the creative artist but acknowledges its base in the natural world.

Ammons uses variations of the word "resemble" in five crucial passages of his "Essay on Poetics," and in each case his emphasis differs from Stevens. Ammons delights in the free exchange, the reversibility of poetic symbol and referential reality, but he does not reduce nature to immanence. In the first instance, Ammons imagines a thousand-acre cattle ranch and delights in how he could in a sense know the habits of the herd and the climatic conditions on the ranch by viewing an aerial photograph of the cowpaths, where "lesser resemblances of / motion" lead to the widest paths. Topographical segments from the smaller to the larger in referential reality allow him to "read" the landscape. Thus, Ammons's perception of the pattern of wear on the grass and near stands of trees would create meaningful significations. Even though Ammons reminds us that he was meditating on a "non-existent" ranch, the shiftings back and forth from aesthetic perception to concrete, referential language give this imaginary ranch a body, and the ranch as organism suddenly becomes analogous to the creation of a poem: "If the organism of the ranch / alters, weeds will grow in old paths and the new waterhole / exist in a new weaving." What kind of poetic weaving the ranch will produce seems dependent on the depth of the poet's perception of that "imagined" reality. The more concrete vision may produce an "entangling" weave of dactylic hexameter; the more surface perception may produce a lyric or manneristic style (ACP 296-98). This is a perfect illustration of the plastic nature of consciousness activating its energies in the act of perception; it reminds one of Merleau-Ponty's phenomenological definition of consciousness as the ability to recognize "a figure on a ground" (VI 191).

In the second instance of resemblance, Ammons creates a poem within his essay/poem, entitled "At Once," to find a middle way of discussing the interplay in the act of creation between the referential tree and the "ideal image-tree" of the mind. Each has its truth, but "when touched" in the act of perception the two create "clusters of entanglement." Hence, the first five lines of "At Once" present the moment of poetic creation as a chiastic interplay of similarity and difference (ACP 302):

Plumage resembles foliage
for camouflage often
and so well at times it's difficult

to know whether nature means
resembler or resembled

So "tree" and "true" swap back and forth together, primarily because
the referential reality, not the poet's overly-intense creative activity, pos-
sesses an integrity that is both vivid and unassailable: "so multiple and
dense is the reality of a tree" (ACP 303).

In the third variant of "resemblance," Ammons explores the
reversibility of mental truth and referential reality as truth, by examining
William Carlos Williams's famous dictum "no ideas but in things." Ammons
states that the mind can go to the extreme of scaling the "higher assimila-
tions" toward the most "lofty reification" or can go another way as it "searches
its culture clutch for meaningful / or recurrent objects" so that the mind

        invests its charge in that concretion, that focus: then

    the symbol carries exactly the syrup of many distillations and
    hard endurance, soft inquiry and turning: the symbol apple and the
    real apple are different apples, though resembled: "no ideas but in

    things" can then be read into alternatives—"no things but in ideas,"
    "no ideas but in ideas," and "no things but in things": one thing
    always to keep in mind is that there are a number of possibilities:

    whatever sways forward implies a backward sway and the mind must
    either go all the way around and come back or it must be prepared
    to fall back and deal with the lost sway
    (ACP 308)

Though either the abstract or the concrete truth achieved in this in-
stance would reside in the domain of the mental, they are variations on
"the symbol apple and the / real apple" where backward and forward inter-
changes of mind and matter appear to be as inevitable in poetic creation as
Newton's Second Law of action and reaction. Again Ammons underscores
a process of reversibility between vision and the sensible world.

An extended analogy between the complex formal disposition of the
"body" of a poem and "strings of nucleation" in the development of bio-
logical organisms in the referential world constitutes Ammons's fourth use
of "resemblance":

> poems, of human make, are
>
> body images, organisms of this human organism: if that isn't
> so I will be terribly disappointed: it sounds as if it ought to
> be right: consonants, vowels, idioms, phrases, clauses (tissues),
>
> sentences (organs), verses (organ systems), poems (living worlds):
> I react to such stuff with a burst of assent resembling for all
> I can tell valuable feeling
> (ACP 312)

The back-and-forth chiastic energy interweaves literary part to bio-
logical organ throughout the passage and convinces the reader of a process
inherent in nature, where our linguistic systems actively exchange energy
with our bodily systems.

Near the conclusion of the "Essay on Poetics" Ammons notes "the
adequacy of the transcendental / vegetative analogy" as he asserts that "a
poem in becoming generates the laws of its / own becoming: that certainly
sounds like a tree . . . " (ACP 315). Then Ammons complicates the analogy
by stating that "art is the craft and lore of preparing / the soil for seed." But
is the seed the poet's germ insight, or the presences in the referential world
that his alert eyes grasp? In his final use of "resemblance" Ammons, with
delicious homespun wit, suggests that the reversibility bond is so strong in
a well-integrated poem that visible referential world and invisible mental
world become one:

> is any yeoman
> dumb enough to think that by much cultivation of the fields wheat
> will sprout: or that saying words over the barren, the seedless,
>
> will make potatoes: son of a gun's been keeping a bag of seed-
> wheat
> in the barn all winter, has sorted out good potatoes and knows how
> to cut their eyes out: it's hard to say whether the distinguishers
>
> or the resemblancers are sillier: they work with noumena every
> day, but speak of the invisible to them and they laugh with
> silver modernity
> (ACP 316-17)

Following the logic of postmodern self-reflexivity, Ammons seems to suggest that barren words crowd the printed page. But at the same time the poet's art impregnates the fallow linguistic field. The made poem takes its place as a material object occupying space and historical time. The carefully chosen eyes of the poet's perceptions become seeds that sprout, completing the poem. The farming homespun (saving seed wheat and potato eyes) is perfectly homologous with storing germ insights for creative use in composing poems.

In *Postmodernism, or the Cultural Logic of Late Capitalism* (1991), Fredric Jameson asserts that one can recover from the structuralists the Lévi-Straussian use of homology without subscribing to any transcendent concept of "structure" (187-93). Homologies for Jameson bring in the rich substance of the natural world; they "imply analogies between objects, content, or raw materials within discourse" and thus question the theories of poststructural language critics who assume the ontological primacy of language (239). Indeed, Lévi-Strauss, in *Totemism* (1963), argues that the tribal mind in early human culture used metaphor and analogy to grasp shared differences among species and thus mediated the limits of the natural world and the needs of human culture without creating the dualistic split between humans and nature that Christianity required (3, 78-82, 91). For Lévi-Strauss the homological method of finding structural relationships that mediate discontinuities is both a "universal feature of human thinking" and *the* essential method of structural anthropology; its purpose is to apprehend the union, the integration, of method and reality, where the opposites are not Derridean linguistic binaries but those of human and nonhuman thinking and social organization (90-91). Lévi-Strauss even suggests that homologous thinking, like much tribal philosophy, presents the intuition, like Bergson's *élan vitale*, of "materialized forms of creative energy" (98).

The word "homology" derives from the Greek *homologous* and the Latin *homologia*. It means "agreeing." Today in the physical sciences such as biology and chemistry, "homology" denotes shared characteristics or corresponding structural features among families of compounds, organs, or creatures deriving from a common ancestor. Unlike analogies, where two dissimilar terms yet have *one* common characteristic, homologies suggest *many* complex corresponding features shared by two entities. Ammons throughout his work suggests that humans, because we derive from the same ancestor, nature, should live in harmony with all other elements and creatures on our planet. By extending homologies to the interface between

parts of a poem and "strings of nucleation" (ACP 306, 311-12) in the de-
velopment of complex biological organisms, Ammons deliberately tries to
eliminate the postmodern gap between the world of language and the world
of referential reality.

In his "Essay on Poetics" Ammons underscores the ecological sense of
observing homologies by introducing paragraph-long quotations from sci-
entific works emphasizing that all "living matter" organizes itself into struc-
tures and that excretion and death in the living world are simply occasions
for the recycling of energy into new life, for both produce worms. Ammons
often uses worms in his longer poems to underscore homologous recyclings
in the human and nonhuman worlds, as with the complex toils of the
elmworm in the "Essay on Poetics" (ACP 305), the worms of "The Ridge
Farm" in whose bellies we are born again and rise up in song (SV 14, 35,
38-39), and the "bird do" that dabbed the poet with "bellyroundworms,
intricate, worky, lily-white / flailing bellyroundworms," giving him hope
of new creative life in *Garbage*: "undone by / do, I forged on" (97-99).

When Ammons, in the "Essay on Poetics," cites a passage from a
scientific text on botany about how all living matter organizes itself into
"appropriately structured cells," he follows the quotation with a general
statement of his homological method:

> poems are verbal
> symbols for these organizations: they imprint upon the mind
> examples of integration in which the energy flows with maximum
>
> effect and economy between the high levels of oneness and the
> numerous subordinations and divisions of diversity
> (ACP 314-15)

Ammons suggests that the energy flow and economy of a concise,
well-organized poem is homologous to the absorption, flow and recovery
of energy in an ecosystem. Philip Fried, in his excellent essay on ecological
influences in early Ammons, notes that Ammons often uses ecology as an
imitative "paradigm" for his compositional technique. Fried also asserts
that Ammons's use of the one and the many, which he may have adapted
from Emerson's essay "Plato; Or, The Philosopher" (Plotinus is another
possible source), is consistent with an ecosystem's balanced management of
diversity within unity, or identity and adaptability (Fried 1989, 90-91).
The interdependency theme in "One : Many" and especially the parable of

the spider weaving his web in "Identity" are prime examples in Ammons's earlier poems. The spider web achieves its individual identity at the periphery, where it intersects with the accidental—the chair knob, the hook near the room corner, and so on, and is most categorically identified as a spider web by the unaltering symmetry of the web center.

Ammons first announced ecology as his theme as he discussed centers and peripheries in the December 27 entry of his *Tape for the Turn of the Year*:

> *ecology* is my word: tag
>   me with that: come
>   in there:
>   you will find yourself
> in a firmless country:
>   centers & peripheries
>   in motion,
>   organic,
>   interrelations!

In that December 27 entry, Ammons follows his announcement with three ecological examples of interconnectedness: how the lichen multiplies around a center that "gathers stability / from bark"; how the cougar "husbands his prey" as he alternately roams the central area and the peripheries of his domain; and how the plains Indians centered their lives in the buffalo chase, "a center / stabilized / in instability" (1965, 111–117).

The "Essay on Poetics" most exemplifies Ammons's homologous method in his extended comparison of the organic organization of the poem to the mature tree. What fascinates Ammons in each case is the phenomonology of perception: how at the point when the referential tree activates human intentionality, a whole complex of "interpenetrations" between the mental and the referential occurs (ACP 307), suggesting the rich inexhaustibility of the encounter. Early in the essay Ammons meditates on how the wind shakes off the snow from the more pliant upper branches of a spruce tree. Snow spills downward, leading to unpredictable minor avalanches on major limbs below, and suddenly the mysterious core of the referential tree is likened to the mysterious heart of the lyric poem (ACP 299). Two pages later Ammons meditates on how an ancient etymological root for the human category "true" concerns the trope "as firm as a tree"; thus, referential facts take on human truth "when touched" by human intentionality in the process of perception (ACP 301). Next Ammons, with light humor, discourses on how impossible it would be to fix the stable location of the unalterable elm tree through altimeter readings and gravity waves; instead, he prefers the delight of the percept where he can simply accept the reality of the elm and stand "quiet in the hands of the marvelous" (ACP 303-4). Finally, Ammons meditates on how seedfall from trees appears totally accidental, peripheral, at first glance, but on second glance we recognize the irreplaceable process through which the tree species reproduces itself through its nearly unalterable genetic code. Through the sheer proliferation of numbers the tree species becomes adaptable, yet centered and resistant to change (ACP 306-7).

Ammons clearly roots his homologous method in the act of perception, where he observes the designs and patterns that exist within the referential world; his lines capture the spontaneous delight of recognition. Thinking is synonymous with seeing resemblances in a certain manner or way that does not violate the factual events under observation:

> the way I think is
> I think what I see: the designs are there: I use
>
> words to draw them out—also because I can't
> draw at all: I don't think: I see: and I see
> the motions of cowpaths
> . . . .
> motion and artificiality (the impositional remove from reality)
> sustain language: nevertheless, language must
> not violate the bit, event, percept,
>
> fact—the concrete—otherwise the separation that means
> the death of language shows
> (ACP 298)

Merleau-Ponty also adopts a painterly metaphor to discuss how a creative artist's style originates in the crucial act of perception, in the primordial encounter of the lived body with the referential world:

> That convergence of all the visible and intellectual vectors of
> the painting towards the same signification, X, is already sketched
> out in the painter's perception. It begins as soon as he perceives—
> that is, as soon as he arranges certain gaps or fissures, figures

and grounds, a top and a bottom, a norm and a deviation in the inaccessible plenum of things. In other words, as soon as certain elements of the world take on the value of dimensions to which from then on we relate all the others and in whose *language* we express them. For each painter, style is the system of equivalences that he makes for himself for the work which manifests the world he sees. (1974, 51)

[My glance] takes up its dwelling in being with authority and conducts itself there as in a conquered country. It is not the object which obtains movements of accommodation and convergence from my eyes. It has been shown that on the contrary I would never see anything clearly, and there would be no object for me, if I did not use my eyes in such a way as to make a view of a single object possible. And it is not the mind which takes the place of the body and anticipates what we are going to see. No; it is my glances themselves—their synergy, their exploration, and their prospecting—which bring the imminent object into focus; and our corrections would never be rapid and precise enough if they had to be based upon an actual calculation of effects. We must therefore recognize that what is designated by the terms "glance," "hand," and in general "body" is a system of systems devoted to the inspection of a world and capable of leaping over distances, piercing the perceptual future, and outlining hollows and reliefs, distances and deviations—a meaning—in the inconceivable flatness of being.

. . . . .

All perception, all action which presupposes it, and in short every human use of the body is already *primordial expression.* Not that derivative labor which substitutes for what is expressed signs which are given elsewhere with their meaning and rule of usage, but the primary operation which first constitutes signs as signs, makes that which is expressed dwell in them through the eloquence of their arrangement and configuration alone, implants a meaning in that which did not have one, and thus—far from exhausting itself in the instant at which it occurs—inaugurates an order and founds an institution or a tradition. (1974, 63-64)

Throughout "Indirect Language and the Voices of Silence" Merleau-

Ponty uses the word "dwell" to signify the originary act of human perception that grasps portions of the referential world anew and thus blurs or deranges the sedimented, conventional meanings of signs in the quest for new signification. Hence, signs are not just sequences of differences without positive terms, as Saussure and Derrida would have us believe, but are repositories for the fresh actions of the lived body's perceptual powers as they inhabit the referential world. The words remain as an abiding, permanent residence for the active energy of perception as it inhabits the signs with new meanings, arrangements that linger or dwell for the reader's delight. According to Merleau-Ponty, the writer does not simply "dwell in already elaborated signs in an already speaking world," for an artist's language is "an originating language" that "gropes around a significative intention which is not guided by any text, and which is precisely in the process of writing the text" (1974, 42-43). Merleau-Ponty asserts that "the theory of perception makes the painter dwell once more in the visible world and once more lays bare the body as spontaneous expression" (1974, 62).

In his more recent poetry volumes, Ammons often conveys the lushness of the referential world through the inhabiting energy of his very self-referential poetic line. In many of the shorter poems of *Sumerian Vistas* such as "Hairy Belly," "A Tendency to Ascendancy," and "The Dwelling," Ammons celebrates the synthetic activity of perception as it moves back and forth from the physical to the mental world, drawing them together. In "Hairy Belly," Ammons plays on the word "gravity" as both a "weak field force" in unified field physics theory and "gravity" as a seriousness of intent in the composition of verse. He creates homologies between physical, biological, and linguistic systems. If the uniform operation of gravity as a physical force suddenly stops, then brooks may stop running. And if the energy that composes verse does not attend to serious pursuits, it may move inaccurately, and "potholes" will "appear in the street" of thin verse. Next Ammons likens gravity to verse in its prevalence: like gravity, verse "dwells" in the shadows of brook ripples and vine threads. As in Stevens's "The Motive for Metaphor," Ammons suggests that verse dwells best in the imperfectly, incompletely known—the shadows. Verse knows reality indirectly, through the human perceptual powers, and can never know absolute reality, the *ding an sich*, the "dominant X" of the Stevens poem. But after Ammons interweaves his gravity/verse/biosystems analogy for five stanzas, he then gives it another twist: verse is like the "vine-skin / cells" of chloroplasts, for vines and the poet's perceptions respond indirectly to sunlight, the visible, the what-can-be-known. Chloroplasts are the parts within the plant cell membranes that contain chlorophyll. Chloroplasts react to sunlight to create sugar and starch, with the help of carbon dioxide and water. Verse is the linguistic starch created by the poet's energy.

Ammons ends "Hairy Belly" with a delightful surprise. The human/verse system is homologically akin to the production of vegetable matter. Not only do we need food to survive, but without the verse photosynthesis of a human responding to the shadows and sunlight of what-can-be-known, the poem (as plant) would wither. Hence a double entendre in the final stanza: "if chloroplasts didn't jiggle-knit / spinning in sunny cells, your / lips' scarlet would not be scarlet long" (78). Without the serious poetic photosynthesis from percept to final poem, the actual words on the page would become anemic, wither and disappear. The hairy belly or nitty-gritty of art is a physical process, an intertwining or chiasm between the referential and the humanly subjective—a tough bonding encoded in both human and plant cells. Like a pinball wizard, Ammons crisscrosses the poles of his subjective/objective chiasm several times in the poem; as the reader tries to keep up with his shifts of territory, one's mind opens up to the possibility that the homology may be true, that the creation of poetry is akin to activities in other significant planetary biosystems. Stevens, in "The Motive for Metaphor," left his reader hyperconscious of human separation and frailty, for we perceive in the oblique shadows of reality's "dominant X." But Ammons emphasizes our connectedness with other significant planetary systems in a way that makes us feel comfortable with our lived body in a livable home.

Ammons's emphasis on chiastic reversibility, the constant flip-flopping from internal to referential worlds every few lines, is not just a poetic technique but carries the substance of his ecological poetic. It suggests that our mental life shares in the energy of other living entities in referential reality and that we are partners with all of life in the energy transfers of interconnected ecosystems. Actually this is no more than an extension of the substance of "Corson's Inlet" (ACP 147-51), one of his finest earlier poems. In "Corson's Inlet," Ammons frees himself from the "perpendiculars" and "straight lines" of thought and also frees himself from "separating inside / from outside." Inner and outer swap around as he permits himself "eddies of meaning" where his "sayings" partake of "swerves of action / like the inlet's cutting edge." Inner and outer worlds meet in the nondualistic "wandering of the mirroring mind" to suggest that humans are always in experience, not just as dominating manipulators and exploiters, but as partakers of energies and motions not unlike Einsteinian force fields. Ammons fuses inner and outer worlds so deftly throughout "Corson's Inlet" that they become indistinguishable and render faithfully our moment-to-moment involvement in direct experience.

The term "ascendancy" in abnormal psychology denotes schizophrenic personality disorders with reciprocal amnesia. W.H. Auden read William McDougall's *Outline of Abnormal Psychology* and used "ascendancy" in his early poem "Consider this and in our time" to analyze a neurotically sick society . Ammons, in "A Tendancy to Ascendancy" (SV 70), suggests that writing poetry is his means of managing his psychological weather. When the winds of poetic inspiration roar, he follows this weather ("I go over") into the verbal world, for he has learned to "dwell in the continuous // sway of the mournful singing." When the psychological tempest abates, he returns to the ground, and in doing so "re-recognize[s]" that ground with a new poem. Just as beach worms and other natural creatures make adjustments, Ammons makes "arrangements," a term he normally reserves for poetic organizations. The poem is the record of his inhabiting spirit, and the words function as the dwelling place of his psychic energy.

On religious questions Ammons also delights in taking an iconoclastic, biocentric position. In "The Dwelling," he argues that humans dwell most properly in our "spiritual / energy"; this "is, the eternal // residence." The comma after "is" underscores the fact that physical existence within a physical world is for Ammons the normal residence of our spiritual energy—that is where life "is," exists. Twice in the poem he equates heaven with "nothing," the Tao of perfected, undifferentiated oneness. This is the place where our spiritual energy periodically returns for purification. But to believe in a static heaven is to place an abiotic "sheen" of perfected "fabrications" before the eyes, fabrications that "ash can't get to," that will not connect with biological processes. Our energy and desire, our "heart's cravings" are satisfied only in "this // jewelry of brick and loft"—which may be either the physical world or the completed poem. The poem ends in a posture of consent to the finished argument—that "the plainest / majesty gave us what it could." Ammons covers ground similar to Stevens in "Sunday Morning" and "The Plain Sense of Things," but affirmatively, without Stevens's sense of religious loss or the depressive "blank cold," the "absence" or winter of the soul in "The Plain Sense of Things."

"The Ridge Farm," the lengthy poem that opens *Sumerian Vistas*, at first appears to be a stern, somber meditation on human finitude. The farm of the title is a large farm on a ridge top near Mecklenberg (26), a town about ten miles west of Ithaca. When Ammons looks toward it as a flock of geese glide overhead, he thinks cold thoughts about the windy ridge in April where "glory is still uncertain and death / not" (18). When he visits it he tries to appreciate its "ineluctable" silence, the speech of the earth before humans and their language (27). The "high farm beseeches [his] mind" (36), and what it most often suggests is a changeless, "showless" permanence in nature, a "durable" limit that places fragile mortal aspirations in a subordinate position:

> but I like the ridge: it was a line
> in the minds of hundreds of generations
> of cold Indians: and it was there
> approximately then what it is now
> five hundred years ago when the white
> man was a whisper on the continent:
> it is what I come up against:
> it regularizes my mind though it has
> nothing to do with me intentionally:
> the shows that arise in and afflict
> nature and man seem papery and
> wrong when wind or time tears
> through them, they seem not only
> unrealistic but unreal: the ridge,
> showless, summary beyond the trappings
> of coming and going, provides a
> measure, almost too much measure,
> that nearly blinds away the present's
> fragile joys from more durable woes
> (10)

Other elements in "The Ridge Farm" also seem at first glance to underscore the theme of mortality and death. Near the midpoint of the poem the poet finds a dead mole in his watering can (19), and the poem on four separate occasions also develops a picaresque odyssey of a squirrel (20, 25-26, 30, 35) that is killed by a car, ignored by the driver and by passing cyclists, ravaged by rigor mortis, and is "chucked off // the road by crow or cop," only to be slung right back to the road's edge eleven days later by the poet as he mows his lawn (the lawn mowing is a dour update of the time and mortality themes in Marvell's mower poems). The durable woes of the animals ironically point to the finitude of the human perceiver.

But if the referential ridge is what Ammons "come[s] up against," it can also function as resistance, as what Stevens calls the "pressure of reality" (NA 13) that initiates new perceptions. Merleau-Ponty considers "perceived things as rivals in my field of vision. I find the means of arbitrating their conflict, which makes depth." The act of creation is "the invention of a world which is dominated and possessed through and through in an instantaneous synthesis which is at best roughed out by our glance when it vainly tries to hold together all these things seeking individually to monopolize it" (1974, 46-47). Furthermore, as the artist fleshes out his creation, his creative energy inhabits the words he uses and "exceeds" the sedimented perspectives of those words. Thus, the creative act of writing poetry must "completely awaken and recall our sheer power of expressing beyond things already said or seen" (1974, 46-47, 49). Even somber meditations on human finitude suggest creative opportunities for new signification. Throughout "The Ridge Farm," Ammons's highly self-reflexive lines launch out beyond sedimented meaning to invest language with "maximum implication and // registration of fact and tension before / integration catches on" (20). In that whir of creative linguistic activity, Ammons is fully in his element: "home is // where the doodle is" (34).

Ammons asserts that the people who own the ridge farm "don't see it or / their part in it." This is because for Ammons "seeing" is a creative act that opens the mind and the visible and exceeds commonplace language by "implicating" it with new perceptions. Like Pound's "MAKE IT NEW" ("Canto LIII"), Ammons winnows linguistic chaff to find firm words that might capture traces of the synergistic energy of perception:

> words cast up
> to see if light
> will pick anything out in them
>
> like sand and trash
> a winnowing:
> though I cast up true
>
> words as far as I know
> (words that truly
> occur) I cannot be

> held wrong when I range
> into winnowing chaff,
> truly chaff: I am
>
> seeing: I am looking to make
> arrangements
> (23)

The light Ammons speaks of in the second line is, as we shall see later in the concluding stanzas of "The Ridge Farm," the illumination of the visible that is the imaginative act of perception itself.

Ammons's real purpose in this poem is to undo death by celebrating the visible, including the human ability to recognize the reversibility that Merleau-Ponty considers the primary element of the visible. One finds chiastic lines in Ammons, like the following in "The Ridge Farm," *Garbage*, and *Glare*, not simply because he likes verbal play but also because he, like Merleau-Ponty, believes that all living entities are both sensible and sentient and inhabit a world where this property exists—as does the omnipresent fluid in an old *New Yorker* cartoon where one fish asks the other "What is all this water we keep hearing about?" For Ammons this reciprocal flesh of the visible is characteristic of his vision and his process of composition:

> since this
> is one place
> going is coming, ending beginning
> (SV 15)
>
> my words
> are, of course, chaff
>
> as assertions are:
> but the motions: as
> the wind blows, so blows
>
> the world: in the
> innerwork of the
> motions one reads what will
>
> be aright

(SV 24-25)

            I go more
than halfway one way
and crosslash back
away: my
splits overlace:
the complication
strengthens me,
interweaving my
fragmentation
. . . .
life, life; because it is
all one it must be divided
and because it is
divided it must be all one
(SV 27-28)

doing what is worth doing is worth
what doing it is worth
(SV 29)

                        today

was a complete chance, a chance at the
complete, the adequate satisfaction
(SV 35)

                  all is one, one all
(G 34)

take, in leavetaking, the leavings
(G 85)

         nonreferentiality is a referentiality

of nonreferentiality: slap the world any way,
it flaps back
(G 88)

        things that go around sometimes go
around so far around they come back around
(G 100)

anything, anything, is poetry: effortlessness

keys the motion; it is a plentiful waste and
waste of plenty: no let up
(G 103)

the terror of emptiness will fill
emptiness with terror
(*Glare* 142)

       first, we artificialize nature
then we naturalize artifice
(*Glare* 198)

suppose some polar opposite is spread apart
there to arrange the coming together of things
(*Glare* 215)

Ammons also emphasizes this chiastic intertwining of subject with object through such self-reflexive language in "The Ridge Farm." When he wants to "implicate" language (16, 20), Ammons means that he wants to invest it in an originary creative fashion with his new perceptions and at the same time make his readers aware of the synergistic energy that inhabits each line as it inhabits the visible world. Most of the synonyms of "implicate" suggest this crisscrossing—to enfold, involve, fold together, intertwine, entangle. As in "Essay on Poetics," Ammons in "The Ridge Farm" accentuates how strongly his energies dwell in energized words that enfold the self with the referential world in moments of revelation, no matter how imperfectly language communicates:

some people say they don't like
thought flowing through illustrative
images (they can't catch much)
they prefer to dwell in one place into
revelation unsuspected
(36)

At the conclusion of a section where he describes with supple accuracy how bush, branch, bird, mouse and other living creatures accommodate themselves to a late snowfall that also cancels classes and leaves him free to observe and draw word pictures, Ammons muses that problem solvers with grants and subsidies "approach solutions but artists / dwell penniless with the central problem"—how to render their participation in the visible (32).

Ammons's mind throughout "The Ridge Farm" dwells on the delight of the visible, especially when, somewhat like his early poem "Mechanism," he captures a perfect intertwining of bird and environment:

lawn full of goldfinches eating
dandelion seeds, the headful whipped
over, held by perchfoot—the yellows
nearly interchangeable
(30)

This passage foreshadows the climactic ending of "The Ridge Farm," where Ammons gazes at a catbird dipping into the water of the brook that meanders along the ridge farm. The highly evocative language highlights how both bird and brook commune in the visible and how language "dwells" in the creative act of perception, how it has the power to evoke their referential reality. Here "the real brook in certain bends dwells, its / stone collections dry-capped, shale shelves / in shade, leaves and falls murmuring / each to the other." Ammons ends his poem with language that Dickinson would love for its slant fascicles and that Crowe Ransom would love for its power to render the thick thinginess of the world's body. The catbird skinnydips in the brook—"dipping into and / breaking the reflective surfaces with mishmashes of tinkling circlets" (41). The death theme becomes a minor element as Ammons celebrates the referential world's potential for offering an unlimited variety of "reflective surfaces" for imaginative perception.

In the penultimate section of "The Ridge Farm," Ammons suggests that poetic perception is possible because "light" or the visible enables perception to portray "human concern working with / what is." The visible empowers the burning human spirit to use language to name, to designate,

and the intensity of the source
blinds out other light: reason

sings the rightness but can do nothing
to oppose the brilliance: it dwells:
it dwells and dwells
(40)

Along with the delight in the visible, so consonant with Merleau-
Ponty, an experience of grounding in the depth of Being occurs when, as
mentioned in chapter 2, Ammons visits the actual farm on a holiday jaunt
and feels an "ineluctible" silence so profound that it "deepens down and
picks up ground" (27). As discussed in chapter 2, Merleau-Ponty believes
that the silent world that precedes language reveals our participation in
Heideggerian Being (VI 165-70). Heidegger discusses dwelling as some-
thing more than simply occupying a building in his essay "Building, Dwell-
ing, Thinking." Some of the most environmentally aware sentences in
Heidegger's writings appear here. To dwell for Heidegger means to "remain
at peace" with nature by "*sparing and preserving*," by allowing things to be
"let free in their presencing" (1979 ["Building"], 149, 151). The renuncia-
tion of egocentric designs and the recognition of the earth as a separate and
equal other are the first steps in experiencing the presencing of Being, and
for Heidegger this leads to preserving the planet: "Mortals dwell in that
they save the earth—taking the word in the old sense still known to Lessing.
Saving does not only snatch something from danger. To save really means
to set something free into its own presencing. To save the earth is more
than to exploit it or even wear it out. Saving the earth does not master the
earth and does not subjugate it, which is merely one step from spoliation"
(1979, 150). Ammons never purchases the Ridge Farm in the poem; he is
at peace simply knowing that it exists. Probably the most sustainable dwell-
ing humans ever produced, a subsistence farm with its unalienated human
labor, frugal recycling, and rootedness with the land embodies for Ammons
an ideal, a benchmark of coherent dwelling within nature. Though Ammons
never becomes sentimental in "The Ridge Farm," the discerning reader
might remember that Ammons's father sold the family farm during the
Depression years, after having failed at converting it from a subsistence
farm to a cash crop farm, and then made his living by dispossessing other
farmers of their land as a court officer or sheriff's deputy (Reiman 1985,
41; SM 59-60, 92, 105). A grim personage, Ammons's father delighted in
scaring people, including his son. Ammons was very attached to the farm
in his youth and missed it terribly. That farm, Ammons revealed, was "where
I got my closeness and attention to the soil, weeds, plants, insects, and

trees" (SM 60, 105). Having a farm nearby while he pursues his academic and creative labors in Ithaca no doubt helps to restore a lost sense of grounding. Ammons lets it be free in its own presencing as a separate and equal other in its own indigenous locale and in the process restores his soul.

The short, pithy poems of "Tombstones," the second section of *Sumerian Vistas*, are in one sense meditations on what poems, the tombstones, can and cannot do—how they function as memorials to human activity and how perception or sight creates light or illumination. In section 19 Ammons denies Cartesian dualism and nature as inert matter. All presences on this earth are "pools of energy cooled into place," coalesced concentrations of light. What poems really memorialize, Ammons suggests in the next section, is "the glint / or glow / once / in someone's eye." Throughout "Tombstones" Ammons connects vision and light in a way that suggests that vision creates light. This is true in a metaphorical sense, if by "light" we substitute "illumination." But Ammons seems to imply in many passages that this light is a property of the referential world. This is exactly Merleau-Ponty's point in his chapter "The Intertwining: The Chiasm," the central chapter of *The Visible and the Invisible* (1968). Merleau-Ponty reasons that, since every living being is both sensible and sentient (I can locate and feel one hand with the other; even a plant will react to my breath and shadow, and I sense a leaf's touch as it touches me), the world possesses a "double reference" (VI 137), a synergistic interweaving or "coiling over" of the visible world onto itself, a "texture" where sensible/sentient beings "all together are a Sentient in general before a Sensible in general" (VI 142, 146). Merleau-Ponty calls this texture, this element or property, this "coiling over" of the visible with itself, the "flesh" of the world—a word that he insists should not be confused with either "matter" or "mind" (VI 139, 146-47, 153-54). Thus, "natural light" (VI 142) exists at the "heart" of the sensible and, chiastically, "that family of sensibles we call lights" (VI 150-51).

Ammons's paean to perception as a human power that engages the flesh of the world and recognizes its referential texture occurs in section 23; its terms echo that early "Note on Incongruence" in its insistence on the primacy of perception and in how the finished poem tries to do justice to the feelings that a referential event initiates:

> the light in an eye
> transfigured in
> frames of feeling—

how is this small well,
so shallow and
deep, so magical

and plain able to
center all
the circumferences—

the eye itself
vision's vision
and visionary sway
(52)

Ammons deepens his meditations on human language and human
detritus in *Garbage*, a prime example of an environmentalist work informed
by the ecological cycles of nature, not the laws of language. The book-
length poem is ostensibly about the huge I-95 landfill outside Miami, which
Ammons presents as a ziggurat (8, 98), a religious edifice of American cul-
ture, and attended by high priests driving bulldozers, spreaders, and gar-
bage trucks. Yet this text is as serious as it is comic; in it one finds a critique
of anthropocentric uses of language and a series of homologies constructed
to orient our perceptions toward greater harmony with the cycles of nature.
As with *Tape for the Turn of the Year*, Ammons wrote *Garbage* on a continu-
ous adding machine tape about a pentameter wider than the earlier poem
(63). The tape's material form underscores its purpose—to suggest conti-
nuities among the elements and beings of the natural world. Often in the
poem Ammons asserts a biocentric acceptance of all life by recognizing his
affinities with animals.

Throughout its lengthy tape *Garbage* emphasizes homologous rela-
tionships between humans and various orders of sentient life. Rather than
valorizing human subjectivity by emphasizing its self-referential desires along
a linguistic chain of signifiers, the work stresses subjective agency through
recognizing in a living language our shared biocentric relationships with all
orders of sentient beings who live in harmony with our planetary ecosys-
tems. In contrast, those engaged in an anthropocentric will to power use a
"styrofoam verbiage" (74) to exploit through unnatural means:

I know the entire language of chickens,
from rooster crows to biddy cheeps: it is a

language sufficient to the forms and procedures
nature assigned to chicken-birds but a language,

as competition goes, not sufficient to protect
them from us: our systems now

change their genes, their forms and procedures,
house them up in all-life houses, trick their

egg laying with artificial days and nights:
our language is something to write home about:

but it is not the world: grooming does for
baboons most of what words do for us.
(51-52)

The satiric barb at the end of this passage, the conclusion of section 7 in the eighteen-section poem, emphasizes that the cart of poststructural language theory must not be placed before the natural horse, its referential source and enabling power.

Ammons uses a homologous method in *Garbage* to reveal the wondrous, joyous, astonishingly beautiful interrelations of the human and the nonhuman worlds that share nature's creative energy. Those familiar with Ammons's earlier work recognize that much of it is built around an ecological application of his One and Many dialectic (SM 13, 103). In *Garbage* Ammons enriches his grasp of the presocratics by noting that their theories are based on homologous relationships: "things are sustained by interrelations and // variety" (40). As he announces that *Garbage* is "a scientific poem, // asserting that nature models values" (20), he freely plays with the homologies of garbage "disposal" and the poetic "disposition" or formal arrangement of the poem's flow. He reveals that "the poem" is "about the pre-socratic idea of the // dispositional axis from stone to wind, wind / to stone" (20). Nature, not language, is the model for the poem's structure, and Ammons's presocratic predecessor now appears to be Anaximines, who argued that the underlying substance of reality was one and infinite, but determinate—air. Of a practical and scientific bent, Anaximines believed that nature's forms are interrelated, composed of degrees of rarified or condensed air. In its rarefied form air is fire, and air slowly descends into more condensed and less active forms of energy from wind to stones (Nahm 1947, 65-67; Warner 1958, 16-18).

Ammons believes that nature offers us active agency, a "globe-round selfempowerment" (49) whose basis is a continual flow of transforming energy. In a way perfectly homologous to the Miami landfill, the poet recycles language by incinerating dead language in the heat of compositional activity: "in the poet's mind dead language is hauled / off to and burned down on, the energy held and // shaped into new turns and clusters, the mind / strengthened by what it strengthens" (20). Again nature, not language, is the model for a series of homologous interrelationships:

>   nature, not
>
> we, gave rise to us: we are not, though, though
> natural, divorced from higher, finer configurations:
>
> tissues and holograms of energy circulate in
> us and seek and find representations of themselves
>
> outside us, so that we can participate in
> celebrations high and know reaches of feeling
>
> and sight and thought that penetrate (really
> penetrate) far, far beyond these our wet cells
> (21)

Ammons's style in *Garbage* "wraps back round" from the high to the low, the sublime to the scatological, giving us not only heaven but "heaven's daunting asshole" (22). He prefers a "chunky intermediacy" between language that apprehends the spiritual and a "gooey language" like the "bird do" that once dabbed his shoulder. Always his poetic energy bubbles with typical Ammonsesque buoyancy: "undone by / do, I forged on," and while "forging" or composing he notes homologous relationships between the bellyroundworms in the "bird do" and the life he creates in the moment of composition. Once again his homologous method flip-flops from the outer world to the inner world every few lines, from the material to the spiritual and back again, to signify our nondualistic participation in each lived moment and note the free energy exchanges in ecosystems. The bathetic "bird

do" meditation wraps around to the spiritual in the space of a few un-
rhymed couplets:

> if you've derived from life
> a going thing called life, life has a right to
>
> derive life from you: ticks, parasites, lice,
> fleas, mites, flukes, crabs, mosquitoes, black
>
> flies, bacteria: in reality, reality is like
> still water, invisible, spiritual: the real
>
> abides, spiritual, while entities come and go
> (98-99)

Incorrigibly comic, Ammons less than a page later meditates on why
men often measure themselves by the size of their penises and women by
the size of their breasts. We seldom find ideal, perfect representatives of
male or female beauty in nature, argues Ammons, because nature "likes a
broad spectrum approaching disorder so // as to maintain the potential of
change with / variety and environment." The ideal resides "implicit and
stable" amid the variations, the "shorties" and "flopsies" (100-101).

As Ammons expatiates on subjects that range from the trivial to the
profound, he rarefies and condenses his meditations in ways that mimic
Anaximines's understanding of nature's movements. He can "mix [his]
motions in with the mix of motions" (G 84). Like the proverbial
blabbermouth, Ammons talks through and around so many topics that
inevitably discussion wraps around to its opposite. In the process the
blabbermouth poet contextualizes his meditations, creating a "common
place" enriched with homologous references, just as the gyrations of earth-
worms enrich the soil by tilling it (78-79). Any homely experience be-
comes a homily on nature's interrelations. In section 11, for instance,
Ammons describes a visit to the Lake Cayuga farmers' market. As he ob-
serves the aging participants, the "wobble-legged," the "toothless, big-bel-
lied, bald, broad-rumped," he realizes that visiting a farmers' market is a
ritual sharing and bonding of humanity that renews life. It is humanity "at
our best, not killing, scheming, abusing" but renewing life, just as the "huge
beech by the water" exfoliates yearly. Then the poet rarefies his discussion
to reach for a moment of faith in the human ability to share, to achieve

community. The simple pleasures of shared glances and kind words suggest that humans are able to police themselves in social gatherings in ways that express a fundamental faith in each other. This complex faith in human solidarity and uniqueness, that we stand "cautious and courageous," as well as "wily with genuine desire," is "the magical exception // to the naturalistic rule" (70-71).

Here Ammons perceives a homology that leads him to recognize that the bonding of humans at such pedestrian events is also a survival tactic, a bit of "science // knowledge, craft" quite within nature's laws. Such human gatherings are homologous to the webworm's ability to camouflage itself and blend its body with the coloration of honeysuckle bushes. As the shared knowledge of planting and harvesting at a farmers' market reinvigorates our ties with nature and merges the isolated individual with the group, so nature gives the webworm a purplish streak down its back "exactly the color" of the buds of "honeysucklebushlimbstems" and colors his feet "exactly the color of the lateralhoneysucklebush / limbstems" to allow him to merge with his environment. Humans share their skills at adapting to the environment at a farmers' market just as the webworm, dangling in air on its thread of web, parades its adaptive skills (71-72).

At times Ammons uses his homologous method to refute anthropocentric heresies. In one short passage where he deliberates on how the chemistry of potato starch enlivens his chemistry, Ammons refutes three kinds of errors in human logic: that of dualists who, like poststructural language critics, assume an initial divorce of humans from nature; that of developers of aesthetic systems based on the polysemous instability of language; and that of anthropocentric inflators of human consciousness who assume that nature does not exist without a human consciousness to perceive it:

> the world is not a show consciousness can pull
>
> off or wipe out: because consciousness can neither
> wipe out nor actualize it it is not a show but
>
> the world: if one does not eat perception-blasted
> potato, one will blast perception by the loss of
>
> perception: starch (in Arch) in the potato
> meets with my chemistry to enliven my chemistry,

clear my eyes, harden, perhaps, my muscle, wag
my tongue (almost certainly): hallelujah: if

death is so persuasive, can't life be: it is
fashionable now to mean nothing, not to exist,

because meaning doesn't hold, and we do not exist
forever; this *is* forever, we are now in it
(87-88)

The starch in potatoes and in the cellular biology of Archie Ammons
suggests that humans share in nondualistic natural processes that place us
"in" nature.

Ammons is most sardonic when he uses homologies to underscore how
far humans have departed from holistic interrelatedness. For Ammons the
culprit is our inflated, anthropocentric trust in language disconnected from
the referential world. In section 12 Ammons meditates on the annual accu-
mulation of waste in the carbon cycle. Though animals such as chipmunks
live off the plethora of sugar-maple seeds that fall each spring, most seeds will
turn to detritus without producing trees. But compacted detritus ultimately
turns into life-nourishing soil. This process has occurred for millennia.

Yet, since our hunter-gatherer ancestors evolved written language six
thousand years ago, "things have gone poorly for the / planet" (74). Too
often we use our words in utilitarian endeavors that disrupt life-sustaining
planetary cycles. Since Sumerian cuneiform and Alexandrian vellum, hu-
mans have developed "surface-mining words" that, though "intricate as the
realities they represent," have gradually polluted and destroyed ecosystems:

all this garbage! all

these words: we may replace our mountains with
trash: leachments may be our creeks flowing

from the distilling bottoms of corruption:
our skies, already browned, may be our brown

skies: fields may rise from cultivation into
suffocation

. . . . . .

we have replaced
the meadows with oilslick: when words have

driven the sludge in billows higher than our
heads—oh, well, by then words will have left

the poor place behind: we'll be settling
elsewhere or floating interminably, the universe

a deep place to spoil
(75-76)

Ammons milks his sardonic mood to its bitter end at the conclusion of section 12, where he suggests that ultimately humans will leave this planet taking only "the equations, cool, lofty, eternal, that were // nowhere here to be found when we came" (76). Ammons mocks our anthropocentric self-inflation by carrying human logic to its ad nauseam, ad absurdum ending in the final couplet of the section, illustrating the apocalyptic end of "styrofoam verbiage" (74): "we'll kick the *l* out of the wor*l*d and cuddle / up with the avenues and byways of the word" (77).

Poststructural language poets such as Robert Hass and Jorie Graham desire to write in the gaps between concepts and the referential world, to write with what Heidegger would call an originary language in the flash moment of creation, without the stale meanings of sedimented language. But this gap too easily becomes a cushy limbo, a safe anthropocentric refuge from the pressures and difficulties of actual life in the referential world. In section 9 of *Garbage*, Ammons presents a parable of a rabbit and a chipmunk that suggests that we weaken our grasp of the referential world at our peril. To stay alive, the "sniffy rabbit" must recognize both his nakedness in the world and his intimate connectedness to his environment. Hence, he often moves just far enough away to survive the pounce of a natural predator such as the local tabby cat. In this middle distance the rabbit stands stone still, blending into his surroundings so intimately and yet so alertly that the predators do not notice him. The chipmunk, on the contrary, is all bursts of undirected energy followed by periods of lolling about on the concrete in sunlight. So into himself as to be disengaged from the environment, he is unaware of the stalking tabby, who soon "in / thrusting gulps and crunches down[s] chippy" (59).

Nathan Scott, in one of the most discerning essays published on

Ammons, wrote that the Heideggerian dialectic between absence and presence "most centrally organizes most of Ammons's poetry" (1988, 731). But Ammons's more recent works suggest that we should also pay attention to his celebration of perception taking place in a corporeal body immersed in the nondualistic quotidian world. For Merleau-Ponty human consciousness is "sustained, subtended, by the prereflective and preobjective unity of my body" (VI 141-42), for the body adheres to the physical world; it "feels the world in feeling itself" (VI 118). The starch in Arch subtends the arc of perception in Ammons and validates Merleau-Ponty's notion of "perceptual faith," the direct "experience, prior to every opinion, of inhabiting the world by our body" (VI 28). Thus, "perception does not come to birth just anywhere . . . it emerges in the recess of a body" (VI 9), for we are in "the midst of Being" (VI 114). One first experiences both Being and the visible "mounted on the axes, the pivots, the dimensions, the generality of my body" (VI 114). In *Garbage* as in Merleau-Ponty, "the body feels the world in feeling itself" (VI 118) because it is always already part of the visible flesh of the world.

Ammons's homologies and chiastic energy reveal his faith in a world where the formless but dynamic Nameless Tao, Anaximinean air, and Einsteinian force fields synthesize in ways that bring delight to human perception and instruct us in how to live lives in harmony with nature. In an interview comment on the moment of perception, Ammons speaks in terms that echo the operations of the Tao as well as suggest Merleau-Ponty's emphasis on the thick texture of the visible in the motions of the elements: "The air between me and that oak tree is invisible and formless. I can't see the air. So I see nothing but form out the window. I know the air is there because I see it work on the trees, and so I begin to think there is an invisible behind the visible, and a formlessness, an ongoing energy that moves in and out of a discrete formation. It remains constant and comes and goes and operates from a world of residual formlessness. That space, at some point, develops what we perceive" (SM 71).

Glare (1997), Ammons's most recent work, follows the long-poem, unrhymed couplet format of *Garbage*, but its perceptions and motions convey less optimism and comic buoyancy. The opening focus on whether a chance meteor from the blue could annihilate us, and confirm our cosmic irrelevancy, introduces the themes of old age and death. We receive candid glimpses of the infirmities of age, of what it feels like to live in a body that is wearing out. Playing the "old fool in a gilded cage" (275), Ammons tells us of the pain in his hipjoint (282), his wrinkled skin (277), constipation (279), how "the knee joint in my / deveined leg hurts" (79), and how that

entire leg swells in the heat (80)—the leg from which veins were taken for
his 1990 heart triple bypass (SM 85). But the meteor, though alluded to a
few times in the text (32, 47, 50, 70, 131, 172, 190, 243), never develops
into as strong a central focus as the Miami landfill in *Garbage*, the assorted
subjects Ammons expatiates on seem more superficial, and the quick move-
ment from one subject to another often appears rambling.

Yet this quick movement is part of Ammons's purpose, for the thin
discussion of subjects allows the formal structure to show through, and one
soon realizes that the poem's structure advances its main themes. The focus
on continual movement suggests that *Glare* is cosmological, as well as eco-
logical, in design. At seventy-one, the aging Ammons is preoccupied with
the unasked question—if I am to die before long, what is or was the signifi-
cance of life? What was life all about? One answer Ammons offers is that
life is the continual movement of spirit coupling with and departing from
recyclable matter. The word "nothing" appears often in the text, and
Ammons frequently equates this word with the source of spirit (39, 68,
124, 163-64, 169, 191, 233, 236, 255). This recalls the nameless Tao of
Lao-tzu (Waley 1958, 141, 159, 193), the formless Nothing of spirit, that
resides at one extreme of Ammons's cosmology. Emanations of the Tao
from the heights into the world couple with matter to inspirit life. The
operations of the Tao in matter, operations consistent with the recycling
energies of ecosystems, provide the internal organization of *Glare*. At one
point, Ammons states that, to integrate "interior impetus" with "external /
shaping," one should "put Laotse in bed with Confucius" (256). The disso-
lution into spiritless matter in nature's recycling process is the nothing at
the other extreme of the cosmology—death by meteor hit (122-23) or in-
ert matter devolving entropically into total dissolution, a black hole (243-
44)—whereas life lives in the middle, where "nature's mixed" (285), where
matter and spirit fuse in living bodies. In section 40, Ammons links his
death theme with his cosmology:

> I must
>
> die: that is what unsettles me:
> . . . .
> but why may I not dwell somewhere in
> luxury besides heaven: material
>
> tries to make it to eternity but
> recycles, and spirit that forever

was forever is: forever, possibly,
because it isn't anything; that is,

it's nothing, or else it's something
time doesn't fool with:
(110)

Ammons wrote *Sphere: The Form of a Motion* (1974) in part as a response to a Cornell faculty meeting where a colleague wanted to initiate a change by placing it in "the form of a motion" (SM 102). In *Glare*, motion signifies the dynamic energy and change that moves living matter in ecosystems, causes seasonal change, and even impels the movement of print from the opening to the conclusion of the poem. Ammons knows that the energy flow of any earthly ecosystem is primarily dependent on the sun's solar power (177), which is almost entirely a one-way transfer of energy that progressively degrades as it cycles through ecosystems and the food chain (E.P. Odum 1993, 46, 76-80). In *Glare*, this energy, highlighted often in the poetry, drives at least three homologies or multifaceted comparisons: (1) the seasonal cycle of birth, growth, and decay, where seeds germinate and grow in water provided by the earth's hydrological cycle; (2) the human biological cycles of sexual desire, procreation, and death; and (3) the motion of the creative mind as it composes, organizes, and types a lengthy poem.

Although solar energy dissipates at every ecosystem transfer, nearly half of the received solar energy warms the earth and drives major ecosystems. Another quarter of the solar energy received by the earth drives the hydrological cycle, earth's major recycling system (E.P. Odum 1993, 76). In *Glare*, Ammons often meditates on the work of water in the seasonal progressions he experiences. The hydrological cycle is homologous to the Tao's emanations; it precipitates from misty clouds at mountaintops and always follows the gravitational motions of the earth. Rain is "like creation beginning" (169), and creation is a synthesis of soil, seed, and water, the place where the "Lord of the rain" sets his seed in the tent of matter (281). Water, like a literary theme, moves around or goes underground when it meets an obstacle, as Ammons suggests in "the water of this movement" in one section of *Glare* (85). Forever animated with the moving spirit, water is immortal in its flow in the hydrological cycle; it can "keep on forever going away and coming // back" (158-59).

Descriptions of the hydrological cycle also elicit deeper meditations on life and death in *Glare*. When brook water flows into a lake, does the water that "flows // through water" integrate to purify time, as perhaps the work of a human may fuse with major movements in the historical era at his death (251)? In another section the poet's rueful meditations on "fatally flawed" humans releases tears, a human rain that waters the grass (282-83). The rain that develops tree roots in the penultimate section of *Glare* fosters cycles that "uphold life" in the poem's conclusion (291-93). At one point Ammons complains that his work does not appear in most nature writing anthologies because "I've been too deep in nature / to notice: nobody noticed" (133). Another answer Ammons suggests for the question of the significance of life is that its beauty consists in immersing oneself in its flow while alive. This is deeply biocentric: wisdom consists not in dominating nature or naturalizing it into benign landscapes, but in acknowledging our position as a subset of grand ecological forces, and living in harmony with them while appreciating their beauty.

The second homology, a seriocomic study of the sex drive of the aging male, leads to both low humor about bodily needs and more serious meditations on how desire in humans participates in the ecological cycle of birth, growth, maturity, and decay. A "deep-energy source" fuels the male's desire "to fill women with food and seed" (18-19). This leads to candid and at times bathetic recitations about the difficulty of excreting in the morning (31-32) or how old fogies take all day to pee (206), as well as voyeuristic fantasies about a couple he encounters, where the woman has "a bottom / broad & warm for planting" and the man has a "schlong adequate to bed the // deepest seed" (34). The "melting spirituality" of women initiates in males a desire to mount them (96). Similarly, the desire for beauty occurs when humans search for knowledge as well as "when your pecker rises" (40).

In *Garbage* as in the work of Merleau-Ponty, one finds in *Glare* an ever-present sense of the corporeality of the human body as the origin of sensation and perception, whether it be in aches and pains or preoccupations with sexuality. In one meditation, Ammons suggests that the begetting of children and the pains of rearing them are what really pushed humans out of paradise (184). The aging Ammons professes that he still has "plenty of seed, it's germination that's the // bust" (223), though the continuance of the species demands that we "must go on fucking as usual" (257). In the middle sections of *Glare* one even finds a discussion of the smell and look of smegma (116, 131), or revelations about adolescent masturbation (144-46). At the end of *Glare* another answer that Ammons provides for the significance of life is that, when one skins the layers of the husk and gets to the core of the seed of love, one finds the naked, "blank will" wanting to go on (285, 293).

Love is the forceful motion that impels life and meditations about life, for "everything is sacred" (201) and "where there is no love // nothing will take root" (70). As in Dante, love connects with spirit and moves feelings toward the divine (146). Yet sometimes the low sexual comedy backfires. Does it really enhance our understanding of life and art to know that the Goldwin Smith Professor of Poetry at Cornell University takes voyeuristic pleasure in noticing that the woman who clicks past his office in her "flimsy skirt" on the way to the bathroom is about to "piddle that pussy" if "she doesn't piddle her pants getting there" (216)? Ammons does want us to know that even in one's golden years sex remains a preoccupation, that desire remains in humans until death, and that sex is part of the love that attaches humans to the ecocycles of life, but some of the sexual innuendo stereotypes the sexes from a male point of view and will cause many women to bristle. The frequent instances of low sexual humor in *Glare* may attract some male readers but may also alienate many women and thus narrow his audience.

As the seed germinates in the warm soil or womb, and as humans prune or care for it during its development, so the poem grows in the third homology. Poems derive from the energy of love and thought set in motion (50-52); even typing the poem requires energy, attention, focus (100-2). The ecologist Eugene Odum avers that "as energy is used and dispersed in a chain of successive transformations, it changes in form and becomes increasingly concentrated or very high in information content. In other words, as energy quantity decreases, its 'quality' increases" (1993, 77). Ecologists use the term "embodied energy" to express this rise in quality; the term defines the "energy required to generate a flow or maintain a process." Reading requires very little energy, but the energy required over the years to educate a child to read is large, and to develop the capacity to think is larger (E.P. Odum 1993, 78-79). Composing a long poem requires much energy, and the words of *Glare* hold and carry some of this embodied energy in the movement from opening to closing lines.

Ammons states that "essential motion for the most part implies / form" (231). As in *Garbage*, Ammons composes on an adding machine tape, and composing on the narrow strip strips his lines, causing breakage much like storms break limbs from trees (175-76). Ammons divides *Glare* into two sections, entitled "Strip" and "Scat Scan." At one point he states that "strip typing is // like strip mining: you peel the / surface off things" and let the clutter drop downhill (108-9). As he trims excess in composing, he prefers to let the residue "drift out of decay // into soil and regrowth" (135-36). The scat or extruded manure can, as in *Garbage*, also promote life. Just as spirit and matter combine in the middle mix to create life, in between the pole of nothingness or pure spirit and the pole of lifeless matter, so the poem gains life by marrying the life of the historical moment to its language. Words, which are empty newsprint unless they partake of the world in the historical moment of their use (41), live not when they function as waywardly disseminating Derridean signifiers but when they negotiate with material realities in the present moment—economics, politics, and the like:

> language operates the same
> way: it holds its consistences,
>
> designations, forms, economies in
> currencies, in motions: let fall
>
> from negotiation, language disappears
> as languages have often done, without
>
> any lasting effect to the material
> world
> (45)

If language lives only when the poet negotiates with the referential world, then the poem does not exist only as a structure of immanence, but rests in a mediate position between the poet's consciousness and the referential world, as a tool for negotiating between the perception of humans and that referential world.

Though *Brink Road* (1996) chronologically precedes *Glare*, it deserves to be placed last in this chapter, for it is quite possibly the best collection of short poems that Ammons, a master craftsman of the short poem, has produced to date. Both the subtlety and the superior substance of the poems in *Brink Road* derive from the fact that Ammons remains aware of nature's integrity and the limits of language throughout the volume. Many poems are superb examples of how biocentric perception incorporates both a highly self-conscious language and a healthy respect for nature's otherness. In a prefatory note, Ammons tells us that a referential Brink Road exists south of Ithaca, "off NY 96 between Candor and Catatonk," about halfway between Ithaca and Route 17. The note also suggests that the relationship between language and referential reality should be one of moderation—not too familiar or intimate, nor too schizophrenically divorced, catatonic.

In "Disclaimer," for instance, Ammons notes that poets who use antiessentialist postmodern language can create nonpoetic poetry, "a voice if it speaks without a voice," and "the world if you will have none of it." But these paradoxes operate only when one divorces language from the referential. The world of nature works with nonreductive, interdependent opposites, only one of which is present at any one moment. Thus, to "give up brook glitter" is to open to view ("betides") the "high world that shines immortal"—the sun that creates the silent shine as well as the possibility of a transphenomenal dimension. Ammons argues, in "Sparklings," that the mind is a product of nature and that consciousness is necessarily attracted to nature and embedded in it. Poetry occurs when consciousness becomes sufficiently enchanted by and entangled with nature to "project structures of design" in the perceptual encounter. Although we are "in" the world of nature's energy ("in" the Taoist "Way") and can control some of that energy in the human will and its technological extensions, our understanding of that power is limited, perspectival, and we do not control it. In "Cool Intimacies," living consists of riding that energy until we drown.

Most of the poems of *Brink Road* are models of grounding oneself in the referential. In "Mind Stone" Ammons worries over the fact that the imagination can produce fantasies in fledgling poets ("balloons in inexperienced hands"). So he coaches himself to "dwell" on "the ground," so much so that he has "talked // pieces of it into not coming off." Poems are attempts at "reconciling opposites, one grab in turf, say, / the other in space." Similarly, in "Erminois," Ammons argues that we cannot reduce reality to linguistic categories such as the "ifs" of subjunctive possibility, or written language only, the synchronic without the energy housed in the movement of syntax in sentences. Like Heidegger, who wrote in *What Is Called Thinking* that recovering Being is being deeply engaged in the activity of recovering Being (1968, 165, 169, 220), so for Ammons "there is forward being / in being." Language developed from the gestures, the energy and motions of human engagements with referential reality. One "dwells there," saying "yes" to "the life that is and is to be." In "Readings by Ways," the monistic or dualistic systems of philosophers throughout world history present "nearly the same story" and are therefore less enticing than the "unread" creek (*référance*) that in its continual process of becoming and changing resists interpretation or absorption into anthropocentric systems.

If one moves in consort with the motions of nature, one learns survival skills at the same time that one learns to appreciate the biocentric harmony of life. The crows in "Abandon" seem exultant as they rise on thermals, cawing and diving in perfect harmony with the winds and seasonal displays of fall. In "Getting About," Ammons notes that bird species know their own strength and know how bold they can be on a windy day: starlings grasp oak branches tenaciously while crows "flap" and "dip" into "spills to check the wind." Only birds as strong as hawks can risk diving "directly ahead into the / blundering wall." October's high skies and "luminous" sunshine in "Hard and Fast" seem to "redress summer / tendencies" and induce in humans a salutary "clarification" that steadies one for the icebound end of the seasonal cycle. The fact that the motions of the water of "Enfield Falls" so accurately depict the persona's own turbulent feelings relaxes his tension and leads to an acceptance of emotional oscillations. As he observes the water "moiling," tensing through a narrow sluice and then easing into "mist-thin" sheets over the falls, the persona finds that being a part of this natural scene makes the burdens he must bear "easier, clearer, more to be expected."

When the Ammons persona tries to anthropomorphize nature and create a dialogue in the poems of *Brink Road*, nature exposes the limitations of human language and logic in ways that enlarge our understanding of life. In "Looking Way Off" the persona asks that a gorgeous moment of sunshine in a winter landscape heal his disquiet, "'Make me right.'" Nature's imagined response, "'You're right wrong,'" conveys an ambiguity where either interpretation redounds on the supplicant. The persona may be very wrong to ask the question ("right" meaning "very"). Or the persona may be left with the contradiction, which suggests that nature reveals that the human logic (right versus wrong) embedded in ethical systems fails to comprehend nature's holistic processes. The persona in "Very High Condition" recognizes that the ridge line is "indifferent to our / settlement here" but recognizes that within that "central indifference" rests a "purity" that dwarfs his need for the forgiveness of wrongs. Here nature's silence and beauty suggest that the persona renegotiate his anthropocentric needs and quiet his spirit without demanding support from others.

Similarly, in "The Category of Last Resort," Ammons suggests that at the center of nature's indifference lies a Taoist "nothing" that purifies all worries of "the unraveling / of a mislived or unlived life." Even human "logic could not attract" that unstained center, and in that center one could find "in nothing / the nearest satisfaction to being everything." Once again nature's silent "everything" sobers and strengthens the soul, cleansing it of comparatively less important anthropocentric cares. Nature's neutrality in the burial poem "Pit Lines" suggests that ecosystems may reveal a spiritual dimension, for the wind, the spirit, goes elsewhere at death, does not follow the body into the grave. In "Death and Silhouettes" the persona ascends a boulder in a glen and wonders, "Harrassed with inquiry," what nature would reveal about the ultimate meaning of life should the world end at this moment. But to humans nature reveals as it conceals: the poem quickly ends with a gull snatching a minnow from the pond's surface—a moment of *référance* where the food chain continues its unspeakable operations, chastening the persona's grandiose request. In all of the *Brink Road* poems where Ammons creates a dialogue between humans and nature, nature has a separate position and offers a transcendent perspective, a larger view that soothes the afflicted spirit, chastens pretentions, or mollifies disquiet by enlarging one's understanding beyond the narrowly anthropocentric.

Throughout *Brink Road* Ammons is openly satiric of humans who create dualistic systems that divorce language and logic from nature. In "Construing Deconstruction," Ammons presents deconstruction as an elitist program that degrades nature by ignoring it, through the extended metaphor of a docking showboat filled with the idle rich. They strut their "agreed // on significances" amid flamingo-feathered parasols (jargon?) on "floating parquet" floors (shifty arguments?). Meanwhile, the dock hands and excluded poor, who "can't or won't know polish & / candy-striped jackets & crystalline sweet-sips," do notice the boat's oilslicks and "dumped garbage" that will find its way into kitchen sinks and the "gouging out of plankton habitats by the sternwheel's / stalling back washes." In "Postmodernist Views," Ammons teasingly suggests that this antiessentialist movement is just a quick fix of the exterior, a re-siding in aluminum or vinyl for the aging house of human culture, with a "prismatic roof" added for the show of multiple views. In "So Long, Descartes," Ammons argues that, though Descartes reduced nature to dualistic calculations and numbers, today's giant computers, able to model Complexity Theory and the operations of ecosystems, return a measure of the "free flow" of "interpenetrant" nature to researchers.

At the end of *Brink Road* Ammons places "Summer Place," an early attempt at the high/low stylistic oscillations and loose structure that later produced *Garbage* and *Glare*. This forty-five-page poem, composed during Fourth of July week in 1975, depends for its organization on the levels of significance that Ammons finds in a number of intersecting themes: trash; locality or place; desire and sex; complaints of various kinds; and the desire to do something for one's country and audience. What this poem lacks in organizational strength, which also gives it the feel of having a very abrupt ending, is the cosmological sweep and swap of opposites that Ammons learned from Lao-tzu and the presocratics and incorporated into the later and more successful *Garbage* and *Glare*.

Ammons's use of the chiastic energy of intersecting opposites is much more deft and revelatory in many of the short poems of *Brink Road*. These opposites are not just structural devices or wooden attempts to trace the motions of *yin* and *yang* in the physical world. They are a serious attempt to portray how ecosystems work. After all, according to Richard Wilhelm, the terms *yin* and *yang* originated in Chinese antiquity from observations of the natural world—the *yin* being the cloudy (feminine) northern side of a mountain or river as seen from above, and the *yang* the sunny or bright (masculine) southern side. The dynamic operations of these two principles suggest to Wilhelm that "change is conceived of partly as the continuous transformation of one force into the other" (1962, xxxvi-xxxvii). As ecosystems use solar energy and process matter, they also move in cycles of continual transformation from one material state to another.

In *Brink Road* the oscillations of weather and ecosystems forestall human attempts at domination and control. In "Middling Seasons," for instance, the mind longs for calm moderation but learns that weather often surges to opposite extremes in a matter of days. The poem ends by questioning the desire to hold onto "some wrong idea about the nature of things." The persona of "Line Drawings" initially wants the pear leaf blister mite to leave the pear trees alone. He then wonders why nature complicates any good it does with "a tantamount negative." With some exasperation he ends his meditation on a sensible note, observing that humans were not made to "figure / out every little thing" in nature. The sexual explosions of spring alienate their opposite, the cancer and HIV patients in hospital wards who have been harmed by extremes of cellular growth, in "Silvering Shadow." The poem ends with a moral about intersecting opposites that is true for all orders of nature, including the human manipulation of language: "splendor has the scariest shade: / in hell, the word-one picks out a heavenly word." "The Deep End" is a celebration of the "ceaseless adjustments" of grand "self-regulating systems." The speaker is "impressed with the way /

things work," with how "ups and downs / work out a way of showing up / from down." Although it is hard to find "the groove itself," the exact path where the "turning / back of going in" resides, the speaker openly suggests that the only moral one can derive from the spectacle is that if you find "something to go / along with, go along with / it." Happiness resides in taking a biocentric position, in following nature's movements, not in trying to dominate the process.

The chiastic energy of opposites produces fine meditations on life's paradoxes in many poems of *Brink Road*. Ammons meditates on the possibility of an afterlife in "Painlessness, to Pain, Is Paradise." He muses on how the delights of the sensuous world are so inexhaustible that one is reluctant to resign oneself to leaving them. Yet resigning oneself to the inevitability of death may produce, in "the going itself," a "rounding back to the beginning," a coming instead of a going, a return that suggests reacquainting oneself with the first light of creation and "beyond, within that, dimly a brighter." In "Eternity's Taciturnity" Ammons avers that history is perspectival and subject to a logic of opposites. The more one learns about a given subject the more that knowledge sweeps everything else from the mind's table. Furthermore, when one sees little that little still "fills up the whole sight," becoming an everything that absents the rest, and when one says little one often implies everything else. Ammons ends with the tantalizing suggestion that when a poem of his says little, it is because he meant to suggest the rest, so to tease the reader into activating his or her imagination.

The referential world we live in is always driven by its logic of opposites, its dynamic *yin* and *yang*. In "Terebene Scene" the state of having nothing left to say, because of this world's energy of opposites, soon generates a desire to move toward "the unspoken unspeakable." The state of indifference quickly reverses to the desire to probe the "well of difference," but we will never be able to speak the unspeakable because movements toward perfection mix with our material world ("terebene" is a mixture of terpenes, the result of mixing sulphuric acid with terpentine) and having to state the thrust of the probe in language qualifies the quest. Any stated position leaves objections from those left out, and "if one tries for the impossible, / no variant of the possible's left out"—and the possible always has its variants. Though nothing is everything in "All's All," it alternates with the least something so that "little and all / alternately disappear." The more you say the emptier you become in "Expropriations," so that wisdom resides in "the plenitude / of speechlessness." Because motion is circular in an

Einsteinian world, bent by mass, motions are always "necessary rondures" in "Weightlessness," and nature forever returns from the transcendent. All stages are "Rosy Transients" and "mix's interpenetrations" produce many subtle balances.

Of the many poems in which Ammons meditates on the process of writing poetry, "Saying Saying Away" is easily the most memorable, for it suggests that the poem ideally "holds its motions" and becomes such a synthesis that its assimilated energies approach the "wordless." The perfectly made poem becomes inexhaustible, forever suggestive because lost in its motions without loose ends or energy loss; it becomes "a place where the distinction / between meaning and being is erased into the meaning of / being." The ideal poem for Ammons becomes not Stevens's planet on a table, but creation itself, an organic recycling structure whose coherent dynamism is homologous with the planet's cycles.

Ammons tires of reviewers who compare him to Stevens, but he is easily more circumspect than Stevens in his grasp of planetary ecosystems and more audacious in his insistence that the imagination must ground itself in those ecosystems and qualify its thirst for the aesthetically pleasurable. Though Ammons only occasionally employs the refined, polished, opulent diction that was Stevens's signature, he does have Stevens's exuberance, his gusto, his endless appetite for enjoying all that nature offers, and the quicksilver energy of his inquiry into the quotidian. Stevens could cup life's concupiscent curds in the early decades of the twentieth century, but Ammons at its end must spend some of his time filtering its fetid flotsam. Maestro of motion, optimist of interlaced opposites, hailer of homologies, Ammons is another sanguine Comedian as the Letter C—the Comedian of Chiasms.

4

The Long Hunter's Vision

Wendell Berry

What I stand for
is what I stand on.

Berry, BCP 207

In a 1992 National Public Radio *Fresh Air* broadcast, Terry Gross tried to coax Wendell Berry into controversy by baiting him on the subject of his reluctance to use machines. "Why do you have horses instead of a tractor?" she teased. A pregnant pause ensued. Then came the familiar basso Kentucky drawl and the very laconic response: "Because I *like* horses better than I like a tractor." Simple, profound, and resonant with significance: horses do not pollute the air, their dung fertilizes the soil, and they satisfy Berry's spirit immensely. Wendell Berry's desire to remain true to local life, to connected life, to the soil, and to ecological cycles of renewal and self-repair while using nonpolluting technology gives his work a unique and unmistakable cast.

In "The Sycamore," (BCP 65), from his second poetry volume *Openings* (1968), Berry articulates ecological principles that have ruled his entire life. Because its bark is intimately related to the living cambium beneath, Berry finds the sycamore to be a "wondrous healer of itself." Symbiotically related to the soil, the sycamore also replenishes the ground when it decomposes. The tree has evolved its unique form, becoming "the intention and radiance of its dark fate," by integrating itself with its local environment, by "bending" to the accidents of seasonal weather and by repairing with its own living fiber the nails, hacks, and whittles that it has suffered through the years. The poem celebrates the act of perceiving the organic relatedness of the sycamore to its local environment where it eats and is eaten. This act of perception integrates the human observer to external nature, forming a biocentric whole that encompasses ethical dimensions:

> I recognize in it a principle, an indwelling
> the same as itself, and greater, that I would be ruled by.
> I see that it stands in its place, and feeds upon it,
> and is fed upon, and is native, and maker.

Unlike Stevens, who celebrates the anthropocentric art of the female singer's song in "The Idea of Order at Key West," the biocentric tree for Berry is the object of reverence. It is its own maker, its rings and bark fabricating its own indwelling song. Berry prefers to conform to nature's pattern rather than celebrate the aesthetically satisfying patterns that humans create. Berry's sycamore retains its separate and equal otherness.

Berry wrote "The Sycamore" soon after a major decision in his career. When invited in 1964 to return to a teaching position at the University of Kentucky, his undergraduate alma mater, Berry expected to lead the intellectual life of the university professor and creative writer of literature. With a degree in that discipline, some poems published, and teaching experience as the director of New York University's freshman writing program, he seemed ready to move home and follow a predictable career track. But soon after his return to the Lexington area, he decided to buy a twelve-acre farm as a second home near his ancestral roots in Port Royal, Henry County, on the Kentucky River, about sixty miles from the university. Reconnecting with his native soil and his ancestral roots and writing about the implications of these native roots soon became the driving force and primary goal of a very prolific writing career that at this date includes fourteen collections of poetry, twelve collections of essays, and ten volumes of fiction. All examine contemporary problems in America from the perspective of one rooted in a distinct locale and living in harmony with it. Berry's commitment to his ancestral soil grew as steadily as his farm, which now consists of a hundred and twenty-five acres. At this writing, Berry still grows most of his family's food on its fifteen arable acres with a team of horses and sells his lambs locally (RE 56-58, 69-70, 329-40; Gross 1992).

Anchored to his locale, Berry in his essays offers an eloquent and often penetrating analysis of the malaise of postindustrial America. Deviat-

ing from the organic wholeness of the individual to his soil, which for
Berry includes one's local community, creates an erosion of character and
culture. Whether he discusses the evils of agribusiness or the strip mining
of Appalachia, the problems of the tobacco farmer (his lawyer/farmer fa-
ther was head of the area Tobacco Growers Association) or the pitfalls of
nuclear energy and dam building, the sixty loads of East Coast garbage
trucked in daily to Henry County or the consumer capitalism of contem-
porary urban America, his plain-spoken directness retains a disarming can-
dor often laced with an intimacy that is both moving and filled with the
integrity of the man who has lived a morally sound life. When assessing the
history of Berry's reception by reviewers and literary critics, especially from
reviews written in the 1970s and early 1980s, one often finds a tone of
deep respect, if not awe, for a man who has lived his life deliberately. Charles
Hudson once wrote that "even more than Thoreau, Wendell Berry has cho-
sen to live an exemplary life" (1982, 223). Page Smith, noting that, "like
Emerson, Berry is a master of the quotable sentence," called him "*the* pro-
phetic American voice of our day" and one much more aware than Emerson
of "the tragic ironies and paradoxes of the human condition" (1987, 764).
Richard King found Berry's work to be in the mold of Thoreau, "a truly
unalienated man" (1973, 21), and Hugh Kenner extolled Berry's essays as
works where he "surpasses Thoreau" as an astute critic of the postmodern
industrial economy (1982, 100).

This praise was justly deserved, for Berry, more than any other envi-
ronmental writer, is able in his essays to penetrate to the heart of our
postmodern malaise by assessing its degree of deviation from the organic
ecological interrelationships that bring humans into a coherent bond with
life. Let me offer just three of many possible examples of the widening
dimensions of Berry's ecological vision. In chapter 7 of *The Unsettling of
America* (1977), Berry argues that contemporary Western culture divides
the body from the soul and the mind from both. In the rift our urban-
industrial society sets up profit-making bureaucracies and abstractions that
fragment what was once a coherent polis into a diseased organism inca-
pable of healing itself:

> The modern urban-industrial society is based on a series of radical
> disconnections between body and soul, husband and wife, mar-
> riage and community, community and the earth. At each of
> these points of disconnection the collaboration of corporation,
> government, and expert sets up a profit-making enterprise that

results in the further dismemberment and impoverishment of the Creation.

Together, these disconnections add up to a condition of critical ill health, which we suffer in common—not just with each other, but with all other creatures. Our economy is based upon this disease. Its aim is to separate us as far as possible from the sources of life (material, social, and spiritual), to put these sources under the control of corporations and specialized professionals, and to sell them to us at the highest profit. It fragments the Creation and sets the fragments into conflict with one another. For the relief of the suffering that comes of this fragmentation and conflict, our economy proposes, not health, but vast "cures" that further centralize power and increase profits: wars, wars on crime, wars on poverty, national schemes of medical aid, insurance, immunization, further industrial and economic "growth," etc.; and these, of course, are followed by more regulatory laws and agencies to see that our health is protected, our freedom preserved, and our money well spent. Although there may be some "good intention" in this, there is little honesty and no hope.

Only by restoring the broken connections can we be healed. Connection *is* health. And what our society does its best to disguise from us is how ordinary, now commonly attainable, health is. We lose our health—and create profitable diseases and dependencies—by failing to see the direct connections between living and eating, eating and working, working and loving. (UA 137-38)

"Cultural solutions" to these problems, argues Berry, "are organisms, not machines, and they cannot be invented deliberately or imposed by prescription" (UA 131). At the center of Berry's understanding of a healthy civilization is a series of hierarchically arranged "nested systems," analogous to natural ecosystems, that he first articulated in *Standing by Words* (1983). These comprise a second example of the widening dimensions of Berry's ecological vision. Here Berry conceives of humans as the center and smallest circle in a set of interrelated circles or "patterns of interdependency" that move outward to family, community, agriculture, and nature. This is, in essence, a visualization of the Greek polis, the family home integrated with the community and its surrounding agricultural landscape. Berry asserts that the individual in the center is most dependent on the interrelations of all the other concentric circles, and disaster happens, as in the Renaissance Great Chain of Being, when the individual, that smallest of centers, presumes that he dominates the other circles (SW 42-49). Berry believes that the autonomous consumer, totally dependent on bureaucracies (from grocery stores to health care) for his survival, signals the complete dissolution of ecological harmony.

We improve the connections between the individual and his wider circles of involvement through work and love in tasks and relationships that are direct and promote bonding. Abstract operations, such as those accomplished on the computer, invite disconnections. For Berry, farming promotes the quintessential labor of connectedness, for respect for "our biological existence, the life of the body," is crucial:

> What relation do we see, if any, between body and mind, or body and soul? What connections or responsibilities do we maintain between our bodies and the earth? These are religious questions. . . . But the questions are also agricultural, for no matter how urban our life, our bodies live by agriculture as we live in flesh. While we live our bodies are moving particles of the earth, joined inextricably both to the soil and to the bodies of other living creatures. It is hardly surprising, then, that there should be some profound resemblances between our treatment of our bodies and our treatment of the earth. (UA 97)

In *What Are People For?* (1990), a more recent volume of essays, Berry extends and deepens his soil analogy to encompass the work of culture—a third dimension of Berry's ecological vision. Often on his walks he would traverse "a wooded hollow on what was once my grandfather's farm." He would see a rusty bucket hanging on a fence post and marvel at how leaves, rain, snow, nuts left by squirrels, and so forth have rotted into soil. Twenty-five years after "The Sycamore," Berry once again expresses his allegiance to the soil cycle, a basic ecological process that has subtle analogies to human activity and culture:

> This slow work of growth and death, gravity and decay, which is the chief work of the world, has by now produced in the bottom of the bucket several inches of black humus . . . . I have seen the same process at work on the tops of boulders in a forest . . . . All creatures die into it, and they live by it.

. . . . .

However small a landmark the old bucket is, it is not trivial. It is one of the signs by which I know my country and myself. And to me it is irresistibly suggestive in the way it collects leaves and other woodland sheddings as they fall through time. It collects stories, too, as they fall through time. It is irresistibly metaphorical. It is doing in a passive way what a human community must do actively and thoughtfully. A human community, too, must collect leaves and stories, and turn them to account. It must build soil, and build that memory of itself—in lore and story and song—that will be its culture. (153-54)

A corollary to these master metaphors of soil, cycles and circles of ecological interdependence, concerns the function of poetic language. For Berry poets write poems not to portray a "seeking of self in words," for a poem reveals "a point of clarification or connection between themselves and the world on the one hand and between themselves and their readers on the other" (SW 7). Although for Berry poetic language may at times be very self-referential, at bottom it is profoundly relational, referential (SW 7–8, 50-54). He stresses this again and again in *Standing by Words*: "The subject of poetry is not words, it is the world, which poets have in common with other people" (SW 8). "If the connection between inward and outward is broken," Berry asserts, "then language fails" (SW 31). A healthy language holds the internal and external in balance in a way that validates both (SW 42). Language must retain its "power of designation," its referential power (SW 52, 54, 59). Fidelity is the ideal condition for language, and this occurs when "words and things, words and deeds, words and people . . . stand in reliable connection" (SW 62). In the title passage of his essay volume, Berry intertwines his soil and interdependency metaphors with their language correlate. Abstract bureaucratic language is diseased because it does not stand by its words; it

is used conscientiously to refer to nothing in particular. Attention rests upon percentages, categories, abstract functions. The reference drifts inevitably toward the merely provisional. It is not language that the user will very likely be required to stand by or to act on, for it does not define any personal ground for standing or acting. Its only practical utility is to support with "expert opinion" a vast, impersonal technological action already begun. And it works directly against the conventionality, the community life, of language, for it holds in contempt, not only all particular grounds of private fidelity and action, but the common ground of human experience, memory, and understanding from which language rises and on which meaning is shaped. (SW 52)

Berry uses these master metaphors of the soil cycle and concentric circles of interdependence, and their corollary in poetic language, very skillfully in his essays, especially to reveal how far from the natural norm our postindustrial society has moved with its profit-making, bureaucratic approach to solving its problems. Reviewers and literary critics have regularly applied these metaphors to Berry's poetry, with fairly successful results. But Berry's essays reveal only a portion of the thematic interest encompassed by the poetry. Frankly, the more one places the collections of prose essays side by side with the poetry volumes in a historical sequence, the more one realizes that the ecological perceptions Berry develops in the essays originate in the poetry and that poetry is primarily a self-reflexive poetry intimately concerned with the process of perception. Especially in the first phase of his oeuvre, Wendell Berry is a phenomenological poet. He roots his soil ecology in the process of perception, and his middle-period satire and later cosmic vision build on that strong base.

Berry published *The Broken Ground* (1968), his first poetry collection, four years after he moved to rural Kentucky and decided to adopt the ancestral values of his Henry County forebears. Not surprisingly, this volume, along with *Findings* (1969), his second volume, concerns house building. Not just the completion of the physical edifice, but the creation of the house or *oikos* (the Greek word from which ecology evolved) and the values that undergird it. The design of a house in the mind of its future owner begins as an ideal and is fleshed out through work, perseverance, and contact with the physical world, the arena of its realization. The prereflective reality of this physical world that Berry so passionately believes in and always remains in close contact with sometimes manifests itself, as it did in Merleau-Ponty, as silence (VI 39, 64, 125-29, 145). Similarly, the adhesiveness of the physical world to the self, what Merleau-Ponty calls the flesh of the visible or light, the inaugurating principle or that according to which one sees (VI lv, 142, 154), is a constant tactile presence in the early poems.

The "Elegy" that opens Berry's *Collected Poems* at first appears to be a poem that takes place outside, in winter, in the grim realities of bereavement. But Berry expresses his love for his maternal grandfather by suggesting that Pryor Thomas Berry's values literally house or organize Berry's inner world, his own perceptions and values. Pryor's sudden absence turns Berry's entire world view askew, out of balance, and in this absence of organizing principles Berry confronts the elemental silence of nature—elemental place: "All day our eyes could find no resting place." As if a family closed the shutters of its house, Pryor's death blots out the sun "in a shutter of clouds," while "no shape or shadow moved the flight / Of winter birds"—"moved" in the sense of motivated, informed with values. In each of the first three sections of the poem, the grandfather's death, his physical silence, becomes a recognition not only of the loss of his values but also a chilling intrusion of the elemental silence of prereflective nature, the brute flesh of the visible that humans organize by attributing values. Berry presents this awareness as physically, psychologically, and phenomenologically disorienting. Pryor Thomas Berry, the central reference point for his understanding of the physical world, has disappeared; in the aftermath, Berry's perceptions struggle like a wobbly cart whose axle has lost its cotter pins.

All five senses become disoriented in sensory depravation. Pryor's afterimage becomes a "Shape of silence in the room," while aurally his death leaves a discordant "Clamor" of steps in "his silence." As snow adorns brute nature, the family members are numbed by his death, their fingers and ears deprived of sensation: "Snow held the earth its silence. / We could pick no birdsong from the wind." Meanwhile, an elegant oxymoron reveals the background of their foregrounded bereavement: "It was this storm of silence shook out his ghost," a storm that deprives the entire poem of the tastes and smells of normalized nature.

As the family performs the burial ritual in the third section, Berry underscores the ritual's connections to the soil cycle with images such as "We have adorned the shuck of him" as they place his body in "the fulcrum dust." The burial replenishes the soil with compost after the church of the earth "heals our father in," just as a farmer gives young roots some contact with the soil before planting. Meanwhile, the river water, nature's elemental flesh of the visible, accomplishes its healing silently: "Water wearing the earth / Is the shape of the earth." In his essay "The Rise," Berry presents the river's main channel as a massed movement of elemental Being, where the hydrological cycle has its greatest force, through imagery of silence (RE 10). In two important passages in his early essays, passages that echo Merleau-Ponty's insistence on living with*in* and being *of* the physical world, Berry speaks of silence as inaugurating a sense of nature's prereflective presence; this restores to us a tactile sense of living within and being dependent on the immediate physical landscape (RE 68, 107). The river water in "Elegy" soon mingles with the poet's "ponderable" words. Language imbues the poet with the solidity of the referential world; it is not divorced from nature, nor held in abeyance in an aesthetic gap.

Berry presents spring in the final stanza of "Elegy" very unconventionally, not as a transcendent rebirth but as a phenomenological restoration of stable vision:

> Spring tangles shadow and light,
> Branches of trees
> Knit vision and wind.
> The shape of the wind is a tree
> Bending, spilling its birds.
> (BCP 5)

The emphasis on the phenomenological in "Elegy" implies that the observer is not a product of Cartesian dualism. The poem instead emphasizes that the death of the grandfather initiates a momentary severance of a bond between the observer and the observed. "Elegy" offers ample evidence of what Merleau-Ponty calls our elementary "openness upon the world," where "he who sees is of it and is in it" (VI 100, 123, 134-35, 137). The chiastic intertwining of vision and light for Merleau-Ponty manifests that flesh of the visible, that nondualistic "return of the sensible upon itself, a carnal adherence of the sentient to the sensed and of the sensed to the sentient. For, as overlapping and fission, identity and difference, it brings to birth a ray of natural light that illuminates all flesh and not only my own" (VI 142). Interestingly enough, when Merleau-Ponty speaks of non-Cartesian perception that simultaneously incorporates duration and physical space, he occasionally uses the metaphor of a tree (VI 111, 131, 136-38). Just as for Berry human interaction with the visible world organizes vision as tree branches "Knit vision and wind," so for Merleau-Ponty's referentially oriented phenomenology, every movement of the human hand or eye implicates itself in a "double and crossed situating of the visible in the tangible and of the tangible in the visible" (VI 134).

An elegy is a puzzling choice for the opening poem of a poet's *Collected Poems* unless it offers a substantial statement of one's poetic. In fact, Berry also emphasizes the phenomenological in his next four poem choices in his *Collected Poems*: "Observance," "Boone," "Green and White," and "A Man Walking and Singing." As if to emphasize the non-Cartesian truth that the eye cannot help but be implicated in what it sees, be of it and in it, Berry in "Observance" presents the consciousness of his river god as fused with what he observes. His innocent absorption in phenomena reveals a healthy "forbearance," an important word in Berry's lexicon. The river god absorbs the picnic songs of the townsmen and their silence when they leave, as if to say that silence is not an emptiness or a Sartrean nothingness, but an adhesion to what Merleau-Ponty calls "brute being," the elemental, prereflective physical reality of which all humans are a part (VI 97, 101, 110, 156-58, 165). Berry ends the poem by portraying the river god's godly freedom phenomenologically, as an ability to attain total absorption in elemental reality through a non-Cartesian integration of mind and physical reality:

> His mind contains
> the river as its banks
> contain it, in a single act
> receiving it and letting it go.
> (BCP 7)

In "The Journey's End," an essay included in *The Unforeseen Wilderness* (1991), Berry recollects a visit to a tiny hut in the Red River Gorge that in 1968 was discovered to have been erected by Daniel Boone—or so the carving "D. boon" in one of its planks proclaimed. This discovery happened at about the time developers were considering a dam on the gorge that would degrade the land and foul it with tourism. Berry's journey to the hut became a moving experience of connecting that hut, already corrupted with tourist refuse, with the pristine beauty of a nearby stand of virgin timber. He mused on the fact that we can preserve wilderness and be familiar with it only by relating to it "on *its* terms" (UW 67). Like Faulkner's Ike McCaslin, Berry actually lost his map on an ensuing hike in the area and found this relinquishment attractive. Although he did not say as much, this hike became an identification with the phenomenological freshness of firsthand exploration in the frontier spirit of Boone and the Long Hunters, the early explorers of pristine America: "Where I am going I have never been before. And since I have no destination that I know, where I am going is always where I am. When I come to good resting places, I rest. I rest whether I am tired or not because the places are good. Each one is an arrival. I am where I have been going" (UW 73).

The poem "Boone" imagines Daniel Boone in his dying recollections of his journeys. Boone freely accepts his past and finds it a graceful movement from dream and desire to marriage with an unnamed locale. He has created his own "final house," a summation of his journeys, and is content to live out his last days with little physical activity but with a tender and growing appreciation of his past. Though his physical powers wane, he enjoys the continual play of his mental powers as he mulls over his past. Even in this stasis his mind, like the iced-over river, still flows, and he delights in mental journeys where "every day is a day's remove / from what I knew." His journeys in virgin America are always originary moments of self-becoming, for no trails exist to become habituated to. Hence the delight in every momentary experience, for "There are no arrivals." Boone's peaceful acceptance of old age at the end of the poem parallels the innocence of "Observance" and the rooted coherent vision of "A Sycamore" in his strong attachment to the seasonal changes in the physical world about him. He wants to be "innocent of my dying" by becoming "submissive / to the weather / as an old tree." The dying Boone, by losing his sense of separateness from nature, attains an ecological vision: his perceptions have integrated him with cyclic physical processes.

Four years after *The Broken Ground*, Berry published *A Continuous Harmony* (1972), his fifth collection of essays and the first to speak openly about ecology as a perception of the Creation, "a great union of interlocking lives and processes and substances" (CH 142). Here Berry emphasizes that ecology is not simply a scientific discipline, a branch of biology, but is rooted in the practices of farming and in the phenomenology of perception: "The discipline proper to agriculture, which survives not just by production but also by return of wastes to the ground, is not economics but ecology. And ecology may well find its proper disciplines in the arts, whose function is to refine and enliven *perception,* for ecological principle, however publicly approved, can be enacted only upon the basis of each man's perception of his relation to the world" (CH 100). The coherent perception of the individual within physical space that Merleau-Ponty ardently believes in and that Berry first articulated in his early poems, later found its way into his more didactic essays.

"Green and White" at first appears to be a simple lyric about white seagulls leaving a bay that shines "like a field of green grass." But the poem actually presents ecology phenomenologically, for it is a meditation on how the seagulls, as white as ideas, need the gestalt of a physical background for recognition. When the gulls leave, they "leave no sign they ever were there" (register no lasting mental impression or "sign"). But the green water "is no memorial to white," no leftover of a more important Cartesian idea that the gulls might represent. The purely ideational is dangerous, needs physical anchoring in the green of nature. Hence the poem's final lines: "There's danger in it. They fly / beyond idea till they come back." Similarly, Merleau-Ponty, using Husserl and gestalt theory to argue against Sartre's dualistic notion of consciousness as a nothingness, a *pour soi* alienated from the *en soi* of Being, affirms the necessity of a horizon or background for vision to affirm that "we are within Being" and that being is not an ideational composition, for "this frontal being before us . . . is cut out upon a horizon which is not nothing" (VI 127-28; also 100, 132, 148-49). Merleau-Ponty goes so far as to argue that, phenomenologically considered, human consciousness resides in the ability to recognize a figure on a ground (VI 191). Thus, to be conscious is to always already adhere nondualistically to the natural world.

"A Man Walking and Singing" asserts Berry's belief in the ability of human perception to organize reality in the moment of its passing, with his "footsteps / beating the measure of his song." Though the poem is dedicated to James Baker Hall, it contains strong echoes of Stevens's "Sunday Morning" in the opening section, where mortality may be the mother of beauty. The remainder of the poem may also echo Stevens's figure of the poet as maker/musician and his habit of composing while on daily walks. The poet composing while walking reveals his moment-by-moment adherence to the visible, to the life lived in the moment of its passing, and his power to introduce the accidental into the poetic composition, so that "His singing becomes conglomerate / of all he sees." The word "conglomerate" suggests the tactile density of physical experience lived in the moment. The ambiguity of the line "He walks and sings to his death" again accentuates the moment-by-moment passing of lived experience. Whether he sings until the moment of his death or in the succession of moments that die as they pass into formality, as his body exhausts a tiny portion of its allotted life with the experience of each instant, the effect is to weld the reader to the referential reality of the moment's passing.

Of the hundreds of reviews of Berry's work that have appeared since 1964, only one, and one of the very first, noted the phenomenological aspect of Berry's verse. In 1965 the poet Robert Hazel, in the *Kenyon Review*, praised Berry for his ability to grasp the density of lived reality. Hazel caught the deliberate phenomenological arrangement of *The Broken Ground*; he thought that the volume "has backbone" because it combines a strong sense of place with a "tension of self juxtaposed to a coherent notion of existence." That coherent notion, according to Hazel, consists of a strong sense of identity confirmed by vivid, moment-by-moment lived experience in the density of the physical world—what he called the "textural flesh and symmetry" of the poems. According to Hazel, "At the heart of Berry's scheme is a confirmation of the identity of a thing and its continuous process of becoming. The effect is a sense of reality as instantaneous; and reality's shifting stages are built into a compulsively causal system of metaphors" (378-79). This holds true for many poems in the volume, for "A Man Walking and Singing" and "Sparrow," as well as for *Broken Ground* poems not included in the *Collected Poems* such as "Diagon" and "Be Still in Haste."

Of all the journal articles and book chapters devoted to Berry, only David Lavery's four-page article (1981) adopts aspects of Merleau-Ponty's phenomenology to comprehend the poetry. Lavery discusses Hart Crane, Wallace Stevens, and one Berry poem, "To the Unseeable Animal," and suggests that what Berry describes in this poem as "Being" is the flesh of light that constitutes our "means of knowing"—the intertwining of seer and seen as the elemental flesh of the world. I agree, but suggest that this is germane to the thrust of Berry's earliest poetry; he did not first discover this elemental adhesion of self to world in one poem published in 1970. "Being" in "To the Unseeable Animal" is a flesh that "dissolves / at our glance," yet is "always here, / dwelling in the oldest sycamores" (CP 140). It was dwelling in the architectonic of Berry's first volume.

Of course, not every Berry poem manifests rich phenomenological dimensions, but enough do in the early work to suggest the deliberate breaking of phenomenological ground. Of the remaining poems in *The Broken Ground*, "An Architecture," "Sparrow," "A Music," "The Fear of Darkness," "The Wild," and "The Broken Ground" demonstrate this nondualistic adhesion of seer and seen. In "An Architecture," the enactment of song fuses the bird with his morning surroundings. Berry suggests that the ability to organize is available at all levels of sentient life; at first light life commences with birdsong, filling space with design like the blueprint of a house. In fact, the bird creates his own house by adhering to the lived moment of his singing: "Around / him his singing is entire." Berry once quoted R.H. Blyth's comment that poetry is not deracinated language in a book, but "an activity in the mind of the poet" (CH 15), the expression of a process of self-actuating organization; "An Architecture" argues that this activity is not limited to humans. Similarly, the "Sparrow" is "his hunger organized." No dualistic separation exists between volition and action; the sparrow is so "filled" with his body and his environment that "he flies / before he knows he's going to." The collocation of "eye-quick / reflex of his flesh" and his ability to depart "without a thought" suggests a holistic involvement in the flesh of the visible.

The instrument of the blind mandolin player in "A Music" is "the lantern of his world," and the persona becomes so absorbed in its music that "It's his music, not the place, I go by." As with Stevens's claviers and oboes, musical instruments speak the highly organized patterns created by the imagination, and in this poem, as in Sylvia Plath's "Snakecharmer," the music actually creates or illuminates the *Métro* station tunnel, the physical space of the poem: "The tunnel is the resonance / and meaning of what he plays." The mandolin player at that moment creates what he can know of the "dark place" of our existence by organizing it, investing it with meaning. The persona insists on seeing the mandolin player's activity as more than scientific fact or economic need; his music adds light to what we normally see through a glass darkly. It bonds human activity to physical place. One of the meanings of "employ" is a phenomenological meaning, to "occupy the attention of"; though the persona employs the mandolin player at the outset of the poem, his music becomes the illuminating intelligence that occupies the persona's attention and creates the poem.

The empty city lot of "The Wild" does not reveal nature as pristine wilderness, but nature unrestricted or uncultivated by human intention— "wild" being in Berry (BCP 19-20) as well as in Merleau-Ponty (VI 13, 102, 110, 115, 121, 158, 165, 167). A few locusts, warblers, and tanagers live "wild as leaves" in this lot and constitute the "habit" or dress that inhabits "this / wasted place." Because they represent unique moments of evolution over millions of years, they should be appreciated in moments of originary perception, "new to the eyes," and not devolve to objects to which city dwellers become habituated. Yet the birds and foliage habitually return to inhabit this wasted lot as if, Berry intimates, they mean to remind us of what pristine nature really is: "They are / its remembrance of what it is."

Merleau-Ponty critiques the Cartesian cogito as a reductive retreat to the mental world that through methodical doubt must objectify an outside (VI 12-49); this is an ontological loss of nerve that inaugurates dualistic splits. As mentioned in chapter 2, Berry identifies dualism as "the most destructive disease that afflicts us" (SEFC 105). An egocentric dualist, the young husband in Berry's "The Fear of Darkness" becomes depressed and fearful. With a new wife and child and an uncertain future mirrored in the attenuated darkness of the rooms and woods outside, he takes refuge in machine technology and vents his nervous energy uselessly in anger and potential violence. He "floorboards" his "third-hand Chevrolet" for the thrill of "let[ting] her go." Unlike Daniel Boone, the husband in his fearful retreat sits in the final darkness of separation from nature at the poem's end.

The title poem of Berry's first volume implicates many senses of "broken ground": spring plowing, the breaking of new literary ground, burial, the final poem stillborn, or our biblical fallen world. Though Berry doubtless intends the ambiguity, especially because many poems in the volume develop these multiple senses of "broken," the lines of "The Broken Ground" convey a sense of perception as process, the ongoing rush of the new that breaks through the sedimented, the old. It is a statement of faith in the power of perception to return a measure of the pristine to each moment, to recover some of what Boone and the Long Hunters must have felt—that mode of experience where "There are no arrivals" and where "where I am going is always where I am" (UW 73). Berry's treatment of Boone affirms our potential to participate in each moment in a nondualistic fusion of self and lived environment that Merleau-Ponty would call "perceptual faith" in the "openness of my perception upon the world," a world that preexists our contemplation (VI 18-19, 23, 29-31, 35, 42, 47, 158). The stillborn poem at the end of "The Broken Ground" is the remnant of a process of continual opening that mimics our participation in life by postponing closure with ever-fresh perceptions of the density of our lived physical experience: "the breaking / through which the new / comes," the continual "bud opening to flower / opening to fruit opening / to the sweet marrow." This experience occurs in the tactile density of the visible world, not in an aesthetic gap.

Berry's work is consonant with the phenomenology of Merleau-Ponty especially because of the deliberateness and passion with which Berry wants to live within the physical world, not removed from it in abstract theory. One of Berry's deepest beliefs is that "the world that environs us, that is around us, is also within us. We are made of it; we eat, drink, and breathe it; it is bone of our bone and flesh of our flesh" (SEFC 34). Conversely, in his essay "The Long-Legged House," Berry expresses his dissatisfaction with most university education as "overtheorized and overvalued" (RE 34). After one year of graduate work, Berry married Tanya Amyx in May 1957 and promptly moved into a two-room Kentucky River cabin built by an ancestor, Curran Mathews, in Henry County during the 1920s. Though the couple lived in the cabin only for that summer, fixing it up for Tanya's arrival and remembering his boyhood haunts there left a strong impression on Berry. He called it an "act of realization" and a "promise" (RE 37-43). During that summer of 1957, Berry began to think of his rootedness in his locale in phenomenological terms "as living within rather than upon the life of the place." He resolved to know his locale intimately, for "If I belonged *in* this place it was because I belonged *to* it" (RE 52). Furthermore, Berry recognized that past and future meet only in present time, the live moment of human consciousness (RE 45). In his early poetry, Berry strove to find poetic cognates for these moments of adhesion to a vividly lived physical reality.

"The Design of a House" in *Findings*, his second volume, contains one of Berry's attempts to portray the creation of a house as something that connects him to his ancestry, his soil, his family, and the present moment of composition. When Berry returned in 1964 to live permanently in Kentucky, the Lanes Landing acreage adjacent to his river cabin became available that November. Berry bought it and soon realized that he and his wife wanted to build not a summer home but an only home on that property, a home in walking distance to his rebuilt long-legged river cabin. Berry's ancestors had lived within five miles of this property since 1803 (RE 329). The building of a family home nearby confirmed a lifelong commitment to ancestral place and polis and became a perfect resting place for the love he felt for his wife and growing family. The poem celebrates how love, vision, desire, and locale become one in the present moment of intensely lived experience:

> Love has visualized a house,
> and out of its expenditure
> fleshed the design
> at this cross ways
> of consciousness and time:
>
> its form is growth
> come to light in it
> (BCP 34)

The "light" of that last line is complex: it signifies inner illumination, rest from physical labor, as a bird lights on a branch, and the gravity of concrete referential realization. In the fourth section of the poem, Berry expresses his recognition that his ancestors actually offered little guidance or opposition. With phenomenological emphasis Berry asserts that history offers only an aggregation of dead facts that "neither sees nor is seen." Berry portrays the house in the fifth section as the living seed of his rootedness to place, a more complete realization of marriage, and in the next section accepts the fact that human lives, as well as houses, are mutable. Throughout the poem, especially in the opening and fifth sections, Berry emphasizes that abstract reason cannot of itself bring desire to realization. Design brought from vision to realization by love and desire needs the physical, the sensible and sentient flesh of the visible that provides the adequate support. This is where desire can "come to light," to visible realization. "The Design of a House" opens with a startling simile of how crucial vision and perception are to the concrete realization of any goal:

> Except in idea, perfection is as wild
> as light; there is no hand laid on it.
> But the house is a shambles
> unless the vision of its perfection
>   upholds it like stone.
> . . . .
> Love has conceived a house,
> and out of its labor
> brought forth its likeness
> —the emblem of desire, continuing
> though the flesh falls away.
> (BCP 29)

In "The Long-Legged House" Berry states that "A house is not simply a building, it is also an enactment," for both perception and vision are necessary: "To ever arrive at what one would call home even for a few days, a decent, thoughtful approach must be made, a clarity, an opening" (RE 33). The house's white color, its integration of various perceptions into values—just as light integrates all colors of the spectrum—combines with the snow at the poem's end to make a nest. Like Merleau-Ponty, Berry gives perception a tactile dimension; vision is the foundation and support that "upholds" the house "like stone." The home provides a necessary background, a gestalt grounding that "the black swifts may come back to." When Berry rebuilt Curran Mathews's decayed river cabin at a higher elevation in 1964, he "began to belong to it" when he set his imagination free by visualizing his plans (RE 57). Here we see a difference of accent between Berry and Ammons: though both write of dwelling or inhabiting in prose essays as well as in poems, Berry is more acutely aware of the labor expended when the energy and vitality of vision overspills from idea into motivation and enactment as one realizes an ideal. During his renovations, Berry had to disturb a nest of phoebes from under the eaves of the old cabin, but they returned to the eaves of the new house the next year, and he "felt honored by this, as though my work had been received into the natural order" (RE 61), creating a new wholeness. In "The Design of a House," the process from imaginative investment to physical and poetic realization is part of the "natural order" of growth from seed to flowering, at all stages an inter-twining of the sentient/sensible visible flesh of the world, not a dualistic process of operating on the physical from a higher mental perspective.

The long, rather digressive poem "The Handing Down" in *Findings* similarly emphasizes the adherence of the sentient/sensible in the physical world. The poem elaborates, in the mind of an elderly man nearing death, the truth of its opening lines, in a section significantly entitled "*The light*": "The mind is the continuity / of its objects, and the coherence / of its objects." Throughout fifteen pages of three-line stanzas, Berry suggests that the old man's "gathering of memories" advances by an attentive adding of new daily experiences that recall and readjust the significance of the old memories. The man has been a lover of family values, symbolized by his interest in the new house being built in another part of town, and has also been an expert at reviving houseplants (BCP 47). The "potted plants," first mentioned in section 2 (BCP 37), gradually become symbolic of the man's ability to grow with his experience, even as his physical powers wane. To-ward the end of the poem, the plants reappear as "The quick plants / of his memory" (BCP 45) and signify an organic wholeness between mind and natural growth in the physical world. His love includes "the green plant leaves in the window" (BCP 46). In section 12, Berry emphasizes the pro-cess of perception as continually interweaving the inner and outer worlds through an organic ordering that is the central significance of the poem's title:

> His intimate the green fern
> lives in his eye, its profusion
> veiling the earthen pot,
>
> the leaves lighted and shadowed
> among the actions of the morning.
> Between the fern and the old man

there has been conversation
all their lives. The leaves
have spoken to his eyes.

He has replied with his hands.
In his handing it has come down
until now—a living

that has survived
all successions and sheddings.
(BCP 46-47)

In the final two sections, Berry suggests that the old man's adherence to the world is so strong that a bonding occurs. He has become intimately and innocently clothed with the earth, "*in the habit of the world*," to prepare himself for "the earth he will become at death" (BCP 47-48). The new house nearing completion at the poem's end comforts the old man as a symbol of the continuity of human adherence to nature.

The old man of "The Handing Down" is Harry Erdman Perry, Berry's maternal grandfather, the subject of the much tighter, more elegant "Three Elegiac Poems." In each elegy, Berry asserts that Perry's body has encompassed many layers of the visible, "flesh and marriage and household" and also the "furrowed hill." These layers intertwine in the second elegy. Berry draws continued sustenance from the man's life and values as he draws water up from a cistern soon after Perry has been lowered into the earth. The grandfather's spirit flies free of the earth in the final section even as his body forever remains among us as compost: "He's hidden among all that is, / and cannot be lost." The poem deftly recreates what Ransom, in *The World's Body*, called the world's body, the "thick *dinglich* substance" of actual sensory experience that can never be reduced to abstractions (1938, 112-13, 123-24, 140-42).

Berry begins *Openings* (1968) with "The old / unaccountable unfolding" of actual sensory experience in "The Thought of Something Else." As spring appears the poet's mind turns away from winter isolation and stasis toward the potential for new growth. But growth does not happen automatically with clear roads and spring travel; it may be simply a renewed interest in renovating the mind, in relocating that habit of perception where the mind can renew itself through prereflective absorption in the physical world—seeing how thought can address the referential world and fill the mind as quietly "as water in a pitcher." In this mode of seeing, the spirit can revel in how perfectly the mind adheres to the world, how the day begins with "a simple wakefulness filling / perfectly / the spaces among the leaves." In this mode, one can also appreciate the silence of the visible, where in "March Snow" the river moves by "taking all falling darkly / into itself."

Except for the deeply meditative "Window Poems," however, the poems of *Openings* are less intricate, less developed, more prosaically limited to the descriptive. One can see why Berry moved the chronologically earlier *Openings* to a position after *Findings* in his *Collected Poems*. What sustains the slighter poems of *Openings* is a continual contrast between poems that emphasize the unity and continuity of natural processes in the physical world and poems that mourn or critique man's divergence from that norm in the Vietnam War, government intervention in the lives of private citizens, and the capitalist degradation of ecosystems. Only in "The Porch over the River," "To a Siberian Woodsman," "A Discipline," and "Window Poems" is Berry able to juxtapose both themes in one poem.

The noise of automobile engines and airplanes scar America with an "audible map" in "The Porch over the River," whereas the inverted tree on the river's surface at dusk, viewed from the poet's long-legged porch perch, suggests a normative calming silence, a density in the physical that exceeds and absorbs all reflection; the river has "a quietness in it / no question can be asked in." The phoebes in the sky near the porch eaves crisscross the jet stream scars, as if stitching the wounds of the day closed, and other natural animal activities at dusk restore the real world by erasing the noisy daytime map that humans have imposed on it. The mirrored tree, available only to the eye, seems to derive life from the water; perception once again connects subjective self to referential reality.

In "To a Siberian Woodsman," Berry compares his rural family life with that of a Siberian woodsman whose picture he had seen in a magazine. Berry supposes that the woodsman's family has a similar intimacy with the land that expresses itself even in their musical entertainments. What saddens Berry in the last three sections of the poem is the governmental enmity, the "official hates" between America and Russia that are supposed to make these otherwise compatible families enemies. Berry ends the poem with simple statements declaring that no government is as worthy of support as his family or the woodsman's. The poem contains a few fine lines that affirm Berry's rootedness in place, such as "I am the outbreathing of this ground. / My words are its words as the wren's song is its song." This echoes a line in the "Long-Legged House" where Berry, sitting on old chimney stones from Curran Mathews's cabin, realizes that "my line issued out of the ground there like a spring, as regardless of itself . . . as water" (RE 21).

But the poetry of simple declarative statement, though capable of candor and tenderness, will not convince unless it conveys intimacy. "To a Siberian Woodsman," like many of Berry's middle-period poems, is too bare and stern—its political edge, honest and direct as it is, chafes with an undertone of self-righteousness. Though Berry's life is certainly exemplary, presenting it as such in bald monotone causes the reader instinctively to stiffen rather than enjoy. "A Discipline" is more convincing in its ascetic directive to turn away from thoughts of holocaust and acquire the personal patience to "be still, and wait," for the seasonal auguries of nature lead one toward forbearance and healing through time.

Berry is more successful at juxtaposing political analysis with the world of nature when he does not tout his own or his family's life as exemplary. In "The Want of Peace," Berry presents the quiet rural life of fisherman and farmer as preferable to the economics of energy and war. As he confesses that he is not always content with simple things and never "wholly in place," his humility rings true. "The Peace of Wild Things" follows on the next page and offers a more hopeful view of attaining grace by relinquishing the analytic ego and gaining "the peace of wild things / who do not tax their lives with forethought / of grief." This poem has more grace in its direct statement, more resonance and less nostalgia than Yeats's "The Lake Isle of Innisfree," which it thematically echoes.

Other poems in *Openings* such as "Grace," "The Meadow," "The Sycamore," "Marriage," and "The Snake" present nature and family life as healing and sustaining; in contrast, a large group of poems critiques American government and the wasteful lifestyle of its citizens: "To My Children, Fearing for Them," "The Dream," "Against the War in Vietnam," "Dark with Power," "To Think of the Life of a Man," and "Do Not Be Ashamed." On the one hand, Berry gains stature for having been a staunch and early critic of the Vietnam War and of wasteful American lifestyles. On the other hand, the hard-hitting directness of these poems does not wear well outside its historical moment.

The social praxis of environmental poetry is vital for planetary survival, but composing salient social criticism without alienating one's audience is a very tricky problem, perhaps *the* problem of environmental literature. In *Openings* one can see Berry trying to confront this problem.

Especially in "The Migrants" and "East Kentucky, 1967," poems he wisely chose not to reprint in *Collected Poems*, one can see the problem: the former poem is unmemorable because its theme is largely unrealized, its anger deflected into generalized language and vague landscapes; the latter poem is too volatile in its moral fervor. Does one palliate one's audience with thin generalizations or risk alienating it with direct accusations or a moral fervor that almost always has an edge of smug self-satisfaction? Berry's best instincts lead him to poems like "The Return," only the final section of which he reprinted in *Collected Poems* as "The Sycamore." In sections 4 and 5 of the original poem, he complains about a man who has tied his yacht to the shore in the night near the long-legged house and left his refuse strewn about the shore the next morning. This causes Berry much anguish of mind, but nature heals in "The Sycamore," the final section. Here he recognizes the personal anguish without self-righteous environmentalism. The final healing offers hope and the potential for renewal. Hence, the wasteful becomes a momentary aberration within the stronger, normative ecological process.

"Window Poems," discussed in part in chapter 2, is Berry's one great triumph in *Openings* of meshing Horace's *dulce et utile*, the delight with the moral instruction, precisely because he begins with natural processes and then houses the social criticism within an anguish of mind that instinctively turns to the cycles of nature for healing. The poem also has the richness of a nondualistic phenomenological view that, like Merleau-Ponty's, sees the sensible and the sentient coiling back each on the other to create the flesh of the visible. When Berry rebuilt Curran Mathews's river cabin a few feet higher up in 1964, a few months before he bought the Lanes Landing property where he erected his permanent family home, he placed within it "a big window, six feet by four and a half feet, with forty panes. This was the eye of the house, and I put it in the wall facing the river and built a long worktable under it." Within the house, "Long-legged as it is, . . . responsive to the natural vibrations," Berry would write every morning, for "here as well as any place I can look out my window and see the world" (RE 58-59, 61, 66). In the poem Berry likens that window to the human eye, to human consciousness interacting with the world and to the formal process of composing the conversation—the poem. Berry deliberately blurs these three distinctions to suggest a nondualistic interactive process where the flesh of the human eye can recognize a formal ordering in nature—its ecology—that can guide human consciousness through tortured meditations on the inhumanity of the Vietnam war:

Window. Window.
The wind's eye
to see into the wind.
The eye in its hollow
looking out
through the black frame
(BCP 72)

       The frame
is a black grid
beyond which the world
flings up the wild
graph of its growth
. . . .
The window is a form
of consciousness, pattern
of formed sense
through which to look
into the wild
that is a pattern too,
but dark and flowing
(BCP 73)

sitting at the window,
he has shed himself
at times, and been renewed.
(BCP 74)

          He is
a wilderness looking out
at the wild.
(BCP 76)

      As the man works
the weather moves
upon his mind, its dreariness
a kind of comfort.
(BCP 77)

Initially Berry knows all too well that the very act of writing, the "notes and remnants" that comprise "the contents of his mind," divide him from the outside, as does his window: "he is set apart / by the black grid of the window" (BCP 79). But from the changes wrought from the rising river, and from the free movement of the birds outside his window, he learns that ultimately words and facts dissolve "into mystery" (BCP 80) and that they really only record or interpret a more primary and necessary process of renewal that in future years will ultimately turn his house into pasture for grazing horses. When Berry rebuilt the long-legged house, he chose a ledge above two sycamore trees, which became the emblem trees of the house (RE 55–56, 60). In section 15 of the poem, the sycamore offers him a signal insight of the more substantial reality of the natural world that humans must follow as model and guide. All of his studies of the tree, all of his poetic attempts to capture it, do not total to a grasp of that tree. He desires "to know it beyond words," but "all he has learned of it / does not add up to it" (BCP 86). Merleau-Ponty often notes how all of our horizons and perspectives are necessarily partial because the world's density is already present—we cannot see into or behind objects precisely because they exist prior to and independent of our conscious cogito. This is the basis of his "perceptual faith" in Being: it necessarily reveals and conceals simultaneously when humans gaze on it (VI 30-31, 77, 113-14, 136). Hence the *référance*, the movement toward a reality beyond words, at the end of section 15: "the world is greater than its words. / To speak of it the mind must bend."

From this point on, the window becomes a concrete symbol of a mode of interrogating the world, past or future, in terms of the present moment: "The window becomes a part / of his mind's history, the entrance / of days into it" (BCP 86). Though he broached the topic of the Vietnam War once earlier in the poem (BCP 82), Berry now has the confidence to agonize through his own hot dislike of those who kill (BCP 84, 88, 93). The window as a mode of interrogating becomes a balance point of connectedness to the physical world. To rail in anger would shatter it into "shards and splinters," whereas to fix his mind steadily and attentively on nature's cyclic renewal will enhance the window's clarity and his psychic balance. Thus, he learns the ecological and phenomenological truth that "it is the mind / turned away from the world / that turns against it" (BCP 88). Those who live at peace with the wild, who conform to the truths of nature, fertilize the soil: "They die and become the place / they lived in" (BCP 89). Berry then dreams a dream of the blessedness of all creation and unites with his wife and locale. In the final two sections of "Window Poems," Berry praises the sentient/sensible flesh of the world, the chiastic intertwining of the visible:

> In the heron's eye
> is one of the dies of change.
> Another
> is in the sun.
> Each thing is carried
> beyond itself.
> The man of the window
> lives at the edge,
> knowing the approach
> of what must be, joy
> and dread.
> . . . . .
> —end and beginning
> without end.
> . . . . .
>   He is one
> with the sun.
> The current's horses graze
> in the shade along the banks.
> The watcher leaves his window
> and goes out.
> He sits in the woods, watched
> by more than he sees.
> (BCP 93-94)

For Merleau-Ponty one evidence of the "adhesion of the seer and the visible" is the moment a painter acknowledges when, so "caught up in what he sees," he feels "looked at by the things" (VI 139). For Berry this happens when, as in the above passage, he becomes so completely absorbed in the physical world that moments of rather complete identification occur. A similar moment occurs in "The Heron," when Berry meditates on the heron's "living eye" and notes that "I see / that I am seen" (BCP 138).

As Berry leaves his house and enters the natural world, he completes what he has always wanted to complete, a Thoreauvian "hypaethral" work, a roofless work freed of walls and enclosures (RE 40). His closing lines recognize that his window, as well as human consciousness, exists in the world, adhering to it in a nondualistic connectedness:

> The window is a fragment
> of the world suspended
> in the world, the known
> adrift in mystery.
> And now the green
> rises. The window has an edge
> that is celestial,
> where the eyes are surpassed
> (BCP 95)

Berry's last line implies that writing, though limited to his own point of view, is also a means for surpassing that point of view. Writing incorporates *référance*, the propensity of consciousness to thrust itself beyond the printed page into the referential world, both to interrogate that world and to redefine the self in relation to that world. It is only natural, or common to all life forms, to develop through a process of curious interrogation of whatever situations occur. Merleau-Ponty believes that it is common to perception to be "surpassed by being" (VI 58); one lives in perpetual solipsism unless one learns that "I live my perception from within, and, from within, it has an incomparable power of ontogenesis. This very power I have to reach the thing and hence to go beyond my private states of consciousness, because it is proper to the perception lived from within, that is, to my own perception, reduces me to solipsism (this time transcendental) the very moment I thought myself delivered from it. This power of ontogenesis becomes my specialty and my difference" (VI 58).

Merleau-Ponty, like Berry, refuses to separate thought from world: "because his relationship with his situation and with his body is a relation of being, his situation, his body, his thoughts do not form a screen between him and the world; on the contrary they are the vehicle of a relation to Being" (VI 62). For Berry, as for all ecopoets, written manifestations of thoughts are more than denatured material signifiers consigned to texts; they are imaginative explorations of what can be uttered about one's originary, firsthand encounters with Being.

Two years before his *Continuous Harmony* essays that first articulated his notions of all-encompassing ecosystems, Berry developed the original perceptions that led to this cosmological view in *Farming: A Hand Book*

(1970). Though the individual poems have separate titles, all are really portions of the almanac or diary of his central persona, the Mad Farmer, who has Hamlet's method in his madness and much sanity beneath his antic disposition. The first poem with the Mad Farmer persona in its title is "The Mad Farmer Revolution," but the voice and values of the Mad Farmer are unmistakably present in "The Man Born to Farming," the opening poem, and in the first-person persona of the next half-dozen poems. The creation of a "mad" or "contrary" central persona allows Berry the distance and narrative line to satirize agribusiness and the conformity of the many to weak, self-serving institutional solutions. Throughout, the satire is subordinate to a cosmological view, a flowering of the poetic that Berry has carefully built in earlier volumes. The Mad Farmer's allegiance is to the soil, sowing, and seasonal cycles; in many poems Berry accentuates this with the analogy of placing one's hand in the soil until, fertilized by nature, it sprouts roots and trees to signify a bonding to the visible physical world.

Moments of *référance* and of phenomenological awareness in the volume accentuate this bonding of the mental to the physical world. In "A Standing Ground" the Mad Farmer stands his ground by being apart and by asserting his values in the peaceful earth: "here the roots branch and weave / their silent passages in the dark." This "healing" relationship with the referential world satisfies as the closing lines thrust the reader's gaze beyond words into the real: "Better than any argument is to rise at dawn / and pick dew-wet berries in a cup" (BCP 116). Imagery of silence (BCP 112-16, 134, 136, 139), like admonitions to be still and quiet in nature (BCP 69, 98, 128, 136, 140, 145), suggest the primacy of the prereflective world of brute nature that preexists our conscious reflection. Imagery of darkness, usually associated with the earth, not only signifies nature's inexhaustible mystery but also the solidity of a real world that our perspectives will never know entirely (BCP 107, 111, 117, 119, 122, 127, 141). Berry echoes Merleau-Ponty's "perceptual faith" (VI 35, 42, 47, 88) in the poem "The Morning's News," where he contrasts conscious death by design, the satanic abstractions of bureaucrats and the military in the Vietnam War, with his young son's more innocent, trusting gaze: "I look at my son, whose eyes are like a young god's, / they are so open to the world" (BCP 109).

The humorous story of daft old Mrs. Gaines in "Meditation in the Spring Rain" (BCP 135-37) also contains moments of *référance*. When the Mad Farmer wants his "words to have the heft and grace, the flight / and weight of the very hill, its life / rising," he thinks of cantankerous Mrs. Gaines, who in her old age has become so "wild" that the townsfolk occasionally must cage her in her room. Her faith is in "One Lord, one Faith, and one / Cornbread," and what most brings her to the Mad Farmer's attention is that as a girl "she must have seen / the virgin forest standing here, the amplitude / of our beginning, of which no speech / remains." The Mad Farmer wishes he were lost in her wild freedom, for here, as the closing lines insinuate, is where the originary rather than the sedimented word is assembled. The strongest moment of *référance* in the poem occurs when the Mad Farmer stands in the drizzle as a congregation of one attesting to the truth of Mrs. Gaines's beliefs. He begins to feel his "thoughts / moving in the hill's flesh" after his wet witnessing:

> For I too am perhaps a little mad,
> standing here wet in the drizzle, listening
> to the clashing syllables of the water. Surely
> there is a great Word being put together here.
> (BCP 136)

"The Farmer, Speaking of Monuments," near the end of the volume, contains the last moment of *référance* in the volume; it also contains a clear statement of Berry's middle period poetic, a phenomenological absorption in elemental reality:

> He remains in what he serves
> by vanishing in it, becoming what he never was.
> He will not be immortal in words.
> All his sentences serve an art of the commonplace,
> to open the body of a woman or a field
> to take him in. His words all turn
> to leaves, answering the sun with mute
> quick reflections. Leaving their seed, his hands
> have had a million graves, from which wonders
> rose, bearing him no likeness.
> (BCP 139)

Throughout *Farming: A Hand Book*, Berry emphasizes that the Mad Farmer's hand, by sowing and tilling the soil (BCP 103-4, 108, 110, 114, 119-20, 127, 130, 139), plants itself in the ground to grow roots that flower into song and values that have the strength and stability of a tree (BCP 103, 107-8, 110, 112, 116, 122-27, 139). The hand, introduced in the first poem, signifies desire, effort, and involvement in the natural world throughout the volume (BCP 103, 105, 110-11, 113, 117, 119, 130, 139). The soil, also a major symbol in Berry's new cosmology, signifies the reality of the preflective physical world, the "divine drug" (BCP 103) of renewal in the cycles of nature, and the firm ground of his values (BCP 103-4, 106, 108, 110-11, 113-17, 119-20, 122, 127-28, 130-32, 136, 139). In "Enriching the Earth" the sowing of nitrogen-fixing legumes to renew the soil connects the farmer to his world naturally, without dualistic distance. For Berry the farmer's hands are intimately connected to the will as well as to the tactile presence of the soil:

> It is the mind's service
> for when the will fails so do the hands
> and one lives at the expense of life.
> After death, willing or not, the body serves,
> entering the earth.
> (BCP 110)

The human hands imagery demonstrates that through the tactile our bodies adhere directly to the physical world, where sensible/sentient matter connects, coils back and intertwines with other sensible/sentient matter. For Merleau-Ponty, the activities of eyes and hands testify to this adhesion:

> Because my eyes which see, my hands which touch, can also be seen and touched, because, therefore, in this sense they see and touch the visible, the tangible, from within, because our flesh lines and even envelops all the visible and tangible things with which nevertheless it is surrounded, the world and I are within one another, and there is no anteriority of the *percipere* to the *percipi*, there is simultaneity . . . a segment of the durable flesh of the world. . . . When I find again the actual world such as it is, under my hands, under my eyes, up against my body, I find much more than an object: a Being of which my vision is a part, a visibility older than my operations or my acts. (VI 123)

Every moment our hands touch a portion of the inexhaustible and therefore dark Being of the world, the "Unseeable Animal" that Berry celebrates in the final poem of the volume. At other points in *The Visible and the Invisible* Merleau-Ponty observes that our two hands, because they can each experience the sense of touching and being touched when they touch each other, offer simple and undeniable evidence of the intertwining of sensible/sentient matter:

> If my hand, while it is felt from within, is also accessible from without, itself tangible, for my other hand, for example, if it takes its place among the things it touches, is in a sense one of them, opens finally upon a tangible being of which it is also a part. Through this crisscrossing within it of the touching and the tangible, its own movements incorporate themselves into the universe they interrogate, are recorded on the same map as it; the two systems are applied upon one another, as the two halves of an orange. (VI 133; see also 9, 134, 141, 147)

Berry's volume is a handbook of ecological relatedness as well as a hand book: he surrounds his hands imagery with organic similes and metaphors to evoke exactly this sense of intimate connectedness to the visible universe: the "wise movements of his hands" are "like fingers locked in the rock ledges / like roots" (BCP 113). Berry articulates his faith in how our hands, eyes, mind, and body become "one with the earth" in a page-long catechism during the "Prayers and Sayings of the Mad Farmer" (BCP 130).

The almanac catechisms, aphorisms, and satire in *Farming: A Hand Book* occur as a minor element within the more healing, integrated, comprehensive cosmology of the Mad Farmer, traced by the soil, hand, sowing, silence, and song imagery. Though Berry savors the perceptions of the common fisherman or farmer in many of his poems and rails against big business, bureaucracies, the military, and passive consumers in his Mad Farmer guise, he is not a Marxist. In his zeal for the common man, his faith in agriculture, his unstinting critique of corporate America and its periodic enshrinement of war, Berry acts much more in the tradition of the La Follette Progressive. But the Mad Farmer's satire in Berry's middle period contains a technique that Marx and Engels in *The German Ideology* suggest is central to an exposure of capitalist ideology.

Fredric Jameson discusses this technique at length in the final chapter of *Marxism and Form* (1971). Just as a camera obscura presents an inverted image, so capitalism reifies society into producers and consumers and the splintered, separated perspectives of government, the military, institutionalized religion, abstract cash value, and the fetishism of consumer products. Marxist critiques rectify these reified mystifications by reinverting the image and exposing the genuine but suppressed class and economic inequalities through a kind of "dialectical shock" (Jameson 1971, 365-415). Part of the purpose of this shock is to restore to the individual a sense of the self as an active producer of history whose free decisions can make a difference. The Mad Farmer, through his lusty or contrary escapades, points to what the splintered capitalist perspectives deny—that the farmer is abused and that capitalist perspectives necessarily lead to the degradation of ecosystems—especially the soil. Similarly, the Worldwatch Institute, a nonprofit, independent environmental research group, reminds us annually that capitalists mystify themselves with statistics such as the gross national product, the stock market averages, and the balance of trade, none of which ever takes environmental degradation into account. Poems such as "Song in a Year of Catastrophe," "The Mad Farmer Revolution," and "The Contrariness of the Mad Farmer" may not have the depth and sophistication of great poetry and may seem elementary to today's environmentalists, but in 1970 they were obviously intended to shock many middle-class urbanites into a recognition of how occluded perceptions lead to ecological disaster.

Two years after he worked out his agrarian cosmology in the poems of *Farming: A Hand Book*, Berry, in an essay in *A Continuous Harmony*, rendered a prose version emphasizing the role of perception. Ecological dependency is necessary precisely because perception is always partial, and no individual in the web can ever comprehend the whole: "Ecologists recognize that the creation is a great union of interlocking lives and processes and substances, all of which are dependent on each other; because they cannot discover the whole pattern of interdependency, they recognize the need for the greatest possible care in the use of the world" (CH 142). The poems in Berry's next volume, *The Country of Marriage* (1973), continue the Mad Farmer cosmology, with Berry proposing marriage as an ecologically sound alternative, a shared bond of dependency that sensitizes us to larger dependencies in ecosystems. A few Mad Farmer poems appear, but these are subordinate to the marriage theme and its cosmological linkages. Nevertheless "Manifesto: The Mad Farmer Liberation Front" deserves mention as one of the best examples of socialist demystification and rectification among the Mad Farmer poems. A sardonic, goading humor alternates with sound ecological wisdom:

Love the quick profit, the annual raise,
vacation with pay. Want more
of everything ready-made. Be afraid

to know your neighbors and to die.
And you will have a window in your head.
Not even your future will be a mystery
any more. Your mind will be punched in a card
and shut away in a little drawer.
When they want you to buy something
they will call you. When they want you
to die for profit they will let you know.
So, friends, every day do something
that won't compute.
. . . .
Invest in the millennium. Plant sequoias.
Say that your main crop is the forest
that you did not plant,
that you will not live to harvest.
Say that the leaves are harvested
when they have rotted into the mold.
Call that profit. Prophesy such returns.
Put your faith in the two inches of humus
that will build under the trees
every thousand years.
(BCP 151)

The Country of Marriage at first appears to be a slight volume, a simple extension of the cosmology of *Farming: A Hand Book*, but in actuality it presents all of the interdependent concentric circles of Berry's middle-period cosmology, later articulated in *Standing by Words* (1983), in perfect integration: the person, the family, the community, agriculture, and nature (SW 46). The poetry of Berry's middle period, so intertwined with the stances he takes on social issues in his essays of the 1970s and early 1980s and the problems that arise in adopting an overly moralistic tone to present the exemplary life he deliberately chooses, offers excellent examples of what Lawrence Buell calls "the text as testament," where the author's life as an agent of historical change and the text as social praxis oscillate dialectically in complex, even conflicted ways with the literary aspects to produce productive labor, the enactment of cultural values (1995, 370-95).

The marriage poems in *The Country of Marriage* extend Berry's soil cosmology by emphasizing that marriage is like good soil, carefully tended, that renews and protects a continuity of values rooted in the place of a relationship. "The Country of Marriage," "Marriage, an Elegy," "A Home-coming," "The Clear Days," "Poem for J.," "Song," and "An Anniversary" present marriage with a quiet dignity, an integrity won from continual rounds of freely entering the embrace of the dark unknown, where originary experience in that undiscovered country, as in "The Long Hunter," de-mands "blind trust." Those who, like Buell, see Berry in this middle period as somewhat patriarchal in equating the male with the planter whose seed fertilizes and husbands the more passive female (161), should read "The Asparagus Bed," a poem from *The Country of Marriage* not reprinted in *Collected Poems*. Here Berry overtly likens his poet-farmer to a woman "la-boring to bring forth the new" by making an asparagus bed or a poem (47). Berry's male/female, nature/culture analogies are often reversible, and in-tend no superiority for the male.

Once again, the accent in the portrayal rests in phenomenology, on vision embracing what it will never completely know. Gradually the un-known does become known, however, for Berry regularly presents sexuality as the planting of the lovers' lives in the ground of their growing relation-ship (BCP 148, 152, 168). This links very smoothly with Mad Farmer poems about planting trees and crocuses, assisting an animal in birth, and observing communal burial rites. The "field of vision" remains clouded and "the eye must stay unlit" until one affirms one's "native piece of ground," that "body's bride" that brings "clear days" (BCP 165-66).

Berry emphasizes how perception integrates subjective desire with the sensible world in short poems such as "Prayer after Eating," where he conveys an intimate relationship with the food he eats, for it is a portion of the elemental visible world, a coherent sentient/sensible intertwining of flesh: "I have taken in the light / that quickened eye and leaf" (BCP 148). In "The Arrival" perception occurs "like a tide," in "wave after wave of foliage and fruit" (BCP 153). While "Planting Crocuses," the Mad Farmer recognizes that his mind is "pressing in / through the earth's / dark motion" as he plants, and planting is analogous to perception, "an opening / to reach through blind / into time" (BCP 160). In these poems Berry under-scores the tactile depth of the visible and the nondualistic adherence of the perceiver to referential reality. The regular emphasis on perception in the volume occasionally incorporates moments of *référance* where language appears more limited than the referential world toward which the line thrusts the reader. In the prereflective world of "The Silence," the "leaves / stir and fall with a sound / that is not a name," and "the world / lives in the death of speech / and sings there" (BCP 156). While the "ignorant money" of banks speaks a "deserted language" (BCP 154), free-hearted men / have the world for words" (BCP 150).

Some poems about light, among the best phenomenological poems in *The Country of Marriage*, do not appear in *Collected Poems*. In "Leaving Home," Berry begins by questioning

> Whose light is this
> that is mine, that
> in the shine of the rain
> flashes from every leaf
> and brightens the rows
> where the young stalks
> rise, as if bidden
> by a knowing woman's hand?
> (34)

Merleau-Ponty sees light as the elemental, generative flesh of the pre-conscious visible world (VI 142, 154). Berry often uses the feminine to describe this property of the visible. In the third stanza, he reverses positions about whose light this is: "the light that is mine is not / mine"; after his death this light would return "like a faithful woman / until the pent stalk rose." He concludes by urging his readers not to wait "to know whose light this is" but rather to act as soon as the heart feels the "ever-wakening / woman's touch of the light" (34-35). Thus, Berry, like Merleau-Ponty, suggests that all sentient matter is involved in creating natural light. In "Leaving Home," natural light signifies the interconnectedness of sentient/ sensible matter; his use of the female for this most significant property of life is certainly not patriarchal. "Zero," "The Strangers," "The Cruel Plumage," and "To William Butler Yeats" also have phenomenological dimensions, and part 2 of "Inland Passages," subtitled "The Lover," (part 1 is collected as "The Long Hunter"), is one of Berry's finest love poems. "The Lover" revels in the process of love making as "the warm opening flower of new desire" that becomes "the return of possibility" in "the opening of the dark, the going in" (50). The meditative yearning of this search in the "unknown country" of loving captures the onrush of new perception along with the tactile density of lived experience where mind is not separated from body or from the referential world.

After his 1970s Mad Farmer poems, where the aesthetic and social themes create a dense and satisfying texture, Berry enters a fallow period until a grand cosmological vision flowers in *The Wheel* (1982). *Clearing* (1977), a transitional volume, opens promisingly with an emphasis on the history of Lanes Landing Farm and the history of America's environmental degradation. "History," the opening poem, summarizes the progressive degradation of the Long Hunters' pristine vision, where the mind regenerates by exploring unnamed places, to the deforestation wrought by "the joyless horsepower of greed" (BCP 173-74). The poem ends with an attempt to comprehend why and how this has happened. "Where," only half of which was reprinted in *Collected Poems*, follows to summarize the real estate history of Lanes Landing, from first survey to first sale and further sales from farmer to farmer, until its final demise in the hands of the developer who sold it to Berry after a three-year standoff. In the middle sections of the poem, the silence of wild nature, the prereflective state of union with referentiality, becomes lost in the machinations of politicians and real estate documents. But "Where" asserts, as does the *Clearing* epigraph from the *I Ching*, that effort and labor can reverse the process. One needs the Taoist patience of water (19) and the persistence of the laborer, for labor heals in "earth and eye and hand" in a reciprocity where "woman, man, and earth" become "each other's metaphor" (10-11).

Only the title poem, however, extends this historical sweep in satisfying ways. "Work Song," "The Bed," "From the Crest," and "Reverdure" suffer from thin, flat narration that covers old thematic ground with tiresome, dogged persistence. In "The Clearing," however, Berry develops a finely focused analogy between the process of clearing a field and the process of composing a poem. He intimates that the pioneer stock that created the frontier spirit has degenerated in the twentieth century into sedentary homebodies who populate rural America because they do not want to be bothered, but effort and a "severity" of vision—vision that is as intense as it is circumspect—can begin to reverse the process. The labor of clearing the field is analogous to the effort of mind continuously involved in acts of perception to clarify vision. As the farmer-poet clears his field, letting all the downed trees and shrubs, save one troublesome elm stump, decompose naturally in an unfired pile, he conveys the arduous effort in simple language that convinces his reader of his involvement in the referential world: "you stand in a clearing whose cost / you know in tendon and bone" (BCP 186). As the elm ash from the one huge stump that he had to fire disappears, Berry further emphasizes a reciprocity of labor that connects one to the earth: "What bore the wind / the wind will bear" (BCP 197).

A Part (1980), Berry's weakest volume, contains many epigrammatic

poems where folk wisdom alternates with satiric complaints at contempo-
rary ecological degradation. The themes are not sufficiently developed in
most of these short poems to satisfy. Moments of *référance* occur in "To
Gary Snyder" and "An Autumn Burning" where language on the printed
page defers to cycles of renewal in real experience. What one does see in
many of these poems is Berry moving toward a cultural syncretism where
he celebrates the cycles of renewal by dovetailing the Tao (in "The Hidden
Singer" and "The Slip") with Christian motifs of paradox and renewal
through experience in the fallen world ("The Necessity of Faith," "To the
Holy Spirit," "Ripening," "The Way of Pain," "We Who Prayed and Wept,"
and "Fall"). The result is the ecological equivalent of the Old Testament
Deuteronomist's cyclic vision: in our craven departures from the path of
faith and ecological rule toward the destructive idolatry of wealth, we peri-
odically learn our limits, the limits of ecosystems, and the God-ordained
path of moderation and sustainability. "The Slip," and "Horses," the final
two poems of the volume, convey the respective Oriental and Occidental
components of this vision with sufficient breadth and depth.

The epigraph of *The Wheel*, a quote from Sir Albert Howard's *The
Soil and Health: A Study of Organic Agriculture* (1947), underscores Berry's
belief that human understanding of ecological stability and sustainability is
first and foremost a matter of perception. Both Howard and Berry see in
the Great Wheel of Buddhist Dharma validations of ancient wisdom pains-
takingly learned from the actual experience of seasonal cycles. The cycle of
Buddhist Dharma, the law or order of things which includes moral prin-
ciple and right conduct, derived from firsthand experience of the cycles of
nature. The finest poems in *The Wheel* celebrate the heavenly vision and
wisdom embodied in these cycles. In these poems, Berry integrates a cel-
ebration of cosmological vision with a continued emphasis on renewed
perception. As in "Traveling at Home," from *A Part*, Berry's ecological vi-
sion necessitates sensitivity to the momentary perceptual changes that re-
new vision as well as our allegiance to the grand agronomical and
hydrological cycles: "The life of the going changes. / The chances change
and make a new way" (BCP 216).

Berry's ecological vision flowers in the grand celebrations of the
agronomical and hydrological cycles in *The Wheel*. "Earth and flesh, pass-
ing / into each other, sing together" in "Desolation." Only the "solitary
will," by turning against this song, severs "the lineage of consequence" (BCP
245). Like the soil's spring renewal, "the world's song is passing / in and out
of deaths" in "The Strait" (BCP 246). By following the temporal rounds of

the "wheel of eternity" as it moves in time in "From the Distance," we recuperate the wisdom of the dead in the work of community. As hands engage in the seasonal labor of the fields, we become "the living of the dead" (BCP 249). Berry's emphasis on agronomical cycles often yields wonderfully anti-Cartesian moments of connectedness, where "In earth, / in blood, in mind, / the dead and living / into each other pass" (BCP 268).

Poems about the hydrological cycle in *The Wheel* develop a biocentric vision where the human will does not dominate nature but instead conforms to nature's cycles. Clarity of vision and biocentric harmony with nature's patterns become two sides of the same coin in "The River Bridged and Forgot" (BCP 255-57). When immoderate plowing and strip mining erodes the soil during heavy rains, the river "in unwearying descent" carries muddy wastes and poisons. But in moderation, in the quiet of summer, evaporation "recovers clouds" and shows its "incorrupt" face, its spiritual source—the Nameless Tao. Taoist "eternal form" and the biocentric mind's "resemblance to the earth" merge in the timeless hydrological cycle, "visible in mystery." Berry celebrates the water cycle in "The Gift of Gravity" and analogizes it to the need for moral gravity in human affairs, for all manifestations of invisible spirit in time are divided, broken into imperfect shapes that need care and attention (BCP 257-59):

> All that passes descends,
> and ascends again unseen
> into the light: the river
> coming down from the sky
> to hills, from hills to sea,
> and carving as it moves,
> to rise invisible,
> gathered to light, to return
> again. "The river's injury
> is its shape." I've learned no more.

Perception in *The Wheel* includes recognizing that events realized in space and time divide the immortal whole into fragmentary parts. Hence, Berry follows his friend and neighbor Owen Flood's phenomenological view in "Elegy": "The Creator is divided in Creation / for the joys of recognition" (BCP 240). We must recognize in the hydrological cycle a pattern, a dance to which we must conform for planetary health. Such is the grand vision of "The Law That Marries All Things." Marriage in *The Wheel* is a function of cosmological perception, the mind harmonizing its attention with the laws of the referential world, the "great chorus / of parts" (BCP 247). By merging mind with referential world, as the kingfisher merges intention and act, airways and waterworld, as he swoops, we lift experience from the physical to the mind, and grasp its spiritual dimensions. We must take our imaginative flights from "what exists," from the prereflective world of nature:

> I am newborn of pain
> to love the new-shaped shore
> where young cottonwoods
> take hold and thrive in the wound,
> kingfishers already nesting
> in a hole in the sheared bank.
> "What is left is what is"—
>
> . . . .
> Imagine what exists
> so that it may shine
> in thought light and day light,
> lifted up in the mind.
> The dark returns to light
> in the kingfisher's blue and white
> richly laid together.
> He falls into flight
> from the broken ground
> (BCP 258)

When the "dark returns to light" or to rest in the kingfisher's raiment, we also have returned to a vision of the density of the referential world, where the dark signifies the solidity and depth of the real extensional world, the what we do not know of it, the concealed part of Merleau-Ponty's visible world.

The fact that we are married to the physical world is often a cause for rejoicing in Berry, for the inexhaustibility of this world is the source of endless perceptual fascination. In all the final poems of cosmic dance in *The Wheel*, poems that rival William Carlos Williams's *Pictures from Brueghel* in their sanguine optimism, the joy depends on our ability to perceive and to revel in the changing present of variable but stable ecosystems. As Berry observes in "The Dance," "we are married / until death, and are betrothed

/ to change" (BCP 262-63). We can delight in this only if we can awaken from the habituated boredom of our consumer world and cleanse the doors of perception. Berry dedicates his poems to achieving just that awakening. We must all periodically become the Long Hunter in "Setting Out" who renews perception by venturing from the "familiar woods of home" into "the forest of the night, / the true wilderness, where renewal / is found" (BCP 248).

A Timbered Choir (1998) represents the most complete flowering of those circular "nested systems" that Berry first articulated in *Standing by Words* (SW 46), as well as the most compelling realization of his drama of ecological perception. The volume collects two earlier publications, *Sabbaths* (1987) and *Sabbaths: 1987-90* (1992), and adds seven more years of Sunday meditations. Many of the poems have a meditative austerity reminiscent of Roethke's "North American Sequence" and a devotional calm reminiscent of Herbert's *Divine Sonnets*. At times, Berry moves freely in traditional forms, including terza rima and Shakespearian sonnet, but just as often forced rhymes cramp the smooth flow of his line. What does work is the grand architectonic of Sabbath meditations, the examination of conscience, the arc upward toward meditative sublimity and the downward return into travail within our broken world. Though only a few of his images are genuinely arresting, the biblical and Taoist references blend with a graceful ease, and the poems generate a lambent simplicity and genuine feeling, with no rancor or vindictive railing in the few moments Berry allows himself to dwell on our century's departure from ecological sense. Here, as in "Window Poems," Berry's best moralizing occurs as a minor subplot within the more substantial drama of nature's healing cycles.

For Sabbath rest from personal cares and labor, and from the noise and destructive work of contemporary civilization, Berry occasionally hikes to the woods above his house. The poems concern his periodic ascents to the woods, his meditations in those woods, and his returns to weekday labor. The woods function not only as a benchmark of wilderness, a coherent ecosystem from which civilization departs, but also a place of self-healing and of mystical vision. In a short preface, Berry states that the poems "were written in silence, in solitude, mainly out of doors," and they were meant to function "as a series, not as a sequence. The poems are about moments when heart and mind are open and aware" (xvii-xviii). Ultimately, the woods are the place where the animating light of the spiritual first meets the land—a "wild" manifestation of the Maker's Art (73). Berry views the trees as "Apostles of the living light"; they are both "Uprisings of their

native ground" and "Downcomings of the distant light" (83). These para-
doxical yokings of opposites often signify, as they do in Oriental poetry,
moments of mystical apprehension of a transphenomenal source.

In the woods, Berry muses on a spider's web shining high in a maple
and contemplates how "The dark / Again has prayed the light to come /
Down into it, to animate / And move it in its heaviness" (75). Here and
throughout the sequence Berry highlights dark and light, *yin* and *yang* im-
agery as he conflates the animating breath of a Christian God with the
cyclic emanations of the Tao as they pass into the fragmentary forms of our
broken world (19-20). Like the womb of the mysterious female in Lao-tzu
(Walcy 1958, 149, 174, 178, 206, 217), for Berry "the dark conceals / All
possibilities," including the message of Christ's death—the necessary pain
that attends all earthly action (21, 25).

The darkness also heals (30), for the Maker accomplishes the work of
creation in sleep and winter stasis (50). Most of all, darkness demarcates
the mysterious unknown within being, whose circumference we will never
know because our knowledge of Being is always partial, perspectival, and
therefore incomplete (74-77), and yet that darkness contains all potential
for future development (21). When Berry counsels himself to "be dark and
still," he courts a mode of experience where, by abandoning the analytic
intellect, he can refresh his soul and his perceptions by an elemental con-
tact with prereflective nature, which the trees primarily symbolize. In a
dark night of the soul Berry examines his fears, willfulness, and anger at
our civilization's destructive habits, and counsels himself. He compre-
hends that he must heal himself before he can experience the integrated
mystical vision and preach to others. The shadowy seed of renewal finally
breaks in a moment of fresh perception, a "shuddering" apprehended by
an awakened spirit, on a plane of perception quite beyond the limits of
language:

> Leave word and argument, be dark and still,
> And come into the joy of healing shade.
> Rest from your work. Be still and dark until
>
> You grow as unapposing, unafraid
> As the young trees, without thought or belief;
> Until the shadow Sabbath light has made
>
> Shudders, breaks open, shines in every leaf. (31)

In a backnote to the first *Sabbaths* volume (1987), Berry reminds us that Christ was mistaken by Mary Magdalene for a gardener (John 20:15). Christ in *A Timbered Choir* is exactly that—earth's heavenly gardener whose loving care animates creation. On the Sabbath our joy is to revel in that ceaseless love and renew our own love of life. To do so is to break into song, as Berry's epigraph (Isaiah 14:7) and many poem passages direct us. Not to do so periodically is to become overmastered by the analytic intellect, which for Berry is blind (30), or to break from the harmonious dance of creation to do the selfish will's destructive work (29; also 14, 16, 51, 58).

Berry's title essay in *The Gift of Good Land* (1981) provides a sure thematic gloss for the poems of *A Timbered Choir*. In the essay, Berry consistently opposes the biblical idea of stewardship (Genesis 2:15) to the abstractions of the analytic intellect. A good steward knows that the soil is a "divine gift to a *fallen* people" (269). In *A Timbered Choir,* that gift expresses itself as grace and light, which warms and animates the soul and the soil, allowing love to grow (168) and crops to germinate (203). The old trees hold the light and teach him to appreciate them as gift, "in a keeping not my own" (111), in rootedness of place, for the trees are "always arriving / from all directions home" (101). The trees are his "praise and prayer"; their rootedness and longevity remind him in his Sabbath rest "Of what you cannot be / And what you cannot do" (147). Berry must accept the trees as pure gift, as part of an ecological process in nature that is beyond his comprehension and control. After travel during the thirty-ninth year of his marriage, Berry stops his car near his home and remembers the whippoorwills singing in a flood of light on the spot where he first envisioned building his home, during his courtship (200). With this backward glance Berry intimates that, by cultivating his marriage and his farm over the decades, he has responded to his gift with a stewardship of love. As an aging man with few possibilities yet a storehouse of memories from relationships and labor, Berry now sees himself as "a sort of tree / standing over a grave," an elder willing to be generous toward whatever wind blows through each day (167).

The long poem in *A Timbered Choir* on the arduous labors of farming attests to Berry's stewardship of that plot of land across four decades (135-49). He has learned from his labor that "To farm, live like a tree / That does not grow beyond / The power of its place" (142). In that place Berry labors daily across the seasons to till the soil, assist the ewes at birth, bring in the hay in the fall, distribute it to the animals in winter, harvest the garden, and cut and pile the wood for winter fuel. The unromantic directness of the poem convinces, and the unhurried lines attest to the fact that Berry enjoys disappearing into his labor to maintain the health of the farm (146). Whereas Berry regularly loses himself in peaceful farm labor, obsessive planners create look-alike cities from abstract designs, bulldozing the land to realize greedy, self-regarding dreams of wealth and possessions (208-09). Locked in these dreams, most humans lack the wholeness and selflessness to appreciate the "all-welcoming, / all-consecrating Sabbath" (88). We need a "quietness of the heart" (88), as well as a quiet landscape (207) and "the eye's clarity" (88), to attain a state of soul where a perception of the Christ-child's innocent manger light can grace any and every ordinary moment, for we "are living in the world / It happened in when it first happened" (94). The grace, light, and tree imagery intersect at so many points in *A Timbered Choir* that they create a cosmological as well as ecological poem.

After meditating on the deaths of Edward Abbey and Loyce Flood, Owen Flood's wife, Berry prays that we all may be a song sung within the "green tree" of Love, an abiding tree that can withstand our century's gasaholic flames (110). Berry hopes for a harmonious world amid golden October oak leaves, "glowing leaves" where vision "made of the light a place / That time and leaf would leave" (111). In this "great mystery" of life "day and dream are one" (112). Machines, whose destructiveness is the result of reducing the mind to regularity, cannot enclose the all-inclusive body of light in created matter, "the being of all." "The mind incarnate / in the body, in community, and in the earth," is an organism "that they cannot confine" (118). Though Martin Rowanberry was killed by our century's destructive hate, his good stays with us like stored cellular information (116) "in light's ordinary miracle" (118). The inclusively organic has its own light and, like the Nameless Tao, "The light he was returns / Unto the Light that is" (116). When a man of peace dies, "He gives a light," provides values and direction, for those who follow (198).

Light as the realization of potential—illumination—shines at the close of *A Timbered Choir,* in the penultimate poem, where Berry contemplates a "familiar carving," a stone that squares the circle of life and time, as in the mystical visions of alchemists. Somewhat like the Taoist *t'ai chi t'u,* the circle within which one finds the dynamic *yin* and *yang* ceaselessly in motion, Berry's stone "doubles / the superficial strip of Möbius" to remind us that past and future "are forever here / now." In the moment of fully illuminated perception, at the completion of his Sabbaths meditations, Berry contemplates the timeless, limitless "dark within light, light / within dark" (214-15). Berry ends *A Timbered Choir* with a short poem where he asserts that his Tao or Way is "not a way but a place" (216). Like Cooper's Natty Bumppo at the end of *The Prairie,* when his time to leave this earth arrives, Berry will answer the call unflinchingly. He will be *here*—at Lanes Landing Farm.

Most of the poems of *Entries* (1994) are occasional pieces, personal poems to family, friends and loved ones to cherish and commemorate events in lives that have touched Berry intimately, but lives that the average reader knows little about. Although the lines are graceful and smooth, the content and the feelings have that unabashed directness and simplicity that works only for small groups who know each other personally. Other poems are slight satirical pieces on familiar Berry subjects—corporation callousness and profiteering, the President stroking his public, the technology of vacations, the limits of the WASP ethic, and even a Mad Farmer poem about seceding from the Union. Section 5 of the sole phenomenological poem in the volume, "Duality," speaks of lovers gazing at each other where the visible and the tactile intertwine in the reciprocal creating and sharing of natural light—a reprise of the theme of ecological vision that Berry developed throughout his major work, and a theme that closely resembles the nondualistic phenomenology of Merleau-Ponty:

> You look at me, you give
> a light, which I bear and return,
> and we are held, and all
> our time is held, in this
> touching look—this touch
> that, pressed against the touch
> returning in the dark,
> is almost sight. We burn
> and see by our own light.
> (48)

In the last three sections of "Duality," Berry states that "Eyes looking into eyes" are "touches that see / in the dark, remember Paradise." Visual interrogation that includes a scrutiny of pain and anguish leads to the renewal of sight, where the lovers, in a moment of *référance,* become "fleshed words, one / another's uttered joy." In the last section Berry asserts that the process of visual interrogation leads to "new clarities"where the "leaf brightens" and the "air / clears" (48-49). The real Paradise for Berry resides in the renewal of perception, in the Long Hunter's vision where there are no arrivals but where every journey leads to refreshed perception.

In *The Soil and Health: A Study of Organic Agriculture* (1947), Howard conveys his perception, tested by thirty years of field research growing crops and observing them as a soil mycologist (an investigator of crop diseases) in England, the West Indies, and India, that soil and animals are healthiest and most resistant to diseases with a minimum of chemical inputs and a maximum of care—proper organic feed for animals, and well-aerated, well-composted, organically fertilized soil for crops. Howard found throughout his experiments with growing crops that chemical inputs gradually weaken the soil and make crops less resistant to disease. Howard perceives soil, plant, animal, and human as one connected chain, with failures in the system attributable to "failure in the first link: the undernourishment of the soil is at the root of all" (12). One can see how Berry developed his ecological "nested systems" from scientific data such as these.

Yet for Berry human health is also dependent on renewing perception, a nondualistic interrogating and ingesting of the detritus of old perception and experience just as plant roots feed from nearby mycorrhizal fungi. We are intimately connected to the soil—not just dependent on it for food, but as organic plants ourselves, growing and decaying. After all, we are, according to Berry's ecological vision, only "brief coherences and articulations of the energy of the place" (RE 80). Howard himself accentuates the role of perception in recognizing the importance and relatedness of ecological cycles to health in the very quote that Berry reprinted as his epigraph for *A Wheel*:

> It needs a more refined perception to recognize throughout this stupendous wealth of varying shapes and forms the principle of stability. Yet this principle dominates. It dominates by means of an ever-recurring cycle, a cycle which, repeating itself silently and ceaselessly, ensures the continuation of living matter. This cycle is constituted of the successive and repeated processes of birth, growth, maturity, death, and decay.
>
> An eastern religion calls this cycle the Wheel of Life and no better name could be given to it. The revolutions of this Wheel never falter and are perfect. Death supersedes life and life rises again from what is dead and decayed. (1947, 18)

Berry is untiring in his literary efforts to show, in Howard's words, "the man in the street how this world of ours can be born again" (13). In *Another Turn of the Crank* (1995), his most recent essay collection, Berry reprints talks given to various local groups about how ecologically aware farming and the conservation of land and forests can lead to health in human communities. "Health is Membership," the final essay in the volume, once again identifies dualism as the primary cultural disease that afflicts us, a disease that leads us to think of the isolated body as a machine to be serviced by corporations. Here Berry argues that in most respects the body "is not at all like a machine," that "Divided from its sources of air, food, drink, clothing, shelter and companionship, a body is, properly speaking, a cadaver" (94). The cure, Berry reasons, is a vision of ecological wholeness, and he directs our attention to Howard's work: "For many years I have returned again and again to the work of the English agriculturalist Sir Albert Howard, who said, in *The Soil and Health*, that 'the whole problem of health in soil, plant, animal, and man [is] one great subject'" (89-90). "Howard saw accurately that the issue of human health is inseparable from the health of the soil" (97). Berry has been meditating on the soil for a long time, at least as long as the prose piece "A Native Hill" in *The Long-Legged House* (1969), his second volume of essays (see RE 105, 113).

To receive the vision of wholeness and health that fertile soil offers us, we need to revise our perceptions periodically. Action follows from motivation, and nothing galvanizes motivation better than a new truth perceived for the first time. The best way to enjoy Berry's poetry is to sensitize oneself to the flexible potential of vision by beginning with his prose piece "A Native Hill." Here Berry, following a gully, walks down Cane Run valley near his home to Camp Branch, where two of the creeks that flow into the Kentucky River meet. Though he knows that "pristine America," the land the first settlers saw, is "as extinct as the passenger pigeon" (RE 91), and though he also meditates on the wanton destruction of the land and woods by two centuries of white settlers, he suggests as Merwin does that we need to recover a sense of awe and reverence for the majesty and mystery of creation (RE 98). He likens himself to a Robinson Crusoe dogged by refuse dropped by "the ubiquitous man Friday" (RE 97), but he is actually more like his Long Hunter, leading readers down the slope with his thirst for renewed vision. In these transfigurings of ordinary sight into visions of ecological relatedness we may find motivation to recreate in our society something closer to the Paradise we first were given. Here is the essence of the Long Hunter's phenomenology, the Long Hunter's vision:

> I stoop between the strands of a barbed-wire fence, and in that
> movement I go out of time into timelessness. I come into a wild

place. The trees grow big, their trunks rising clean, free of un-
dergrowth. The place has a serenity and dignity that one feels
immediately; the creation is whole in it and unobstructed. It is
free of the strivings and dissatisfactions, the partialities and im-
perfections of places under the mechanical dominance of men.
Here, what to a housekeeper's eye might seem disorderly is none-
theless orderly and within order; what might seem arbitrary or
accidental is included in the design of the whole; what might
seem evil or violent is a comfortable member of the household.
Where the creation is whole nothing is extraneous. (RE 103)

Berry is Thoreauvian not only in having lived an exemplary life delib-
erately but also because his poetry shares a hermeneutic of perception that
William C. Johnson, Jr., considers the essence of *Walden*—the demand
"that readers conceive and reproduce in themselves a system of thinking
and imagining as an active, habitually renewable, event" (1991, 55). Though
an uneven poet who shuns the experimental and delights in traditional
agronomical wisdom, Berry in his best work proves that his "art of the
commonplace" (BCP 139) can convey the density and mystery of lived
experience, especially experience deeply felt in the actual moment of per-
ception, while granting nature its irreducible otherness.

5

Closing the *Écarts* through the Moment of Green

W.S. Merwin

Once
a single cell
found that it was full of light
and for the first time there was seeing

Merwin, RT 35

Oscillating between the gnomic and the oracular, the apocalyptic and the incantatory, the serene and the satirical, W.S. Merwin's poetry has, across its span of five decades and fourteen major volumes, provoked an equally broad spectrum of critical responses. This was especially true once Merwin left the late modernist mythmaking of his first four volumes, deconstructed the domains of self and presence, and questioned what nourishes language in his postmodern middle period, the work of the 1970s and 1980s. Critics during this period wondered whether the "elusive pallors" of his abstract language needed to be force fed to "raise sturdier offspring" (Vendler 1980, 236) or, conversely, whether Merwin succeeded in creating "generic experiences" that "fenc[e] back the blind silence as little as possible" through "a pursuit of darkness, of silence, of the soul moving in ways so unlike abstract thought that it burrows into or 'eats' its immobile paradise" (Pinsky 1976, 94). Richard Howard, however, saw the pursuit of silence and darkness positively, as the visionary's way to access the "integrity" of "darkness, unconditional life" through an "ecstasy of loss" (1970, 634-35), stripping away appearances and divisions in poem after poem finally to implore the integral white ash tree at the conclusion of *The Carrier of Ladders* (1970) to sing to him.

In a dense and sinewy 1987 essay that remains a significant assessment of Merwin's middle period, Charles Altieri argues that Merwin's major achievement occurred in the postmodern "poetics of absence" of *The Moving Target* (1963) and *The Lice* (1967). According to Altieri, Merwin's progress resembles a Heideggerian mode of becoming a stranger to the ordinary world and stripping oneself of conventions and ordinary experience to realize in the soul's pain and melancholy momentary glimpses of the still, the unborn, the silent, primordial Being beneath the flux of appearances. Disembodied speakers and pale, generic images create a space wherein the poet struggles to achieve "hard-won glimpses of deeper forms of presence" (Altieri 1987, 193). But as Merwin slowly placed confidence in notions of necessity, process, and plenitude, located an abiding permanence beneath the flux of appearances and restored his faith in language in *The Carrier of Ladders* (1970) and *Writings to an Unfinished Accompaniment* (1973), his poetic line, according to Altieri, lost tension and his cadences slackened. By the time of *The Compass Flower* (1977) and *Finding the Islands* (1982), direct lyric affirmations rendered through casual observation and a language "fully present as speech" now "deprives Merwin's poetry of its tension, its life, and its possible significance as an attitude. In saving his soul, Merwin is risking the loss of poetic immortality" (Altieri 1987, 193).

The assumptions behind Altieri's assessment entail the typical postmodern critique of presence in language and the privileging of human consciousness or hermetically sealed subjectivity as the arena where the poet resolves conflicts. Here nature exists only as a neutral plenum with mystical auras passively awaiting the tense poetic psyche to dispel its fears and demons and its distrust of language in order to recognize the central current of the psyche's life. Acts of the mind in the imaginative, subjective space of the poem provide the sole locus of value. These dualistic assumptions, however, represent only one reading of Merwin's middle period. Edward Hirsch, for instance, found significant attentiveness to the referential world in *The Moving Target* and *The Lice*. "Everything in them is written under the sign of 'a coming extinction.' His work has always had an ecological consciousness, but these poems take up our desperate vulnerability and our plight as a species, our relentless drive to exterminate ourselves and our environment" (1988, 20). Altieri's assumptions, accurate and just for the historical moment when he wrote them and relevant for one reading of Merwin's middle period, cannot comprehend Merwin's second major period, the poetry from *The Rain in the Trees* (1988), through *Travels* (1993) and *The Vixen* (1996).

Merwin, in this latest phase of his career, has saved his soul, but not through an aestheticist pursuit of poetic immortality. Instead he has restored the primacy of its dialectical other, nature. He has accomplished this without resorting to dualisms or to suspect doctrines of linguistic presence. Mark Christhilf once quipped that for Merwin "poetry is primarily a matter of perception or of 'seeing'" (1986, 39). In this phenomenological area Merwin finds a cure for the agony and melancholy of the postmodern soul. In his latest work Merwin emphasizes his environmentalism without reverting to a "poetics of absence"; he crafts a new ecological poetic by becoming intensely absorbed in the present moment of human interaction with nature. The result has been salutary, for Merwin, as mentioned in the opening chapter, gained a measure of poetic immortality by winning two prestigious awards in 1994: the Lila Wallace—Readers' Digest Fellowship and the Tanning Prize from the Academy of American Poets.

One can readily find a reverential treatment of nature in Merwin's work from its very beginnings, and his environmental consciousness became explicit in the mid-sixties. It was not just the obvious poems about species extinction like "The Last One" or "For a Coming Extinction" in *The Lice*, or poems where the persona communes closely with place and process in nature, as in "Looking for Mushrooms at Sunrise." Yes, Merwin retained these and other nature poems in his 1988 *Selected Poems*, but his strong environmental emphasis is even more unmistakable in his seminal first statement on poetics, the 1966 "Notes for a Preface." Here Merwin observes that "man . . . has chosen to pass mutilated into the modern world" because he has abandoned immediate experience and settled for mass media substitutes. On three or four occasions in this short piece Merwin analogizes our truncated sensual life to a story of a bee that continues to ingest honey for some minutes after its abdomen is amputated. Merwin's central point is that poetry today must revitalize our capacity for integrating our five senses with our capacity for "seeing," because monolithic institutions and materialist economics have created the passive consumer, an entity with severed senses, supplied with media prosthetics, whereas historically in the arts "the non-human world" has always "enter[ed] into the definition" of man:

The arts and their source were fed from the senses, and the circumstances that have been conceived and are being developed in the name of economics are relegating these anarchistic voices to the bee's abdomen. Indeed they must do so, for the senses if they were not uniformed, duped, and cowed, would constitute a continuous judgment of the world they touched on, and not only of its means but of its ends. Instead of the world of the senses . . . the creature that is replacing the Old Adam has substituted comfort and erotic daydreams (whether or not physically enacted) and tells you that they are not only more convenient and more fun, but cleaner. (271)

From this preface one can see the entire curve of Merwin's environmentalist treatment of nature, not only in the obviously satiric treatments of destructive corporate power and generic consumers in *The Rain in the Trees* ("Now Renting," "Glasses," "Airport," "Thanks," and "Liberty") or poems like "Questions to Tourists Stopped by a Pineapple Field" in *Opening the Hand* (1983) but also in his poetic treatment of what one might call a phenomenology of perception that structures his second, more recent, major period. The directness of *The Compass Flower* and *Finding the Islands* was a pause for breath, an invigorating splash in nature's lyric pond before moulting into a new aesthetic, a new attempt to connect us to the life of the senses through our faculty of perception.

The lyricism of *Finding the Islands*, as well as the new environmental aesthetic, evolved from a momentous event. Merwin, who always thinks of himself as a vagabond and who spent most of his adult life wandering from New York City to London, southern France, and Mexico, rooted himself permanently in 1979 on rain forest acreage in the village of Haiku, Maui. From that vantage point Merwin learned firsthand about the environmental degradation of a unique, self-contained ecosystem, the Hawaiian Islands. This tropical paradise, where the temperature remains between 75 and 90 degrees fahrenheit for three hundred days each year and where strong northeast trade winds expel the humidity every hour, was created by undersea volcanic eruptions about seventy million years ago. Approximately once in every fifty thousand years, a plant seed or spore fell on the islands, usually deposited by a wandering bird. Today the unique ecosystem that evolved boasts ten thousand original insect species, more than ninety unique varieties of lobelia, fifty different varieties of honeycreeper birds, and a silver sword plant found nowhere else on this planet.

The Polynesians who discovered the Hawaiian Islands shortly after the time of Christ brought some new species, but in the two hundred years since Europeans discovered the islands, thousands of imported species changed and often degraded this paradise. Mosquitoes introduced with feral pigs spawned in wallows and spread avian malaria, which has resulted in the disappearance of seventy percent of the bird population and the elimination of many bird species. None of the cash crops we associate with Hawaii—sugar cane, coconut, and pineapple—was native to the islands; as American and European entrepreneurs introduced and developed these crops on hillsides, the lush topsoil eroded into the bays, strangling the coral. Today Hawaii has one million residents, but six million tourists each year use up precious fresh water, trample coral with snorkeling fins, and turn intact rain forest into golf courses (sixty at present and another hundred in the planning stages). What Edward Abbey used to call "Industrial Tourism" (1971, 45-67) has left the Hawaiian natives with menial jobs (servicing rental cars, playing ukeleles, and plaiting bowls at luaus), bereft of cultural dignity or waterfront property.

The numbers of native Hawaiians have dropped steadily as European and American entrepreneurs exploited the islands and then seized them in the Bayonet Treaty of 1887 and the bloodless coup of 1893. Although President Cleveland directed the United States to return the islands to the Hawaiian people, his successor, William McKinley, ignored this directive; the islands were formally annexed to the United States in 1900. When Captain Cook "discovered" the Hawaiian islands in 1778, more than a half-million pure Hawaiians lived there, but measles, chicken pox, syphilis, gonorrhea, imported sugar plantation laborers who intermarried with the natives, and finally poverty have decimated this people. In 1993 less than nine thousand pure Hawaiians remain on the islands, and by 2044 demographers predict they will vanish altogether (Kapu'uwailani Lindsey 1996).

While absorbing this Hawaiian history, Merwin strengthened his commitment to the environment. In a 1991 television production, the Arts and Humanities segment of *Assignment Discovery* on the Discovery Channel (Alexander), Merwin read poetry on the Maui shoreline while wearing a Kaho'olawe tee shirt. Kaho'olawe is the small island near Maui that for centuries held sacred Hawaiian burial and temple sites. The United States confiscated the island during World War II and for fifty years used it for naval target practice and military maneuvers; during this period the United States severely restricted access to the sacred grounds until returning the island to the Hawaiian people in 1990. Merwin has also occasionally published activist letters in newspapers and journals, as with his letter in *American Poetry Review* (March 1990, 43-45) about the folly of an American scheme to bore huge geothermal wells for unneeded energy (expected tourist expansion?) on the Big Island; the scheme cut to pieces the largest intact lowland rain forest on the islands. The project is presently stalled because funds evaporated.

Merwin's growing comprehension of stressed Hawaiian ecosystems transformed both his poetic style and his aesthetic principles. His formerly stripped language and "poetics of absence" now expresses a simple but fierce adherence to the natural world. In a 1988 interview with David Elliott, Merwin explained his new preference: "I wanted to accept more and more aspects of the world. Certain things are no more acceptable than ever, of course; but wanting to be more intimate and closer to things and to be able to take the real day-to-day details of existence and use them, and to have that kind of closeness—that's been the real intent" (Elliott 1988, 10). This closeness does not, however, necessitate reverting to a discredited language of presence. When Elliott quizzed him about his use in *The Compass Flower* of things "with their names" and "without their names" (cf. "Kore," "June Rain"), Merwin responded with care, directing us to the heart of his new aesthetic:

Q. . . . What is it that naming does?

A. It sets up a concept betweeen you and what you are looking at. The cat doesn't know it's a cat until you teach it that it is a cat.

Q. And then by setting up that concept do we feel that we have possession over it?

A. I think so. We feel that we have some control over it. The names are important to us; we can't do without them. But on the other hand you can be trapped in the names and they can keep that barrier between you and things. I don't know his writing very well, but I believe that Heidegger talks about that.

Q. So then when you say things like "with no names," in a sense you are talking about a relationship between you and something else where you are able to perceive the suchness directly;

there is no name interposed, no concept of your own which you think somehow draws it into you.

A.Well, there is an evocation of the thing that is there before there's a name, before there's a concept of it. The rain falls whether we know it's the rain falling or not. (16-17)

Heidegger in his late essay "The Nature of Language" in *On the Way to Language* avers that in the modern world most language conveys basic information in thoroughly conventional, generic ways. It is mostly a heap of cliches and conventions filled with sedimented meanings collected over centuries for ingestion by what Heidegger himself called "the modern mind, whose ideas about everything are punched out in the die presses of technical-scientific calculation" (1971, 91). The poet, however, undergoes a real "experience with language" (57, 59, 63, 90-91), a "thinking experience" (69-70), a "quest for essential being" (72), a quest to find "the appropriate and therefore competent word [that] names a thing as being" (63). It is a "face to face" (82, 90, 106-8) encounter of nature and the poet to facilitate moments of originary experience where one renounces cliches and above all else "listens" (71, 76) until the right word arrives for that unique experience. Often a silence ensues that reveals the poet's attainment of "the most intimate kinship" (78) with nature. The poet necessarily conveys his sense of mystery and wonder (89) as he approaches kinship with nature and refreshes his own sense of grounding in Being: "as all nature has the character of a ground, a search for it is the founding and grounding of the ground or foundation" (71).

Yet this operation for Heidegger is not essentialistic, for though language itself is a material thing (86-88), in the process of composition the poet and his readers refresh, redefine, and renew their fundamental relation to language and Being. Heidegger throughout the essay insists on the relational exchange (65, 73, 80, 82-83, 87) between language and the Being of nature; even the most successful poetic quest leaves the quester cognizant of the fact that language does not reveal its origins, and Being conceals as it reveals glimpses. This thrust beyond language toward glimpses of the Being of the natural world explains in philosophical terms what I have been calling *référance*. When the poet clears away sedimented language and frees his perceptions, he is on the way (Heidegger does allude to the Taoist "Way"—92) to a revelation of the relationship of words to things, to a way "that reaches out sufficiently, the way is that by which we reach—which lets us reach what reaches out for us by touching us, by being our concern" (91). Thus originary language has the capacity to point toward and direct our attention toward the referential world.

For Heidegger this quest "transforms our relation to language" (93) and results in an originary "saying," a "dwelling in nearness" that relates to the Old Norse notion of "saying": "to make appear, set free, that is, to offer and extend what we call World, lighting and concealing it" (93). The poet in his originary "saying" comes as near as is humanly possible to nature, but what he redefines is our essential relationship to the other beyond the self. Thus language does not have presence inherent in its workings, nor does it capture essence; in profoundly moving poetic experiences it refreshes the essential relation of human consciousness to the other of nature. It offers a fresh "encounter" (100, 108). This encounter for Merwin is not essentialistic, as Edward Hoeppner suggests (1988, 263, 276), but dialectical. For Merwin, who believes that humans have always (until the postmodern present) defined themselves in relation to physical nature through their senses, poetry is first and foremost a moving experience of a poet's close dialectical encounter with that necessary other. It is an attempt to use poetic language to thrust beyond sedimented language and achieve what Merwin described as "an evocation of the thing that is there before there's a name."

In *The Rain in the Trees* (1988a) the rain is indeed almost palpably there, residing on the other side of the "one syllable" of language, in "Utterance." The poet's goal is to evoke what he can never really capture:

Sitting over words
very late I have heard a kind of whispered sighing
not far
like a night wind in pines or like the sea in the dark
the echo of everything that has ever
been spoken
still spinning its one syllable
between the earth and silence
(44)

What the poet can convey is his melancholy—the "whispered sighing" in his words—at trying to coax the ineffable from a nearly exhausted language whose echoes betray its age, its jumbled mass of worn syntactical parts, its historical "everything" that has been uttered. The closest his lexicon can come in this instance to evoking the silent encounter are the similes in line four—honest, humble, frugal in their simplicity, and deliberately not very original. Yet the encounter is "not far": it has the aura of that Heideggerian nearness in the "neighborhood" of Being (79-82; 103-5) and is honest in its questioning of the relationship of words, firsthand experience, and being. Its self-reflexiveness is very postmodern, but the thrust is not centripetal, toward the world of words as a self-contained synchronic system. It mourns the loss of a naive encounter with nature as it foregrounds the impedence of language and conceptuality. It wishes it could recover something more from the silence, to convey the quality of a silent apprehension of the earth, and therefore the thrust is centrifugal, towards the nature that lies beyond the power of language. It is a moment of *référance*.

The poems about the dying Hawaiian language in *The Rain in the Trees* suggest that Merwin believes a healthy language in a vibrant, indigenous culture reflects a people's unique relationship with their environment. This was especially true for the Hawaiians, whose Polynesian heritage flowered intact and uninterrupted in a tropical paradise for nearly fifteen centuries before European discovery. The Hawaiian language remained entirely oral until nineteenth-century missionaries systematized the long flowing sounds to American English by using the five major vowels and twelve consonants. Over the last twenty years, a renaissance of interest in national heritage has led Hawaiians to teach their language to their children in the elementary education system. Merwin, however, mourns the loss of the unique *relation* of language to environment in an indigenous people and also decries the abstractions and materialistic assumptions of American English that infect the perceptions of the natives who learn it. The breath of an oral, animistic culture has left the Hawaiian language in "Losing a Language"; by following American influences, the natives have confused their identity, placed a conceptual wedge between their self-image and their experience, eroded their close, empathic relationship between self and nature, and created distanced simulacra of what one ought to emulate:

> the young have fewer words

> many of the things the words were about
> no longer exist

> the noun for standing in mist by a haunted tree
> the verb for I

the children will not repeat
the phrases their parents speak

somebody has persuaded them
that it is better to say everything differently

so that they can be admired somewhere
farther and farther away

where nothing that is here is known
(67)

Merwin, an interloper from the conquering culture, confesses in *The Rain in the Trees* his inability to learn the Hawaiian language, but for important reasons: he has not himself experienced the unique *relationship* of environment to perception as a native. He can only lament the victory of the "Conqueror" language and express a faith in the resiliency of natives who persist and wait for the conquerors to abdicate: "do you know who is praying // for you not to be here." In "Hearing the Names of the Valleys," Merwin confesses he cannot retain the Hawaiian names for objects; this is not just because he is too old to learn another language (he is, of course, an accomplished translator), but because he never lived in Hawaii at a formative age to ground these words in firsthand experience. When the old Hawaiian man articulates the Hawaiian names for particular stones and water from particular rocks, Merwin cannot retain the sounds: "as he says it I forget it." Merwin wants to be able to speak the "name for the color of water," but he cannot retain it for lack of firsthand experience; he wants "to be able to say it / as though I had known it all my life / without giving it a thought." One can with application learn names in other languages than one's native language, but one must experience the events and the stories that pass through these places—their "water."

A consciousness of this loss of cultural heritage leads to "The Lost Originals," a moving poem with a complex tone. At first glance, the poem, with its subjunctive mood, appears to adopt a reverential posture toward the beset Hawaiians: if the Hawaiians had lived nearby and written American English, we would have empathized with their plight and become "ashamed and indignant / and righteous." This is to some extent true, for the sufferings of others, untranslatable in their anguish and pain, do mean more to us when the sufferers speak our own language. But ironies soon appear: if one accepts this point at face value, one must conclude that the persona is clueless about the obvious facts of the American takeover and the lack of indignation by most Americans in the last fifteen years of the nineteenth century. The irony suggests a Browningesque dramatic monologue that indicts the persona. It is arrogant to assume that the impoverished natives, who were taught only agriculture and homemaking by the missionaries, could quickly attain sufficient command of English and the political clout in that century of American expansionism and gunboat diplomacy to make a difference. Why could not Americans have learned to widen their grasp and appreciation of other cultures? Of course, the reverse happened. By 1890 our government and its cavalry had succeeded in obliterating the Native Americans, so vanquishing the Hawaiians in a bloodless coup three years later and turning a deaf ear to the cries of Queen Liliuokalani and the few educated Hawaiians who did protest was no problem at all. "The Lost Originals" thus suggests a mordant undercurrent of cultural obtuseness. The main thrust in Merwin's volume, thankfully, is toward achieving an appreciation of the Hawaiian environment through a reverence for its culture and through the more discerning perceptions of the awakened persona in the majority of the poems.

When Merwin, in *The Rain in the Trees*, wants to suggest the positive potential of originary encounters with nature's otherness, he often resorts to a dialectical drama of perception, a seeing for the first time. When Stephen Daedalus and Leopold Bloom achieve their closest moment of communion in the "Ithaca" chapter of Joyce's *Ulysses*, they awaken to refreshed perception as they exit the house to urinate. They see the night sky anew, with aweful reverence: "the heaventree of stars hung with humid nightblue fruit" (1961, 698). Similarly, when Merwin tries to evoke refreshed perception in close communion with his new wife Paula, he uses the word "first" in "The First Year" as a trope for a sort of Eliadian world-creating originary perception that sweeps away all sedimented language, revealing "green sunlight" on the leaves of the "tree of heaven." The lovers, newly awakened, are the "first" to see these leaves, and they "knew" them experientially, not conceptually, in modes at once childlike or participatory, and biblical, as a deep encounter with world-creating being. Thus the "first day" begins for this new Adam and Eve, while "the words had been used / for other things" and "all the languages were foreign." As in Dylan Thomas's "Refusal to Mourn the Death, by Fire, of a Child in London," Merwin abolishes the need for words with words. But this is not a reversion to romanticism, because the experience is momentary, relational, grounded in the limits of human perception, and does not need a supratemporal empyrean or transcendental realm beyond the physical world to endorse the character of the encounter.

Seeing for the first time serves as an organizational and epistemological focus in *The Rain in the Trees*. In "The Overpass" and "The Strangers from the Horizon," the "first thing in the morning" or "the first light of the morning" is a moment of privileged seeing, the former a nostalgic vision of what has since been despoiled by concrete roadways and the latter a premonition of the loss of the Hawaiian culture with the advent of European "discovery." In "Summer '82" seeing "in first light" recollects a privileged place of natural beauty on the Hawaiian islands that defines an intimate relationship shared by two lovers; it sustains them through the hot weather, the "blurred sirens and the commercials" of a New York City summer. In "The Rose Beetle" a Chinese insect, also a foreign interloper, becomes a pest that devours many native species. But the persona sympathizes with the beetle's plight: disrupted from its natural place, it seems to persist in its lace-creating operations in memory of its dispossession, longing to return to that "sky long ago over China." Its ancestors arrived "blind in eggs," and the rose beetle's awakening "for the first time" is now indissoluably connected with a sense of privation, a loss of place. Yet its hungers connect it to its new locale; it *relates* itself to its new place by relying on its saving sense of smell to know what to eat to survive.

A phenomenological dimension resides in the poet's desire for "the tree that stands / in the earth for the first time" in "Place." In this apocalyptic vision of the "last day of the world" and the end of the earth "full of the dead," Merwin, whose persona functions in the poems as the biblical one just man, emphatically desires to affirm his faith in the ontological primacy of perception. He plants "not for the fruit" or for landscaping, but for the fructification of vision. The poem intimates a reciprocity. Stieglitz once described the purpose of his Fifth Avenue studio with the statement that "we have to learn how to see. We have to learn how to use our eyes" (Dijkstra 1969, 12), and Merleau-Ponty opined that "true philosophy consists in re-learning to look at the world" (PP xx). Environmentalists like Thoreau agree: "Wisdom does not inspect, but behold. We must look a long time before we can see" (1980, 29). Merwin suggests that if we could learn to see in awe and wonder the richness and mystery of the earth, perhaps we would manage our relationship with it sustainably and not annihilate it. Seeing "for the first time" refurbishes our *relational* bond with nature. The poem conveys in its elegant simplicity a firm and blunt statement of the moral imperative of art.

James Atlas once charged that Merwin's "ornate, peculiar diction"

and "derivative, self-conscious voice" do not "engage our imaginative ener-
gies." These features of his writing have supposedly plagued his work ever
since he decided to adopt an aetheticist position that avoided a "direct
treatment" of the issue behind the poem (1973, 69, 72-73). Though this
may have been true of his early modernist mythmaking and his postmodern
middle period, Merwin has become quite outspoken about environmental
issues, and his more recent poetry often confronts these concerns very di-
rectly. In 1988 he stated in the Elliott interview that he does not

> see that our culture and our species are behaving in a more
> enlightened and gentle and harmonious fashion now than we
> were twenty years ago. And the cause of [my] anger is, I sup-
> pose, the feeling of destruction, watching the destruction of
> things that I care passionately about. If we're so stupid that we
> choose to destroy each other and ourselves, that's bad enough;
> but if we destroy the whole life on the planet! And I'm not
> talking about a big bang; I'm talking about it—the destruction
> of the seas, the destruction of species after species, the destruc-
> tion of the forests. These are not replaceable. We can't suddenly
> decide years down the line that we made a mistake and put it all
> back. The feeling of awe—something that we seem to be los-
> ing—is essential for survival. (6)

That feeling of awe, that capacity to perceive things "for the first
time," is precisely what Merwin senses as absent in the satiric poems of *The
Rain in the Trees* that describe environmental degradation in Hawaii and in
mainland American cities. Here Merwin's language often becomes generic
and repetitive to expose the sedimented, habituated perceptions that have
solidified into compulsively destructive habits (see Merwin's remarks on
language as habit in the Folsom and Nelson interview [1992], 47). Much
of the destruction derives from the perceptions of entrepreneurs. Using
Cartesian logic, they create dualistic divides between themselves and nature's
otherness. They convert the sensuous and particular to the economic, the
cash nexus, the most abstract and distanced level of perception. This is
what happened, Merwin surmises in "Rain at Night," during the turn of
the century in the pineapple and cattle farming boom in Hawaii:

> after an age of leaves and feathers
> someone dead

thought of this mountain as money
and cut the trees
that were here in the wind
in the rain at night
it is hard to say it
but they cut the sacred 'ohias then
the sacred koas then
the sandlewood and the halas
holding aloft their green fires
and somebody dead turned cattle loose
among the stumps until killing time

but the trees have risen one more time
and the night wind makes them sound
like the sea that is yet unknown
the black clouds race over the moon
the rain is falling on the last place
(26)

That "last place" is page 26 of *The Rain in the Trees*, where the isolated poem rests amid a saltier rain, the tears of the poet's lament for the lost "green fires" of native species.

When I visited him on Maui in June 1994, I learned that Merwin's daily regimen consists of reading and writing in the morning and early afternoon, but in the mid-afternoon he dons a tattered straw hat, slips a machete under the belt of his faded jeans, and gardens on his fifteen acres of reclaimed rain forest soil. Merwin now plants endangered species on soil restored from its red clay base, the result of erosion from fly-by-night pine-apple farms. Some of his exotic palms are more than twenty feet high. This is Merwin's way of going "Native": he takes the detritus of abstract numbers and capitalist economics and converts it into sustainable contexts:

Most afternoons
of this year which is written as a number
in my own hand
on the white plastic labels

I go down the slope
where mules I never saw

plowed in the sun and died
while I was in school

They were beaten to go
straight up the hill
so that in three years the rain
had washed all the topsoil

out past sea cliffs
(63)

Merwin creates just the right note of dry gallows humor at the end of the poem by observing that the seedlings he grows in his potting shed are labeled with Latin names, a dead language. A loving, caring *relation* of perceiver with the other of nature results in the one just man's partial restoration of environmental balance. The labor described at the end of the poem reconnects the linguistic signifier with the contextual referent in a bioregional ethic. Thus "Native" models sustainable behavior.

Many poems in *The Rain in the Trees* reveal how thoroughly our postmodern American civilization is disconnected from any sense of place. Our mass media and consumer practices, our architecture, workplaces, vacation habits, and nomadic, minimal contact Toffleresque lifestyles betray the lack of any essential connection to place. Merwin's ascerbic wit and generic language in most of the satiric poems reinforce the old Orwellian maxim about the reciprocal *relationship* of language to experience that Edward Brunner refurbished in his study of "links" in *The Rain in the Trees*: we need a rich vocabulary won from much firsthand experience (seeing "for the first time"), and we also need the referential objects to which the words refer (1991, 277-84). Scaffolding, for instance, has become so much a feature of New York City architecture that it permanently obscures the referential landscape. Nobody can remember what lies beneath the structure; the abstract concept of rental space has obliterated the site in "Now Renting." The final glass building is "home" to no one and is "never built" because never noticed as integral to the place. Equally displaced, the worker zombies of "Glasses" are "real glass" who never notice the celestial movements above them; they perform generic operations in amorphous groups while being insulated, severed from firsthand experience by windows or glass partitions. Their lives lack individuality and they don't notice what happens around them: "There is no eye to catch." They see things through glass eyes. Made callous by mind-forged manacles derived from mass practices, they are unreachable. The books they read fail to alter their perceptions: "they have just read a book / they have never read a book."

Similarly, American travel and vacationing practices disconnect the individual from any enduring sense of place while the native ability to see "for the first time" atrophies. Merwin placed "Airport," "Liberty," and "Thanks" near the center of the volume because they are deeper, more profound studies—political environmental poems about the spiritual atrophy beneath capitalist practices. The spiritual portion of the psyche, "that Biblical waif" that Merwin mentioned in his "Notes for a Preface," atrophies, and a profound lassitude results, a willingness to rely on robotic habit and to forsake the wakefulness needed to see things "for the first time." As he asserted in "Notes for a Preface," Western civilization substituted material goods and secondhand media for firsthand experience (270). Thus we created the airport, a building that is not "a place / but a container with signs / directing a process." Here people glance at their tickets but "nobody knows" the "way home." Dispensers and glass enclosures adorn "a facility / devoted to absence in life." Airports are people movers; as we use them to turn over the dollar in our business engagements and career advancement, or for convenience in our tourist travels and visits with relatives, we lose our sense of place: "we forget / where we have been."

What has "Liberty" become when its chief symbol is a locked statue serviced by crews and visited by hordes who pass ceaselessly through turnstiles and elevators? We move on line through disconnected facts and "whatever is safe," although historically cries for liberty have never been safe. Resting on its "cemented pedestal," the Statue of Liberty offers vacationers and tourists another mass practice disconnected from place. We "follow signs / to the ticket booths / vendors conveniences" as our spirits devolve in submissive routine. For the price of a ticket we trudge through a dead museum piece dedicated to disconnecting facts and names from sensual experience. As we say "Thanks" for being serviced by anaesthetizing mass practices, we become amnesiac spectators hurrying along our mazes, oblivious to our deadened senses; in this mode the reciprocal relationship of words to place and experience atrophies. Meanwhile we see through a glass darkly; capitalism continues to degrade planetary ecosystems and cause species extinction while its practices inhibit our senses and our ability to perceive the destruction. The robotic "thank you" glosses it all with plastic approval as we shrink wrap the world:

with the animals dying around us
taking our feelings we are saying thank you
with the forests falling faster than the minutes
of our lives we are saying thank you
with the words going out like cells of a brain
with the cities growing over us
we are saying thank you faster and faster
with nobody listening we are saying thank you
thank you we are saying and waving
dark though it is
(46)

When we live in close communion with planetary ecosystems, we
periodically perceive Joyce's and Merwin's heaventree of stars "for the first
time." The mythologies of tribal cultures testify to their ability to attain a
perception of the wholeness of life—the Egyptian or East Indian World
Tree with all species on it, the Norse Yggdrasil with its roots deep in the soil
and its leaves embracing the heavens like a giant vertical cotter pin con-
necting earth to sky, the Central Asian Cosmic Tree or the tepee tent pole
of American Indian and Eskimo culture as another Cosmic Tree where the
shaman ascends to the smoke hole to experience visionary seeing (Eliade
1964, 120, 270-71). The gridlock and earthquake catastrophe of "The
Crust" is caused, in the opinion of a witness from one of these earlier cul-
tures (the persona uses the medieval "Sire"), by contemporary Western
culture's inability to believe in holistic vision. Where once our *relation* with
nature was integrated, reciprocal, now we have the vertigo of the poem's
conclusion. Today we have fewer sustaining trees but more furniture, and a
complete divorce of humans from their environment: "from the tree your
chair was made / with the earth falling away from under it." Although fifty
percent of tree fiber is fixated carbon dioxide that trees eliminate from our
polluted atmosphere, the forests are indeed "falling faster than the min-
utes."

Instead of the music of the spheres, planetary harmony devolves to
Cartesian abstractions—cords of wood, units of combustible biomass sev-
ering a sustainable tree/earth/humans ecosystem. This is the view Merwin
offers in "Chord." In the 1820s, while Keats was writing his lush, opulent,
sensuous odes to attest to our connectedness to nature, entrepreneurs as
well as natives forced from their family farms by an imperious, feudal social
system were cutting down the Hawaiian sandlewood and the forests of

Europe for the battleships and mercantile vessels that have hastened planetary exploitation. The reasoning was foreign to the natives, who nevertheless were victimized by accepting a prosperity that was never more than a few crumbs from the tables of entrepreneurs. Centuries later, we explain this collossal conversion of unique ecosystems and indigenous cultures into sameness in the temperate latitudes of this planet in fine books, written in a language foreign to the natives, such as Alfred Crosby's excellent *Ecological Imperialism* (1986). The severing of conceptual language from indigenous experience is the culprit; we have lost our sustainable *relation* with our environment. Keats was ignorant of economics and nineteenth-century practices usually divorced economics from culture.

Today the horizons of the rooms in which we live ("The Horizon of Rooms") lead us to perceive experience as boxed and packaged; they offer no Keatsian "season of mists and mellow fruitfulness," and the computers we busy ourselves with print words more disconnected from experience than ever. Our exhausted perceptions ensure that precious little of our real involvement in the world reaches the printed page. We suffer the aloneness of disconnected words surrounded by white space "here in this place hard to see / on a piece of paper" ("Paper"). As real pastures disappear and more and more citizens experience childhood and adult life solely in urban areas, we lose important sensual contact with nature. We become severed bees. Because Merwin experienced pastures as a child, he knows that the word "named something / with a real sky" ("Pastures") where one could periodically reinvigorate one's contact with nature. This for Merwin is part of what pastures are for—for a synesthetic "hearing our breaths" in "the chill twilight."

Without awakening the faculty of perception, without developing the capacity periodically to see things "for the first time," our vocabularies atrophy; this leads to a callousness that, whether silently or actively, promotes the eradication of species and rain forest and the degradation of good topsoil and clean air and water. Then our dictionaries become "full of graves," which signify the final absence of the referential object ("Before Us"). Merwin in "Native Trees" remembers that as a child he asked his parents to name the trees near the house where he was born. But they could not remember them. With impoverished senses and perceptions, his parents could feel only "surfaces of furniture." Their forgetfulness becomes the first step on the road to environmental degradation.

On the page facing "Native Trees" in *The Rain in the Trees*, however, rests "Touching the Tree," a poem that evokes the richer, more participatory and relational world of childhood perception. The child with his lively imagination sees the macadam as a black river through his "green fence"; the blackness is part of the adult world of superego discipline that reproves with its everlasting "no." Yet for the child who sees "for the first time," all is alive; even the street car sings its iron song. The lively imagination of the child creates a personal relationship with his environment: at the end of the poem the child digs a cave for a lion at the foot of his integrated tree of perception.

This conclusion alludes to the prophecy of Isaiah 11:6, where the calf and the lion lie down with the other animals of the field in perfect harmony when "a little child shall lead them." Compounding this allusion is a backward glance toward "The Child" in *The Lice*, where the persona desires to escape the blinkered world of adult perception by trying to "learn the word for yes," which would return him to himself, "the child that will lead you." That "yes" and the affirmation of childlike vision at the conclusion of "Touching the Tree" perhaps both allude to the metamorphosis of the spirit that Nietzsche suggests in the opening chapter of *Thus Spake Zarathustra*. One must locate the power of the lion within the self to vanquish the imposition of conventional duty, and roar an emphatic "no" to the "no" of social restrictions. Then one must begin anew with the innocence and forgetting of the child's sacred yes that "wills his own will" (1964, 25-27).

One of the most riveting moments of childhood vision in *The Rain in the Trees* occurs in the beautiful short poem "The Duck." Here Merwin remembers "the first time" that an adult reversed the prohibitive "no" and allowed him to take the canoe across the lake one midsummer evening. An intense originary moment of perception follows when the child sees a duck "catching / the colors of fire." The poem ends with the poet acknowledging what he has found "long afterwards / the world of the living." Having as a child developed that capacity for originary perception, Merwin late in his life can periodically refresh his thoughts by reviving that mode of perception.

Further inquiry into the epistemological import of childlike vision will clarify "Sight" and "The Biology of Art," two of the more enigmatic poems of *The Rain in the Trees*, and also uncover the dimensions of Merwin's ecological vision in his most recent work. Lacan's interpretation of the mirror stage of the child's development is perhaps the most well known postmodern gloss on the consequences of what happens when the infant first recognizes an other as distinct from the self, but it is by no means the only way to interpret this critical stage in a child's development. For Lacan the child's early recognition of itself in a mirror, at the age of six to eighteen months, causes a rush of libidinal energy that helps the unsteady child achieve balance and coordination. But it also causes the child to identify with that specular image in a way that creates "an alienating identity, which will mark with its rigid structure the subject's entire mental development" (1977a, 4). From this point on, the child's unconscious is structured by language to accept roles imposed by society. The child's ego is from the start objectified and inscripted by a culturally determined language into a series of passive social roles, with his or her behavior always mediated by language and its attendant cultural assumptions. Lacan believes that "I identify myself in language, but only by losing myself in it like an object" (1979a, 86). As Smith (1988, 71-79), Bowie (1979, 131-37), and Levin (1991, 58-62, 69) have noted, the adult who develops from this schema is a marionette, subjected into an aggregate of passive social roles; Lacan's *objet petit a* is a wooden stand-in, pulled by the interpellating strings of socially constructed signifiers.

This is not the case for Merwin. In "Sight" seeing begins with the awakening of a biologically inherent ability to develop self-awareness, in a reciprocal dialogue with the other of nature. Merleau-Ponty believes we cannot automatically restore our lost immediacy of involvement with nature, for we must think of nature at a distance (*écart*) to begin the process of fusion. But with fresh, renewed perception, we may recover a sense of the fullness of being that envelops all nature and the perceivers who experience it, so that "the visible things about us rest in themselves, and their natural being is so full that it seems to envelop their perceived being, as if our perception of them were formed within them" (VI 122). Instead of alienation and objectification, intense identification with all orders of the natural world may ensue from such reciprocal dialogue. In stanzas 2–4 of "Sight" the persona, seeing "for the first time," experiences empathic identification with a bird, a mountain goat, and a fish and in so doing integrates the subjective ego with the realms of air, land, and sea to produce a coherent whole. The result in the last stanza is a dilation of time, a stretching out of the moment in intense poetic involvement in nature:

I
look at you
in the first light of the morning
for as long as I can
(35)

Merwin is not only implying that originary perception extends the moment; he is also suggesting that seeing "for the first time" involves an intensely reciprocal and developmental relationship between the subjective ego and the other of nature, not a complete alienation that is to be the price for the signifying power of Lacan's Name of the Father. None of the major postmodern theorists—Derrida, Lyotard, Lacan, Foucault—can elucidate "Sight," for Merwin's pithy poem at first glance seems to belong in the tradition of objective, naturalistic vitalism, originating with Lamarck and Shaw, that includes contributions such as Jung's Self, his Child archetype (symbolic of an adult's potential future), the social genetics of Theodosius Dobzhansky (1962), and the deep, spontaneous energies of Thomas Berry (1988, 194-215). Actually, "Sight" most properly belongs in Merleau-Ponty's complete transformation of that vitalism.

For Merwin, as with Merleau-Ponty, the awakening of self-awareness is primordially constitutive in a dialectical, self-developmental way, for both believe that inherent in the lived body is the will and the power to become not only the resistant self, but the unique self, the self-determining self, the potential agent of change. Both "Sight" and "The Biology of Art" in *The Rain in the Trees* equate the process of childhood development with the phylogenetic development of all biological organisms and with a dialectical process of awareness where self and the other of nature are equal, reciprocating participants in the maintenance of ecosystems. Each is open to the embrace of the other in ways that encourage the enhancement of awareness. This development of awareness in humans provokes a reciprocal respect for the other of nature.

Merleau-Ponty, in his essay "The Child's Relations with Others," argues that children from birth onward organize their actions and responses through their perceptions of others and the world outside them. "The child in no way distinguishes at first between what is furnished by introception and what comes from external perception"; "he cannot separate what *he* lives from what *others* live" (PriP 133, 135). Hence, when an infant hears the cries of other infants in a nursery, he also cries, and he smiles back at his mother's smile even before he has control of his visual or motor system (PriP 124). According to Merleau-Ponty, the child does not merely imitate in ways that always interpellate him into rigid social norms, for the child from the outset has self-developmental capacities that lead to creative problem-solving (as we noticed in Merwin's "Touching the Tree"):

It is as though there is in the child a sort of elasticity that sometimes makes him react to the influences of his surroundings by finding his own solutions to the problems they pose. And so the internal characteristics of the subject always intervene in his way of establishing his relations with what is outside him. It is never simply the outside which moulds him; it is himself who takes a position in the face of the external conditions. (PriP 108)

Merleau-Ponty critiques Lacan in this essay and in so doing views the alienation of the mirror phase as both a learning experience and an opportunity for developmental social interaction, inciting the child either to sympathize with others through the images they have of him, or respond aggressively (PriP 135-39). The ego first realizes itself within a child's body after understanding other bodies through sociable interaction and postural play (PriP 141-50) in a reciprocal, dialectical process of self-development:

> In the initial state of perception there is consciousness not of being enclosed in a perspective and guessing—picking out across it an object which is outside—but of being in direct touch with things across a personal-universal vision. The *I* arises when the child understands that every *you* that is addressed to him is for him an *I*; that is, that there must be a consciousness of the reciprocity of points of view in order that the word *I* may be used. (PriP 150)

Perception even for the child is circumscribed, for Merleau-Ponty, by the primacy of perception, by the openness of self to the external world and the adherence of self and world that is necessary for perception. Hence, we develop referentially, through our social interactions with the world, not with signifiers in texts:

> We must abandon the fundamental prejudice according to which the psyche is that which is accessible only to myself and cannot be seen from outside. My "psyche" is not a series of "states of consciousness" that are rigorously closed in on themselves and inaccessible to anyone but me. My consciousness is turned primarily toward the world, turned toward things; it is above all a relation to the world. (PriP 116-17)

David Levin, in his excellent essay on intersubjectivity in Merleau-

Ponty, argues that, whereas Descartes, Freud, and Lacan see alienation in the mirroring of narcissistic subjectivity, Merleau-Ponty rather sees "a larger, nonegological identity, radically decentered by its dialectical experiencing of the intertwining of self and other." In the child's first awareness of otherness he awakens a "primordial sociality" that "frees" the ego to "continue its individuation, beyond socially imposed roles, by taking part in the communicativeness and reciprocity of an embodied social existence" (1991, 64-65).

Merwin's statement in stanza 1 of "Sight" that sight first occurs when "a single cell / found that it was full of light" conveys an awareness and involvement of self-in-the-world, the visible whole that impinges on the retina. Just as the light-sensitive retina cannot help but perceive the whole of the visible in the object it focuses on, both the light reflected by the object and the object, which contains the remaindered portion of the light spectrum (Davis 1991, 33), so all corporeal bodies are part of the visible, exchanging sensations, sensing and being sensed. We are all, for Merleau-Ponty, part of the visible flesh of the world, portions of the "formative medium" of the subject-object intertwining (VI 147). We participate in "wild Being" where the sentient and the sensible intertwine, where "every reflection is after the model of the reflection of the hand touching by the hand touched" (VI 204). Hence, Levin believes that for Merleau-Ponty "the presence of the other . . . enables me to see myself as *always already social*—as having *already been social*, social from the very beginning" (66). The undifferentiated "you" that Merwin looks at for as long as he can in the last stanza of "Sight" encompasses his wife Paula, the reader, and the whole of the visible world, in a reciprocal, sociable gaze.

In "The Biology of Art" Merwin extends his treatment of perception by asserting that the artistic impulse is inherent in human biology. It is a capacity for becoming awakened to "the first light" and to our deeply rooted connectedness to the other of nature before sedimented knowledge labels things with names. It is most fundamentally a childlike identification with the phenomena of that otherness as sacred—trees, valleys, water. That awakening is a matter of perception, a flexibility that Merleau-Ponty believes intersects with our biologically encoded ability as children to develop by organizing our experience (PriP 98-100). If we realize that perception is both introceptive and extroperceptive, then we can abandon the dualistic separation of classical psychology that one's own psyche is unique and inaccessible by others. Next we should consider Merleau-Ponty's notion that cenesthesia (or coenesthesia), the body's experiential awareness of itself as a sensed schema or differentiated corporeal scheme of sensations, joints, muscles, and organs, leads to a reciprocal relationship of the body's posture towards the extroperceptive dimensions of the vertical, horizontal, and other coordinates of its external environment (PriP 114-19). Then it is not hard to see how the hypersensitive poet can transfer his cenesthetic sense of self and experience himself as tree, valley, and water, as Merwin does in "The Biology of Art." Merwin is trying to describe the poet's acute awareness of his moment-by-moment adherence to the visible world as a prerequisite for art. This is far from a withdrawn, dualistically self-absorbed Cartesian cogito engaged in a hermetically sealed textuality.

In fact, Merwin seems in some of the poems of *The Rain in the Trees* to attempt the impossible, to convey in words our subtle biological adjustments to prove how deeply the physical presence of the other can affect one's own perceptions and sensations. If the lived body is sentient and sensible at every moment and is intimately attached in a reciprocal relationship with the visible world, can we not be occasionally so affected by other humans and by our environment as to absorb some of their behaviors, take on their gestures and perspectives as our own—in a phrase, be so deeply *influenced* that our own behavior as well as our own perceptions change?

Merwin suggests exactly this in the chiastic cross-stitching of "West Wall." The "unmade light" at the outset of the poem is a moment of *référance*, a deliberate pointing toward the real world sunlight beyond the makings of linguistic signifiers. In that real light Merwin perceives the world, and focuses intensely on apricots that he has often passed by, but "never saw." Now the quality of the "first" experience of seeing the apricots transforms his entire awareness of his environment. He sees the entire day through the fluid perception of newly seen apricots. The air becomes ripe, his wife's skin suddenly has the velvety touch of apricot skin, and he tastes in her mouth the sunlight that he tastes in the apricots.

In "West Wall" Merwin suggests that poetic seeing is a learning experience so intense that it reconfigures his entire way of perceiving the world. This is possible because the lived body is open to the world. One's cenesthetic sense of one's own body is to some extent malleable, can adjust its psychophysiological sculpture when deeply affected by others. If one jettisons the dualism of classical psychology, one can note, as did Merleau-Ponty, that "I gradually become aware of my body, of what radically distinguishes it from the other's body, at the same time that I begin to live my intentions in the facial expressions of the other and likewise begin to live the other's volitions in my own gestures" (PriP 119).

This cenesthetic empathy and developmental identification with the other is never complete, however, and does not, for either Merleau-Ponty or Merwin, depend on outmoded doctrines of presence in language—the belief that language has a naive purchase on extralinguistic reality or that it captures in an unmediated way the essence of events in the referential world. For Merleau-Ponty, the body is ambiguous flesh (that which I can see and that which makes seeing possible) endowed with consciousness, and in order for that consciousness to think of itself temporally, it must recognize the bodily self at a distance, present to a transcendent other (VI 123-24, 136-39). When consciousness locates the actual world, "this does not mean that there was a fusion or coinciding of me with it: on the contrary, this occurs because of a sort of dehiscence opens my body in two, and because between my body looked at and my body looking, my body touched and my body touching, there is overlapping and encroachment, so that we must say that the things pass into us as well as we into the things" (VI 123).

To be conscious is not a coincidence with the bodily self, but "a separation (*écart*), such as the corporeal schema, which is the foundation of space and time" (VI 191). "To touch *oneself*, to see *oneself*, accordingly, is not to apprehend oneself as an ob-ject, it is to be open to oneself, destined to oneself (narcissism)," for one reaches the self "by divergence (*d'écart*)" (VI 249). Of this passage in Merleau-Ponty, Levin notes that "the 'narcissism' to which this passage alludes is *not* the immediate narcissism of Cartesian self-absorption and epistemic coincidence, but rather the mediated narcissism of a passage through the *écarts*, the ecstatic disseminations of the flesh: I see myself mirrored in the body of the other; I see myself from the viewpoint of the other, as the other sees me. I *need* the other as my mirror, if I am to see and know myself; and in the mirroring, I get to see this—this passage—through alterity" (68).

Merwin, in the 1991 Discovery Channel video, stated that he feels very close to the Polynesian deity Kanaloa. Part of this closeness derives from his application of Kanaloa mythology to the epistemological problems of knowing and self-knowledge. As with Merleau-Ponty, knowing the self in Merwin's poem "Kanaloa" happens through a separation from the self that is also the foundation of space and time. In Hawaiian mythology Kanaloa is a demiurge and culture hero, the god of the squid and octopus, an expert sailor who finds freshwater springs and is associated with fish-ponds and the cultivation of crops. Because not allowed to drink awa, a narcotic drink prepared from a pepper shrub root, Kanaloa and his followers rebel from his brother god Kane. Kanaloa is sent to the underworld and becomes the first of the spirits placed on earth after it is separated from heaven. Other stories identify Kanaloa as the devilish one who curses man to die, seduces the first man's wife, and drives them out of their god-given garden spot because he becomes angry when his drawing of man in the earth does not live, while Kane's does (Beckwith 1970, 60-64, 94-95).

Merwin emphasizes Kanaloa's dawning awareness of consciousness as a separation from paradisial unity. With this separation, as in Merleau-Ponty's *écart*, comes the first consciousness of temporality, of sequence in time. Kanaloa becomes aware of the other of nature through temporal sequence: the elements—the sun, moon, wind, stars, comets, sea, day and night—come toward him in succession. His first mistake, as with Blake's Albion, is to further separate himself from nature through imagining abstractions: "he had imagined the first mistake / all the humans are coming toward him with numbers." Consciousness does have its positive side, however, for Kanaloa is also able to "house" the "ghosts of the trees // the ghosts of the animals / of the whales and the insects" in language, memory, and his imagination. Yet this process of awakening to the other of nature does not result in identification or doctrines of presence, for Kanaloa is always elsewhere in time, "the one who is already gone," when he brings the things of the world home to consciousness. Time is inexorably the foundation of consciousness and perception.

The aesthetic of Merwin's next poetry collection, *Travels* (1993), revolves on this axis of knowing through the *écarts*, through separation and identification. One of the correlates of Merleau-Ponty's epistemology is that knowing through dialectical separation and reciprocity necessitates an other for consciousness to know anything (what would humans come to know of themselves if they were born and raised in a vacuum?). The narrative, historical poems of *Travels* not only recapitulate the sad history of exploitation and ecological degradation in the temperate zones of the world from the Renaissance to the present; they also imply that travel is satisfying only when driven by the inner necessity and moral imperative of adhering to the other of nature. The aesthetic of the entire volume responds to the humble admissions of the first poem, "Cover Note," with its meek postmodern lack of confidence in "one track of syllables" and its urgency about species destruction and mass practices that will soon rob our "free trees" as well as our "uncaught / voices" of their liberty. The entreaty in the opening stanzas of "Cover Note" rings through the entire volume: in the 1990s we must recognize that "the world we / cling to in common is //

burning." Is the burning a reference to global warming, rain forest and species destruction, or a more positive burning of imaginative perception that can respond to the duck's "colors of fire"?

A number of important poems in *Travels* are narratives that concern the history of Merwin's own past travels as well as those of European explorers and naturalists. These frame the ecological issues as well as point toward the way one can close the *écarts*, through a cenesthetic adherence to the visible. In "Writing Lives," dedicated to Leon Edel, the biographer of Henry James, Merwin suggests that two ways exist for "the author in the words" of the poem to develop historical material:

> one way with the words is to tell
> the lives of others
> using the distance as a lens
>
> and another way
> is when there is no distance
> so that water
> is looking at water
> (9)

The first way is the usual practice of limited omniscience historical realism; the second a cenesthetic identification with the subject that can be so intense that the author momentarily becomes the protagonist of the narrative. Actually, the poems of *Travels* suggest that whether one uses the external perception of the realist or imaginative cenesthetic identification, the progression of the poem depends on the fortunes of the sensible/sentient protagonist in reciprocal dialogue with the other of nature, touching it and being touched by it. The most worthwhile poems are those where the persona or historical character is so touched by "the moment of green," the title of the poem about Gregorio Bondar, that he learns truths about preserving nature's ecosystems, perhaps even dedicating his life to this project after the epiphany. Other poems depict failures to find in nature anything more than possessions wrested from the calculating distance of capitalist self-interest that furthers planetary exploitation.

"Manini" and "The Real World of Manuel Cordova" present historical figures who ultimately fail to grasp anything beyond the prevailing Cartesian dualism and post-Renaissance exploitation of newly discovered lands. The Spanish adventurer Don Francisco de Paula Marin (1774-1837), called

"Manini" by his friends, deserted for the Hawaiian Islands during naval service for the Spanish at their fur trading base on Nootka Sound, British Columbia, in 1793 or 1794. Adept at languages, he fled to Hawaii and followed the fortunes of the native warrior Kamehameha, serving him as his chief interpreter, pilot, architect, accountant, financial advisor, herbalist healer, and distiller of wine and brandy. After many scrapes, captures, and threats to his life, Marin prospered in lands and goods as Kamehameha united the islands and became the first king of Hawaii. When Kamehameha died in 1819, and Protestant missionaries arrived a year later, Marin's fortunes slowly declined. He became parsimonious (to be ungenerous might provoke in a native the reply "*Manini,* huh?"—Gast and Conrad 1977, 16) and was dispossessed of much of his lands and fortune in political imbroglios with power-seeking missionaries. Marin interests Merwin as Hawaii's first horticulturalist, healer, and a shrewd trader who functioned as a catalyst during the period when Hawaii gradually came under the burden of foreign dominance and exploitation.

"Manini" presents Marin as a dispossessed, restless Spanish wanderer in search of a homeland, never fully comfortable under the favors and tensions of Kamehameha, who nevertheless had a keen eye for the worth of plants, vines, the pearl or sandlewood trade, and trade of any advantageous kind. Yet his commonsense mercantilism leaves him anxious about his adopted place. He knows that Kamehameha needs his translating and business skills, and he knows that he needs "protection" from the warrior's enemies, so he accepts his economic role without question: "we found what each of us / needed from the other." Meanwhile the poem conveys his rueful but resigned acceptance of the despoilation of the earth in the illegal fur trade he witnessed as a youth and the cutting of the sandalwood forests of Hawaii for the Chinese market through a contract with New England merchants that Marin himself helped to draft and execute. In the poem Marin is conscious of spirit leaving the forests with the dead animals and cut trees, but all he can do is guard his own precarious position.

Merwin concludes the poem with Marin late in life still longing for a garden as large as a valley and for a "place / like somewhere I thought I had come from." But the capitalist ethic Marin labored under gives him, instead of permanent satisfaction to crown his years, the regret that essential depths of experience in nature have evaded him. His hunger remains as goods, duties, and the responsibilities of family life (according to the biographers Gast and Conrad, he had three wives and fathered nearly twoscore children) run through his fingers like the pearls over which Kamehameha exercised a trading monopoly. A servant under the sometimes whimsical or preemptory demands of a native king, Marin died as a traveler whose restless spirit never found satisfaction in a life dedicated to gaining favor and personal wealth under the yoke of coarse trading interests. He remained a functionary in a system that drained his energies and never satisfied his spirit. His involvement with the other of nature has been too thin, too momentary, too much a matter of goods traded. The colors of his life evade the touch of his hands in the poem's concluding lines.

"The Real World of Manuel Cordova" recounts the true story of the Peruvian Manuel Cordova-Rios (born 1887), who was captured while on a rubber-tapping expedition in 1902 by the Huni Kui or Amahuaca Indians of the Brazilian/Peruvian border. Cordova lived with these natives for seven years, and after months of initiation into tribal practices that included the hallucinogenic *nixi honi xuma* or *ayahuasca* vision drink, he learned that his captors have been fleeing brutal invasions by rubber tappers for years, have decided to live in peace in a remote part of the forest far from navigable rivers, and have the foresight to choose as their next leader one—Cordova himself—who could teach them the rubber-cutting trade so they could exchange latex for guns to defend themselves. Cordova gradually learned the medicinal herbal practices of the Huni Kui and became sympathetic to their plight. Most memorable in F. Bruce Lamb's account, *The Wizard of the Upper Amazon*, are the passages where Cordova describes the capacity of drug-induced visions to make him one with nature and with a group consciousness shared by all in the tribe that guides their decision making (1975, 87-97, 156-59, 167-69, 182-88). Habituation to the drug makes Cordova light and noiseless in his forest movements, hyperaware in his perceptions of forest birds, plants, and animals, and grants him a sixth sense that aids him in guiding his tribe once the old chief died. But after continuing drops in the price of latex and repeated attempts on his life by enemy tribes who wanted to weaken the cohesion of the Huni Kui, Cordova experiences black visions of death and destruction, escapes to freedom by boat from the rubber trader's hut, and uses his herbal wizardry to become a revered healer of dignitaries in his home town of Iquitos, Peru.

Merwin is most eloquent in his descriptions of how the *ayahuasca* causes a cenesthetic absorption in nature in Cordova (compare with Lamb 184, where Cordova could "follow in great detail the coursing of blood" through his body; 91, where "every leaf, as my attention settled on it, seemed to glow with a greenish golden light"; and 94, where "all the senses seemed to be intensely acute and integrated into a single system"):

and the visions rose
out of the darkening voice
out of the night voice the secret voice
the rain voice the root voice
through the chant he saw his
blood in the veins of trees
he appeared in the green of his eyes
he felt the snake that was
his skin and the monkeys
of his hands he saw his faces
in all the leaves and could recognize
those that were poison and those
that could save he was helpless
when bones came to chase

him and they were
his own the fire
of his teeth climbed after
his eyes he could hear
through his night the river
of no color that ended nowhere
echoing in his ear
(103-4)

Lacking punctuation and usually couched in syllabics, Merwin's po-
etic line in his recent poetry often has the effect, like Jorie Graham's hector-
ing parenthetical asides (are you there, reader?), of keeping today's short
attention span reader involved, for one must either remain alert enough to
make sense of the syntax or risk losing the thread of the narrative. More
importantly, the cramming together of nouns and adjectives, and the use
of parallel structure to create hypnotic effects, as in the above passage, con-
veys the persona's intense cenesthetic adherence to the moment of firsthand
experience. Or, as in "Among Bells," the cramming together of nouns that
point toward concrete objects takes us out of our flattened world of news-
print and computer screens by evoking the plenitude of referential nature.

By weakening the artificial boundaries among humans and between
humans and nature, the *ayahuasca* drug in both Lamb's and Merwin's ren-
ditions induces a sympathy for all creation and heightens Cordova's ethical
resolve to guide his adopted tribespeople toward sustainable living. Yet the

latex for guns swap is at best a holding action, and Cordova soon becomes vaguely anxious over how the incursions of civilization (Abbey's syphiliza- tion?—183) are destroying the Huni Kui's sustainable lifestyle. The mer- chandise he buys seems "weightless," the noisy guns are of little use for hunting in the dense forest, and the alien rubber tappers infect the "wild fabric" of nature and the village where the Huni Kui's "first world wakens" (106-8). Cordova's increased ecological awareness and moral purpose seems finally to come at the expense of the Huni Kui, as their unity and hardi- hood decreases.

Merwin's conclusion, which follows Lamb's account fairly closely, emphasizes Cordova's final vision of a sickness in the tribe that is met- onymic of a sickness in civilization, and this foreshadows the final devolu- tion of the Huni Kui into cannibalistic attacks on neighboring tribes. Merwin does not, however, mention Cordova's final career as a Peruvian healer; the poem ends with a powerful image of cultural, as well as ecological, erasure: "whatever he might need / was somewhere that could not be said / as though it had never existed." Both "Manini" and "The Real World of Manuel Cordova" echo Merwin's 1966 remarks in "Notes for a Preface" about how modern economic practices have severed humans from their referential context, world, bioregion.

The second poem of *Travels*, "The Blind Seer of Ambon," inaugu- rates a group of historical poems spaced throughout the volume that present more successful passages through the *écarts* of separation to achieve unity in a firsthand grasp of nature. "The Blind Seer of Ambon" could be a figure for Merwin himself as wandering naturalist. In this poem Merwin praises the tenacity and love for nature of the German Georg Everard Rumpf (1628- 1702) who, after early exploits as a soldier, enlisted in the Dutch East India Company in 1652 and spent the rest of his life on the island of Ambon in the Moluccas of the Malay Achipelago. As Rumpf succeeded in advancing a career as a civil servant of the Dutch merchant class, and as a mathemati- cian and architect, he developed such a love for plants that he wrote the *Ambonese Herbal*, the first work to describe systematically the plants of the East Indies. Composing the first chapter in Latin some time after 1654, Rumpf changed his name to Rumphius and used his adopted Dutch lan- guage and his son as an amanuensis after glaucoma and blindness struck him in 1670. Published before the taxonomical standardizations of Linnaeus, the *Ambonese Herbal* reveals Rumphius's intense imaginative involvement in the singularity of each plant described and a vivid imagination filled with metonymies and lively descriptions of exotic plants.

Most evident in Merwin's poem is Rumphius's close, firsthand grasp of nature, which sustains him throughout the majority of the composition of the *Herbal* during years of blindness. The opening stanzas assert that the reciprocal touching and being touched by the other of nature is more important than whatever language one uses to convey the experience: the referential world is paramount for Rumphius. His grasp of shells now is like "hearing after music," and the final stanza presents his continuing liveliness, his moment-by-moment awakening to the newness of the moment of green. The middle stanzas recite the hardships that Rumphius endured, which attest to his tenacious dedication to his project. Along with his blindness, which made his financial situation precarious in those callous mercantile times, Rumphius lost his wife and daughter in a 1674 earthquake (they were found under a collapsed brick wall). Half the drawings executed for the *Ambonese Herbal* by Rumphius and other draftsmen were lost in a 1687 fire, and the first six books of the manuscript of the *Herbal* were lost at sea in 1692 as the French sunk the Dutch vessel bound for Holland. Rumphius sent all twelve books to Holland in 1697 and in 1701 sent the final "Actuarium" to the *Herbal,* but the Dutch East India Company refused publication because the knowledge in it might give their competitors some advantage. The full text was finally published in seven volumes in 1755, more than fifty years after Rumphius's death (Beekman 1981, 1–40). Yet in Merwin's rendering, all these adversities are secondary to the continual moment of surprise, with the looking cenesthetically transferred in the blind seer to a touching and feeling of newness which for Merwin is the absolutely necessary prelude to artistic composition: "everything takes me by surprise / it is all awake in the darkness."

Rumphius in "The Blind Seer of Ambon," like David Douglas in "After Douglas," seems delighted and amused at how his cenesthetic involvement in the lived moment translates into human languages. Rumphius first spoke German, then Latin, wrote most of the *Herbal* in Dutch, and spoke fluent Arabic and Malay, yet he has no doubt that firsthand experience and the actual objects in the referential world are primary, more important than whatever signifiers humans adopt. The signifiers barely scrape the surface of the referential world and can only "echo / the untold light and depth." Hence the moment of *référance* in the opening stanzas of the poem:

I always knew that I came from
another language

and now even when I can no longer see
I continue to arrive at words

but the leaves
and the shells were already here
and my fingers finding them echo
the untold light and depth
(3)

In "After Douglas" Merwin presents the Scottish botanist and adventurer David Douglas (1799-1834), for whom the Douglas Fir received its signifier, as the restless, intrepid explorer that he was in real life. In the poem he is so preoccupied with the imperative to "go on" that he becomes aware of the great distance between his cenesthetic life, his moment-by-moment experience of his body, and his persona and reputation, which "seemed to be moving / away." The Northwest Coast American Indians did call him "grass man" (Davies 1980, 60, 76, 90) for his earnest collecting of seeds and dried specimens, and Douglas himself used that name to make himself more mythically imposing when he had to reprove natives for pilfering his knife or tobacco pouch while they were ostensibly engaged in group smoking socials. Yet to Douglas each moment is beyond words and public images; each moment of experience is a much more originary, self-creating moment that seems in stanza 4 like the perpetual sound of stones breaking, as in a continual birth dream (Douglas's father was a stone mason). His cenesthetic life announces him to himself "not as a name" but as a center of three-dimensional sensory experience. At times he understands himself in a way that only Merleau-Ponty's epistemology can comprehend, as one voice engaged in reciprocal interaction with other animals ("I see in the eyes of my first birds / where I am coming along this path") and from direct cenesthetic involvement in the moment, as when he feels that North America is "so deep that I reach out my hand to touch it / and feel that I am air moving along / the black mosses."

In Merwin's rendition of Douglas's adventures, the anger that Douglas felt at the difficulties of trying to get his notes published while in London vanishes when he later recognizes that his firsthand encounters with "the lives," the living specimens and travelling acquaintances, not the journal entries that followed, "are the guides," the only adequate record of his adventures—a singular moment of *référance*. This is an important realization (actually an inference by Merwin), for Douglas, as he left North

America for the last time, lost his botanical notes, journal entries, and about four hundred specimens (including two hundred fifty moss specimens) as his canoe was "dashed to atoms" on rocks in a whitewater stretch of the Fraser River in May 1834, just two months before his death. Douglas, in a letter to a friend, stated that this event left him "broken" in "strength and spirits" (Davies 1980, 163-64), but the environmentalist in Merwin intervenes to offer a more sanguine portrait of Douglas in his last months.

Merwin wrote "After Douglas" as if Douglas were reviewing his life at the moment of his death and embracing that life as fitting and worthwhile. Merwin's back note reminds us that Douglas was killed while hiking the volcanoes of Hawaii in July 1834. Exceedingly short sighted by now, Douglas evidently hiked too close to a bull pit, though he was warned about it by its creator, one Ned Gurney, an ex-Botany Bay convict who made his living capturing wild bulls, imported animals that wreaked environmental havoc on the islands. Apparently the intrepid but myopic Douglas edged too close to the pit to inspect yet one more living specimen, one more life, and the loose ground gave way. Later that morning, natives found the bull in the pit standing on the foot and shoulder of the dead body, and an autopsy weeks later confirmed a death by bull trampling (Davies 1980, 155-56). In his last moments of consciousness, Douglas in Merwin's poem reviews "the lives," his encounters with referential nature, the substance of his life, and finds his life good: "the lives one by one / are the guides and know me yes and I / recognize // each life" until the moment of his death, where he "forgets." Human and nonhuman vision reciprocate while nature provides the guidance, the cynosure.

"The Moment of Green" is Merwin's most direct statement of his epistemological aesthetic in *Travels*, his most direct attempt to close the gap between the *écarts*, the interior cenesthetic sense of living in one's body and experiencing nature firsthand, and the objectifications of oneself that accrue in time from the mirror stage through adulthood. In this poem Gregorio Gregorievich Bondar (1881-1959), a Russian entomologist and plant pathologist who spent most of the first half of his adult life studying palm trees in Brazil and writing scholarly botanical studies in Portuguese, suddenly decides to return to his homeland in 1916, during World War I and just before the Russian Revolution. He is completely unable to provide logical reasons for his return after so many years, and his interrogators therefore suspect that he is a spy. Bondar slips past the interrogators' suspicions when they realize that he has the scientific knowledge to help them control the pests that are invading their crops and threatening their harvests. He is unable to provide rational explanations for his travel because human logic in words comes nowhere near his immersion in firsthand experience. Bondar's goal since childhood has been to know nature, and his desire was so strong that as a child his hand "grew" (not "drew") pictures of nature, that other he felt so compelled to bond with, until all distance vanishes:

> and his hand grew
> pictures of her he traced the legs
> of her grasses lengthening he
> followed the lace of her veins to
> find where they opened from he drew
> the bees in her flowers and on
> her leaves the cicada one of
> her voices and the grasshopper
> part cloud part paper who became
>
> his guide through the dust and winter
> and the tissues of days farther
> and farther afield ticking through
> libraries stations the glitter
> of alien cities westward
> into trees of strange talk until
> he knew the leaves and tenants of
> summer to be one as he was
> one with the calling that found him
> (77)

Sent east to inspect crops for pests, Bondar continues his wanderlust through Manchuria, Korea, and Japan, all the while integrating himself with a music in nature that is unconformable to words; he can know it only in the moment of originary experience. This everlasting "shimmer of sound" was "what he / had to go on listening to." Travel compelled by inner necessity gives Bondar a rich life, and the music he hears continues "through the decades / of research and the more than four / hundred published descriptions of / insects and as many of plants," beyond his attempts at description, in continual *référance*, "after everything had been said." The lives indeed are the guides, even if they are insect lives: in Merwin's poetry living nature creates cynosure, pointing readers past the limited linguistic world toward the inexhaustible referential world.

Music, whether it be Douglas hearing the sound of stones breaking or Bondar hearing nature's "shimmer of sound," is a frequent trope in *Travels* for a more direct immersion in momentary experience that defies logical description. Merwin introduces this theme early in the volume, in "Rimbaud's Piano," to suggest that the artist's life follows the psychostructural logic of a music orchestrated by the deep personal centers in the psyche, the intuition and creative imagination. Rimbaud in Merwin's poem follows the promptings of his creative gifts; words and discursive logic certainly could not offer rational explanations for his bizarre conduct and careless treatment of his mother. "Rimbaud's Piano" begins with Rimbaud having already finished his poems at twenty-one and, having lost faith "in the alchemy of the word," making a few pennies from teaching German and "trying to turn / some words into money into numbers." But Merwin, through Rimbaud, observes with *référance* that "there must be something to which the numbers / were still witness." Rimbaud's obsession for a piano, according to Merwin, derives from an attempt to pierce the veil of nature and become one with a more essential music at the heart of experience, a music that words can barely evoke but that artists can listen for. Nature is the orchestra, the context or unfinished accompaniment with which the artist as soloist interacts (as in the title of Merwin's 1973 *Writings to an Unfinished Accompaniment*).

The lesser historical narratives in *Travels* primarily present ironic tragedies of how naturalists and singular individuals who try to preserve their experiences in nature are beaten by the historical power of capitalist empire building. In some, such as "Cinchona" and "The Lost Camelia of the Bartrams," naturalists and botanists struggle to transplant specimens of newly found species in the mother country while capitalists exploit the indigenous ecosystem where that species thrived, annihilating its natural habitat. A tree in the Peruvian Andes becomes "something of value" only when its bark, which contains a substance much like quinine, cures the malarial fever of the Countess of Chinchon, the wife of a seventeenth-century Peruvian viceroy. When it suddenly has anthropocentric value, the tree gets a name and becomes sought after by empires. While the indigenous habitat of the Cinchona trees becomes so "plundered," so "flayed and rummaged" that no seedlings remain, the Dutch transplant Cinchona seeds in Java and the English in India, so that their colonial slaves could tend the trees. The seeds resist sprouting in these nonnative habitats, though various naturalists perform heroic feats, sometimes after being jailed, to smuggle these seeds out of Peru, whose government wants to monopolize the business.

"Cinchona" ends with the incredible feats of the Englishman Richard Spruce to haul thousands of carefully packed cinchona seeds and cuttings from Peru to India amid severe hardships and health so poor that he was "deaf / in left ear unable to walk or sit / without //great pain." But Spruce becomes so desperately involved in his travels, so smitten by the moment-to-moment experience of defying craggy mountains, fearsome river currents, and smashed rafts, that he becomes "stunned in the sound of the river" and so wedded to his seeds and cuttings that they seem the cenesthetic extensions of the bones in his body: the cases of cuttings after the ordeals feel to the intrepid travelers "as though they were touching bones / of their own after a fall." Spruce's intense involvement in nature becomes another kind of fever, and so exhilarating that it displaces the original purpose of the expedition. The travel itself welds him to nature and has its own necessity; the journey is worthwhile even though the seeds, once they reach India, will probably "be planted and come to nothing."

When John Bartram, the father of American botany, and his son William lose their way and travel without artificial guides or maps, they find a "nameless" tree with "beautiful / good fruit" and exquisite flowers that "were of the first order for / beauty and fragrance." Merwin spends four stanzas of "The Lost Camelia of the Bartrams" describing this gorgeous flower. Twelve years later William returns to Florida and, when he once again finds this camelia, takes seeds and cuttings, and names it (William Bartram described it in part 3, chapter 9, of his *Travels*). But by the time William has turned fifty, this camelia disappears altogether from the altered landscape, and then it is left to grow only in botanical gardens "as a cultivated / foreigner." Again the wild plant becomes domesticated in faraway places while the incursions of civilization erase it from its original habitat.

The American Indian Frank Henderson wanted to preserve through drawings the vanishing prairie landscapes and customs of his Arapaho tribe in "The Lives of the Artists," but civilization seems dedicated to obliterating the attempt. Henderson is shot twice through the back by American cavalry; the bullets pierce the book of drawings he had so meticulously tied with rawhide strips to his back. An agency foundling, Henderson was given a name by a passing white man. But this white man's name has no relation to the natural world, as do the names of real Indians such as Black Wolf Hill Man, so Henderson resolves to render the birds, animals, Indian dances, and landscapes of his life in drawings, with "no names," to evoke their sounds and activities through his animated visual artistry. These moments of *référance* would be better than learning "white words" at school. But after broken treaties, Henderson dies in his early twenties in an escape attempt from Fort Robinson, Nebraska, the same fort where Crazy Horse died. What leaks out of the bullet holes in Henderson's defaced book is the intensity of his involvement in nature and his sustainable culture.

Naming in most of the lesser narratives of *Travels* leads to possession, exploitation, and environmental degradation, whereas intense firsthand involvement in nature seems to augur the preservation of ecosystems. Throughout the volume Merwin foregrounds language through comments about how limiting is the act of naming and then points the reader's attention back toward the referential world objects and less limited firsthand experiences that have always been the sources for the words. *Référance* permeates the entire volume.

Most of the remaining poems of *Travels* divide into two groups that follow the epistemological bent of the narrative poems. Poems with subject matter where Merwin closes the *écarts* of temporal separation receive positive treatments; poems with subject matter that rigidifies distances from the natural world receive more acerb scrutiny. In "Kites" the kites look down "from their own element" on the smoky dumps, the "cooked" city air and noisy, claustral train stations. The kites suggest a cleaner, clearer place; their dancing and leaping seem to embody aspirations for freedom among the cramped train station travelers. The referential world of nature beyond crowds, machines, and cities holds promise for travelers; the kites "beckon as guides" and suggest "a new life with afternoon light." The kites symbolize the mysterious other of nature that is not reducible to human emotions or logic; they neither hope nor promise and exist in a strange non-anthropocentric element, "neither living as the living know / of it nor dead with the dead." Yet the poem suggests that the referential kites do offer access to self-realization, for they seem to draw humans toward free-spirited, unfettered involvement in nature as the proper context for the realization of their hopes and aspirations.

Similarly, Merwin asserts in "One Story" that the main purpose of the thousands of fables, quest romances, and heroic adventure stories that concern being lost like Dante in a dark wood is to recognize the moment of ignorance, the moment when one must launch into Heideggerian originary naming for the self. The individual must confront the demons within and the mysterious referential other, just as Dante did as he turned his dark forest into an entire *Divine Comedy*. To win the self-defining struggle with making meaning, we must "be led at last by the wiles / of ignorance" into seeing "for the first time." Surviving the demons and mysteries is a process of "recognizing them with / no names and again surviving / seizing something alive / to take home." Merwin discussed the importance of ignorance in his 1982 interview with Ed Folsom and Cary Nelson:

> It would not be an authentic poem if the *intellectual* intention were the real, final guiding force in the poem. This is another way of recognizing that other dimension; I think a real poem comes out of what you don't know. You write it with what you know, but finally its source is what you don't know. There's a passage where Thoreau says, "How can someone find his ignorance if he has to use his knowledge all the time?" The arrogance would be the assumption that what you know has some kind of final value and you can depend upon it, and it will get rid of a whole world which you will never know, which really informs it . . . . Both of these worlds, in my view, are without meaning; there is absolutely no meaning in either, but the *sense* of the world of relation comes from them nonetheless. (45)

Merwin's final comments in the above quotation reinforce my opening discussion of Heidegger and naming in this chapter, where naming comes from recognizing anew the right *relation* of personal experience to referential context. Merleau-Ponty takes much the same view, holding that language is a "tool or instrument," an "open system of expression" that a child learns piecemeal, not as a synchronic linguistic system, as he or she acquires habits that relate the physical body to its operations in the referential world. Hence language facilitates "a structure of conduct" in the flesh of the world (PriP 99). Merwin suggests that naming should never be an arrogant device to "get rid of a whole world which you will never know," but much of postmodern theory seems to chart that course, as does our rampant degradation of ecosystems. The final stanza of "One Story" takes this point one step further. "Part of the story" *is* the referential context; if "there is no forest," then "there is no more / story that will be our / story." Here we should remember Merwin's point in "Notes for a Preface" about how humans until now have always defined themselves as rooted in the context of nature. What will happen when we have annihilated the forests, the unknown other that draws us on toward mystery and self-definition?

Willard Spiegelman, in the *Yale Review*, called Merwin an epistemological poet in his review of *Travels* (1993, 141). "Rain Travel" is a splendid short poem with a surprise ending that hits the epistemological theme of *Travels* dead center. The poem begins with Merwin awakening next to his still-sleeping wife one rainy morning when travel is imminent. But the poem ends by suggesting that real travel is epistemological; it is recognizing that awakening moment where the self positions itself in the normal, objectified way in temporal experience, the moment of dehiscence or *écart*, and then collapsing that distance by uniting more intimately with the rain. By the end of the poem the persona recognizes that the only train leaving the station is the rain train; rain travel is merging one's cenesthetic self with the rushing train of the falling rain: "all at once there is no sound but rain / and the stream below us roaring / away into the rushing darkness."

Other poems in *Travels* also direct the reader toward the referential world. In "Writing Lives" Merwin avers that "if a single moment could be seen / complete it would disclose the whole." "Among Bells" is Merwin's attempt to do just that through a full imagistic inventory of what is happening in the whole three-dimensional surround (the hills, the city square, the streets, roofs, windows, train station) when a swift effortlessly vanishes from its perch in a belfry. "Mirage" is its opposite, where the poet admits that a skein of words cannot possibly render the whole experience. This fond belief is perhaps the poet's necessary mirage; the child in the poet runs frantically with arms raised and open toward the clouds and the vanishing crow. The witty Harvard Phi Beta Kappa graduation poem, "The Day Itself," rests in a middle distance, bringing to consciousness all the knowledge and experience that we want to glean from a day's inexhaustible wealth, and recognizing, as in Emerson's "Days," how little of this we do garner.

"The Palms" celebrates their great variety and usefulness for animals and humans. These trees are alive in the referential world, and they "learn from the splashing water / and the falling water and the wind." They are part of Merleau-Ponty's flesh of the visible and know how to find water and shade when young, and how to propagate themselves across great distances. Though they may not share the sentient consciousness of humans, they seem in their survival abilities capable of more than just purely physical responses to sensation. Many palm species antedate the first humans, and their genetic encoding contains much stored survival knowledge, a referential "writing / from long before speech." Similarly, "Field Mushrooms" teach the poet of the depth of the referential world and its "texture of flesh / scarcely born." The mushrooms house a portion of nature's ineluctable substance.

Poems in *Travels* that convey Merwin's censure discuss environmental degradation, or express how the persona's cenesthetic sense of firsthand involvement in nature has atrophied. "Immortelles" and "Another Place" continue Merwin's critique of his parents. Like "Native Trees" in *The Rain in the Trees*, his parents in the *Travels* poems do not experience nature intensely; coldness, hollowness, and superficiality predominate. The flowers of "Immortelles" are so artificial that Merwin as a child had trouble recognizing them as flowers. Made of wire and beads, with leaves the colors of "unlit / church windows," the flowers function purely as aesthetic decoration and are completely detached from the natural world of growth and change. These flowers, which his mother says "must never be touched," rest isolated in imagery where blackness and inaccessibility predominate—even the black marble fireplace is "never used." Merwin's mother is pleased that these flowers need no water and "would never change," but this is unnatural. They do change in time anyway, for his mother throws them out long before her lonely, eerily silent death (another change) when she "stood / up and died" after contemplating "black waving / trees." The entire poem is bereft of any cenesthetic involvement of a lived body in the concrete flesh of the natural world.

More chilling is Merwin's penetrating portrait of his Presbyterian minister father in "Another Place." That other place is the self-enclosed mind of the Protestant ethic, coldly removed from familial contact. The poem recounts Merwin's father's habit of leaving his family after an early supper and walking to his empty church, in whose cavernous and "heedless dark" he would ascend the pulpit stairs and practice his sermons aloud when "there was nobody there." His two children, who knew him only as one who was never "able // really to touch them or / address them except in anger" had "turned from him," and later could remember him "only as the author / of everything forbidden." Merwin presents his father as doubly distanced, for while practicing his sermons to pews as empty as his soul, he seems to lose himself in delusions of yesterday. He envisions himself as a younger figure, a minister impeccably dressed, "without error," the confident, self-assured one who always had the right answer. Yet Protestant ministers must be itinerants, and Merwin's father never gave his son a sense of place. The poem reveals that in his rootless wanderings Merwin's father was also hounded by rumors of infidelity with a favorite parishioner who was seen with him in his car on many of the late evening auto jaunts that followed those lonely sermon-practicing sessions.

Twice Merwin punctuates his presentation with a tableau of his father gazing from "the top stair / of the new manse" across the street to the "austere / facade" of his church, wanting to capture it in a black and white photo for the first page of every Sunday's Order of Service announcement. The linguistic signifiers and hymn numbers in these bulletins are also a facade, Merwin seems to say; they exist, like his minister father, in complete disjunction from his family and the town's lived reality. Here words and cenesthetic experience part completely. The poem ends with a fitting picture of a boarded area in an empty field that encloses "nothing visible" (Merleau-Ponty would have loved the irony), with a "Danger / Keep Out" sign. The church, long since a victim of fire, finally exposes its empty, ashen rubble; it is "naked to the public air."

Many environmentalists agree with Joseph Campbell's belief that the Animal Master rituals of indigenous tribes fostered a reverence not only for the principal food source, but for all of nature. A sense of the spiritual value of the natural world combined with a censure for excess and waste to produce sustainable lifestyles in the tribal cultures that practiced these rituals (1988, 69-89). In "Fulfillment" Merwin presents a sad portrait of tribesmen—probably the Northwest Coast AmerIndians that Marin knew in his early wanderings—who have fallen victim to the invading capitalists' fur-trading practices. Merwin summarizes Animal Master rituals, where the principal food source was feted as a departing spiritual emissary, in stanzas 3 and 4. Practicing these rituals seems to have given the natives a premonition of the negative consequences of invasions by whites, but the natives are powerless to stop this. Worst is the poem's sad conclusion where, after environmental degradation has turned their villages and hunting grounds to smoke, the invaders in a moment of ironic *référance* tell the villagers that no one will even care if the natives themselves are annihilated, for the only record will be an edited one in the language of the conqueror: "*only in our words will anyone hear / what we choose to say of you.*" The natives conclude that these conquerors define themselves by words that are not only distant from lived experience but cover an erased referential reality that they have turned to smoke: "they are what they forget and they make / records of all they are not." The natives cannot stop this voracious "wind with no home."

"Inheritance" laments the erasure of several thousand varieties of French pears over the last century. Inhabitants of each village once took pride in their botanical accomplishments; they were "a settled careful cunning people / who compared their seedlings" and knew how to graft "those rare exceptional strains." Then the names of the varieties were heard in "syllables ripe with anticipation" and "weighted down with a sensuous longing." Such a profusion of varieties occurred that tastes and names blurred, and the townsfolk finally pick an all-male jury to decide which varieties should survive. But this jury relies on artificial means; it votes after creating abstract categories and "a few clear / standards on a scale of one to ten." The process of course is reductive, and Merwin ends the poem by stating that it matters little which varieties received the strong and the weak votes, for the interposition of distanced, abstract processes ruins the sensuous connectedness between referential reality and the villagers' cenesthetic life. The jury procedure has opened a Pandora's box of *écarts* that in the end leaves just a few simple, store-bought varieties "compiled from our sweeping erasures."

Some of the shorter poems in *Travels* lament the pressures placed on the landscape by postmodern mass practices. At an airport Merwin writes notes to himself "On the Back of the Boarding Pass" as a hedge against the dislocation from place that one experiences in these facilities. To resist the dislocation, he remembers that that morning he mended a fence on his property, and as he writes on the boarding pass he fuses that experience with his commitment to write poetry that awakens us to preserve our bioregions. Hence, his poems, like his fence mending, are knots tied around the Hawaiian valleys to better preserve them. Recollecting this obvious point becomes a necessary mantra in an airport, which obliterates any sense of place. In "Last Morning at Punta Arena," Merwin enjoys the first rays of the morning sun as they hit the mountain ridge, but the gradually intensifying color, moving from peach to orange, reminds him of all the landscapes that civilization has burned to ashes. Humans seem to have become the greatest threat to the survival of wild nature, and the "wild dogs," the coyotes who lope away from Merwin at the end of the poem, "all the time looking back over their shoulders," seem to confirm this truth. "Lunar Landscape" is actually a very funny poem, written as if to a jaded consumer for whom moonlight is a simple fact known not from discerning personal experience but from the secondhand filters of culture—in "the words of others" or from photographs or the rhymes of poems. Since it is neither useful nor profitable, Merwin needles, one should ignore the moonlight. Thus, it is "not there," and this leaves the consumer in a quandary over whether he ever really experienced its beauty through firsthand experience. This is Merwin in an Edward Abbey mode, wanting to awaken his readers by irritating them.

"The Hill of Evening," "Barn," and the last six poems of *Travels* concern Merwin's reflections on the people and countryside of the south of France and presage the landscape of *The Vixen* (1996). With a small inheritance from an aunt, Merwin bought a half-ruined farmhouse at Lacan in 1954, before he married Dido Milroy. As the *Vixen* poem "Late" reveals, Merwin once believed this residence to be the ideal place for him. Merwin has written prose memoirs of his life in the south of France and of the rustics and villagers of the area (see "Hotel" in *Unframed Originals* [1982]); he prefers their rural practicality and simple joy in honest agricultural labor to the din of cities and their media culture alienations. But Merwin and Dido separated in the late 1960s, and Dido chose to remain in Lacan and London while Merwin returned to the United States and settled in Hawaii.

The Vixen was written in the years after 1990, when Merwin occasionally returned to Lacan. The poems concern meditations about the value of place and the erosions of time. The autumnal imagery of many of the poems reflect the fact that Merwin is in the autumn of his life and has chosen to place his roots elsewhere. The poems are a palimpsest occasioned by a parallax, an apparent distance in space and time; they reinvestigate memories of past experience in the south of France reviewed in the light of recent visits. What of the sharply individualized neighbors and townsfolk he used to know, all of whom are now dead and cannot see what Merwin now sees of this landscape ("Other Time")? What of the daily rhythms of farm life, the leading out of the cows in the morning ("One Time"), the planting of gardens ("The Furrow"), the mowing of hay, the grafting of trees ("Bodies of Water")? What of Louis the carpenter's dying walnut trees ("Legacies"), what of the oldest man in town, who so reveres his father's blacksmith craft that the name stamped into sickles and knives has inestimable value to him ("Authority")? What happened to Mentieres, whose plum alcohol kept him warm in the World War I trenches ("A Taste"), or Adrienne, whose sausage making was so renowned that she was always in demand at a pig killing ("Thread")? What do the cares and concerns of that time mean to Merwin now? Has distance and time altered their meaning in any final way?

"Fox Sleep," the opening poem of *The Vixen*, functions as an induction that frames the themes of the volume. At the heart of the poem is a fable about an old man who regularly attended the poet's readings, his discourse about "waking." Five hundred lives ago that old man was a poet and was asked the question "When someone has wakened to what is really there / is that person free of the chain of consequences"? He answered "yes" and was changed into a fox. Now the old man asks the question again and, when the Merwin persona offers an epistemological answer, "that person sees it as it is," the old man is relieved of the "body of the fox" and asks the Merwin persona to conduct a burial for the dead fox body.

The "chain of consequences" is, of course, Buddhist karma, the cause-effect ethical debt incurred for temporal actions. The probable source for this portion of "Fox Sleep" is a Zen story recited by D. T. Suzuki to illustrate his discussion of karma:

> When Hyakujo Ekai, one of the most noted Zen masters of the T'ang dynasty, had one day finished his preaching, an old man who regularly attended his sermons came to him and said, "In the days of Kasyapa-Buddha, innumerable *Kalpas* ago, I lived here on this mountain, and one day a student asked me 'Does an enlightened man fall into cause-effect [i.e. moral causation] or not? I answered, 'No,' and for this answer I have lived in the form of a wild fox ever since. Will you give the proper answer that I may be freed from this fox form? Does an enlightened man fall into cause-effect or not?"
>
> The master answered, "He does not ignore cause-effect." The fox man was enlightened and liberated. Next day the master preformed a funeral service for the fox form left behind by the old man.
>
> The meaning of the story is this: The enlightened man allows the law of causation, moral and physical, to take its course, that is, he submits himself to it, he does not sever himself from it, he does not make any distinction between it and himself, he becomes it, he is it. (D.T. Suzuki 1962, 407-8)

Later in this passage Suzuki asserted that a Zen adept would not sever himself from the law and his deeds, so Hyakujo correctly upholds "self-identity," whereas the old man suffered because he was a "dualist" who believed in an "external agent" (408). The poems in *The Vixen* recount Merwin's wrestling with the ethical consequences of his absence from Lacan, its landscape and its people. Merwin refuses the easy dualistic manner of dealing with external causes; he rather brings into his conscience the aspirations, labors, and pain of his friends; he learns to absorb the pain and burn it away by suffering with the people in the act of writing the poems. Instead of dualistic objectification, the best poems of *The Vixen* convey moments of bonding, where the townsfolk's concerns become Merwin's concerns and where he sympathetically relives the natural stresses in climate and landscape from long ago.

An autumnal visit to a disused mill converted into a sort of antique shop precedes the "Fox Sleep" fable of the old man and the poet. There Merwin buys a hand mill, once used for grinding grain and salt, that has figured in its iron handle a fox with his nose in his tail. This uroboros image of renewal also emphasizes the acceptance of suffering as the way out of suffering. Merwin may have freely borrowed millstone symbolism from a Hindu *Panchatantra* story (book 5, fable 3, in the Arthur Ryder translation [1925]) that Joseph Campbell discussed in his *Masks of God: Creative Mythology* (1968, 413-16). Four poor friends are each given a magic quill by the magician Terror-Joy, which will produce treasure when dropped. The first is content to find copper, the second silver, the third gold. The fourth holds out for the best, gems, and wanders until he meets a Bodhisattva in excruciating pain because a whirling wheel has been affixed to his head. When the fourth asks a compassionate question and shows his quill, the Bodhisattva is relieved of his suffering and the millstone becomes affixed to the head of the questioner, the fourth poor Brahmin. The point of the story is that a truly awakened man asks not for personal wealth or the quick liberation of nirvana but accepts the sufferings and burdens of all with whom he comes in contact. As Merwin buys his hand mill, he does much the same. The poems of *The Vixen* record his final acceptance of his past life in France and the sufferings of others. Accepting the suffering means becoming the suffering, denying dualism and closing the *écarts* by refusing to keep cooly distant from his past, by eliminating the temporal distance between past and present, by reliving the burdens and letting their meaning come home to him.

A vixen is, of course, a female fox, a silent, seldom seen, wary, and resourceful creature. She symbolizes nature, who reveals as she conceals and vanishes. In "Oak Time," the second poem of the volume, a fox barks and is gone, while the ivy, which may know the way of resurrection (Graves 1966, 183), primarily functions as time the destroyer. The vixen reintroduces Merwin to the natural world and, more specifically, to his memories, his grasp of a specific time and place. The vixen's presence initiates an intense reassessment of that past, an examination felt so intensely that the poet merges his cenesthetic body and his imaginative sympathies with the referential world in nondualistic ways. At the heart of these poems resides an investigation of exactly what nature means to one who has aged and transplanted his roots into an entirely different locale. "Letters," addressed to an older male friend, reinvestigates the meaning of a friendship made difficult by what had never been possible to say in that relationship. Merwin remembers how empty the friend felt at turning forty and how he habitually associated that emptiness with the dropping of the wind in the bay at Aulis as the Greeks advanced toward Troy, the moment where Iphigeneia is sacrificed to appease the gods and expedite the battle fleet in Aeschylus's *Agamemnon*. As Merwin wrestles with his memories, he remembers how the friend compounded his self-pitying accusations with a maladaptation to nature: a restless, egocentric "vertigo" in the male habitually turned nature into an anthropocentric straw man for pummelling: "you wrote from England / alluding to pastoral scenery as though it / belonged to you." Merwin closes the poem with a gorgeous image of light passing through quince petals; he must become the quince petal accepting the light of his past, absorbing it, but also letting it pass through him without permanent karmic debt. He suffers through the revived memories.

Another flawed incarnation of the vixen resides in the foxy eyes of the vineyard owners engrossed in worrying over their investment as the dry summer withers the grapevines in "Dry Ground." Merwin counters by seeing more. Perception and a reverence for nature lead the poet's imaginative eyes below ground, whereas the vineyard owners care only about their vines and grapes above. Here Merwin expresses faith in sentient-sensible nature's own knowledge. As the dry summer passes, tap roots know exactly what to do: the dry weather that they feel activates their desire for survival. They waken and probe deeper for moisture, just as Merwin probes his past for sustenance.

Most of the poems of *The Vixen* are short, half-page meditations on the intersections or lack thereof of time, place, memory, and mortality. They begin with Merwin's feeling despondent over his inability to connect with his past in Lacan, and progress through a process of winnowing and sorting to finally grasping the root, the essence of what his past at Lacan means to him now. "Gate" presents Merwin with his own illusion of the past, a warm memory of all his friends and the townsfolk he knew gathered together in the autumn light to greet each other and to talk of their experiences, "believing there were other words." But this is a fond illusion, for not only does the past rust in the memory ("Forgotten Streams"), but all of the townsfolk he once knew are now dead ("Other Time").

As Merwin probes deeper, he recognizes that he needs to be honest about that past rather than idealize it. He admits that even as he lived through his life in Lacan, part of his attention, his furrow of consciousness or his Derridean trace (Merleau-Ponty also characterized consciousness as a trace or furrow with a certain negativity impelling it—VI 151; PP 137), was occupied elsewhere ("Completion," "The View")—he was partly "thinking of something different"—so how could he possibly make that past "abide as it was forever" in words ("The Furrow"). He is not so easily freed of the "old chain" of consequences and should not use poetry to evade issues ("Old Walls"). Although he once thought he would like to be buried in the French countryside ("Old Walls"), and considered his life there to be heavenly ("Returning Season"), in fact he left a failed marriage and moved on. He also realizes that his grasp of the life he lived in Lacan has eroded in time, that his memories of that past life are filled with lacunae and absences, and admits that his grasp of events in Lacan is limited to what he feels in the present moment of composition ("Late," "Season").

Along with these meditations on his past in Lacan, Merwin intersperses more philosophical meditations about what can be recovered from separations in place, time, memory, and mortality. "Threshold" asserts a vintage Merwin theme, the recognition of ignorance as a necessary prelude to new knowledge. Merleau-Ponty agrees with Heidegger and Merwin about the necessity of ignorance: "when one speaks . . . of what one does not know . . . . [the words created] most energetically open upon Being, because they more closely convey the life of the whole and make our habitual evidences vibrate until they disjoin" (VI 102). "The West Window" affirms the necessity of the otherness of nature, for knowledge occurs only through a reciprocal interaction with an other that has its own voice, as in Merleau-Ponty, and is not conscripted into a purely anthropocentric design. "Ill Wind," like "Letters," warns not to ascribe human designs and motivations to natural processes, and "The Bird" contains the recognition that humans can only expect to hold what we can of the moment of our reciprocal interaction with nature delicately and uncertainly in that present moment, as in the fragile blossoms that the wind of time blows down in a day, or in the golden, translucent, easily bruised mirabelle plums ("Present"). Merwin's father in "Passing" offers the reverse; preoccupied with currency exchange rates and trains to the Holy Land, he sees nothing of the countryside during his visit to France.

"In the Doorway" renders the moment of perception cenesthetically, as breath, smell, and touch: it is the moment of sensing and being sensed by nature. Merwin recognizes that the sensible/sentient physical body is paramount, for all knowledge is both within us and without, in nature, and necessarily experiences separation or *écart* as the first stage of knowing. States of ordinary consciousness under the *écarts* seem oxymoronic: "the breath of belonging / and being distant," "that smell of abiding / and not staying," and "the smell of touching and not being there." In our normal consciousness we are partly in the present moment of experience, and partly wool gathering or preoccupied with past or future considerations. Yet it is only in the present moment of actual sensuous experience, according to Heidegger, that we can have opportunities to get in touch with Being, to touch the elusive vixen, in "night breeze remembered only / in passing of fox shadow."

In "Untouched" Merwin longs for an instance of what Merleau-Ponty calls "reciprocity." Part of what we can know and part of what we want to know lies hidden in the gaze of others. Their responses to our desires and questionings are a part of what can be known. This theme of friendship as reciprocity, as a guide to self-worth and self-knowledge, is at least as old as Shakespeare's *Sonnets* (Hubler 1952, 129-31), but Merwin gives the theme an environmental twist. Part of what Merwin needs to remember and evaluate about his years in France lies hidden in "the presence of each" of his friends as they inhabit their unique landscape and perform their tasks in inimitable ways. But the reciprocity Merwin desires does not end with recalling friendships. Remembering how Esther would call "the hens at dusk *petit petit*," how Viellescazes often would be "sucking the last joints of a story" and how Edouard would bend "into shadows to pick up walnuts" brings to mind the need for a Proustian *recherche* of the uniqueness and solidity in the passing village culture of France.

Words cannot capture these touches; they can only help us to recollect our memories. But being touched periodically by that other is important. Without it we have no access to the Heideggerian blossoming of Being. What haunts Merwin in "Untouched" is that "something was missing" before he left Lacan—something was not brought to complete realization in the experiences and friendships. For Merleau-Ponty full reciprocity lies in the experience of inhabiting one's world so intensely that the tactile human body and the tactile world overlay like "the two halves of an orange" (VI 133). When does one experience that intense, full touch, so that one is not, as in ordinary consciousness, partly here and not here? Does that fullness ever happen in the moment of the original experience, or only in the Wordsworthian recollection? Merwin ends the poem by noting that in missing these touches he is now untouched and has "left the stream running under the mossy cliff." That stream is probably what flows from the "clear spring of being" in "A Given Day," the final poem of the volume: knowing the "water" of Lacan would be having the full knowledge, the full heft, weight, and gravity of the stories that passed through these places.

In "Romanesque" the persona receives a vision of the creative force that sustains all of living nature. It is located in the stone that rests at the heart of light, in the flesh of the visible. The stone imagery recollects the philosopher's stone, the perfected Self that the alchemists quested for (Jung wrote three volumes on this subject: *Alchemical Studies* [1967], *Psychology and Alchemy* [1968], and *Mysterium Coniunctionis* [1963]) and the *lapis exillis* that sustained the Grail Knights in Wolfram von Eschenbach's *Parzival* (1961, 251). Stone symbolism also derives from Peter's exhortation to the Christians to become "living stones" and build a "spiritual house" in 1 Peter 2:5–7. The cornerstone of that spiritual house was to be a discarded stone: "the stone which the builders disallowed, that same is made the head of the corner." As the persona of "Romanesque" sees everything as stone, he discerns a universal first principle that fuses subjective self and objective nature into one whole, one substance. The stone "mother of us all," with the stone serpent coiled around her thigh, expresses a faith in a universal force of regeneration and productivity akin to the stone statues and wall carvings of Lilith or the pre-Christian Snake Goddess of Old Europe (Gimbutas 1974, 112-51). The stone statue sustains a perpetual smile, fructifying nature at each and every moment. An epiphany of that regenerating power is the subject of "Snake," where Merwin sees a green snake in the sunlight outside the same room at the Lacan house where years ago he found a delicate snake skin "with the day / still moving in it." Scales loosen and fall from the persona's eyes, for he realizes that this power of renewal is the magnet that holds him there and brings him back periodically to this landscape. The snake, nature's emissary, knows him intimately because he is part of the visible flesh of nature.

"One Time" contains a significant realization that foreshadows the thematic resolution of *The Vixen*. Though Merwin as a child did not know about the villages of southern France, he did experience moments when his sensing/sensible body was refreshed by the purity of nature. Once in the rumble seat of a car, while being driven home from the circus, Merwin sat in an adult woman's lap and thought of her as "fragrant, strange and as hard to believe / as Christmas" as he watched her breath fly away into the "cold night" and "naked stars." At that same historical moment on the other side of the Atlantic, the older Merwin hypothesizes, the father of his future neighbor in Lacan must have been taking the cows out "onto / the untouched frost of the lanes" where the "woods furred the ridge." The realization hinted at in the poem is that a particular physical place may not be an absolute; one can experience the power of the vixen, the "mother of us all," at any time and place on this planet. One can transcend time and space if one can close the separations, for nature is the one persistent common denominator of experience.

Like "Kanaloa" in *The Rain in the Trees*, Merwin in "The View" learns that memory is hopeless; it can never recapture the essence of the original experience, for that original experience occurred mostly in ordinary consciousness, when he was partly immersed in the moment and partly elsewhere, under the strictures of the *écarts*, and what he was experiencing was passing and "already gone" as soon as he experienced it. Time moves at the speed of light, just as we experience the solar radiation we call sunlight long after it has left the sun. Relying on memory is a "way of forgetting," for it can never recollect the fleeting, complex moment of originary experience.

In "Completion" Merwin again realizes that ordinary experience is divided by time and the *écarts* of perspectival separation where consciousness is always partly immersed in the experience and partly outside of it. Hence, in nature experience is normally "coming together" and "moving apart," and "home was a knowledge that did not suit every occasion / but remained familiar and foreign." But privileged moments do occur when intense experiences emblason themselves in memory. These are instants when the vixen grants special privileges, when "the fox would bark in the cold night" to herald unitary moments that close the usual separations.

The last dozen or so poems resolve the themes of *The Vixen* in a thoroughly ecological fashion. Here Merwin realizes that the one home he is always coming home to is not an enclosure with four walls but the planet itself and his conscious interaction with it. The constants of sunlight, water, and animals give solidity and unity to his life. Experience is a matter of touching and being touched by the sentient-sensible flesh of the visible, a medium shared by all living creatures. In "Upland House" the sunlight arrives each moment through the boards of the unlocked door, "tracing the way." "Through each of the lives there the one life of sunlight" that moves slowly and silently, but cenesthetically; it moves by "fingering the fireplace," tablecloth, and ceiling cobwebs, but "not taking anything with it." It traces a unitary path through the necessary divisions and separations of time, experience, memory and mortality. The human retina instantly acknowledges that sunlight illuminates all.

Before Merwin saw the south of France, the cyclic round of seasonal labor over the centuries ground the villagers to a dust that obliterated their individuality. In "The Time Before," the unending temporal round of rural life erased the names of the people and the words they spoke. The animals themselves, the denizens of the referential world beyond human consciousness, bear the "Substance" of it, the "weight and place / of the hour as it happened." Cow and trout "were bearing the sense of it"—the meaning of it in their senses and in what they sensed—without the separations of subjectivity.

In "Ancestral Voices" the blackbird, nightingale, and goldfinches sang on this planet "long before the first / of our kind had come to be able to listen." The birds are totally themselves, enduring portions of the flesh of the visible, and they believe in the visible flesh that clothes and sustains them each moment of their lives. Hence "the blackbird came believing in the habit / of the light." In "Distant Morning" Merwin offers a catalogue of animals doing their several things in a supportive ecosystem that is its own meaning. As Thomas Berry once quipped in a talk given at the Unitarian Fellowship in my adoptive hometown of Blacksburg, Virginia (May 5, 1996), nature is the only text without a context; all the meanings provided by humans are comparatively confining, limited by the rules of logic and language and their dependence on the less limited context of nature for their efficacy. In "Distant Morning" the redstart, kite, weasel, wryneck, owl, nuthatch, adder, cricket, nightwalkers, hedgehogs, badgers, foxes, and bats live "in their home ground," the one real home for us all. This home survives its momentary incidents, and it cannot be encompassed by the interpositions of human logic: "none of it could be held or denied or summoned back / none of it would be given its meaning later." Existence and meaning inhere in the moment of observation and action, without the need for human logic to grant meaning. This moment of *référance* points us back to the less limited natural world that is our true home.

Collecting rainwater in cisterns is a sound practice of sustainable living but a lost art today. In "The Cisterns" Merwin presents water as part of the substance of the natural world, the most durable and necessary ingredient for growth next to sunlight, and an element that shows the way by cleansing itself regularly in the hydrological cycle. A patient, yielding, unassertive acceptor of experience in Lao-tzu (Waley 1958, 151, 217, 238), water was the ground of Being for the presocratic Thales, and for Merwin it is "the one still continuo" that underlies all and remembers all voices. Once again, the referential world is primary and the human voices that the water absorbs secondary. In "Bodies of Water" humans embody their aspirations in their projects in the referential world. The stone masons are remembered by their basins and cisterns, and the old man by his grafted walnut trees that give him "something to look forward to." In the stone basin Merwin sees the faces of masons who have embodied their worth in their work in the referential world. Patient and yielding to simple tasks, the water reflects the "speechless daylight" and embodies a stillness and a depth, an unmovable solidity of place whose silence reflects the worth of those who toiled on the land.

The more Merwin meditates on constants in the referential world such as sunlight and water, the more he sees the house in Lacan as part of an almost primordial landscape. By the time Merwin first saw that house, it "had stood / empty for half a lifetime and been abandoned." Many generations of villagers had peered out its windows and built fires in its corners. But seeing nature recover it by shrouding it in brambles and ivy, by taking its own back so to speak, gives Merwin a changed perspective that he did not have while living inside its walls. The walls begin to crumble in his perceptions just as nature assists in the deterioration of "broken limestone" and the "faded mortar containing the rusted earth / of the place itself." "Green Fields," the next poem, continues the process of obliterating walls. Merwin's English friend Peter, a veteran of the Great War, comes to live in the south of France because he still believes in heaven and believes this landscape to be an "earthly / model of it." Like Stevens's poem on the last hours of Santayana, "To an Old Philosopher in Rome," Merwin ends his poem with Peter in a retirement home seeing the walls of his room vanish each day as he views once again the green field he and his mother had planted when he was a child. Peter's most persistent vision of heaven is not an enclosure but an open landscape of green fields.

In "A Given Day," the final poem of *The Vixen*, Merwin finally recognizes that home is not a physical enclosure in Lacan or Maui but his moment-by-moment adherence to the physical world, guided by the cynosure of family, friends, and the endurance of animals. Part of his feeling of wholeness and permanence is "the eyes of the animals upon me," the reciprocal gaze of a portion of the sensible/sentient flesh of the world. It is autumn again, but now the veteran poet in Merwin knows the natural way to content himself with "the flowers of winter." Now he affirms that "I am home," and home is not a four-walled physical dwelling but a mode of perception, his periodic experience of "the first light" of morning in the referential world, "the gradual sweetness of morning / the clear spring of being here as it rises one by one / in silence and without a pause." As discussed in chapter 2, Merleau-Ponty's phenomenology (VI 165-71) can elucidate the import of these moments of silence in ecopoets. Here Merwin experiences a deeply moving moment of grounding in Being, a silent blossoming of the source at the heart of the perceptual world, and a sense of its infinite plenitude and potential, that Merleau-Ponty would have no difficulty comprehending: "this perceptual world is at bottom Being in Heidegger's sense, which is more than all painting, than all speech, than every 'attitude,' and containing everything that will ever be said, and yet leaving us to create it" (VI 170).

Merwin finds comfort in locating stability and solidity in the visible flesh of the referential world, a home available to him anywhere on this planet. The cause of his joy is really a reinvigoration of what nature means to him. Hence, it is fitting that Merwin leaves the title poem for the penultimate poem in the volume, as part of the distillation of his meditations on time, place, and mortality. It is an invocation to nature, the vixen or mysterious other that conceals as she reveals. When she comes close and the poet catches a momentary glimpse, the *écarts* of separation close and he has "waked and slipped from the calendars." Merwin passionately wants his words to find their appropriate "places" in the history of encounters with Being, but all the while he recognizes that the vixen resides in an "aura of complete darkness." She is the "keeper of the kept secrets" and the source of *référance*, "the sentences / never caught in words." She exists in the less limited referential world that will forever supercede human concepts, logic, and discourse.

In the 1991 Discovery Channel video, Merwin replied to the question of what effect would you like your poetry to have on your readers with the statement that "I would like it to make them feel that it had helped them to come awake to something and, having wakened, that they stayed awake" (Alexander). To become awake, a frequent term in Merwin's recent poetry, is in Zen Buddhism to achieve the state of enlightenment, of *bodhi*, to abandon dualistic, rational thinking, material possessions, and the selfish subjective ego, in order to see the self as part of the totality of creation, as undivided is-ness (D.T. Suzuki 1962, 71-94). The Buddhist words *bodhi* and *Buddha*, D.T. Suzuki reminds us, both derive from the Sanskrit root *budh*, "to wake" (71). The *Katha Upanishad* (4:15) likens that undivided state of enlightenment is-ness to "pure water poured forth into pure" water, which "becomes the very same" (Hume 1931, 355; D.T. Suzuki 1962, 86). This adds to the import of Merwin's second way of "Writing Lives" in *Travels*, the way "when there is no distance / so that water / is looking at water." The true guides to writing lives are those, like Rumphius, Douglas, Bartram, Henderson, and Bondar, who bonded their cenesthetic bodies to the referential world so that water is indeed looking at water.

Of course, Merwin does not expect to convert his readers to Zen

Buddhist philosophy, nor can he hope to achieve with any regularity moments when his mind is not divided into the *écarts* of heres and elsewheres. Yet his ecological phenomenology of perception offers masterful personal testament to his capacity to immerse his wakened body in the living fabric of nature. In that Discovery Channel video, Merwin asserts that his "emotional involvement" in the "green world . . . gets stronger as I get older." Wendell Berry, in *Standing by Words*, wrote the most eloquent prose defence of the language of referentiality. But Merwin, by conveying a riveting sense of our cenesthetic body's moment-to-moment involvement in the referential world, is the most eloquent poetic craftsman of *référance*. His "poetics of absence" has flowered into an ecological poetics of wakefulness.

6

Wild Nature and Joyful Interpenetration

Gary Snyder

(What's this talk about not understanding!
you're just a person who refuses to see.)
. . . .
See or go blind!

Snyder, Myths & Texts, 48, 21

In chapter 2 of *The Spell of the Sensuous*, David Abram summarizes the development of phenomenology from Husserl to Merleau-Ponty. According to Abram, Husserl's focus on perception was at least in part his attempt to return scientific inquiry to "the forgotten ground of our directly felt and lived experience" (1996, 43). Husserl countered the charge of solipsism by positing that "the subjective field of experience, mediated by the body, opens onto other subjectivities" (37). Perceived phenomena are intersubjective, "experienced by a multiplicity of sensing subjects" (38). For Husserl, the "real world" or the intersubjective world, is the *Lebenswelt*, the "life-world" of "our immediately lived experience," an "intertwined matrix of sensations and perceptions, a collective field of experiences lived through from many different angles" (39-40).

Merleau-Ponty develops Husserl's thoughts on intersubjectivity and the *Lebenswelt.* He argues that the sensing body is constantly involved in a reciprocal interchange between itself and the entities that surround it. Neither self nor the visible world is passive, as in the Cartesian paradigm, for sensible things are alive in the moment of perception. According to Abram, "Merleau-Ponty writes of the perceived things as entities, of sensible qualities as powers, and of the sensible itself as a field of animate presences, in order to acknowledge and underscore their active, dynamic contribution to perceptual experience. To describe the animate life of particular things is simply the most precise and parsimonious way to articulate the things *as we spontaneously experience them,* prior to our conceptualizations and definitions" (56). Thus, Abram understands that for Merleau-Ponty "perception always involves, at its most intimate level, the experience of an active interplay, or coupling, between the perceiving body and that which it perceives" (57).

Gary Snyder believes that the real work of poetry is not only "the work of social change," but also the work of reconfiguring our perceptions. His goal is to awaken us to our participation in the energy exchanges that bond all living matter in our ecological *Lebenswelt.* In a 1976 interview, he declared that "the work of poetry . . . . has to do with bringing us back to our original, true natures from whatever habit-molds that our perceptions, that our thinking and feeling get formed into. And bringing us back to original true mind, seeing the universe freshly in eternity, yet any moment" (RW 72).

Of the four ecopoets discussed in this volume, Gary Snyder throughout his lengthy career best expresses the "active interplay" of the lived body in contact with the sensible/sentient environment. Especially in his poetry Snyder consistently conveys a sense of the free-flowing, joyous play of energy and desire in the ordinary quotidian world, whether he is laboring at Kitkitdizze, his hand-built home in the San Juan Ridge area of California, conversing with neighbors or traveling companions, or appreciating nature while hiking or camping. In his many essays, Snyder extends his commitment to the physical world through his tireless championing of a bioregional ethic that contains an activist component. Snyder's work evinces a rich and coherent combination of influences from his working class roots to his Forest Service work, his apprenticeship in Zen Buddhism, his study of the cultural anthropology of indigenous peoples, and his readings in the science of ecology. All are available in his poems during active play of energy and desire in the moment of perception as Snyder's consciousness immerses itself in the sensible/sentient ecology of nature.

In the "Plain Talk" prose section of *Turtle Island* (1974), his Pulitzer Prize–winning poetry collection, Snyder includes a short essay with a title quote from Blake's *Marriage of Heaven and Hell:* "Energy is Eternal Delight." Delight in the energy that interpenetrates all living matter has been Snyder's persistent theme, a theme that denies Cartesian dualism and emerges most formidably in the present moment of perception. As the "Plain Talk" essays of *Turtle Island* reveal, Snyder's readings from the ecologists Eugene and H.T. Odum on biomass information storage and on energy transfers within ecosystems (104, 107-8) combine with his allegiance to the Kegon school of Zen Buddhism, and his commitment to the *Avatamsaka Sutra* (Yamazato 1991, 232), to produce a poetics where "wild nature" or "the wilderness outside" fuses with "the wilderness within" the mind of the poet (106) and where the practice of poetry leads to ethical commitments to nonhuman nature and a bioregional ethic.

Snyder studied Zen for ten years in Japan, including six years of formal Zen training, through most of the late fifties and sixties, with one stint under the direction of the Rinzai Zen master Oda Sesso Roshi at the Daitoku-ji Temple, Kyoto (Murphy 1992, 6–8.) The plain-talking Snyder believes that "at the root of the problem where our civilization goes wrong is the mistaken belief that nature is something less than authentic, that nature is not as alive as man is, or as intelligent, that in a sense it is dead, and that animals are of so low an order of intelligence and feeling, we need not take their feelings into account" (107). By considering Snyder's "Plain Talk" meditation on Eugene Odum's use of "biomass," we can recognize the depth of his ecological poetics: "Life-biomass, [Odum] says, is stored information; living matter is stored information in the cells and in the genes. He believes there is more information of a higher order of sophistication and complexity stored in a few square yards of forest than there is in all the libraries of mankind. Obviously, that is a different order of information. It is the information that has been flowing for millions of years. In this total information context, man may not be necessarily the highest or most interesting product" (107-8).

In his prose diary *Earth House Hold* (1969), Snyder discusses the ecological interconnectedness of Indra's net in the *Avatamsaka Sutra* (129). He conflates this ecology of energy interpenetration with Indra's net in his 1977 essay collection *The Old Ways* to suggest how a sense of place "out there" and one's subjective self "in here" can achieve unity:

> The biological-ecological sciences have been laying out (implicitly) a spiritual dimension. We must find our way to seeing the mineral cycles, the water cycles, air cycles, nutrient cycles, as sacramental—and we must incorporate that insight into our

own personal spiritual quest and integrate it with all the wisdom teachings we have received from the nearer past. The expression of it is simple: gratitude to all, taking responsibility for your own acts; keeping contact with the sources of the energy that flow into your own life (i.e. dirt, water, flesh).

Another question is raised: Is not the purpose of all this living and studying the achievement of self-knowledge, self-realization? How does knowledge of place help us know the Self? The answer, simply put, is that we are all composite beings, not only physically but intellectually, whose sole individual identifying feature is a particular form or structure changing constantly in time. There is no "self" to be found in that, and yet oddly enough, there is. Part of you is out there waiting to come into you, and another part of you is behind you, and the "just this" of the ever-present moment holds all the transitory little selves in its mirror. The Avatamsaka ("Flower Wreath") jeweled-net-interpenetration-ecological-systems-emptiness-consciousness tells us, no self-realization without the Whole Self, and the whole self is the whole thing. (63-64)

Interpenetration is the main theme of the *Avatamsaka Sutra*, where Indra's net, with a gemstone on each of its knots, endlessly reflects all the facets of the world as they interanimate each other (Yamazato 1991, 232).

Snyder's early poetry often expresses delight in the ordinary and the interpenetration of all reality with the energy of life, even though it may at first appear stern and austere in its championing of disciplined labor, both physical and intellectual, and sweeping, if not dismissive, in its critique of American expansionism and the Puritan ethic. Snyder's own 1965 interview comments, recollected in part in *The Real Work*, and his afterword to the 1990 edition of *Riprap and Cold Mountain Poems* (1965), provide the best glosses on the early poetry. In 1965, Snyder discussed the background to "Milton by Firelight" by contrasting book knowledge with his direct experience of very strenuous daytime labor for weeks on end developing trails at Yosemite Park. Only when Snyder jettisons his attempt to carry on separate, purely intellectual university-type self-colloquies with Milton and other readings and trusts to direct experience to weave mind and body together does he remove the frustration. What he gains is integral to his early poetics—the technique of juxtaposing outdated or ineffective intellectual knowledge and inherited cultural myths with the *référance* of joyous immersion in direct experience: "Finally, I gave up trying to carry on an intellectual interior life separate from the work, and I said the hell with it, I'll just work. And instead of losing something, I got something much greater. By just working, I found myself being completely there, having the whole mountain inside of me, and finally having a whole language inside of me that became one with the rocks and with the trees. And that was where I first learned the possibility of being one with what you were doing, and not losing anything of the mind thereby" (RW 8).

Other poems in *Riprap and Cold Mountain Poems* valorize direct experience over bookish cerebration. In "Riprap," Snyder's first announcement of his poetics in a poem, words must mesh with a sense of place and be the fruit of physical and mental labor accomplished by the poet, not inherited or read from a book. The words of a poem must be "placed solid" in "space and time" by actual "hands / In choice of place." And this activity must happen in consort with the referential reality of nature, where changes are as complex and inevitable as an "endless / four-dimensional" Chinese game of Go. In his afterword to the 1990 edition, Snyder wrote that the title poem "celebrates the work of hands, the placing of rock, and my first glimpse of the image of the whole universe as interconnected, interpenetrating, mutually reflecting, and mutually embracing" (65-66). Similarly, the mere words on the page, the finished poem, are less important than the referential reality of having to repaint a wall in "Goofing Again." Both "Water" and "Thin Ice" lead the reader away from words toward a quick drop into cold water. In "Migration of Birds" Snyder stops studying when the arrival of spring distracts him with the whir of a hummingbird and the yellow flowers entangling a redwood post. "That big abstraction's at our door" may not simply refer to the depiction of Kerouac and Snyder reading about life through books in the poem but also that big abstraction, spring, which begins on a calendar date for most, but not for Snyder, who dates the poem "April 1956." Spring arrives when the birds and flowers return, not when an abstraction on a calendar says so.

The most haunting lines in Snyder's early poetry, from "Piute Creek," seem to suggest Merleau-Ponty's doctrine of reciprocity, that the activity of perception is an active engagement of both the perceiver and nature. Thus, "A clear, attentive mind / Has no meaning but that / Which sees is truly seen." Most critics focus on the Zen enlightenment of the "clear attentive mind," but one possible explication of the "what which sees" is the human eyeball. Then comes the odd passive-voice construction of "is truly seen." Seen by whom? By other orders of sentient/sensible nature. This thrusts us forward to the poem's conclusion, the "Cold proud eyes / Of Cougar or Coyote" that watch the poet's every move. Nonhuman sentient/sensible nature has eyes that probe; he is seen by other eyes that are as alive as the human eye. At the very least, this indicates that Merleau-Ponty's phenomenology is consonant with the nondualism of Zen Buddhism and the animated world of the Native American myths that Snyder prefers to the Protestant ethic capitalism of white interlopers. "Nooksack Valley" offers a perfect moment of *référance* as Snyder prepares himself for his first trip to Japan. Here he confesses that he is more "Awake" and "Caught more on this land" than ever. To prepare himself for his Zen apprenticeship, he must rid his mind of the "damned memories, / Whole wasted theories, failures and worse success" that keep trying to infect his poetry. The disciplined ascetic perception in the *Cold Mountain* section indicates considerable progress in writing a poetry that is more purely attentive to referential reality.

The modernist structural juxtapositions of *Myths & Texts* (1960) consistently suggest that if the direct perception of nature in the present moment yields instance after instance of ecological disaster, then something must be wrong with America's progress myth, which incorporates none of the environmental degradation. If we perceive nature through the dim spectacles of this progress myth, we repress the degradation. The cryptic lines of "Burning 13" suggest this: "(What's this talk about not understanding! / you're just a person who refuses to see.)." Snyder presents many episodes of the wanton killing of birds and deer and the clear cutting and burning of forests in the volume, and suggests with pithy quotations from Exodus (34:13) and the Acts of the Apostles (19:27) that part of the problem in Western perception derives from adhering to inherited cultural myths. This habituation has become more questionable than ever now, for the practices that derive from these myths are wrecking the planet. In the two biblical quotes Snyder juxtaposes ancient Judaic and Christian admonitions to destroy the groves and temples of animistic, nature-worshiping cultures with the inherently more reverential and nonwasteful treatments of nature in those maligned cultures.

In contrast to those unable to revise their perceptions, the Snyder persona in the early poems delights in venturing beyond the mind-forged manacles, the narrowly rational sight of Blake's "Single vision & Newtons sleep" (722). Sherman Paul, in his excellent essay on Snyder's early work, believes that the true revolutionary is one who is able, as Snyder wrote in an early journal, "to look within and adjust the mechanism of perception" (1970, 62). When the Snyder persona looks within, his contrasting sight offers alternatives to Western progress myths. The Kwakiutl horn spoon ritual of "Hunting 5" shows a reverence and respect for the dead animal and the recycling of all body parts, and "Hunting 8" opens with a mythic song that emphasizes the sacredness of the deer. Snyder then juxtaposes this with the second half of "Hunting 8," where a drunken redneck shoots a deer that has been momentarily blinded by his headlights. This ironically echoes the message from the swifts in "Hunting 3"—"See or go blind!" We must reperceive our mythic heritage in the light of our direct experience of nature. The bulldozers and Cats of other poems are problematic technological extensions of a people raised in a culture that can "Believe in god, but can't / Believe their own senses" ("Logging 15").

Many of the poems of *The Back Country* (1968) present what Snyder in *Earth House Hold* called the "joyous and voluntary poverty of Buddhism" (91). *Back Country* poems such as "Yase: September," "Work to Do Toward Town," and most of the sections of "Six Years" present Snyder's experiences in a Zen monastery and in Japanese villages during his periods of voluntary training in the 1960s as a deeply satisfying housecleaning of the mind and perception. But often dissonance occurs in other poems, such as "Mt. Hiei," "Out West," "This Tokyo," "Vapor Trails," "The Public Bath," and "A Volcano in Kyushu," for Snyder cannot help but note the atrocities at Hiroshima and Nagasaki during World War II and the ongoing human and ecological carnage of the Vietnam War, nor can he fail to note how his idealized vision of monastic serenity in Japan often does not correspond with the postwar capitalism, Americanization, and industrialism in its major cities during this period. At times Snyder experiences self-doubts over his choice of monastic life, increased loneliness and separation from family, anguish over the poverty and malnutrition he witnessed on a trip to India, and long periods without a steady female companion. As Patrick Murphy has shown, the four sections of *Back Country*, very deliberately arranged by Snyder, follow an archetypal quest motif of "separation, initiation, and return," with increased Buddhist enlightenment (1992, 75-89). At least a partial resolution of many of the dissonances of the psychic underworld created in the volume occurs in the final section, with its emphasis on being grounded in place ("Through the Smoke Hole"), in cultural practice, and in the wild plenty ("Oysters") of the ever-giving earth.

Few instances of self-reflexive *référance* occur in these poems, but, as Altieri has shown in an excellent discussion of *Back Country*, Snyder seems more intent on expanding the referential reach of his style by using participles divorced from human referents and parataxis to create a sense of actions and objects existing independent of subjective consciousness. The preponderance of concrete details in these poems suggests a deliberateness to Altieri: "so much pointing asserts the referential power of language" (1970, 51). Altieri's main point is that a dialectic of balances characterizes Snyder's 1960s style: he expands his vision outward toward the reaches of the cosmos at the same time that he deepens his inward grasp, indicating how one generates meaning by participating in nature's cycles. One sees this especially in the "Far West," the opening section of *Back Country*, in Snyder's meshing of his saw sharpening and the swallows that flit in and out of his shed in "Sixth-Month Song in the Foothills" and in the expansion of space to encompass the stars in "Burning the Small Dead." Altieri is especially sharp in noticing how Snyder in such poems balances humanized space with a referential emphasis on nonhuman ecology (48-58).

The essence of philosophy for Merleau-Ponty is an interrogation by the psychophysical body (VI 168) of the preobjective, prereflective "wild being" that contains our bodies and our minds (VI 13). It is a "reconquest of brute or wild being" where "the words most charged with philosophy" are those "that most energetically open upon Being" (VI 102). We interrogate the world through vision, which is first and foremost a recognition of the invisible flesh of this world, "that which inhabits this world, sustains it, and renders it visible" (VI 151-153). From Snyder's *Regarding Wave* (1970) forward, his joyous recognition of the satisfactions of the present moment lived fully convey more than just a sense of the interanimating energy transfers of ecological perception; they open out to a genuine philosophical interrogation of this palpable but invisible flesh. The volume not only celebrates his marriage to Masa Uehara (as in the epithalamion "Burning Island"), his pleasurable sexual encounters with her, and the birth and infancy of his sons Gen and Kai but also celebrates the stuff of life, wild being, the fullness and plenitude of the preobjective, prereflective referential world. Consider the vibrant dance of intelligent living beings within the Whitmanesque catalogue of "All the Spirit Powers went to their Dancing Place":

> Wild beings sweeping on cities—spirits and ghosts—
> cougar, eagle, grizzly bear, coyote, hummingbird
> intelligences
> directing destructing instructing; us all
> as through music:
> songs filling the sky.
> (62)

Or the interanimating dance of life-sustaining water, "Flowing free ! / With you / in me" in "Running Water Music II." Or the eating of the deer, which brings deer energy into Snyder's hair, in "Long Hair." Snyder passionately desires to connect language with wild nature; in "The Wild Edge" the "two steel spring-up prongs" that hold paper on his Hermes typewriter become the wings of a gull, and his words and vision sail mercurially out the window, inhabiting the referential world of cliffs, parking lots, and gravel, in a fine moment of *référance*, until his infant son's cry breaks his moment of green connectedness. But all babies, Snyder avers in "Kyoto Born in Spring Again," are "wild babies," nature's pure emanations or energy transfers, the "dance of Vajra power." Snyder revels in pointing out to his readers again and again that there are no voids or dualistic splits in experience; like primordial Play-doh, the stuff of life is a fluid texture that keeps changing shapes and contexts, moving outside as well as inside our skin. Snyder would hasten to say that life is also in the skin itself—there is no line of demarcation between inside and outside. The concept of wild nature, as we shall see later in this chapter, will play a most important part in Snyder's essays and poetry.

Thus, it is no wonder that in *Regarding Wave* Snyder, like Yeats before him, finds in coitus the most adequate symbol of our interconnectedness to the world. Murphy and others have developed Snyder's comments in "The Voice as a Girl" section of *Earth House Hold* (123-26) that pertain to the writing of poetry as a sacramental experience of the Goddess Vak or Sarasvati as lover and creative energy of Brahma in Indian tradition (*Understanding* 97-98). This relates of course to Snyder's celebration of his deep union with Masa and his explicit allusion in this section of *Earth House Hold* to the title of *Regarding Wave*: "As Vak is wife to Brahma ('wife' means 'wave' means 'vibrator' in Indo-European etymology) so the voice, in every one, is a mirror of his own deepest self. The voice rises to answer an inner need" (125). But Snyder layers his essay and the poetry of *Regarding Wave* with other phenomenological levels. In the very next paragraph in his essay, Snyder links the conch shell (and, implicitly, the nautilus shell in the cover photo of *Earth House Hold*), and ancient engravings of animals licking abstract penises and vulvas, with "the mystery of voice becom[ing] one with the mystery of body." Here Snyder does not mean just male and female human bodies but all bodies in the flesh of the world. The opening paragraphs of "The Voice as a Girl" focus on the tribal religious perception of the oneness of the phenomenal world. The animistic perspectives of tribal cultures are for Snyder

a pure perception of beauty. The phenomenal world experi-
enced at certain pitches is totally living, exciting, mysterious,
filling one with a trembling awe, leaving one grateful and
humble. The wonder of the mystery returns direct to one's
own senses and consciousness: inside and outside; the voice
breathes, "Ah!"

Breath is the outer world coming into one's body. With
pulse—the two always harmonizing—the source of our inward
sense of rhythm. Breath is spirit, "inspiration." Expiration,
"voiced," makes the signals by which the species connects. (123)

Snyder is here suggesting what, according to Robert Hume, is the
primal experience of the *Upanishads*—the moment when inner and outer
space become one, when inspiration and expiration unite to banish dual-
isms and create the realistic monism of Indian thought, the moment when
Ātman or the inner self unites with the *Brahma* of "all space" to produce the
unity of being of Brahma worship (Hume 1931, 42-52). In this moment,
states Hume, "individuality and all distinctions are overcome" (52). In
Brahma we find a perception kindred to Merleau-Ponty's flesh of the vis-
ible, with Snyder's poetry implicitly confirming both.

"The body is a thing among things," it is "*of them*," a portion of the
visible, according to Merleau-Ponty (VI 137). When "the seer is caught up
in what he sees," one experiences "this strange adhesion of the seer and the
visible" (VI 139), "when a certain visible, a certain tangible, turns back
upon the whole of the visible, the whole of the tangible, of which it is a
part, or when suddenly it finds itself *surrounded* by them" (VI 139). At
such moments, Merleau-Ponty suggests, we feel "a quality pregnant with a
texture, the surface of a depth, a cross section upon a massive being, a grain
or corpuscle borne by a wave of Being" (VI 136). When we experience our
entanglement within the visible, that texture is sometimes experienced by
our perception as a "folding back, invagination, or padding" within the
perceptual field (VI 152).

Snyder conveys the joyous, nondualistic, Brahmanic entanglement
of his body within the visible through unabashed sexual imagery in many
of the most memorable poems of *Regarding Wave*. The grain of things in
"Wave," the opening poem, is a textured layering caused by the pulsations
of energy in all living things. The grooves on a clam shell, the depth of
growth rings of trees when exposed by rip-cutting, the layerings in cooled
lava flows, the waves of sand dunes, forkings in a bird's foot—all are evi-

dence of a depth in the plenum. Vision folds back from the background of "sawtooth ranges" to the foregrounded intricacies of "veins on the back of the hand" to prove that we are in it and of it. The texture or "dancing grain of things" excites Snyder's ecstatic vision throughout the poem.

The sexuality of "Song of the Tangle" and "Song of the Slip" is so overt that it perhaps at first overpowers imagery that relates to the "folds" of "the whole," the tactile stuff of the visible, the little-noticed underbrush that we brush up against, "through which we push." Glacier Peak visions occur within the visible; we push "through" the "banks and windings" of the visible flesh of the world at every stage of the journey ("For Jack Spicer"). Hence, we know that exalted vision is possible when the referential route opens, when the ice melts and bark chips from the path above wash down. Even when Snyder celebrates the vagina, it is with an emphasis on the space it holds within it, the potency for new life that made it one of Lao-tzu's favorite symbols for the Tao, the Nameless, the Valley Spirit or Mysterious Female from which all created matter emanates (Waley 1958, 149, 174, 178, 206):

O!   cunt

that which you suck in-
      to yourself, that you
         hold
     there,

hover over,
excellent emptiness your
     whole flesh is wrappt around
(16)

Similarly, the explicit sexual imagery of "Seed Pods" controls a series of analogies that emphasize the nondualistic bonding of matter in the visible world. The poem opens with the line "Seed pods seen inside while high." Snyder may be suggesting a synaesthesia induced by drugs, but the "seen inside" suggests the kind of perception that we saw in Merwin's "Sight" and "The Biology of Art," which in Merleau-Ponty is characteristic of a realization of the texture of the world's "durable flesh" (VI 122-23). The "sticky fluid" of sex is like "cyprus resin" and the seed released adheres like the seeds of plants in the fur of animals (or the fertilized egg to the uterine wall). Snyder implicates the reader in the adherence of the visible by suggesting that the words of his poem are his seed that will "float into you." The entire poem argues against dualisms and for the participation of all beings who are "of" the visible. The ova of women are

moons
later let it be
    come—
  staind
on their soil ledge tilth
    fucking bed.
(44)

In other less overtly sexual poems in *Regarding Wave*, Snyder also celebrates his entanglement in the whole web of life in sharply visual and tactile imagery. In "Song of the Cloud" he experiences clouds as if from the inside, as being one with them, and rejoices at the slow buildup of mass, voluminousness, as masses group and "pile up, pile up, our deep-mounting / pleasure in our richness." Snyder celebrates friends and poets feasting on grilled squid and cups of shochu in "By the Tama River at the North End of the Plain in April." What makes this poem intriguing is Snyder's focus on what is simultaneously happening across the river. Trucks are loading gravel that was just sorted from river stones by a screen drum. Snyder symbolically links these "smooth round stones" with the philosopher's stone, the *lapis* or completed Self; hence the poets and friends gathered are examples of completely developed, whole Selfs. But at the same time the stones remain an important part of his tactile and visual memories of the event. The referential stones remain part of the nonhuman nature that forms the ground of our experience at the end of the poem.

When fishermen catch a shark in their nets and share portions of the big catch with other islanders, Snyder in "Shark Meat" muses on both energy transfers and the wholeness of life on this globe that the shark on his many journeys has encircled before giving humans his flesh. Snyder persistently sees the grim realities of the food chain as a joyous transfer of energy from body to body. As the entire island eats the flesh at noon, Snyder ends the poem by blessing the shark for "re-crossing his own paths / to tangle our net / to be part of / this loom." In *A Place in Space* (1995, 38, 70-72, 76-77, 186) Snyder often meditates on the interchange of energy in the food chain as a sacramental sharing where the sole crime is waste:

Everything that lives eats food and is food in turn. This compli-
cated animal, the human being, rests on a vast and delicate pyra-
mid of energy transformations. To grossly use more than you
need, to destroy, is biologically unsound. (38)

. . . . .

A key transaction in natural systems is energy exchange, which
includes the food chains and the food webs, and this means
that many living beings live by eating other beings. Our bod-
ies—or the energy they represent—are thus continually being
passed around. We are all guests at the feast, and we are also the
meal! All of biological nature can be seen as an enormous *puja*,
a ceremony of offering and sharing. (76-77).

The poems of *Turtle Island* (1974) are just as openly engaged in a
joyous celebration of the senses and the energy transfers among all the
interdependent living beings on planet earth. The dancing curves of naked
women in "Charms" evoke "the Delight / at the heart of creation." Snyder
observes in "By Frazier Creek Falls" that "we are" the "living flowing land"
that "sings through us" without dualistic separations. In the "Plain Talk"
section he is quick to note that his ecological Buddhism has no place for
Cartesian dualism, for the poet is engaged in perceiving "the delight of
being alive":

Delight is the innocent joy arising
with the perception and realization of
the wonderful, empty, intricate,
inter-penetrating,
mutually-embracing, shining
single world beyond all discrimination
or opposites.
(113)

Even past loves and children are "twinning and knotting / through
each other" in "On San Gabriel Ridges." In "It Pleases," the intricate "Earth-
sky-bird patterns / idly interlacing" do what they please above the idle D.C.
Capitol dome and its bureaucracies. Snyder's vision merges with "A whoosh
of birds" to create "one swift // empty / dancing mind" in "Straight-Creek—

Great Burn." He regularly delights at perceiving the oneness of creative energy animating created matter, knitting the human with the nonhuman.

The "snake center / fire" of Tantra Yoga pushes the energy of creation from Snyder's son Kai's buttocks through his mouth to his eye—the third eye of transphenomenal wisdom in Mahayana wisdom (D.T. Suzuki 1992, 396, 400), in "The Egg." Here language is the end product of information energy stored in the root—the genes in the fertilized egg that flowered into Kai:

> Kai's hand
> in my fist
> the neck bones,
> a little thread,
> a garland,
> of consonants and vowels
> from the third eye
> through the body's flowers
> a string of peaks,
> a whirlpool
> sucking to the root.
>
> It all gathers,
> humming,
> in the egg.
> (37-38)

Here, as in "What Steps," all things move in and out of creation, "the Mother," stepping obediently "to the power within."

"Night Herons" conveys Snyder's joyous immersion in creation when his perceptions locate affinities between the birds that nest in the stationary boilers of San Francisco's water plant and his own tough survival skills. While fishing at the water's edge, Snyder is surprised and intrigued by the presence of these birds nesting within city limits. He first wonders why would herons return like him to San Francisco to fish in "this noisy place on the bay." He answers his question by affirming the toughness, the parallel survival adaptations, of all living matter: "the joy of all the beings / is in being / older and tougher and eaten / up."

The finest celebration of life in *Turtle Island* is, of course, "The Bath," where Snyder and his wife enter naked into their sauna to wash their young son Kai. The refrain "*is this our body?*" becomes an affirmative "*this is our body*" for the first time when Snyder contemplates his son's genitals and notes the energy paths that unite them and that led to his son's conception:

> Kai's little scrotum up close to his groin,
>   the seed still tucked away, that moved from us to him
> In flows that lifted with the same joys forces
>   as his nursing Masa later,
>   playing with her breast,
> Or me within her,
> Or him emerging,
>   *this is our body*
> (13)

This energy creates the "veins net flow across the ribs" that in Masa "peaks up in a nipple" in the previous stanza. This creative flow opposes the logging and the land developments that create "rot at the heart / In the sick fat veins of Amerika" in "Front Lines."

In "Toward Climax" Snyder meditates on the climax and food web theories used by the Spanish ecologist Ramon Margalef. Snyder muses that the "nets" of science have "many knots." The "skin is border-guard" while "detritus pathways" are "'delayed and complex ways / to pass the food through webs.'" Margalef notes that an ecosystem is most stable in the "climax" or "final stage of succession, when the ecosystem is in equilibrium with the existing supply of species and the properties of the local environment" (1968, 32). When each ecological niche remains filled, the ecosystem gains self-regulating strength; when some of the living members of an ecosystem are destroyed, the simpler ecosystem weakens. Similarly, though some energy is lost in feeding along the food chain, ecosystems often develop negative or stabilizing food webs, with a portion of the lost energy recovered as survival information ("General Concepts" 664 ff.; Margalef 1968, 5). In *The Real Work*, Snyder explains Margalef's reasoning in ways that mesh the Zen Buddhist doctrine of Enlightenment with his proclivity for perceiving nondualistic energy webs, in a series of homologies that Ammons would love. The following excerpt is long, but its length captures the syncretic sweep of Snyder's thought, his proclivity for direct experience where inner and outer labor mesh, and his delight in the recycling of energy:

The communities of creatures in forests, ponds, oceans, or grass-lands seem to tend toward a condition called climax, "virgin forest"—many species, old bones, lots of rotten leaves, complex energy pathways, woodpeckers living in snags, and conies har-vesting tiny piles of grass. This condition has considerable sta-bility and holds much energy in its web—energy that in simpler systems (a field of weeds after a bulldozer) is lost back into the sky or down the drain. All of evolution may have been as much shaped by this pull towards climax as it has by simple competi-tion between individuals or species . . . . Our human awareness and eager poking, probing, and studying is our beginning con-tribution to planet-system energy-conserving; another level of climax!

In a climax situation a high percentage of the energy is de-rived not from grazing off the annual production of biomass, but from recycling dead biomass, the duff on the forest floor, the trees that have fallen, the bodies of dead animals. Recycled. Detritus cycle energy is liberated by fungi and lots of insects. I would then suggest: as climax forest is to biome, and fungus is to the recycling of energy, so "enlightened mind" is to daily ego-mind, and art to the recycling of neglected inner potential. When we deepen and enrich ourselves, looking within, under-standing ourselves, we come closer to being like a climax sys-tem. Turning away from grazing on the "immediate biomass" of perception, sensation, and thrill; and reviewing memory, in-ternalized perception, blocks of inner energies, dreams, the leaf-fall of day-to-day consciousness, liberates the energy of our own sense-detritus. Art is an assimilator of unfelt experience, per-ception, sensation, and memory for the whole society. (173-74)

Snyder's characterization of perception as an openness that moves through the "immediate biomass" conveys that sense of the intertwining of the flesh of the visible that forms the backbone of Merleau-Ponty's phe-nomenology.

Nets other than Indra's or Masa's veins or the nets of science also exist. For Chuang Tzu language is a net that can entrap us in words rather than point us toward the more important referential reality. Hence, in chap-ter 26 of his *Works*, Chuang Tzu reminds us that "The fishing net is used to catch fish; let us have the fish and forget the net. The snare is used to catch rabbits; let us have the rabbit and forget the snare. Words are used to convey ideas; let us have the ideas and forget the words" (Chang 1963, 13). Snyder in *Axe Handles* (1983) develops a tripartite structure to convey his delight in the ordinary, his Buddhist interpenetration theme, and his emphasis on referential language. Part 1 details the simple joys of family living on San Juan Ridge. Part 2 deepens the interpenetration theme by adding Snyder's poetic response to Lovelock's Gaia theory. Part 3, entitled "Nets," contains many moments of *référance* as Snyder cautions us about how capitalism, government, and other institutional bureaucracies use abstract words as nets to extend technological power and despoil the land. Words that immediately point toward referential realities convey Snyder's joyous interpenetration with nature, whereas the cliches and abstractions of technological language usually invite Snyder's satiric censure because they turn their backs on referential realities. Bureaucracies are trapped in power-laden words and hierarchies that deny the vitality of creation and substitute a listless sameness.

Part 1 of *Axe Handles* intimately develops Snyder's bioregional ethic. Snyder welcomes the hearing and review process of the Environmental Protection Agency because it allows the citizens of a given region to evaluate and challenge proposed changes. Thus, for Snyder, "the *ecological* benefits of bioregionalism, of cultivating a sense of place, are that there will then be a *people* to be the People in the place, when it comes down to the line, in terms of implementing and carrying through legislation that is mandated. But we shouldn't forget that no legislation is any better than the ultimate will of the people at the grassroots level to have it happen" (RW 139-40). For Snyder a bioregional ethic starts at home and flows into community practice (RW 136). The dedication of *Axe Handles* to a place, not a person, underscores its bioregional theme: "This book is for San Juan Ridge." The subtitle for section 1, "Loops," emphasizes how the poet transmits and reenergizes culture in his creative thinking and in his family and community practices. The prefacing fifth century C.B.C. Chinese folk song and the title poem suggest that one's elders, in this case Snyder himself, are the models or completed axes who transmit cultural knowledge and practice to the young—Snyder's son Kai as axe head. The transmitted knowledge gives Kai a handle on life, just as Pound once gave Snyder advice on poetry, and the Chinese masters in turn taught Pound.

When Snyder in "For/From Lew" has a dream about the California poet Lew Welch (who disappeared in 1973 with some clothes borrowed from Snyder and left a suicide note), the gist of it is the directive to "teach the children about the cycles." Similarly, the poet's creative energy digests the past and reenergizes it, refashions it for use in the present. Snyder believes that "poets are more like mushrooms, or fungus—they can digest the symbol-detritus" (RW 71). "On Top," a poem ostensibly about working a compost heap, is actually a poem about the process of creating poetry, of working over the symbol detritus of the cultural cycles with "A mind like compost."

Other poems in part 1 of *Axe Handles* present Snyder *en famille* in his bioregion, completing necessary chores at Kitkitdizze, delighting in nature's local pleasures, and getting to know the San Juan Ridge watershed. Often the cultural mesocosm and psychic microcosm intertwine in the activity of living in the present moment, or Snyder's reflections locate analogical relationships between human and nonhuman nature. In "The Cool Around the Fire," the labor of burning brush to lessen the chance of forest fires is also a way to cleanse "the tangle of the heart," to remove excess bile, while felling and splitting dead trees gives the poet the simple satisfaction of the fruits of his labor, four cords of wood, in "Getting in the Wood." The stewardship of watering an apple tree by bending to work the pump handle becomes at the same time a reverential bow to nature in "Bows to Drouth."

The nature that reveals as it conceals gives Wendell Berry and Snyder joy in "Berry Territory." As Snyder walks with Wendell Berry at his Lanes Landing Farm, Berry uncovers part of a wild ecosystem by using his sense of smell to discover a fox hole. "Among" is a celebration of the Douglas Fir's difficult struggle to survive the dry California summers, and "All in the Family" celebrates the interrelatedness of disparate members of the mint family, which is analogous to the disparate activities of the Snyder family. As August rain exceeds the zero average in San Juan Ridge, so the Snyder family gets more than the average work done in "Beating the Average." Poems such as "Fence Posts," "Soy Sauce," and "Working on the '58 Willys Pickup" celebrate the simple joys of recycling, and "So Old—" celebrates the timeless endurance of nature as the Snyder family learn more about their watershed by driving down old dirt roads.

Many other "Loops" exist in part 1 of *Axe Handles*. A few poems celebrate Japanese traditions that knit generations together by handing down the knowledge, the cultural handles. Or Snyder takes pleasure in recognizing that his labor ethic and his California Forest Service work of thirty years ago have implanted psychophysical roots that have recurring benefits in his later life. Snyder delights in perceiving the timeless correspondence of the activities of beetles to the itineraries of tourists as he revisits a Japanese village he once knew, which turns out to be Masa's childhood home, in "Delicate Criss-crossing Beetle Trails Left in the Sand." The trails of humans and insects alike crisscross timelessly in the dunes. The sailors, monks, and old-stand pine trees are all "Ancient Ones," timeless recyclers of cultural and biological information, in "Walking Through Myoshin-ji." Like "*mu*," the nonsense response in Zen *kōans* that signifies the limits of human logic and reason (*mu* means "not" or "none"—D.T. Suzuki 1962, 291), the dividing Cartesian categories of reason are insufficient to encompass the interrelatedness of these ancient ones. Cultural transmission continues as elders drink and sing songs to commemorate their dead in a specific village graveyard in "At the Ibaru Family Tomb Tagami village, Great Loo Choo: Grandfathers of my sons."

Recycled energy leads to ecological wisdom and stable family values in *Axe Handles*. As a Texas waitress, eyeing the black hair of Snyder's sons, mistakenly suggests that they are Vietnamese, Snyder privately delights in how the continuance of his sons' Japanese heritage is validated in their genes—their black hair—in "Eastward Across Texas." In a foreshadowing of the language theme of part 3 of *Axe Handles*, Snyder delights in the actual labor of "Painting the North San Juan School," even though the names and mathematical abstractions taught in our "shaky" culture will in part disconnect the students from their bioregion. Snyder feels very ambivalent about the fact that students will be taught "games of numbers," geography and history by the dominant culture, in "written signs" assigned by "those who / think they know" the truth, but he is content that the human energy spent recycling the old building is worthwhile; it will provide education in a stable bioregion where families care.

"River in the Valley" and "True Night," two of the best poems in Part I of *Axe Handles*, show Snyder handling the activity of transmitting culture with delicacy and grace. In the former Snyder, as Murphy noted (1992, 137), conveys three different but congruent ways of participating in nature's lively energies. Gen "runs in little circles" to imitate the "swoops of swallows," while Kai tries "to hold with his eyes the course / of a single darting bird." In a more practical fashion, Snyder participates in seed dispersal by removing seeds from his socks. But Snyder's participatory gaze becomes more intense at the poem's close. When one son asks "'where do rivers start?,'" Snyder relates a moment of oneness with nature, a paradoxical yet mystical vision of movement and stillness that Taoists sometimes experience when they perceive the spiritual unity of all things (Chang 1963, 203-8):

in threads in hills, and gather down to here—
but the river
is all of it everywhere,
all flowing at once,
all one place.
(9)

Similarly, after chasing raccoons from his kitchen one night, Snyder experiences a moment of Zen *satori*, a sudden explosion of perception in stanzas 3 and 4 of "True Night," where time and eternity fuse in an absolute present where no difference exists between the self and what one perceives (D.T. Suzuki 1962, 44, 201-6). But Snyder does not linger too long in this aesthetic night; he is even more true to his family and community duties.

In part 2 of *Axe Handles* Snyder shifts his gaze from the family to celebrate the interdependence of cycles and energy transfers of the macrocosm, "this slow-paced / system of systems," in twenty short poems (I-XX) entitled "Little Songs for Gaia." Snyder had absorbed Lovelock's Gaia theory in the mid-seventies and discussed it in *The Old Ways* (38-40, 93). In his "introductory Note" to *Turtle Island*, Snyder spoke of nondualistic "energy pathways that sustain life. Each living being is a swirl in the flow . . . . The land, the planet itself, is also a living being—at another pace." His allusions to the Gaia hypothesis in the later essay collections *The Practice of the Wild* (16, 29, 39, 90, 177) and *A Place in Space* (86, 96, 244) indicate that he has synthesized Lovelock with his nondualistic ecology of energy transfers. This synthesis now has complex interconnections. In *The Practice of the Wild* he conflates wild nature with what Merleau-Ponty would call our "lived bodies" and what Lovelock would call homeostatic or self-regulating cybernetic loops in human bodies (see Lovelock [1979], 10-11, 65-57, 127, 131-32, 146), the conscious and unconscious minds to which these bodies are attached, and the living space, akin to Merleau-Ponty's flesh of the visible, in which they dwell:

> Our bodies are wild. The involuntary quick turn of the head at
> a shout, the vertigo at looking off a precipice, the heart-in-the-
> throat in a moment of danger, the catch of the breath, the quiet
> moments relaxing, staring, reflecting—all universal responses
> of this mammal body. They can be seen throughout the class.
> The body does not require the intercession of some conscious

intellect to make it breathe, to keep the heart beating. It is to a great extent self-regulating, it is a life of its own. Sensation and perception do not exactly come from the outside, and the unremitting thought and image-flow are not exactly outside. The world is our consciousness, and it surrounds us. . . . The body is, so to speak, in the mind. They are both wild. (PW 16)

As with the nondualistic "all space" of Indian Brahma, Gaia for Snyder also encompasses the surrounding world as a series of wild but ultimately interconnected Lovelockian feedback systems: "the source of fertility is the 'wild.' . . . The power that gives us good land is none other than Gaia herself, the whole network" (PW 90).

Lovelock intends no teleological First Cause that directs his Gaia hypothesis. His main evidence for his hypothesis that the planet has evolved through natural selection into a sentient, potentially self-regulating biosphere over the past three eons is that during this time period the planet has always maintained optimal conditions for the growth of life. Life sustains life. The oceans have never frozen completely or boiled away, ocean salinity remains at 3.5 percent (the electrical bonds of cell walls would deteriorate if salinity within or in its external environment exceeded 6 percent), fresh water ph stays near 8 (optimal for life unless polluted by humans), and oxygen in the air remains near 21 percent. If oxygen in the air were more than 25 percent, forest fires would not stop at wet wood, and at lower than 15 percent the higher mammals, including humans, would not have evolved. Complex processes originating at ground level interact with the air and rainwater: methane rises and turns the excess oxygen produced by plant respiration and carbon burial into carbon dioxide and water vapor, while ammonia gas, also produced at ground level, rises and takes excess acidity out of rainwater.

Though Lovelock's evidence coincides with what scientists know about biogeochemical cycles, his hypothesis is scientifically untestable and unfalsifiable and has no predictive value. Biological processes and the geophysical environment do influence one another, but Lovelock uses both negative and positive feedback loops in his theory, so it is not possible to determine if Gaia maintains optimal conditions for life because of or in spite of biotic processes (Kirchner 1989, 223-35). Nevertheless, scientists such as James Kirchner (1989, 231, 233) and Carolyn Merchant (1992, 98-100) agree that it is useful to stress the holistic interactions rather than the dualistic separations of environmental processes, in part because humans interact with the environment and influence it. According to Merchant, Lovelock's hypothesis "might provide alternative ethical guidelines for humanity's relationship with the environment" (1992, 100).

Snyder's "Little Songs for Gaia" stress both the aesthetic and ethical implications of perceiving our planet as a series of interacting, self-regulating feedback systems. The opening poem highlights, like the Aesop's fable about the grasshopper and the ants, humankind's myopic laziness and its twentieth-century technological insulation from nature—"grasshopper man in his car driving through." Yet the opening poem also suggests that technological man is but a small aberration, a blip on Gaia's radar screen, a dust mote in this more powerful "slow-paced / system of systems." Log trucks may desecrate the forests (XIII) and automobiles may produce road kills (XV), but Snyder's gaze so accentuates the biocentric beauty of the system in the majority of the poems that the reader cannot help but reflect ethically on what Abbey once called the *Slobivius americanus* in us (215).

Many of the short poems celebrate nature by offering a biocentric view that emphasizes the dependence of humans on nonhuman nature or shows how all orders of nature are codependent. Manzanita, a shrub of the heath family, is one of the plants that will help reclaim a clear cut and jump start forest succession in California; hence the celebration of its powers in poem III. The ouzel, or dipper bird, actually swims under water for its food; thus, it symbolizes how species often interact harmoniously with air, land, and water—the major components of Gaia. Poem V offers a biocentric view of humans as dependent on other orders of nature. We are only the middle term in a series of analogies; we are longer lived than the cricket, but shorter lived than trees, which are shorter lived than the enduring rocks and hills. Snyder presents an epiphany of the Great Goddess of nature from Native American Corn Goddess myths, staples of Pueblo, Chippewa, and Pawnee tribes, in poem VI. The call of the flicker woodpecker in poem VIII inaugurates a meditation on nature that brings together all the five senses, while the biocentric view of poem IX is subversive, suggesting that in some senses humans are the servants of the Red Hens that Snyder once kept at Kitkitdizze.

The playful mating rituals of bucks skirmishing in wild nature in poem X contrasts with the road kill caused by human interference in nature in poem XV. Poem XI presents the P'eng Bird of Chuang Tzu's first chapter, who wanders freely in the boundless all because he affixes no boundaries, dichotomies, hierarchies: "all he sees is / blue." Snyder previously discussed the "Seed syllable" idea in this poem in *The Old Ways* (35) as a fundamental sound/energy level that permeates all, as in a mantra. The flickers of poem XVIII emphasize total absorption in the present moment, while in poem XIX Gaia appears not only as a Diana-like Huntress, but also the Matriarchal Fertility Goddess whose continual expenditure of sexual energy keeps creation alive, for her "sheath" is a translation of the Latin *vagina*, and her "quiver" suggests sexual response as well as the arrow-like swift motion of creation. The final poem of "Little Songs for Gaia" relates a moment of *référance*. Here Snyder humbly apologizes for his messy inadequacy, his having to use language to convey what cannot be captured in language—Gaia's power and informing energy in the referential world. Snyder presents this metaphorically, as if he had raided Gaia's library to help him understand her. This sudden drop into *référance*, into self-conscious language use, foreshadows the language theme of part 3.

"Nets," part 3 of *Axe Handles*, contrasts poems where Snyder uses language to present the animated participation of the lived body in the present moment with poems where reductive, power-laden abstractions lead us away from the referential world and induce environmental degradation. *Référance* permeates part 3. The opening poem of "Nets I," "Walked Two Days in Snow, Then It Cleared for Five," relates an epiphany of Gaia's energy in the alert activities of animals at home in their environments. Snyder notices the actions of otters, moose, eagles, hawks, and badgers on a forest hike; together they suddenly make him aware of "each lift and stamp" of Gaia's "high-arched feet." The conclusion of "Geese Gone Beyond" definitely conveys a moment of *satori* as the "carpet of canada geese" suddenly become one in flight at the trigger-swift moment when one becomes "the first to feel to go."

Soon the poems complicate the bucolic mood with *référance*. Coyote's language in "Three Deer One Coyote Running in the Snow" is a language of signs and tracks in the referential world; when Snyder wants to study this unpredictable but largely beneficent nature spirit's news, he must walk through the area where it ran, and spot evidence like a scout (see *The Old Ways* 84). The poem reminds us that animals have their own language, and that human language, for Snyder, "belongs to our biological nature and writing is just moose tracks in the snow" (PW 69). In "White Sticky" the common name that adequately conveys what this mushroom looks and feels like is preferable to the taxonomical Latin name that no one can find in books. As in Snyder's earliest work, book knowledge once again is less effective than knowledge of the lived reality. Similar to Bashō's haiku of the same name, "Old Pond" leads the reader to a point where Snyder himself becomes the "naked bug / with a white body and brown hair" who splashes into the pond in an ecstatic moment of unity with the lived environment.

Snyder believes that "on one level there is no hierarchy of qualities in life" (RW 17). This statement offers a perfect gloss on the next poem, an epiphany of Gaia at a very specific place and time, where Snyder bows in humility on ordinary "roadside gravel" at a revelation of Gaia as the Taoist Nameless, the source of all things in the phenomenal world. The words in the poem, carefully arranged to be spaced equally across the page, not only suggest the nonhierarchical interpenetration of all created matter that Julia Martin noted, but also conveys an emanationalism as one moves left to right across the page. The sky becomes the gateway into the phenomenal world where mists become clouds and Mother Gaia's sustaining milk becomes the pure snow. Snyder in the next line plays with the Sanskrit word *nirvana*, which literally means the cessation of wind, to reverse the process by indicating how Gaia is the source of all wind and breath, including the poet's words. In several "Nets" poems, including the lengthy title of this poem, Snyder uses dates such as 40075 instead of 1975, for he believes that human brain size, skills, and imagination peaked at the high point of Cro-Magnon man, who did the first cave paintings in the Upper Paleolithic. Humans have had about the same skills and brain power for the last 40,000 years, and a 40,000–year time frame makes us realize how comparatively recent is the development of agriculture (about 12,000 years ago), how even more recent is the development of civilization (about 8,000 years ago) and general literacy (about 200 years ago), and yet how frighteningly recent is almost all of the environmental degradation we have become complacent about—just this past 150 years. Snyder suggests that narrowed perceptions induced by society may be the cause for the reduction in brain size since Cro-Magnon man and for the pollution we face (see *Earth House Hold* 143; *The Old Ways* 16-21, 62).

Language and money, two of the chief inventions of civilization, may be very flexible tools for transferring knowledge and goods, but their power may also be the primary causes of our present environmental malaise. Snyder's meditations on these tools certainly inform part 3 poems such as "Glamour" and "Money Goes Upstream." Our desire for wealth and consumer goods also creates the ersatz need for fossil fuels, which the ecologists Paul and Anne Ehrlich call "The One-Time Bonanza" that will not last (1990, 24-45). In "Alaska" and "Dillingham, Alaska, the Willow Tree Bar," Snyder suggests that we will not return to a bioregional ethic until the oil runs dry. Meanwhile, auto and factory exhausts not only pollute the air but also fuel a mass media whose power constricts cultural diversity. One hears "the same new songs" in bars in Iran, Italy, Texas, Australia, or Alaska, and in the process one loses the respect that the indigenous cultures had for the environment. "Uluru Wild Fig Song" is Snyder's attempt to counter mass culture sameness by reminding us of the respect that Australian aborigines have for the land that sustains them. The sand on the naked skin and the song that arises from labor and the dance of the spirit connect the body to the flesh of the visible, whereas abstractions and the glut of consumer goods continue to alienate the civilized psyche.

Society also creates powerful hierarchies that develop abstract terms to control ever larger domains. "The Grand Entry," which begins "Nets II," is a satiric send-up of America's beef cattle industry. Here Snyder introduces us to the "High biomass priest-accountants / Who invented writing" and created false needs for high-protein diets—those red, white, and blue hamburgers at the poem's end. Implied in Snyder's critique of our gustatory practices are facts that many environmentalists know: that it takes from seven to sixteen pounds of grain to produce one pound of beef (Lappé 1982, 69, 463-64), and if Americans alone reduced their meat intake by 10 percent (say one meatless lunch and dinner per week), the liberated feedlot grain, if it indeed reached the hands of the needy, would keep healthy every one of the sixty million who die each year of starvation (Robbins 1987, 352).

Snyder himself prefers low-level and appropriate technology that helps him to manage and sustain his own land and the life of San Juan Ridge. When Governor Jerry Brown appointed Snyder to the California Arts Council in the 1970s, Snyder had no phone at Kitkitdizze and periodically drove twelve miles to Toki's Okinawan Noodle and Bait Shop to use their pay phone for necessary Arts Council communications (RW 131-33). Yet Snyder pokes fun at his attempt to use the high technology of language transmission over long distance telephone lines in "Under the Sign of Toki's." The telephone calls quickly become a silly misadventure in miscommunication as Snyder dials wrong area codes and converses with strangers thousands of miles away. The greater the distance, the more abstract and inhuman the technological process: dialing a one and ten digits will take anyone anywhere in America, but at the same time the technology will obliterate any referential connection to one's bioregion. Gaia intrudes with *référance* to poke fun at Snyder in the poem, for her snow on nearby tree limbs drips onto Snyder's notebook and smudges the telephone numbers. The smudged numbers reveal the hubris of a society that has become blind to its referential base.

Similarly, when Snyder meets with Governor Brown in "Talking Late with the Governor about the Budget," he sympathizes with the impossible tasks imposed on governors of California. The technology allows one man in a Sacramento office to make sweeping decisions that affect the lives of people from at least six distinct bioregions "In this land of twenty million / From desert to ocean." The energy of oil allows such technological power to collect atop pyramids of power, but even the neophyte environmentalist knows that the oil will indeed run out in another hundred or so years. Snyder wistfully acknowledges the futility of mass media concepts such as "the People"; these are meaningless abstractions that overreach the needs of any particular group, and the governor cannot possibly satisfy so many diverse groups. All Snyder can do is gaze at the far heavens and then bring things down to earth by wondering if it is raining at San Juan Ridge, his intimate bioregion. In the next poem, Snyder and the governor, after day-dreams about how automobiles will become relics after the oil runs out, laughingly decide to live in the simple present. As they enjoy the recreation of shooting arrows at hay bales, they eschew abstractions and become one with the moment in the disciplined inattention of Zen (RW 33), as in Eugen Herrigel's book on Zen and archery (1989).

The *kōan*-like circular reasoning of "Arts Councils" also suggests that civilization has become specialized in ways that induce an atrophy of Cro-Magnon man's prodigious imaginative powers. In many tribal societies *everyone* created art, so museums, buyers, Arts Councils and "artists" were unnecessary. But today most individuals do not create their own art. So we have specialists called artists and abstractions like money assisting a process divorced from any coherent culture—the nonexistent "we" is replaced with the amorphous "I," who develops a substitute craving for what he must buy instead of produce himself.

The last six poems of *Axe Handles* are all celebrations of Gaia, the "Beautiful body we walk on" (105). The celebrations include the Backaskog woman's power to give birth nine times, the power of the breast to filter poisons, the recycling of forest compost into the "quick life" of the "woodpecker's cry," and the sustenance of "Old Woman Nature," a crone "calmly gathering firewood in the moon" while "heating you some soup." The song of "The Canyon Wren" that follows Snyder as he shoots the whitewater rapids of the Stanislaus River, purifies his ears as he undergoes what appears to be a moment of enlightenment in the mystical vision of water that seems to rest in its permanence at the same time that it speeds the raft downwards. Snyder ends *Axe Handles* with "For All," a restatement of its main theme. He pledges allegiance to the Turtle Island of his vision, a place that has "joyful interpenetration for all."

Snyder's next volume, *Left Out in the Rain* (1986), primarily contains previously unpublished poems written before *Axe Handles*. Like *Back Country*, the poems convey his doubts at his vocation and Japanese culture during his years in Japan, his loneliness and regret for lost love, and also reveal how early and how persistent in Snyder's career was the conviction that underlies part 3 of *Axe Handles*—that twentieth-century urban/industrial civilization is an energy-glut aberration that nature will soon erase in geologic time (see 11, 13-15, 54, 65-66, 76, 125, 136). Against the artificial highways of our culture Snyder juxtaposes the ancient wandering trails of elk in the opening poem, "Elk Trails," and suggests in many other poems that the important trail is the one that you open and keep clear in your moment-to-moment perceptions (123, 127-28, 130, 133). This state of fresh perception is the place where one writes poetry, the "Eagle of Experience" (128). In "Epistemological Fancies" Snyder cautions us not to obstruct our gazes with the "superficial depth" of illusory phenomena but to keep the real Noumenon, enlightenment vision, before us. It's all a matter of perception: "For all that's real, or ought to be, / Is what one can, or cannot, see" (189). In "Geological Meditation" Snyder states that what is real is geological change in the referential world; hence we should not obscure our referential gaze with chimerical dreams of pleasure, the "hallucinations" caused by the brain's "chemical trick" (43-44).

In *Left Out in the Rain* Snyder celebrates in poems too numerous to mention the continual practice of leading the simple life and engaging in ordinary labor that cleanses the mind and reinforces convictions. Wild nature (108-10, 191), like the Banyan tree in Waikiki whose roots underlie the twenty-five-thousand-room hotel, is the reality of the present and the hope for the future (145). Living the simple life reinforces our grasp of this important truth. Nature's language is stronger and more ubiquitous than human language (18, 136, 140, 144-45); it speaks the fructifying power of Gaia and the plant hands of Rhea, whose labor makes the sap swell each spring (141). Throughout the volume seeing resides in the ability to pierce the illusions created by our urban culture and live in harmony with nature's changing ecosystems. Human words and the pure ideas of theories and philosophical systems create a purblind grammar that "is not the goal" in "Numerous Broken Eggs," for "Unstuck from objects, meanings are unsure" (36-37). Poems that survive being left out in the rain are poems made from grasping referential rock.

The new poems in the last section of *No Nature* (1992) present Snyder openly embracing advanced age with the serenity of a man who is very happy with his values and still thoroughly satisfied with the simple joys of hiking, building, and caring for his family and the neighbors in his watershed. Sitting naked in a sweat lodge with Aleut women reminds him of "seals hauled out for sunning," and this leads to remarks such as "Older is smarter and more tasty," or "We get old enough and finally really like it!" (364-65). "Building" celebrates the labors of Snyder and his neighbors to erect first a schoolhouse and then a community hall. Unlike buildings built by construction companies, this firsthand engagement in unalienated labor in the "dance with Matter" leads to "solid" buildings that "are constantly wet from the pool / that renews all things" (366-67). Hikes bring the simple joys of smelling the unique odor of particular pine trees that Piutes admire ("Kusiwoqqobi" 363) or red cypress trees that Taiwanese revere ("Kisiabaton" 379). The words used by these indigenous peoples to describe the trees have a closer correspondence to lived experience in referential reality, and that is precisely the experience Snyder wants to share. While sitting in the kitchen and reading a student's doctoral dissertation about Lew Welch in "For Lew Welch in a Snowfall," Snyder is moved not by the student's concepts but by his own vivid memories of discussing poetry with Welch in the kitchen amid similar snowfalls. Poetry comes not from theory but from the referential world, as a "blundering" or "Frightened" animal that coaxes Snyder out of his habits and into unique encounters with wild nature ("How Poetry Comes to Me" 361).

In *The Practice of the Wild* Snyder defines precisely what he means by "wild" (9–12, 16-24, 151). "Wild" is both ecological and Taoist. It is the full, rich energy potential and wholeness of systems where all living members are present (12), and thus similar to Margalef's use of climax theory in fully formed ecosystems. "Wild" is also the free, direct experience of nature unmediated, uninfluenced by human intentions or preconceptions, and thus similar to the Taoist Way or an unconstructed, free-flowing path, "both empty and real at the same time" (10, 151). Both are similar to Merleau-Ponty's phenomenological understanding of "wild" as the referential surround that preexists human contemplation, the complex living context from which we derive human language. When we go lightly through nature we see ourselves as integral parts of ecosystems, but not superior to other living, functioning parts of these ecosystems. Hence, in *No Nature*, Snyder delights at biocentric comparisons of a file of turkeys moving through the brush to a family of humans passing through their appointed time on the green planet earth ("Surrounded by Wild Turkeys" 368). Or he stares with "honor" and "humor" at a chance encounter with the language of huge bearscats on a trail hike as "a peek into her whole wild system," a system that has a language, a "message for all species," a "sign / That is not found in books / Or transmitted in letters" ("Right in the Trail" 375-76). When Snyder hikes "Off the Trail" (369-70), he rejoices in a free, unpremeditated journey where the hikers "find our own way," whichever way their moment-to-moment choices in the wild take them. Hence the reference to the opening of chapter 1 of Lao-tzu:

> The dense matted floor
> Of Red Fir needles and twigs. This is wild!
> We laugh, wild for sure,
> Because no place is more than another,
> All places total,
> And our ankles, knees, shoulders &
> Haunches know right where they are.
> Recall how the *Dao De*
> *Jing* puts it: the trail's not the way.
> No path will get you there, we're off the trail,
> You and I, and we chose it!
> (369-70)

No Nature receives its title from the state of Buddhist enlightenment where, as D.T. Suzuki notes, one does not discriminate among particular objects in the ten thousand things but participates in the oneness of nature in the absolute present (1962, 142-43, 204-6). This is a prelinguistic state where concepts would only interfere and cause pigeonholing into Aristotelian empirical categories. Hence, there is no concept called "nature" but a perpetual newness in each moment of participation in what Snyder calls the ecological "thusness" of "the nature of the nature of nature. The wild in the wild" (PW 103). When Snyder in *No Nature* leaves the freeways, housing projects, and academies to hike "At Tower Peak," he awakens to fresh participation in the allness of creation: "Wake to the same old world of no names, / No things, new as ever, rock and water" (373). In "Ripples on the Surface," the final poem of *No Nature*, Snyder observes that nature is "not a book, but a *performance*," with "Ever-fresh events / scraped out, rubbed out, and used, used, again—" (381). In his "Preface" to *No Nature*, Snyder quotes Hakuin Zenji: "'self-nature that is no nature/ . . . far beyond mere doctrine.' An open space to move in, with the whole body, the whole mind. My gesture has been with language." Thus at the conclusion of "Ripples on the Surface" we have "No nature," where "The vast wild" is the entire planet and the separate "self" is an illusion.

To maintain this ecological perspective Snyder strongly suggests in *The Practice of the Wild* that we follow the example of Dōgen Zenji, the Zen monk who believed in continual labor and everyday practice: "Dōgen was fond of saying that 'practice *is* the path'" (PW 153). In this practice we must learn to forget the intellect, the ego, and attachment to worldly goods, so that we can become one with nature: "'We study the self to forget the self.' said Dōgen. 'When you forget the self, you become one with the ten thousand things.' Ten thousand things means all of the phenomenal world. When we are open that world can occupy us" (PW 150).

Mountains and Rivers without End (1996) brings to a triumphant close forty years of hiking meditations among Gaia's rocks and waters. Snyder begins the volume with an enigmatic epigraph from Dōgen Zenji's *Gabyō*, his "Painting of a Rice Cake." By abstracting the main argumentative progression from Dōgen's five-page meditation, Snyder highlights Dōgen's tantalizing question, a question that directs readers toward the all-important issue of the relation of artistic text, its language and representational artifice, to lived life. What is "painted hunger" and how can a "painted rice cake" become "a remedy for satisfying hunger?" Given our Western heritage of empirical dualism, we would initially want to agree with Xiangyan Zhixian's comment that "a painting of a rice-cake does not satisfy hunger" (*Moon* 134, 251). Yet if we do agree with this perspective, we will never get on Snyder's boat, or Dōgen's boat, nor will we gain the enlightenment of fanning ourselves in the moment-by-moment Zen realization that Snyder achieved in the poems of *Mountains and Rivers without End*. By elucidating the references to Dōgen in *Mountains and Rivers without End*, we can see how practice includes both artistic text and absorption in the wild of nature at the referential moment of realization—the moment of joyous, participatory delight in the practice of Gaia's energy transfers. Snyder's allusions to Dōgen also underscore Merleau-Ponty's belief that consciousness is always embodied and placed—at work in visible, tangible, tactile nature.

In his lengthy biographical note appended to *Mountains and Rivers without End*, Snyder states that his reading of Dōgen's translated works in the late seventies was crucial both to his understanding of the practice of walking through landscapes, and to the composition of the poems of *Mountains and Rivers*, most of which are intimately concerned with landscape journeys (157). Like Snyder, this thirteenth-century Japanese Zen master (1200-1253) struggled with the relation of everyday labor to the realization of enlightenment. As Thomas Cleary has noted, Dōgen travailed in a decaying spiritual tradition. Although Dōgen championed monastic life for its nonattachment to ego, fame, and worldly goods, he was painfully aware of the fact that in his time Japanese monasteries were public institutions supported by land grants and under government control. Many students flocked to famous Zen masters because exceptional monastic conduct often lead to court career advancement. Decadent practices crept in where many believed that the mechanical following of rules and the recitations of names, or the passive intellectual study of Zen scriptures, could produce enlightenment (Cleary 1993, 1–36).

Dōgen passionately believed that direct experience and disciplined daily labor were necessary, for enlightenment occurs as realization in regular labor and practice. At the conclusion of his *Genjō Kōan*, Dōgen solidified this teaching with a parable:

> Zen master Baoche of Mt. Mayu was fanning himself. A monk approached and said, "Master, the nature of wind is permanent and there is no place it does not reach. Why, then, do you fan yourself?"
>
> "Although you understand that the nature of the wind is permanent," Baoche replied, "you do not understand the meaning of its reaching everywhere."
>
> "What is the meaning of its reaching everywhere?" asked the monk again. The master just kept fanning himself. The monk bowed deeply. (*Moon* 72-73)

Dōgen ended with the observation that if you assume "that you do not need to fan yourself . . . you will understand neither permanence nor the nature of wind" (*Moon* 73). Stephen Heine interpreted the waving of the fan as "symbolic of sustained practice" (1985, 25). Indeed, in "*Bendō-wa*," "On the Endeavor of the Way," Dōgen wrote that to read and chant sutras mechanically is to be "ignorant of the way of practice" (*Moon* 148). Whereas "this inconceivable dharma is abundant in each person, it is not actualized without practice, and it is not experienced without realization" (*Moon* 143). For Dōgen practice and the realization of enlightenment "are inseparable" (*Moon* 151). Heine argued that in this "identity of theory and practice" resided one of Dōgen's most unique contributions to Zen philosophy; here "awakening does not happen once, but must be ever-continuing and ever renewed" (*Existential* 26, 28). Enlightenment can occur with regularity in the practice of simple worldly tasks, so long as we do not become attached to fame or possessions. The practice or muscular effort of moving the fan is necessary.

What does an appreciation of Dōgen's historical moment and his contributions to Zen do for our understanding of Snyder's *Mountains and Rivers without End*? Many things. Historically, both men seriously pursued the discipline and asceticism of monastic life. Both men left their home countries in their mid-twenties to seek spiritual rejuvenation elsewhere: Dōgen abandoned the "hidebound dogma" of a "moribund" Japanese Buddhism as he journeyed to China in 1223 (Cleary 1993, 18-19; Heine 1989, 29); Snyder rejected McCarthyism and consumer America when he sailed for Japan in 1956. Dōgen returned to Japan, founded what was later to become the Soto sect of Zen, and opened his own temple, the first independent Zen center in Japan, in 1236 (Heine, *Blade* 29). In 1244 Dōgen left Kyoto altogether and established a strict monastic order in the remote mountains of Echizen province (Heine, *Blade* 5). Snyder studied Zen in Japan for nearly a decade and has spent the rest of his life living frugally in California in his rural San Juan Ridge home, Kitkitdizze, while integrating Zen teachings and practice into an environmental vision of wholeness and harmony.

Like Dōgen, Snyder does not accept a decadent, dualistic split between the virtues of textual appreciation and our labor in everyday reality. The entire effort of the artifice of *Mountains and Rivers without End* works to deny any attempt to privilege a hermetically sealed aesthetic appreciation of the text that can wall out our worldly filiations with daily labor and our tussles with an aggressive late capitalism that infects our economic and political situation. Snyder's essays in *The Practice of the Wild* always accentuate the necessity of combining Zen and environmental philosophy with daily labor and social action. Theory and practice, aesthetics and realization, life and literature, are necessarily inseparable for Snyder. This is the message within the artifice of *Mountains and Rivers without End*.

Consider that lengthy rice cake epigraph, for instance. If one recognizes, as Kazuaki Tanahashi does in his notes to "Painting of a Rice-cake," that "painting" often means "words useless for realization" (*Moon* 251), one can appreciate Dōgen's reversal of this position in his rice cake meditation. The key is to recognize, as Tanahashi does in his seventh note, that "the enlightenment of various buddhas cannot be separated from verbal expressions of enlightenment." The labor of artistic creation though words is just another of the many ways that one can realize enlightenment. It is inseparable from everyday practice. "Painted hunger" is the creative effort to achieve in the practice of writing the state of emptiness, the *śūnyatā* of hunger, through which one achieves enlightenment. Thus "painted hunger" is indeed a "remedy" for "satisfying hunger," for hunger should remain unsatisfied, in a continual courting of emptiness. Ideally, the "painted hunger" and the entire rice cake meditation of *Gabyō* function as *kōans* meant to explode the conscious mind's reliance on reason, logic, and words.

Snyder's emphasis on his calligraphy training at the outset of his biographical note (153-54), as well as both his painterly induction in the opening poem, "Endless Streams and Mountains," and his painterly phrasing in the final words of the concluding poem, "Finding the Space in the Heart," all corroborate this inseparability of the labor of artistic creation and everyday life. Snyder concludes his opening poem by emphasizing the continuity of practice—from walking the paths to grinding the ink to composing each line. Text and practice are inseparable, and Snyder's "moist black line" dispels the late capitalist illusion that signifiers are unattached commodities, Baudrillardian simulacras of surfaces mechanically reproduced for middle-class consumption in ways that insulate us within language games of aesthetic appreciation. Snyder implies that the aesthetic appreciation of the "moist black line" is inseparable from the labor of experience in the everyday that evolved the perceptions that motivated, guided, and enacted the process of artistic composition.

Within the nondualistic labor of realization in "Endless Streams and Mountains," the *"streams and mountains never stay the same,"* for one is engaged in walking through the labors of everyday practice. Snyder offers a Zen ecology of numerous intersecting themes on this point in his *Practice* essay on Dōgen's *Sansui-kyō*, the "Mountains and Waters Sutra." In "Blue Mountains Constantly Walking," Snyder suggests that mountains and rivers are interconnected; they "form each other" because peaks precipitate the moisture that continually carves these geological formations (PW 101-2). Furthermore, mountains walk when we walk, not simply because our perspective of them changes with each step, but also because with each step we alter the streams and paths. Mountains and waters are our necessary environmental second skin, and they change as we change. Tectonic plates move mountains ever so slowly each day. Philosophically considered, "mountains and waters" is, according to Snyder, a Zen way of referring "to the totality of the process of nature" (PW 102), in which humans are insepara-

bly linked. We are all part of the practice of the wild. So Snyder, meditating
on Dōgen, waxes philosophical:

> Dōgen is not concerned with "sacred mountains"—or pilgrim-
> ages, or spirit allies, or wilderness as some special quality. His
> mountains and streams are the processes of this earth, all of
> existence, process, essence, action, absence; they roll being and
> nonbeing together. They are what we are, we are what they are.
> For those who would see directly into essential nature, the idea
> of the sacred is a delusion and an obstruction: it diverts us from
> seeing what is before our eyes: plain thusness. Roots, stems, and
> branches are all equally scratchy. No hierarchy, no equality. No
> occult and exoteric, no gifted kids and slow achievers. No wild
> and tame, no bound or free, no natural and artificial. Each to-
> tality its own frail self. Even though connected all which ways;
> even *because* connected all which ways.
>
> This, *thusness*, is the nature of the nature of nature. The wild
> in the wild.
>
> So the blue mountains walk to the kitchen and back to the
> shop, to the desk, to the stove. (PW 103)

So, too, the mountains and rivers walk with each brush stroke through-
out the lines of *Mountains and Rivers without End*. Finally, when the effort
of walking through forty years of journeys has achieved its full realization
in composing the final line of the final poem, the moist brush lifts away:

> *Walking on walking,*
> 　　*under foot　earth turns*
>
> *Streams and mountains never stay the same.*
>
> 　　　　　　The space goes on.
> 　　　　　　But the wet black brush
> 　　　　　　tip drawn to a point,
> 　　　　　　　　lifts away.
>
> (152)

The process of artistic composition is not analogous to the actual
walking, the real life journeys, it is an inseparable part of a nondualistic
process forever advancing in time.

While evaluating Dōgen's *waka* poetry, Heine emphasizes Dōgen's unique response to transience as one where he "overcome[s] the distinction between absolute and relative by concretizing the former in the latter" (1989, 6). For Heine the "full aesthetic or intuitive immersion" in the "impermanent unfolding of nature" overcomes "the separation of self and other, subject and object, man and nature" (1989, 6–7). Since all phenomena are interdependent (32), language can be both "revelatory" of Dharma and demonstrative of "the inherent unity of language and reality" (12, 22). Dōgen's unitive gaze exploits both sides of the paradox of "the simultaneous identity and distinction of absolute and relative" (21). We see this fusion of the absolute and the transient, especially in Dōgen's *waka* poem "*Shōbōgenzō*," or "Treasury of the true Dharma-eye." By giving this short *waka* poem the same title as his major prose collection, Dōgen accords it special prominence among his *waka* poems. Whether or not the sea or the wind is agitated, the serene mind is a boat so fully immersed in the temporal flow of experience that it remains solitary, tenaciously absorbed and independent:

Shōbōgenzō	Treasury of the true Dharma-eye
Nami mo hiki	In the heart of the night,
Kaze mo tsunaganu	The moonlight framing
Sute obune	A small boat drifting;
Tsuki koso yawa no	Tossed not by the waves
Sakai nari keri	Nor swayed by the breeze.
(1989, 101)	

In section 5 of his *Zenki* or "Undivided Activity," Dōgen himself offered the best gloss on his boat symbol. Here one's "riding makes the boat what it is" and the boat's temporal movement encompasses in undivided unity the sky, water and shore, so that "there is nothing but the world of the boat." This total immersion of subjectivity and temporality leads to perpetual, moment-to-moment birth as enlightenment realization. Hence "the entire earth and the entire sky are both the undivided activity of the boat. Thus birth is nothing but you; you are nothing but birth" (*Moon* 84-85).

In the very first stanza of the opening poem of *Mountains and Rivers without End*, Snyder invites us to take a ride on his boat. Throughout all of the following poems of the volume, the artifice suggests that we experience

Snyder's journeys from the perspective of Dōgen's boat ride, a ride where subjective and objective, absolute and temporal, language and social action, interconnect in perpetual nondualistic birth:

> Clearing the mind and sliding in
>   to that created space,
> a web of waters streaming over rocks,
> air misty but not raining,
>   seeing this land from a boat on a lake
>   or a broad slow river,
>   coasting by.
> (5)

Snyder's boat is not Huck's escapist raft; it links with Dōgen's boat, fan and rice cake to offer the reader keys to the artifice and the union of text and context that Snyder wishes us to realize as our enlightenment experience in reading the poems of *Mountains and Rivers without End*. Thus, in all of the journeys of the volume "there / IS no" Highway 99 (24), no goal to be attained, for realization is an "IS" that occurs every moment to a mind totally immersed in the phenomenal now. The dream river and the real river should be *one*, not a fantasy construct imposed on reality, in "The Elwha River." "Goodwill" in "Bubbs Creek Haircut" means recognizing that language confers no a priori essence for worldly things like chairs, for in our phenomenal hell all is a flowing Shiva / Parvati dance of forms where things continually recycle, as in the Goodwill Store that provides Snyder with a green hat that moves him with the flow of nature and lures mosquitoes as well as free rides. On "the roof of the world" in the Brooks Range of Alaska in another poem, Snyder follows a sheep trail to a point where the spiritual and the phenomenal worlds merge in an "emptiness of intelligence" where the "Vajra sheep" on their mountains teach the "Koyukuk waters" below true "suchness" (92-95). He follows that sheep trail to the "sweet rank smell" of their "hidden / sheltered beds" and meditates like a Tantric yogin on the white dot of a Dall sheep to learn "how uniquely *at home* each life-form must be in its own unique 'buddha-field'" and to "begin to imagine, to visualize, the nested hierarchies and webs of the actual nondualistic world" (PW 108-9).

It is important to recognize that Snyder had integrated Zen into his writing and personal lifestyle, especially the practice of hiking on journeys, in the early fifties, about twenty-five years before translations of Dōgen influenced him. One can readily see the direct influence of Han Shan and Oriental perspectives in his earliest poetry volumes, *Riprap* (1959) and *Riprap and Cold Mountain Poems* (1965). Portions of Kerouac's 1958 *Dharma Bums* and 1955 entries in Snyder's journals attest to Snyder's struggle to synthesize the mundane and the spiritual in the present moment of lived experience and at the same time purify the self of American consumerism. Kerouac and Snyder lived and hiked together in the San Francisco area in 1955. Although Snyder has sought to distance himself from the fictional character over the years, David Robertson, after a May 26, 1989, interview with Snyder and an inspection of Snyder's own journal account of the actual May 1–2 Mount Tamalpais hike with Kerouac, concluded that *Dharma Bums* is often quite reliable for Snyder's views on the Zen of hiking. Many of the following short quotes relate directly to the search for wholeness through the labor of hiking and to the exorcism of consumer America in the 1966 poem "The Circumambulation of Mt. Tamalpais," which Snyder included in *Mountains and Rivers without End*:

> "Great." I wondered why Han Shan was Japhy's hero. "Because, said he, "he was a poet, a mountain man, a Buddhist dedicated to the principle of meditation on the essence of all things. . . ."
>
> . . . . .
>
> "there is a definite mysterious form in the arrangement of the rocks. It's only through form that we can realize emptiness." (Kerouac 1958, chap. 3)

> With my sneakers it was as easy as pie to just dance nimbly from boulder to boulder, but after a while I noticed how gracefully Japhy was doing it . . . . I learned it was better for me to just spontaneously pick my own boulders and make a ragged dance of my own.
> "The secret of this kind of climbing," said Japhy, "is like Zen. Don't think. Just dance along."
>
> . . . . .
>
> "They're so silent!" I said.
> "Yeah man, you know to me [Japhy] a mountain is a Buddha. Think of the patience, hundreds of thousands of years just sittin there bein perfectly perfectly silent and like praying for all

living creatures in that silence and just waitin for us to stop all our frettin and foolin." (Kerouac 1958, chap. 9)

Japhy leaping up: "I've been reading Whitman, know what he says, Cheer up slaves, *and horrify foreign despots,* he means that's the attitude for the Bard, the Zen Lunacy bard of old desert paths, see the whole thing is a world full of rucksack wanderers, Dharma Bums refusing to subscribe to the general demand that they consume production and therefore have to work for the privilege of consuming . . . all of them imprisoned in a system of work, produce, consume, work, produce, consume, I see a vision of a great rucksack revolution thousands or even millions of young Americans wandering around with rucksacks, going up to mountains to pray . . . ."

. . . . .

"I'm goin to Marin County in a few weeks," said Japhy, "go walk a hunnerd times around Tamalpais and help purify the atmosphere and accustom the local spirits to the sound of sutra." (Kerouac 1958, chap. 13)

"The closer you get to real matter, rock air fire and wood, boy, the more spiritual the world is." (Kerouac 1958, chap. 29)

"THIS WORLD viewed with love & detachment is *nirvana.*" (November 13, 1955, journal entry; see Robertson 1992, 220)

"I am not able to see it or know it—this enormous inhuman beauty—and yet, letting go, I am simply it, being part of it, in me as well as outside." (August 27, 1955, journal entry; see Robertson 1992, 221)

From the mid-fifties on, Snyder carefully and deliberately built an aesthetic where literature derived from work, from practice, from activity and energy and meditation all flowing together (see Japhy and "activity" [Kerouac 1958, chaps. 24 and 25]). When Snyder revisited his 1950s trail crew work in the Sawtooths of the Sierras in 1978, near the northern boundary of Yosemite Park, he wrote "Look Back," a poem that recollected a labor crew friend and reconfirmed the worth of his Zen hiking aesthetic.

Snyder smiles with satisfaction at the fact that work accomplished decades ago has flowered into worthwhile values. Though the foreman of the trail crew supposed that Snyder was slinking away for better wages elsewhere ("Bechtel" is an American-based multinational construction company that built, among other things, oil pipelines in Iran—*The Old Ways* 58) because he studied Chinese at night, left the crew early, and said he was going to Japan, Snyder now knows that he no longer need be nervous about his decision to study Zen in Japan. The poem ends with the lines "Jimmy Jones, and these mountains and creeks. / The up and down of it / stays in my feet" (*Axe Handles* 28-29). With Dōgen as with Snyder, the up and the down of walking stays in one's poetic feet as well as in one's memories and practice. In the "Tiny Energies" section of *Left Out in the Rain*, Snyder found further confirmation of this nondualistic interpenetration of mind and labor in the ecologist H.T. Odum's observation that tiny amounts of energy are amplified along the food chain when transferred in the right form (153; see H.T. Odum 1971, 172).

Reading Dōgen in the late seventies reconfirmed for Snyder the emphasis on labor and practice as a vehicle for purification and enlightenment realization. In the *Axe Handles* poem "The Canyon Wren," reprinted in *Mountains and Rivers without End*, Snyder experienced the dragon vision of Chuang Tzu (163) and Dōgen, the state of highest enlightenment according to Chang Chung-yuan (125, 159), when he integrated the canyon wren's downward song into his consciousness as he shot down California's Stanislaus River rapids in 1981. Naturally he quoted Dōgen on dragon vision from his "Mountains and Waters Sutra" (*Moon* 102, 104-5, 107), a sutra composed at midnight, the "hour of the Rat": "mountains flow / water is the palace of the dragon / it does not flow away" (90-91).

Once again riding on Dōgen's boat of "undivided activity" (*Moon* 85), Snyder experienced self and lived environment as a single totality flowing through the succession of temporal moments. Dōgen in the "Mountains and Waters Sutra" characterized water as the place of liberation, an intuitive abiding in its "own phenomenal expression," unsupported by place and realized in all things within a ceaselessly flowing hydrological cycle (*Moon* 102-3).

Similarly, as Dōgen incorporated poetic meditations into Zen training-hall meal practices, so Snyder recycled one of these cultural transmissions from Dōgen's *Keisei-Sanshōku*, his "Valley Sounds, Mountain Sights" lecture (*Flowers* 261-68), as he washed camping utensils in Pacific Coast water in "We Wash Our Bowls in This Water." Awakened humans are the "valley streams and looming / mountains," just as for Su Tung-p'o a stream is a tongue and a mountain is "a wide-awake body" (139). So Dōgen wrote in his "*Genjō Kōan*" that moving water suggests that nothing is permanent, whereas "to forget the self is to be actualized by myriad things" (*Moon* 70).

What Snyder particularly noticed in Dōgen, and developed in the final design of *Mountains and Rivers without End*, is the Zen master's unique emphasis on the activity of writing as part of the effort of enlightenment realization. Dōgen's sutras are heady intellectual exercises in part designed as teaching tools. By turning inherited teachings on their ears, a practice engaged with relish in Song dynasty China (Cleary 7), Dōgen often teased out new preceptions that fostered enlightenment education while simultaneously using the *kōan* exercise's emphasis upon exploding the mind's tendency to rest secure in the dualisms fostered by rational, empirical logic. Throughout his sutras Dōgen emphasized that writing is not separable from other labor and lived experience, as is often the case with poststructural theoreticians. In the opening poem of *Mountains and Rivers without End*, Snyder emphasizes the inseparability of writing and practice as he wrote that "The watching boat has floated off the page" of Ch'i Shan Wu Chin's "Endless Streams and Mountains" landscape scroll, and then included his personal translations of portions of the Chinese colophons that were added in the historical transmission of this great Song Dynasty painting.

By connecting writing to other labors in the historical transmission of lived life, Snyder is able to incorporate dozens of social and ethical issues into *Mountains and Rivers without End*. The list includes the bruised heroism of labor unions in "Night Highway 99," the limitations of American education in "The Elwha River"; critiques of consumerism and pollution in "The Circumambulation of Mt. Tamalpais," of the energy glut that fuels American economics in "Walking the New York Bedrock Alive in the Sea of Information," and of urban sprawl in "Covers the Ground"; advice on how to enjoy the West Coast economically, through a celebration of Goodwill Stores in "Bubbs Creek Haircut" and a practical list of how to have fun without being bilked at tourist traps in "Three Worlds, Three Realms, Six Roads"; ecological meditations on the use and sharing of our earth's resources, such as "Earrings Dangling and Miles of Desert"; celebrations of animal life (and, implicitly, animal rights) such as "Macaques in the Sky"; and pleas for compassion toward our fellow humans in "The Blue Sky," "With This Flesh," and "Finding the Space in the Heart." For Snyder nondualism means nondiscrimination between aesthetics and practice, or locating the spiritual within the practical as enlightenment realization flows through time.

Snyder also used the artifice of Chinese landscape painting to make us feel at home in a nondualistic world. According to Sherman E. Lee and Wen Fong, although Northern Sung landscape paintings such as the Ch'i Shan Wu Chin's "Endless Streams and Mountains" are conceptually, not representationally organized, one of the essential features of these landscape paintings is the appearance of a "consistent, natural, and understandable way through the endless mountains and over or around the endless streams" (1967, 10, 6). Dōgen's way provides both the conceptual and natural means of realizing the journeys and the artifice of *Mountains and Rivers without End.* Another essential feature in Chinese landscape paintings is the appearance of peasants laboring in their journeys up and down the paths. Here we might find Snyder smiling as he "leans into the grade" (6), fanning himself, eating a painted rice cake, and walking with a mind like a boat moving. Under the *pentimenti* overlays of the "Endless Streams and Mountains" we might just find a faint trace of Dōgen, too. Both are realizing a space in our hearts and a language that connects with environmental praxis in the practice of our everyday lives.

Snyder's readings in Zen and ecology, and his contentment in the everyday practice of his beliefs, give his poetry a phenomenological depth and exuberance that is unmatched among contemporary poets. His life is a model of environmental sanity, and the coherence of his poetry and essays with his lived life make him our most complete ecopoet. His poetry is so rich at least in part because of his persistent willingness to contest prevailing Cartesian notions of experience. Snyder's Buddhist mind or consciousness is the place where inner and outer worlds interpenetrate at the moment of perception. Merleau-Ponty would find the plain-talking author of this *Turtle Island* quote most agreeable, so long as we understand that *Mind* for Buddhists, as well as for Merleau-Ponty, is not Cartesian immanence, but the entire field of the living world in which the human mind/body complex participates: "Now, we are both in, and outside, the world at once. The only place this can be is the *Mind.* Ah, what a poem. It is what is, completely, in the past, present, and future simultaneously, seeing being, and being seen" (114).

Postscript

The Green Referential Fuse

"The poet has lit the fuse of speech." The French poststructuralist historian Michel de Certeau (1925-86), editor of *Études*, saw this sentence on a flyer on May 13, 1968, the day that he watched students take over the Sorbonne in the Paris uprisings—the event that ignited the poststructuralist reexamination of the uses of language (1997a, 13). De Certeau saw this uprising as a "capture of speech," a contestation by those marginalized, silenced or repressed in a power structure suddenly brought into question. Once belief is withdrawn from a system of representation, observed de Certeau, that system becomes a hollow symbolic shell, and those symbols become vulnerable to inversion and subversion by new symbols that demystify sites formerly laden with the silencing aura of the power structure. A photograph of an unkempt student sitting in an aloof professor's regal chair, barricades on campus streets (causing consternation in parents), insurgent red or black flags carried by mixed groups of students and workers (classes normally kept apart in the rigid social structure)—these symbolic confrontations suddenly made fragile and open to contestatory interrogation what had been silently accepted. De Certeau saw this as a poetic or creative explosion of repressed energy, the creation of a hole, a *punctum*, in a system whose slogans no longer commanded blind obedience and servitude. Such captures of speech create sites where we can realize new possibilities through ruses and creative play by those who use language against the ideological grain in the practice of everyday life (1997a, 1–10).

For de Certeau the practice of everyday life fundamentally involves the relations of language to the referential world. Notice that the flyer did *not* state that the poet has lit the fuse of textuality or language theory. Not all poststructural theory limits inquiry to texts—to *différance* and dissemination, antireferential language, bland discussions of deictic shifters in aesthetic grammars, or Wittgensteinian language games restricted to the printed page. Some poststructural theory also refuses the deterministic inscription of potential agents into postures of subjection, including subjection to an art-for-art's sake decadence. De Certeau was well aware that "two centuries of linguistic analysis have shown that language does not make manifest the presence of things, no longer yields presences, and no longer produces a world of transparence. Rather, it is an organized place that allows things to happen. It does not give what it says: it lacks being" (1997b, 30). But language also produces powerful boilerplate—it does organize and codify systems of legally binding human socioeconomic relations. So one must question how language is used, what practices it allows or prohibits. When language is used anonymously by a power regime, with tacit silence or without personal accountability, one needs to capture speech, according to de Certeau, shatter the decayed symbols, and restore to life the network of living human cultural and socioeconomic relations in referential reality that the language of a healthy culture codifies. The 1968 Paris uprisings were for de Certeau "a *symbolic* revolution," inasmuch as students and workers used language to contest "given social and historical *relations* in order to create authentic ones" (1997b, 5). At least the unrest in the spring of 1968 pressured the ossified postwar de Gaulle regime into concessions that made the educational system less impersonal and gave workers something closer to a living wage.

Why introduce the socially inflected theory of de Certeau—new material—in a "Postscript" to a study of ecopoetry? First of all, to illustrate that the poststructural treatment of language can be a positive, enabling pursuit that does not necessitate an attenuation of referential reality by restricting language to the aesthetics of texts. But, more importantly, for an illuminating analogy. Similar to de Certeau's social treatment of language, ecopoets inspect the relations between human language and ecosystem health or damage, thus creating a more authentic picture of our actual, lived lives—how we interact with the environmental context that sustains us at the close of the twentieth century. The texts of ecopoets are the historical records of their encounters with nature, of their embodied perceptions in the flesh of the visible, and constitute the record of their attempts to capture speech in order to promote a balance between the needs of humans and the health of earth's ecosystems. Especially when ecopoets use *référance*, they highlight the relations between language and environmental context as they point toward our lived experience in that context. In their activist mode, ecopoets capture a green speech to contest both the environmental degradation caused by capitalism and the blinkered vision, the restricted aestheticist use of language in texts, in the academy.

Nowhere in de Certeau's poststructural treatment of history and culture do we find language divorced from the speech and experience of humans and their interactions with their social environment, with the concrete symbols of institutionalized power in the lived historical moment. By emphasizing an embodied consciousness interacting in interdisciplinary ways with planetary ecosystems, ecopoets also underscore the relation of language to the referential world. Nowhere does de Certeau limit the uprising of language to texts, to language games or aesthetic grammars based on synchronic linguistic systems. Though he is very aware of the Lacanian deferral of desire and the absence of the thing behind the word on the printed page, as well as Foucault's investigation of panoptic institutional discipline, de Certeau never divorced text from context or opted for determinism by text or institution. He analyzed, for instance, the ubiquitous advertisements for pleasure and happiness in postindustrial societies as signs that point to the absence of pleasure and happiness in the stressed office workers who view them (1997b, 18-23). Frankly, de Certeau's theory depends on an acute appreciation of how language derives from the social, economic, cultural, and ecological context of a group.

De Certeau, by the way, saw the primary value of Wittgenstein to be his deconstruction of privileged authority in language. By emphasizing the ordinary use value of language, Wittgenstein denied any scientific, metaphysical, or philosophical position beyond what can be said in the everyday practice of language by the ordinary citizen. Hence, one cannot assume a superior position of authority, dominance, or mastery beyond or above language to determine meaning. In de Certeau's understanding of Wittgenstein, the only competence that language has comes from within language, from its daily use, its "practical activity" (1984, 8–14). De Certeau would find the academic treatment of Wittgenstein by establishment literary scholars reductive, for this approach limits language to a synchronic semiotic system for textual exploration and the attribution of aesthetic value. It attenuates the referential use value of language in the practical lives of its practitioners. To be certain, the referential emphasis accorded language by ecopoets and environmental scholars restores to language much of the relational use value that Wittgenstein intended.

An astute critic of how university systems propagate culture, de Certeau celebrated the interdisciplinary inquiry into language of poststructuralists, for "structural innovation takes place only in interdisciplinarity, wherever *relations* can be grasped and debated, wherever boundaries and significant divisions of a system can be challenged" (1997b, 98). The academy, de Certeau observed, is heavily vested in textuality and disciplinarity, not in the oral culture of the masses or the mix of actions in the referential world that produces policy. So one must analyze what system of relations academic language produces. "The privilege enjoyed by written culture," wrote de Certeau, is a privilege that "belongs to scholars," for the assumption "that the learned class can change the world is the assumption of the learned class. It is also what they are doomed to *repeat* in myriad ways. A culture of teachers, professors, and readers will silence 'the remainder' because it wants to be and calls itself the origins of all things. A *theoretical interpretation* is thus tied to the *power of a group* and to the structure of a society in which it conquered this position" (1997b, 87). Ecopoetry and ecocriticism challenges the elitism that resides in some areas of the academy.

Texts are not created simply from amalgams of other texts, from linguistic *jouissance*, theory, cultural determinism, or adherence to aesthetic ideals. Texts are interdisciplinary amalgams produced in concrete historical moments of referential complexity. As schoolchildren we learned that the French Revolution was fought for the Enlightenment ideals of *liberté*, *fraternité*, and *egalité*, but a more interdisciplinary approach comes closer to the full story. Behaviorists such as B.F. Skinner (1971) remind us that the French Revolution was fought for the bread that the nobility gave or withheld as a controller or negative reinforcer. Environmentalists such as Gore note that the crop failures and poor harvests in France for the six years prior to the Revolution that galvanized the hungry proletarians into action were caused in large part by cold weather and constant dry fog, the result of volcanic eruptions in Iceland—on Hecla and Skapter Jokul, as Ben Franklin noted—and in Japan—on Asama (Gore 1992, 59-60). De Certeau noted that, once the folk withdrew belief in the ancien régime, the Bastille became a negative physical symbol and the folk erupted with a capturing of speech that altered perceptual habits and promoted change (1997a, 10). As Ammons reminds us, things happen in a mix of motions, a mix that usually includes the social as well as the environmental.

The interdisciplinary pursuits of ecopoets and environmental critics reveal what is lacking in establishment poetry and criticism: a healthy sense of a sustainable relationship with nature conceived as a series of interrelated, potentially self-regulating cyclic feedback systems. Actions are sustainable when they do not neglect the resource base; in sustainable poetry the ecosystems in referential nature that bore and sustain us constitute the resource base. Hence, ecopoets model salutary behaviors that harmonize with nature, or at least treat nature as an equal and separate other in the quest for balance between human needs and environmental health. These behaviors are meant to revise perceptions and coax sustainable actions in readers. When Berry farms his land, meditates in the woods, and models his values after a sycamore tree's tenacity and healing powers; when Ammons flits in milliseconds from the micro, the starch in Arch, to the macro, the starch in our food supply; when Merwin muses on the dead Latin names for the endangered species that he pots with affection in his Maui shed or collapses the distance between Maui and Lacan; and when Snyder actively enjoys the sensual body and its energy exchanges with nature or celebrates the practice of gathering brush to forestall dangerous California brushfires, the poems that record these actions suggest that we should enjoy the perceptual delight of immersing our bodies in nature as we engage in similar sustainable tasks. An establishment poetry that regularly neutralizes nature into benign, homogenized landscapes for anthropocentric discussions about language simply throws in the towel and abets the degradation of our planetary ecosystems by ignoring the referential reality—the laissez-faire work of the hands of humans, individual or corporate. Such poetry can create an art of lying that even Oscar Wilde could not condone were he alive today, precisely because the conditions in referential reality demand more socioeconomic and environmental probity than an occasional rap on the knuckles at commodification.

Merleau-Ponty's prereflective cogito, embodied consciousness, and flesh of the visible restore our immersion in what Murray Bookchin calls the world of first nature (1987, 21), the world of our five senses in contact with dynamic planetary ecosystems. Human speech to other humans is mediated or modified, but certainly *not* determined, by the structure, syntax, and vocabulary of language. But our moments of private immersion in nature do not necessitate an egocentric cogito constantly evaluating experience in language to promote the numero uno "I," the "what's in it for me" perspective. Frankly, one of the prime motivations for a nature walk or a hike in the woods is to give that analytic ego a rest and bathe the five senses in the natural world to recoup and revitalize our embodied, cenesthetic awareness of our connectedness to that world.

The analytic ego mediated by language is not always hyperactive in consciousness. When one hits a pothole that one did not notice beforehand while riding a bicycle at dusk, one's body rights its balance before the brain can utter linguistic commands. In gridlock one's hands immediately turn the wheel to the left, without language-induced volition, when one's eyes notice an opening in the passing lane, even if one is immersed in cassette music. And when a friend telephones while one is cooking breakfast eggs and one mistakenly grabs the iron skillet handle while continuing the conversation, one's fingers drop it without the brain producing sentences about how hot that handle is. Before conscious thought produces language, the corporeal schema of the lived body is always cenesthetically immersed in reciprocities between the tactile and the visible.

Before the self-conscious "I" intervenes, we experience nature in a tacit or prereflective cogito, according to Merleau-Ponty, within a lived body that experiences nature through that body as well as through its sensing of referential nature. And that lived body is immersed in a three-dimensional surround where we interact with other orders of sensing nature that palpate us as we palpate them. At this moment, as I type into my computer, if I move my left hand one foot to the left of my keyboard, my cat Cam, slumbering away in my study chair three feet to my left, will alter her position, become semialert to the presence of a human encroaching on her safe space. Sensitive to her space, I will make slow movements to my left if I must, so not to disturb her unduly (Cam is nearly seventeen years old). Such small rearrangements in lived space happen constantly as other orders of living nature readjust to nonlinguistic human signals. Even the fly on the inside of my study window screen will readjust its position if my right hand moves toward the printer to my right. The foregoing four sentences are text, a historical *re*collection of actions in referential reality. The text would not exist without the first-hand experience, without the reciprocity Merleau-Ponty considers inbuilt in the flesh of the visible, in the sensing/sensible actions of living entities in nature.

By attenuating the relationship of language to referential reality, poststructural theory can devolve into a dangerous relativism. This is the subject of a group of essays edited by Michael Soulé, the founder of the Society for Conservation Biology and chair of the Environmental Studies Board at the University of California, Santa Cruz, and Gary Lease, Dean of Humanities at Santa Cruz. The essays in *Reinventing Nature? Responses to Postmodern Deconstruction* (1995), respond to an extreme poststructuralist position, that of the social constructionists. This position asserts that we can never know first nature, that "nature" is a social construction of humans. In his essay in this volume, the environmentalist Paul Shepard cites the work of Derrida, Foucault, Lacan, Lyotard, Rorty, and critics of visual arts such as Hal Foster, for creating the illusion that "the referent does not exist" and "the text—the only reality—is comparable only to other texts" (1995, 20-22). If so, why bother with wilderness conservation? Poststructural language theorists who evaluate contemporary American poetry can often approximate this position by naturalizing or ignoring nature.

As I write this postscript in early May 1998, the world is burning, as Merwin suggests in his "Cover Note" to *Travels*. Massive rain forest fires are entirely out of control in the northern Amazon, in Mexico, and in Indonesia. The Amazon blaze has destroyed the native home of the Yanomami, one of the last hunter-gatherer cultures left on earth. The Mexico fire is so intense that its smoke has traveled hundreds of miles north to mix with auto exhausts and bathe Dallas, Texas, in daily smog for many weeks. The Indonesian fire is pumping as much carbon dioxide into the atmosphere each day as the entirety of Europe. The conditions for all three fires were created by El Niño–induced drought in areas unaccustomed to drought, and the fires in each area began with the hands of humans—slash-and-burn agriculture condoned by government policy or neglect. Only significant rain can quell these fires, for they are entirely beyond the response capacities of human technology. As we lose rain forest trees, we not only lose their substantial carbon dioxide absorption but the extra carbon dioxide in the atmosphere warms the planet, which warms the oceans. The warmed water holds less carbon dioxide at the same time that it hastens more El Niños. Not only does this process create dangerous positive feedback loops, but enormous inertial forces can develop below the threshold of human awareness that may create future environmental catastrophe.

The Erlichs's instructive story of the pond weed comes to mind. If a weed begins to grow in a pond, and it doubles every day to cover the pond in a month, how much weed covers the pond on the twenty-ninth day? Only half. But taking notice on the twenty-ninth day is taking notice when the inertial forces in the process are too advanced to reverse (1990, 15). The inertial forces of ecosystems are more important than statistics, but more difficult to comprehend because too widespread or not readily discernible to the naked human eye. Though mentioned earlier, Berry's ecological point, consonant with Merleau-Ponty's perspectival approach to vision, is worth repeating at this juncture: since ecologists themselves can never comprehend the operations of all of the interconnected and interdependent systems on this planet, they "recognize the need for the greatest possible care in the use of the world" (CH 142).

As I conclude this postscript, I note that the most recent issue of the *Worldwatch* magazine to arrive at my door (May/June 1998) contains a provocative essay by Aaron Sachs, a former Worldwatch research associate, entitled "The Other Side of the World: Why Does Anyone Care About Sustainability?" Sachs had just returned from a visit to India, where his well-educated Indian friends opened his eyes to why India would never pay for the kind of sanitation systems we have in America. Sachs learned that India is culturally habituated to scavenging, to systematically inspecting any refuse for reuse, for "everything has value here." Hence, elaborate sanitation systems would never gain approval in Indian culture. How can one communicate global environmental concerns across such cross-cultural divides, wondered Sachs. He then noted a cross-cultural limitation in America, a kind of American detritus that inhibits environmental awareness: "Warnings about impending environmental catastrophes simply get lost in the barrage of information and images each of us receives daily through our computers and televisions." Sachs comes to the conclusion that one cannot expect to "persuade people to change their bad environmental habits" in either India or America by simply reciting statistical data.

Sachs's conclusion to his dilemma underscores the value of ecopoetry, though he does not explicitly discuss poetry. Sachs observes that "we generally value things to which we have some personal connection," and we must correlate "cultural diversity with biological diversity." "One of the most compelling features of environmentalism is precisely its potential to promote connectedness," Sachs notes, and "Ecology shows us that we're all in the same boat and we had better plug the leaks." Thus, we will promote cross-cultural environmental solidarity not through doomsday statistics but through "personal incentives—stories and articles and television shows and eco-tours [and poems!] that seek not to terrify and dismay, nor merely to entertain and enchant, but to foster connections. Without these connections, the international environmental movement risks not only investing in culturally inappropriate solutions, but also alienating potential activists." Through using *référance* and by modeling behaviors that bind us to our referential world, ecopoets remind us of the importance of the labors and pleasures that connect us to nature, the context that produces our texts. They suggest that we need to lift our eyes from the single vision of our computer screen sleep and reinvigorate our understanding of the nature that sustains our every waking moment. The ecopoet has lit the fuse of a green speech that revises our perceptions from the anthropocentric to the biocentric—a sustainable practice. May the force that, through the green fuse of ecopoetry, creates new flowers of perception in altered eyes, also create more environmentally friendly practices in our everyday lives.

Works Cited

Abbey, Edward. *Desert Solitaire: A Season in the Wilderness*. New York: Ballantine, 1971.

Abram, David. *The Spell of the Sensuous: Perception and Language in a More-Than-Human World*. New York: Pantheon, 1996.

Aeschylus. *The Oresteia*. Trans. Richmond Lattimore. New York: Washington Square/Simon & Schuster, 1967.

Alexander, Carol, dir. *Assignment Discovery: Othello, Oates, and Merwin*. Discovery Channel. 1991.

Allen, Paula Gunn. "The Sacred Hoop: A Contemporary Perspective." *Studies in American Indian Literature*. Ed. Paula Gunn Allen. New York: MLA, 1983. 7–17.

Altieri, Charles. *Canons and Consequences: Reflections on the Ethical Force of Imaginative Ideals*. Evanston, Ill.: Northwestern UP, 1990.

———. "Contemporary Poetry as Philosophy: Subjective Agency in John Ashbery and C. K. Williams." *Contemporary Literature*, 33 (summer 1992): 214-41.

———. "From Symbolist Thought to Immanence: The Ground of Postmodern American Poetics." *Boundary 2*, 1 (1973): 605-41.

———. "Gary Snyder's Lyric Poetry: Dialectic as Ecology." *Far Point*, 4 (1970): 55–65. Rpt. *Critical Essays on Gary Snyder*. Ed. Patrick D. Murphy. Boston: G.K. Hall, 1991. 48-58.

———. "The Powers and the Limits of Oppositional Postmodernism." *American Literary History*, 2 (fall 1990): 443-81.

———. "Situating Merwin's Poetry since 1970." *W.S. Merwin: Essays on the Poetry*. Ed. Cary Nelson and Ed Folsom. Urbana and Chicago: U of Illinois P, 1987. 159-97.

———. "Some Problems about Agency in the Theories of Radical Poetics." *Contemporary Literature*, 37 (summer 1996): 207-36.

———. *Subjective Agency: A Theory of First-person Expressivity and Its Social Implications*. Oxford and Cambridge, Mass.: Blackwell, 1994.

———. "Temporality and the Necessity for Dialectic: The Missing Dimension of Contemporary Theory." *New Literary History*, 23 (winter 1992): 133-58.

———. "When the Self Became the Subject: A Review Essay on Paul Smith." *Southern Humanities Review*, 23 (summer 1989): 255-63.

Ammons, A.R. "A Note on Incongruence." *Epoch*, 15 (winter 1966): 192. Rpt. SM 8–9.

———. *Brink Road*. New York and London: Norton, 1996.

———. *Collected Poems: 1951-1971*. New York: Norton, 1972.

———. *Garbage*. New York: Norton, 1993.

———. *Glare*. New York and London: Norton, 1997.

———. *Ommateum*. Philadelphia: Dorrance, 1955.

———. *Set in Motion: Essays, Interviews, & Dialogues*. Ed. Zofia Burr. Ann Arbor: U of Michigan P, 1996.

———. *The Snow Poems*. New York: Norton, 1977.

———. *Sphere: The Form of a Motion*. New York: Norton, 1974.

———. *Sumerian Vistas*. New York: Norton, 1987.

———. *Tape for the Turn of the Year*. Ithaca, N.Y.: Cornell UP, 1965.

Ashbery, John. "In the American Grain." *A.R. Ammons*. Ed. Harold Bloom. New York, Chelsea House, 1986. 57-61.

Astor, Michael. "Brazil Fiddles While the Amazon Burns." *Roanoke Times*, August 24, 1997. H1, 5.

Atlas, James. "Diminishing Returns: The Writings of W.S. Merwin." *American Poetry since 1960: Some Critical Perspectives*. Ed. Robert B. Shaw. Chatham, England: W. & J. Mackay, 1973. 69-81.

Auden, Wystan Hugh. *Selected Poems: New Edition*. Ed. Edward Mendelson. New York: Random House, 1979.

Avise, John C. "The Real Message of Biosphere 2." *Conservation Biology*, 8 (June 1994): 327-29.

Barthes, Roland. *The Pleasure of the Text*. Trans. Richard Miller. New York: Hill & Wang, 1975.

Bartram, William. *The Travels of William Bartram*. Ed. Francis Harper. New Haven, Conn.: Yale UP, 1958.

Bate, Jonathan. *Romantic Ecology: Wordsworth and the Environmental Tradition*. London and New York: Routledge, 1991.

Baudrillard, Jean. "The Precession of Simularca." *Art & Text*, no. 11 (September 1983): 3–47.

Beckwith, Martha. *Hawaiian Mythology*. Honolulu: U of Hawaii P, 1970.

Beekman, E.M., ed. and trans. *The Poison Tree: Selected Writings of Rumphius on the Natural History of the Indies*. Amherst: U of Massachusetts P, 1981.

Berry, Thomas. *The Dream of the Earth*. San Francisco: Sierra Club, 1988.

Berry, Wendell. *Another Turn of the Crank*. Washington, D.C.: Counterpoint, 1995.

———. *The Broken Ground*. New York: Harcourt, Brace & World, 1964.

———. *Clearing*. New York: Harcourt, Brace, Jovanovich, 1977.

———. *Collected Poems*. San Francisco: North Point, 1984.

———. *A Continuous Harmony: Essays Cultural and Agricultural*. New York: Harcourt, Brace, Jovanovich, 1972.

———. *The Country of Marriage.* New York: Harcourt, Brace, Jovanovich, 1972.

———. *Entries.* New York and San Francisco: Pantheon, 1994.

———. *Farming: A Hand Book.* New York: Harcourt, Brace, Jovanovich, 1970.

———. *The Gift of Good Land.* San Francisco, North Point, 1981.

———. *The Long-Legged House.* New York: Harcourt, Brace & World, 1969.

———. *Openings.* New York: Harcourt, Brace & World, 1968.

———. *A Part.* San Francisco: North Point, 1980.

———. *Recollected Essays.* San Francisco: North Point, 1981.

———. *Sabbaths.* San Francisco: North Point, 1987.

———. *Sabbaths: 1987-90.* Ipswich, England: Golgonooza, 1992.

———. *Sex, Economy, Freedom, & Community.* New York and San Francisco: Pantheon, 1993.

———. *Standing by Words.* San Francisco: North Point, 1983.

———. *A Timbered Choir: The Sabbath Poems 1979-1997.* Washington, D.C.: Counterpoint, 1998.

———. *The Unforeseen Wilderness: Kentucky's Red River Gorge.* San Francisco: North Point, 1991.

———. *The Unsettling of America.* San Francisco: Sierra Club, 1977.

———. *What Are People For?* San Francisco: North Point, 1990.

———. *The Wheel.* San Francisco: North Point, 1982.

Blake, William. *The Complete Poetry and Prose of William Blake.* Ed. David V. Erdman. Revised ed. Berkeley and Los Angeles: U of California P, 1982.

Bloom, Harold. *The Ringers in the Tower: Studies in Romantic Tradition.* Chicago: U of Chicago P, 1971.

———, ed. *A.R. Ammons.* New York: Chelsea House, 1986.

Bloor, David. *Wittgenstein: A Social Theory of Knowledge.* New York: Columbia UP, 1983.

Bohm, David. "Postmodern Science and a Postmodern World." *The Reenchantment of Science.* Ed. David Ray Griffin. Albany: SUNY P, 1988. 57-68.

———. *Wholeness and the Implicate Order.* London, Boston, and Sidney: Routledge & Kegan Paul, 1980.

Bondar, Gregorio. *Palmeras do Brasil.* Sao Paolo, Brasil: Instituto de Botanica, 1964.

Bookchin, Murray. "Social Ecology versus 'Deep Ecology': A Challenge for the Ecology Movement," *Green Perspectives, Newsletter of the Green Program Project,* 4–5 (summer 1987): 20-27.

Bowie, Malcolm. "Jacques Lacan." *Structuralism and Since: From Lévi-Strauss to Derrida.* Ed. John Sturrock. New York: Oxford UP, 1979. 116-53.

Bramwell, Anna. *Ecology in the Twentieth Century: A History.* New Haven, Conn., and London: Yale UP, 1989.

Bristow, Jeremy, prod. *El Niño.* Discovery Channel. BBC News Discovery: Sci-Tech. 1997.

Brown, Lester, et al. *State of the World: 1996.* New York: Norton, 1996.

———. *State of the World: 1997*. New York: Norton, 1997.

———. *State of the World: 1998*. New York: Norton, 1998.

Brunner, Edward. *Poetry as Labor and Privilege: The Writings of W.S. Merwin*. Urbana and Chicago: U of Illinois P, 1991.

Buell, Lawrence. *The Environmental Imagination: Thoreau, Nature Writing, and the Formation of American Culture*. Cambridge: Harvard UP, 1995.

Caldicott, Helen. *If You Love This Planet: A Plan to Heal the Earth*. New York and London: Norton, 1992.

Campbell, Joseph. *The Masks of God: Creative Mythology*. New York: Viking, 1968.

Campbell, Joseph, with Bill Moyers. *The Power of Myth*. Ed. Betty Sue Flowers. New York: Doubleday, 1988.

de Certeau, Michel. *The Capture of Speech and Other Political Writings*. Trans. Tom Conley. Minneapolis and London: U of Minnesota P, 1997a.

———. *Culture in the Plural*. Trans. Tom Conley. Minneapolis and London: U of Minnesota P, 1997b.

———. *The Practice of Everyday Life*. Trans. Steven Rendall. Berkeley, Los Angeles and London: U of California P, 1984.

Chang, Chung-Yuan. *Creativity and Taoism: A Study of Chinese Philosophy, Art, and Poetry*. 1963; rpt. New York: Harper & Row, 1970.

Christhilf, Mark. *W.S. Merwin the Mythmaker*. Columbia: U. of Missouri P, 1986.

Chuang Tzu. *The Complete Works of Chuang Tzu*. Trans. Burton Watson. New York: Columbia UP, 1968.

Cleary, Thomas. *Rational Zen: The Mind of Dōgen Zenji*. Boston: Shambala, 1993.

Collis, John Stewart. *The Triumph of the Tree*. London: Cape, 1950; New York: Sloane, 1954.

Cooper, James Fenimore. *The Prairie*. New York: Holt, Rinehart & Winston, 1967.

Crosby, Alfred. *Ecological Imperialism: The Biological Expansion of Europe, 900-1900*. Cambridge: Cambridge UP, 1986.

Davies, John. *Douglas of the Forests: The North American Journals of David Douglas*. Seattle: U of Washington P, 1980.

Davis, Duane H. "Reversible Subjectivity: The Problem of Transcendence and Language." *Merleau-Ponty Vivant*. Ed. M.C. Dillon. Albany: SUNY P, 1991. 31-45.

Deleuze, Giles, and Felix Guattari. *A Thousand Plateaus: Capitalism and Schizophrenia*. Trans. Brian Massumi. Minneapolis and London: U of Minnesota P, 1987.

Derrida, Jacques. *"Différance." Margins of Philosophy*. Trans. Alan Bass. Chicago: U of Chicago P, 1982. 3–27.

———. *The Ear of the Other: Otobiography, Transference, Translation*. Trans. Peggy Kamuf. Ed. Christie V. McDonald. New York: Schocken, 1985.

———. *Of Grammatology*. Translated by Gayatri Chakravorty Spivak. Baltimore: Johns Hopkins UP, 1976.

———. *Limited Inc.* Trans. Samuel Weber and Jeffrey Mehlman. Evanston: Northwestern UP, 1988.

———. *Writing and Difference.* Translated by Alan Bass. Chicago: U of Chicago P, 1978.

Descartes, René. *Meditations on First Philosophy.* Trans. Haldane and Ross. The Philosophical Works of Descartes. Eds. Haldane and Ross. New York: Dover, 1955.

———. *Rules for the Direction of the Mind.* Trans. Haldane and Ross. The Philosophical Works of Descartes. Eds. Haldane and Ross. New York: Dover, 1955.

Dijkstra, Bram. *The Hieroglyphics of a New Speech: Cubism, Stieglitz, and the Early Poetry of William Carlos Williams.* Princeton, N.J.: Princeton UP, 1969.

Dillon, M.C. *Merleau-Ponty's Ontology.* Bloomington: Indiana UP, 1988.

———, ed. *Merleau-Ponty Vivant.* Albany: SUNY P, 1991.

Dobzhansky, Theodosius. *Mankind Evolving: The Evolution of the Human Species.* New Haven, Conn.: Yale UP, 1962.

Dōgen. *Moon in a Dewdrop: Writings of Zen Master Dōgen.* Trans. Kazuaki Tanahashi. San Francisco: North Point, 1985.

———. *Flowers of Emptiness: Selections from Dōgen's Shōbōgenzō.* Trans. Hee-Jin Kim. Lewiston, New York: Edwin Mellen, 1985.

Eagleton, Terry. *Marxism and Literary Criticism.* Berkeley and Los Angeles: U of California P, 1976.

———. *Literary Theory: An Introduction.* Minneapolis: U of Minnesota P, 1983.

Edelman, Gerald M. *The Remembered Present: A Biological Theory of Consciousness.* New York: Basic Books, 1989.

Ehrlich, Anne H. and Paul R. Ehrlich. *The Population Explosion.* New York: Simon & Schuster, 1990.

———, and Gretchen C. Daily. *The Stork and the Plow: The Equity Answer to the Human Dilemma.* New York: G.P. Putnam's Sons, 1995.

Elder, John. *Imagining the Earth: Poetry and the Vision of Nature.* 2d ed. Athens and London: U of Georgia P, 1996.

Eliade, Mircea. *Shamanism: Archaic Techniques of Ecstasy.* Trans. Willard R. Trask. Princeton, N.J.: Princeton UP, 1964.

Elliott, David L. "An Interview with W.S. Merwin." *Contemporary Literature,* 39 (spring 1988): 1–25.

Ellis, John M. *Against Deconstruction.* Princeton, N.J.: Princeton UP, 1989.

Emerson, Ralph Waldo. *Poems: The Complete Works of Ralph Waldo Emerson.* Vol. 9. Ed. Edward Waldo Emerson and James Eliot Cabot. New York and Boston: Houghton Mifflin, 1904.

Eschenbach, Wolfram von. *Parzival.* Trans. Helen M. Mustard and Charles E. Passage. New York: Vintage/Random House, 1961.

Faulkner, William. "The Bear." *Go Down, Moses.* New York: Modern Library, 1955. 191-331.

Finch, Robert, and John Elder, eds. *The Norton Book of Nature Writing.* New York and London: Norton, 1990.

Folsom, Ed, and Cary Nelson. "'Fact Has Two Faces': An Interview with W.S. Merwin." *Iowa Review,* 13 (winter 1982): 30-66.

Foster, Hal. *The Return of the Real: The Avant-Garde at the End of the Century.* London and Cambridge, Mass.: MIT P, 1996.

Foucault, Michel. *Discipline and Punish: The Birth of the Prison.* Trans. Alan Sheridan. New York: Vintage, 1979.

Fried, Philip. "Some Influences of Evolution and Ecology on the Poetry of A. R. Ammons." *Pembroke Magazine,* no. 21 (1989): 79-101.

Galvin, Brendan. *Great Blue: New and Selected Poems.* Urbana: U of Illinois P, 1990.

Gast, Ross H., and Agnes C. Conrad, eds. *Don Francisco de Paula Marin.* Honolulu: UP of Hawaii, 1977.

Gifford, Terry. *Green Voices: Understanding Contemporary Nature Poetry.* Manchester: Manchester UP; New York: St. Martin's P, 1995.

Gimbutas, Marija. *The Gods and Goddesses of Old Europe: 7000 to 3500 BC.* Berkeley and Los Angeles: U of California P, 1974.

Glotfelty, Cheryl, and Harold Fromm, eds. *The Ecocriticism Reader.* Athens and London: U of Georgia P, 1996.

Gore, Albert. *Earth in the Balance: Ecology and the Human Spirit.* Boston: Houghton Mifflin, 1992.

Graham, Jorie. *Dream of the Unified Field: Selected Poems, 1974-1994.* Hopewell, N.J.: Ecco P, 1995.

———. *The End of Beauty.* New York: Ecco P, 1987.

———. *Erosion.* Princeton, N.J.: Princeton UP, 1983.

———. *Materialism.* New York: Ecco P, 1993.

———. *Region of Unlikeness.* New York: Ecco P, 1991.

Graves, Robert. *The White Goddess: A Historical Grammar of Poetic Myth.* Amended and enlarged ed. New York: Farrar, Straus and Giroux, 1966.

Gross, Terry. Interview with Wendell Berry. *Fresh Air.* National Public Radio. 1992.

Guetti, James. *Wittgenstein and the Grammar of Literary Experience.* Athens and London: U of Georgia P, 1993.

Haeckel, Ernst. *Generelle Morphologie dur Organismen.* Berlin: G. Reimer, 1866.

Harjo, Joy. *In Mad Love and War.* Middletown, Conn.: Wesleyan UP, 1990.

Hass, Robert. *Human Wishes.* New York: Ecco P, 1989.

———. *Praise.* New York: Ecco P, 1979.

———. *Sun Under Wood.* Hopewell, N.J.: Ecco P, 1996.

Hazel, Robert. "Reality's Shifting Stages." *Kenyon Review,* 27 (spring 1965): 378-80.

Heidegger, Martin. "Building Dwelling Thinking." *Poetry, Language, Thought.* Trans. Albert Hofstadter. New York: Harper & Row, 1979. 143-61.

———. *On the Way to Language.* Trans. Peter D. Hertz. New York: Harper & Row, 1971.

———. *What Is Called Thinking.* Trans. J. Glenn Gray. New York: Harper & Row, 1968.

Heine, Stephen. *A Blade of Grass: Japanese Poetry and Aesthetics in Dōgen Zen.* New York: Peter Lang, 1989.

———. *Existential and Ontological Dimensions of Time in Heidegger and Dōgen.* Albany: State University of New York P, 1985.

Herbert, George. *The Works of George Herbert.* Ed. F.E. Hutchinson. London: Oxford UP, 1941.

Herrigel, Eugen. *Zen and the Art of Archery.* Trans. R.F.C. Hull. New York: Vintage, 1989.

Hertsgaard, Mark. "Who's Afraid of Global Warming?" *Washington Post,* January 21, 1996. C1, 4.

Heyen, William. *Pterodactyl Rose: Poems of Ecology.* St. Louis, Missouri: Time Being Books, 1991.

Hirsch, Edward. "The Art of Poetry: XXXVIII: W.S. Merwin." *Paris Review,* 29 (spring 1987): 57-81.

———. "Bleak Visions, Hand-Clapping Lessons." *New York Times Book Review,* 93 (July 31, 1988): 20-21.

Hoeppner, Edward H. "A Nest of Bones: Transcendence, Topology, and the Theory of the Word in W.S. Merwin's Poetry." *Modern Language Quarterly,* 49 (September 1988): 262-84.

Horace. *Ars Poetica.* Trans. Walter Jackson Bate. *Criticism: The Major Texts.* Ed. Walter Jackson Bate. New York: Harcourt, Brace & World, 1952. 49-58.

Howard, Richard. "A Poetry of Darkness." *Nation,* December 14, 1970: 634-35.

Howard, Sir Albert. *The Soil and Health: A Study of Organic Agriculture.* New York: Devin-Adair, 1947.

Hubler, Edward. *The Sense of Shakespeare's Sonnets.* New York: Hill & Wang, 1952.

Hudson, Charles. Review of *Recollected Essays,* by Wendell Berry. *Georgia Review,* 36 (spring 1982): 220-23.

Hume, Robert Ernest. *The Thirteen Principal Upanishads.* 2d ed., rev. London: Oxford UP, 1931.

Hunt, Tim. "Robinson Jeffers: The Modern Poet as Antimodernist." *Critical Essays on Robinson Jeffers.* Ed. James Karman. Boston: G.K. Hall, 1990. 245-52.

Husserl, Edmund. *The Crisis of the European Sciences and Transcendental Phenomenology: An Introduction to Phenomenological Philosophy.* Trans. David Carr. Evanston, Ill.: Northwestern UP, 1970.

———. *Ideas Pertaining to a Pure Phenomenology II.* Trans. Richard Rozcewicz and Andre Schuwer. London: Kluwer Academic, 1989.

Information Please Environmental Almanac: 1991. Boston: Houghton Mifflin, 1992.

Jacobson, Joseph and Sandra. "Intellectual Impairment in Children Exposed to Polychlorinated Biphenyls in Utero." *New England Journal of Medicine,* 335, no. 11(1996): 783-89.

Jameson, Fredric. *Marxism and Form: Twentieth-Century Dialectical Theories of Literature.* Princeton, N.J.: Princeton UP, 1971.

———. *Postmodernism, or the Cultural Logic of Late Capitalism.* Durham, N.C.: Duke UP, 1991.

Jeffers, Robinson. *The Double Axe and Other Poems: Including Eleven Suppressed Poems.* 1948; rpt. New York: Liveright, 1977.

Johnson, William C., Jr. *What Thoreau Said: Walden and the Unsayable.* Moscow: U of Idaho P, 1991.

Joyce, James. *Ulysses.* New York: Modern Library, 1961.

Jung, Carl Gustav. *Alchemical Studies.* Trans. R.F.C. Hull. Ed. Sir Herbert Read, et al. Bollingen series 20, vol. 13. Princeton, N.J.: Princeton UP, 1967.

———. *Mysterium Coniunctionis: An Inquiry into the Separation and Synthesis of Psychic Opposites in Alchemy.* Trans. R.F.C. Hull. Ed. Sir Herbert Read et al. Bollingen series 20, vol. 14. New York: Pantheon, 1963.

———. *Psychology and Alchemy.* Trans. R.F.C. Hull. Ed. Sir Herbert Read et al. Bollingen series 20, vol. 12. Princeton, N.J.: Princeton UP, 1968.

———. "The Psychology of the Child Archetype." *Essays on a Science of Mythology.* Trans. R.F.C. Hull. Ed. Carl G. Jung and Karl Kerenyi. 1949; rpt. Princeton, N.J.: Princeton UP, 1969. 70-100.

Kapu'uwailani Lindsey, Elizabeth. *Then There Were None.* PBS, 1996.

Keats, John. *Poetical Works of John Keats.* Ed. H.W. Garrod. 2d ed. Oxford: Clarendon P, 1958.

Kenner, Hugh. "Contempt Causes Insanity." *Harper's,* 264 (April 1982): 100.

Kerouac, Jack. *The Dharma Bums.* New York: Viking, 1958.

King, Richard H. "Down to Earth." *New Leader,* 56 (February 19, 1973): 20-21.

Kirchner, James W. "The Gaia Hypothesis: Can It Be Tested?" *Reviews of Geophysics,* 27, no. 2 (May 1989): 223-35.

Klinkowitz, Jerome. *Rosenberg/Barthes/Hassan: The Postmodern Habit of Thought.* Athens and London: U of Georgia P, 1988.

Krieger, Murray. *The New Apologists for Poetry.* 1956; rpt. Bloomington and London: Indiana UP, 1963.

Kroeber, Karl. *Ecological Literary Criticism: Romantic Imagining and the Biology of Mind.* New York: Columbia UP, 1994.

———. "'Home at Grasmere': Ecological Holiness." *PMLA,* 89 (January 1974): 132-41.

Krupat, Arnold. *The Voice in the Margin: Native American Literature and the Canon.* Berkeley: U of California P, 1989.

Lacan, Jacques. *Écrits.* Trans. Alan Sheridan. London: Tavistock, 1977*a.*

————. *The Four Fundamental Concepts of Psycho-analysis.* Trans. Alan Sheridan. Ed. Jacques-Alain Miller. London: Hogarth P, 1977*b*.

Lamb, F. Bruce. *Wizard of the Upper Amazon: The Story of Manuel Cordova-Rios.* Boston: Houghton Mifflin, 1975.

Lappé, Frances Moore. *Diet for a Small Planet.* Rev. ed. New York: Ballantine, 1982.

Lavery, David L. "The Eye as Inspiration in Modern Poetry." *New Orleans Review,* 8 (winter 1981): 10-13.

Lee, Sherman E., and Wen Fong. *Streams and Mountains without End.* Rev. ed. Ascona, Switzerland: Artibus Asiae, 1967.

Lentricchia, Frank. *After the New Criticism.* Chicago: U of Chicago P, 1980.

Leopold, Aldo. *A Sand County Almanac.* New York: Oxford UP, 1949.

Levin, David Michael. "Visions of Narcissism: Intersubjectivity and the Reversals of Reflection." *Merleau-Ponty Vivant.* Ed. M. C. Dillon. Albany: SUNY P, 1991. 47-90.

Lévi-Strauss, Claude. *Totemism.* Trans. Rodney Needham. Boston: Beacon, 1963.

Liu, Alan. *Wordsworth: The Sense of History.* Stanford: Stanford UP, 1989.

Lopez, Barry. *Arctic Dreams: Imagination and Desire in a Northern Landscape.* New York: Charles Scribner's Sons, 1986.

Love, Glen A. "Revaluing Nature: Toward an Ecological Criticism." *Western American Literature,* 25 (fall 1990): 201-15.

Lovelock, J.E. *Gaia: A New Look at Life on Earth.* New York: Oxford UP, 1979.

Lucas, Thomas A., dir. *Great Lakes: A Bitter Legacy.* National Audubon Society. 1991.

de Man, Paul. *The Rhetoric of Romanticism.* New York: Columbia UP, 1984.

Margalef, Ramon. "General Concepts of Population Dynamics and Food Links." *Marine Ecology.* Ed. Otto Kinne. Volume 4: *Dynamics.* New York: John Wiley & Sons, 1978. 617-704.

————. *Perspectives in Ecological Theory.* Chicago: U of Chicago P, 1968.

Martin, Julia. "The Pattern Which Connects: Metaphor in Gary Snyder's Later Poetry." *Western American Literature,* 22, no. 2 (summer 1970): 99–121. Rpt. *Critical Essays on Gary Snyder.* Ed. Patrick D. Murphy. Boston: G.K. Hall, 1991. 188-210.

Marx, Karl, and Friedrich Engels. *The German Ideology.* Trans. R. Pascal. New York: International, 1947.

McIntosh, Robert. "Ecosystems, Evolution, and Relationship Patterns of Living Organisms." *American Scientist,* 52 (1963): 246-68.

McKibben, Bill. *The End of Nature.* New York: Random House, 1989.

Meeker, Joseph. *The Comedy of Survival: Studies in Literary Ecology.* New York: Scribner's, 1972.

Merchant, Carolyn. *The Death of Nature: Women, Ecology and the Scientific Revolution.* 1980; rpt. New York and San Francisco: Harper & Row, 1990.

————. *Radical Ecology: The Search for a Livable World.* New York and London: Routledge, 1992.

Merleau-Ponty, Maurice. "Indirect Language and the Voices of Silence." *Phenomenology, Language, and Sociology.* Ed. John O'Neill. London: Heinemann, 1974. 36-80.

————. *The Phenomenology of Perception.* Trans. Colin Smith. London: Routledge & Kegan Paul, 1962; New York: Humanities P, 1962.

————. *The Primacy of Perception.* Ed. James M. Edie. Evanston, Ill.: Northwestern UP, 1964.

————. *Signs.* Trans. Richard C. McCleary. Evanston, Ill.: Northwestern UP, 1964.

————. *The Visible and the Invisible.* Trans. Alphonso Lingis. Ed. Claude Lefort. Evanston, Ill.: Northwestern UP, 1968.

Merwin, W.S. *The Carrier of Ladders.* New York: Atheneum, 1970.

————. *The Compass Flower.* New York: Atheneum, 1977.

————. *Finding the Islands.* San Francisco: North Point, 1982.

————. *The First Four Books of Poems.* New York: Atheneum, 1975.

————. "Foreword." *A Zen Wave: Basho's Haiku and Zen.* Ed. Robert Aitken. New York: Weatherhill, 1978. 11–15.

————. *The Lice.* New York: Atheneum, 1967.

————. *The Moving Target.* New York: Atheneum, 1963.

————. "Notes for a Preface." *The Distinctive Voice: Twentieth-Century American Poetry.* Ed. William J. Martz. Glenview, Ill.: Scott, Foresman, 1966. 268-73.

————. *Opening the Hand.* New York: Atheneum, 1983.

————. *The Rain in the Trees.* New York: Knopf, 1988a.

————. *Selected Poems.* New York: Atheneum, 1988b.

————. *Travels.* New York: Knopf, 1993.

————. *Unframed Originals.* New York: Atheneum, 1982.

————. *The Vixen.* New York: Knopf, 1996.

————. *Writings to an Unfinished Accompaniment.* New York: Atheneum, 1973.

Mowitt, John. *Text: The Geneology of an Antidisciplinary Object.* Durham, N.C.: Duke UP, 1992.

Murphy, Patrick D. *Understanding Gary Snyder.* Columbia: University of South Carolina P, 1992.

Murphy, Patrick D., ed. *Critical Essays on Gary Snyder.* Boston: G.K. Hall, 1991.

Nahm, Milton C., ed. *Selections From Early Greek Philosophy.* 3d ed. New York: Appleton-Century-Crofts, 1947.

Nash, Roderick. *The Rights of Nature: A History of Environmental Ethics.* Madison: U of Wisconsin P, 1989.

————. *Wilderness and the American Mind.* 3d ed. New Haven, Conn., and London: Yale UP, 1982.

Nielsen, Dorothy M. "Prosopopoeia and the Ethics of Ecological Advocacy in the

Poetry of Denise Levertov and Gary Snyder." *Contemporary Literature*, 34 (winter 1993): 691-713.

Nietzsche, Friedrich. *Thus Spake Zarathustra*. Trans. Thomas Common. Ed. Oscar Levy. New York: Russell & Russell, 1964.

Odum, Eugene P. *Ecology and our Endangered Life-Support Systems*. 2d ed. Sunderland, Mass.: Sinauer, 1993.

Odum, Howard T. *Environment, Power, and Society*. New York, London, Sydney, and Toronto: John Wiley & Sons, 1971.

Pack, Robert, and Jay Parini, eds. *Poems for a Small Planet: Contemporary American Nature Poetry*. Hanover, N.H., and London: UP of New England, 1993.

Paul, Sherman. "From Lookout to Ashram: The Way of Gary Snyder." *Iowa Review* (1970). Rpt. Murphy, ed. *Critical Essays on Gary Snyder*. 58-80.

Perloff, Marjorie. *Radical Artifice: Writing Poetry in the Age of Media*. Chicago: U of Chicago P, 1991.

———. "Toward a Wittgensteinian Poetics." *Contemporary Literature*, 33 (summer 1992): 191-213.

———. *Wittgenstein's Ladder: Poetic Language and the Strangeness of the Ordinary*. Chicago and London: U of Chicago P, 1996.

Piercy, Marge. *Mars and Her Children*. New York: Knopf, 1992.

Pinsky, Robert. *The Situation of Poetry: Contemporary Poetry and Its Traditions*. Princeton, N.J.: Princeton UP, 1976.

Plath, Sylvia. *Collected Poems*. New York: Harper & Row, 1981.

Pound, Ezra. *Cantos*. New York: New Directions, 1965.

———. "Vorticism." *Fortnightly Review*, New Series, 96 (1 September 1914): 461-71.

Ransom, John Crowe. *The New Criticism*. Norfolk, Conn.: New Directions, 1941.

———. *The World's Body*. Baton Rouge: Louisiana State UP, 1938.

Reiman, Donald H. "A.R. Ammons: Ecological Naturalism and the Romantic Tradition." *Twentieth-Century Literature*, 31 (spring 1985): 22–54.

Rich, Adrienne. *An Atlas of the Difficult World*. New York: Norton, 1991.

———. *Blood, Bread, and Poetry: Selected Prose, 1979-1985*. New York: Norton, 1986a.

———. *Your Native Land, Your Life*. New York: Norton, 1986b.

Roanoke Times. "Asian Loggers Strip World's Rain Forests." August 26, 1996. A1, 5.

———. "2000 Dirty Beaches Were Closed in 1991." July 24, 1992. A1

Robbins, John. *Diet for a New America*. Walpole, N.H.: Stillpoint, 1987.

Robertson, David. "Real Matter, Spiritual Mountain: Gary Snyder and Jack Kerouac on Mt. Tamalpais." *Western American Literature*, 27 (Fall 1992): 209-26.

Roethke, Theodore. *Collected Poems*. Garden City, New York: Doubleday/Anchor, 1975.

Roszak, Theodore. *Person/Planet: The Creative Disintegration of Industrial Society*. Garden City, New York: Anchor P/Doubleday, 1978.

Rushdie, Salman. "Outside the Whale." *Imaginary Homelands: Essays in Criticism: 1981-1991.* London: Granta/Viking, 1991. 87-101.

Ryder, Arthur, trans. *The Panchatantra.* Chicago: U of Chicago P, 1925. 434-41.

Sachs, Aaron. "The Other Side of the World: Why Does Anyone Care about Sustainability?" *Worldwatch,* 11, no. 3 (May/June 1998): 31-38.

Said, Edward W. *Culture and Imperialism.* New York: Random House, 1993.

————. *The World, the Text, and the Critic.* Cambridge, Mass.: Harvard UP, 1983.

Sartre, Jean-Paul. *Being and Nothingness: An Essay on Phenomenological Ontology.* Trans. Hazel E. Barnes. New York: Simon & Schuster/Pocket Books, 1966.

————. *No Exit and Three Other Plays.* Trans. S. Gilbert and L. Abel. New York: Random House/Vintage, 1955.

de Saussure, Ferdinand. *Course in General Linguistics.* Edited by Charles Bally and Albert Sechehaye, in collaboration with Albert Riedlinger. Translated by Wade Baskin. New York: McGraw-Hill, 1966.

Scheese, Don. "Thoreau's Journal: The Creation of a Sacred Place." *Mapping American Culture.* Ed. Wayne Franklin and Michael Steiner. Iowa City: U of Iowa P, 1992. 139-51.

Scigaj, Leonard M. "The Painterly Plath That Nobody Knows." *Centennial Review,* 32 (summer 1988): 220-49.

————. "Reveling in the Referential Flux: Involution and Merleau-Ponty's Flesh of the Visible in Pattiann Rogers." *Under the Sign of Nature.* Ed. John Tallmadge and Hank Harrington. Madison: U of Wisconsin P, 1999 (forthcoming).

Scigaj, Leonard, and Nancy C. Simmons. "Ecofeminist Cosmology in Thoreau's Walden." *Interdisciplinary Studies in Literature and Environment,* 1 (spring 1993): 121-29.

Scott, Nathan. "The Poetry of Ammons." *Southern Review,* 24 (autumn 1988): 717-43.

Sears, Paul. "Ecology—A Subversive Subject." *Bioscience* 14, no. 7 (July 1964): 11–13.

Shaw, Bernard. *Man and Superman. Complete Plays with Prefaces.* Vol. 3. New York: Dodd, Mead, 1963.

Shepard, Paul. "Introduction: Ecology and Man—A Viewpoint." *The Subversive Science: Essays Toward an Ecology of Man.* Eds. Paul Shepard and Daniel McKinley. Boston: Houghton Mifflin, 1969. 1–10.

————. "Virtually Hunting Reality in the Forests of Simulacra." Soulé and Lease, eds., *Reinventing.* 17-29.

Sitarz, Daniel, ed. *Agenda 21: The Earth Summit Strategy to Save Our Planet.* Boulder, Colo.: Earthpress, 1994.

Skinner, B.F. *Beyond Freedom and Dignity.* New York: Knopf, 1971.

Smith, Page. "Responsibility at Home in the Great Economy." *Christian Science Monitor,* 79 (July 3, 1987): B1, B8.

Smith, Paul. *Discerning the Subject.* Minneapolis: U of Minnesota P, 1988.

Snyder, Gary. *Axe Handles.* San Francisco: North Point, 1983.

———. *The Back Country.* London: Fulcrum, 1967; New York: New Directions, 1968.

———. *Earth House Hold: Technical Notes and Queries to Fellow Dharma Revolutionaries.* New York: New Directions, 1969; London, Jonathan Cape, 1970.

———. *Left Out in the Rain: New Poems, 1947-1985.* San Francisco: North Point, 1986.

———. *Mountains and Rivers without End.* Washington, D.C.: Counterpoint, 1996.

———. *Myths and Texts.* New York: Totem/Corinth, 1960; New York: New Directions, 1978.

———. *No Nature: New and Selected Poems.* New York: Pantheon, 1992.

———. *The Old Ways: Six Essays.* San Francisco: City Lights, 1977.

———. *A Place in Space: Ethics, Aesthetics, and Watersheds.* Washington, D. C.: Counterpoint, 1995.

———. "Poetry, Community, and Climax." *Field,* 20 (spring 1979): 21-35.

———. "Poetry and the Primitive: Notes on Poetry as an Ecological Survival Technique." Rpt. *The Poetics of the New American Poetry.* Ed. Donald Allen and Warren Tallman. New York: Grove, 1973. 395-415.

———. *The Practice of the Wild.* San Francisco: North Point, 1990.

———. *The Real Work: Interviews and Talks: 1964-1979.* New York: New Directions, 1980.

———. *Regarding Wave.* New York: New Directions, 1970. London: Fulcrum, 1970.

———. *Riprap.* Ashland, Massachusetts: Origin, 1959.

———. *Riprap and Cold Mountain Poems.* San Francisco: North Point, 1990.

———. *Turtle Island.* New York: New Directions, 1974.

Soulé, Michael, and Gary Lease, eds. *Reinventing Nature? Responses to Postmodern Deconstruction.* Wachington, D.C.: Island P, 1995.

Spanos, William. "What Was Postmodernism." *Contemporary Literature,* 31 (spring 1990): 108-15.

Spiegelman, Willard. "Poetry in Review." *Yale Review,* 81 (July 1993): 134-51.

Stahl, Jim. "Interview with A.R. Ammons." *Pembroke Magazine,* no. 18 (1986): 77–85. Rpt. SM 41-55.

Stephenson, Shelby. "An Interview with A.R. Ammons." *Pembroke Magazine,* no. 18 (1986): 196-202.

Stevens, Wallace. *Collected Poems.* New York: Random House/Vintage, 1982.

———. *The Necessary Angel: Essays on Reality and the Imagination.* New York: Random House/Vintage, 1951.

Suzuki, D.T. *The Essentials of Zen Buddhism.* Ed. Bernard Phillips. New York: E.P. Dutton, 1962.

Suzuki, David, and Anita Gordon. *It's a Matter of Survival*. Cambridge: Harvard UP, 1991.

Thiher, Allen. "Wittgenstein, Heidegger, the Unnamable, and Some Thoughts on the Status of Voice in Fiction." *Samuel Beckett: Humanistic Perspectives*. Ed. Morris Beja, S.E. Gontarski, and Pierre Astier. Columbus: Ohio State UP, 1983. 80-90.

Thomas, Dylan. *Collected Poems: 1934-1952*. Rev. ed. New York: New Directions, 1956.

Thoreau, Henry David. "The Natural History of Massachusetts." *Henry David Thoreau: The Natural History Essays*. Ed. Robert Sattelmeyer. Salt Lake City: Peregrine Smith, 1980. 1–29.

Time. November 16, 1992. 48.

Toffler, Alvin. *Future Shock*. New York: Random House, 1970.

Vendler, Helen. *On Extended Wings: Wallace Stevens's Longer Poems*. Cambridge, Mass.: Harvard UP, 1969.

———. *Part of Nature, Part of Us: Modern American Poets*. Cambridge, Mass.: Harvard, 1980. 233-36.

———. *Wallace Stevens: Words Chosen Out of Desire*. Knoxville: U of Tennessee P, 1984.

———. "What We Have Loved, Others Will Love." *Falling into Theory: Conflicting Views on Reading Literature*. Ed. David H. Richter. New York and Boston: St. Martin's P, 1994. 27-36.

Voros, Gyorgyi. *Notations of the Wild: Ecology in the Poetry of Wallace Stevens*. Iowa City: U of Iowa P, 1997.

Waley, Arthur, trans. and ed. *The Way and Its Power: A Study of the Tao Te Ching and its Place in Chinese Thought*. New York: Grove, 1958.

Warner, Rex. *The Greek Philosophers*. New York: New American Library, 1958.

Wilde, Oscar. "The Decay of Lying." *Victorians on Literature and Art*. Ed. Robert L. Peters. New York: Appleton-Century-Crofts, 1961. 147-61.

Wilhelm, Richard, ed. *The I Ching or Book of Changes*. Trans. Cary F. Baynes. 2d ed. 1961; rpt. New York: Pantheon, 1962.

Williams, Raymond. *The Country and the City*. New York: Oxford UP, 1973.

Williams, William Carlos. *Pictures from Brueghel and Other Poems*. New York: New Directions, 1962.

Wittgenstein, Ludwig. *Philosophical Investigations*. 3d. ed. Trans. G.E.M. Anscombe. New York: Macmillan, 1968.

———. *Tractatus Logico-Philosophicus*. Trans. D.F. Pears and B.F. McGuiness. London: Routledge & Kegan Paul, 1974.

Worster, Donald. *Nature's Economy: The Roots of Ecology*. Garden City: Anchor P/ Doubleday, 1979.

Yamazato, Katsunori. "How to Be in This Crisis: Gary Snyder's Cross-Cultural

Vision in Turtle Island." *Critical Essays on Gary Snyder.* Ed. Patrick D. Murphy. Boston: G.K. Hall, 1991. 230-47.

Yeats, William Butler. *Collected Poems.* 2d ed. New York: Macmillan, 1951.

Zaller, Robert. "Spherical Eternity: Time, Form, and Meaning in Robinson Jeffers." *Critical Essays on Robinson Jeffers.* Ed. James Karman. Boston: G.K. Hall, 1990. 252-65.

Index

DATE DUE

HIGHSMITH #45115